Margaret Heffernan is an award-winning chief executive, author and playwright and blogs for BNET, *Real Business* and the *Huffington Post*. *Wilful Blindness* was her third book. She lives near Bath, England.

ALSO BY MARGARET HEFFERNAN

The Naked Truth: A Working Woman's Manifesto
About Business And What Really Matters

Women On Top: How Women Entrepreneurs Are
Rewriting The Rules Of Business Success

Wilful Blindness: Why We Ignore The Obvious
At Our Peril

A Bigger Prize: How Competition Isn't Everything
And How We Do Better

A BIGGER PRIZE

Why Competition Isn't Everything
and How We Do Better

MARGARET HEFFERNAN

**SIMON &
SCHUSTER**

London · New York · Sydney · Toronto · New Delhi

A CBS COMPANY

For Lindsay

First published in Great Britain by Simon & Schuster UK Ltd, 2014
This paperback edition published by Simon & Schuster UK Ltd, 2015
A CBS COMPANY

1 3 5 7 9 10 8 6 4 2

Simon & Schuster UK Ltd
1st Floor
222 Gray's Inn Road
London WC1X 8HB

www.simonandschuster.co.uk

Simon & Schuster Australia, Sydney
Simon & Schuster India, New Delhi

A CIP catalogue record for this book
is available from the British Library

ISBN: 978-1-47110-076-5
ebook ISBN: 978-1-47110-077-2

Typeset in the UK by M Rules
Printed and bound by CPI Group (UK) Ltd, Croydon, CR0 4YY

CONTENTS

INTRODUCTION

On a beautiful August day, the New Hampshire sunshine streamed through the tall pine trees surrounding the Cheshire County Fair. On the outer perimeter, carthorses and pigs were scrutinized and judged, some garnering rosettes, others returned to their owners, for whom they were both livelihood and pets. Kids could try their hand at milking cows and goats or driving their first tractor. After lunch, Slackwire Sam unicycled up and down his loose clothesline; in the far corner of the fairground, tug-of-war was scheduled for the end of the day.

An inner circle of food stalls offered fried dough, blossoming onions, corn dogs and cotton candy. Families four abreast carried paper cartons of calamari and chili fries, or cones overflowing with fluorescent ice cream. Clutching goldfish in plastic bags, three young girls compared prizes while twin brothers walked side by side, sporting matching t-shirts: 'The 2nd amendment: America's original homeland security'. In the dusty heat, we all sauntered slowly, eating, talking and seeking out small patches of shade when, over the loudspeaker, came the announcement: the demolition derby was about to begin.

Gently – it was too hot to rush – the direction of the crowd turned towards the central stadium and up the bleachers, where the seats in the shade were soon occupied. Conceding defeat, the rest of the spectators shifted reluctantly towards the sunny side, spread out and donned hats. Aficionados placed towels carefully on their laps.

In the centre of the arena, eight rusty wrecked cars rev their engines. Car 49 sports flags decorated with skulls; car 38 proudly promotes its sponsor – WB Paint Worx – in hand-painted electric red, white and blue logos. Car 72 displays steer horns on its roof while car 3 advertises McCue's billiard hall in nearby Keene.

'Are you ready?' the loudspeaker blares. The crowd starts to join in the countdown: 5 ... 4 ... 3 ... 2 ... 1 – and the cars reverse out of their alignment, struggling to gain traction in the dust. Now they're off, whirling and spinning as they drag themselves into collisions. The goal is demolition and the last car left running wins the prize.

'Get serious guys – we need some contact!'

As the cars drag themselves around the arena, radiators steaming, the spinning tyres throw up dirt made damp from oil spills and water. The crowd screams and ducks as it goes flying, landing on laps and smearing my sunglasses. Now I understand why the woman next to me brought her towel: this is part of the fun.

'Eileen, you gotta hit somebody!'

Driving car 23, Eileen can't possibly hear the crowd through her crash helmet but she knows what to do. Whizzing around, she heads off to smash into car 49, an easy target as its under-carriage drags along the ground. Then she backs up and charges into the corner where Kyle in car 25 is stuck, trapped by three dilapidated vehicles that back up, accelerate and smash into him. The radiator explodes against the arena wall, the car accordions and Kyle is out of the game. Once a car can't move, all the rest move in to pulverize it.

With doors, bonnets and fenders now dispersed across the dirt, just four vehicles remain. 72 can only drive in reverse now and limps with a flat tyre. Everyone is starting to lose power but the derby can't finish until one more goes down. As if sensing blood, cars 35, 66 and 72 head for Eileen but she outmanoeuvres them, gets behind 35 and, catching it on her front fender, rams it against the wall.

'We've got our three!' and the crowd erupts into applause as the local fire brigade walks onto the field to clear the wreckage and prepare for the final.

As I sat in the stands, on that beautiful August day, I couldn't help but think I was watching some kind of parable. All around the world, rusty, dilapidated institutions and ideas seemed to be crashing into each other, driven by a competitive spirit that offered the brutal simplicity of winners and losers. After five years of corporate breakdowns, ethical corrosion, financial crashes, stalled politics and overheated rhetoric, all that remained was the grim drama of the contest.

Wherever I looked, competition had become the default motivator, as though, exhausted and demoralized, no culture or politics could proffer a superior driver or decisive alternative. As complex social, financial, legal and environmental challenges piled up on one another, a kind of despair seemed to descend: we don't know what to do, let the market decide. Put it out to competition, make people compete, the best will rise to the top – won't it?

Fans of competition regularly looked to Charles Darwin for intellectual support. Most cited 'survival of the fittest' without recognizing that the term came, not from Darwin, but from Herbert Spencer, who had handily translated 'natural selection', giving it his own favoured political spin. Since a world of winners and losers was natural, the social Darwinians argued, we would do better to tone our competitive muscles than question the ways of nature. We are, after all, the product of an evolutionary contest in which the best of our genetic inheritance has survived while the rest perished. Although even Darwin scholars couldn't agree whether Darwin himself would have been a social Darwinian, nature itself seemingly provided the ultimate alibi.

They were hugely aided by the many people familiar with (but had never read) Richard Dawkins's *The Selfish Gene*. No wonder publisher Tom Maschler suggested the book might better be called *The Immortal Gene*. As Dawkins himself conceded in the thirtieth-anniversary edition, many people took the title at face value, didn't bother to read the text and concluded that the book must be a vindication of raw, unbridled selfishness. The selfish gene is only out for itself, it is who we are, and there's nothing we can do about it. That the book said nothing of the kind – in fact mounted an eloquent and powerful counter-blast – didn't matter. The title had become the work.

Nor were the avid competitors devoid of data. At the end of the nineteenth century, one of the world's first social psychologists, Norman Triplett, had demonstrated that cyclists rode faster against a competitor than when cycling alone. And, even though much of Triplett's subsequent work added layers of refinement and contingency to his result, the headline stuck: everyone works harder, faster, better when they're up against each other. Sport became the ubiquitous metaphor, profusely obscuring what it sought to illuminate.

As a consequence, organizations – public and private – have come to rely on competition to choose and motivate people; to inspire investors and consumers; to justify everything from doomed mergers to sweatshops and price hikes. What's been tested by competition must be better. Never mind the cost, never mind that competition is designed to benefit the few, not the many – we live in a dog-eat-dog world and what matters now is to be top dog. Schools may no longer be about learning, work may not be about self-fulfilment and society may not be about relationships anymore; what matters is to read the manuals, bone up on techniques, buy the equipment, pay the trainer, swallow the supplements and always keep score.

Winners were, of course, always more susceptible to this argument. Since competitions work for them, they find it understandably hard to see what might be wrong with their strategy. Losers rarely write history. And, anyway, competition is fun; it's dramatic and exciting; there's a winner and you always know just where you stand. At a moment in time when no one seems to know where to go or what to do, isn't that clarity good enough?

And yet, just as we'd learned that individuals weren't rational and markets weren't efficient but went ahead operating as though they were, so we also recognized that competition quite regularly didn't work, the best did not always rise to the top and the so-called efficiency of competition seemed to throw off a very great deal of waste. It was comforting to designate these ideas 'perverse outcomes' as though each one was an anomaly; but as aberrations mounted, they started to look more like a norm.

This is where the Prisoner's Dilemma* came into its own.

---

* The Dilemma poses what looks like a simple scenario: two members of a gang are arrested and placed in solitary confinement where they have no means of communicating with each other. The police don't have enough evidence to convict the two on the main charge, so they plan to sentence each to a year's imprisonment on a lesser charge. But they also offer a bargain: if one testifies against his partner, he will go free and the partner will get three years in prison on the more serious charge. As in all good socialscience scenarios, there is a catch: if both prisoners testify against each other, they each get two years in jail.

Dreamed up and given its name by a Canadian mathematician, Albert W. Tucker, the game has been used to model competition and the variety of ways in which it can play out. It has been applied to so many problems and settings – from the Cold War to drugs in sports – that it has been called the 'e-coli of social science'. Game theory is largely absent from this book – I'm far more interested in practice – but in all its many permutations, one finding remains critical: when each prisoner competes for himself, instead of collaborating with his fellow, they both lose. The individual pursuit of self-interest proves collectively defeating.

Over the last fifty years, we have seen this played out on an epic scale. In our quasi-religious fervour to compete, we have expected fabulous efficiencies, miraculous economies, infinite creativity and dazzling innovation. Instead, we've found ourselves gasping for air in a sea of corruption, dysfunction, environmental degradation, waste, disenchantment and inequality – and the harder we compete, the more unequal we become. This is no coincidence but the inevitable outcome of our faith in competition as a simple panacea for the many and complex challenges that we face.

Winning always incurs costs. When siblings grow up in rivalry, they struggle to relate with trust and generosity. When schools celebrate the top of the class, they demotivate the rest. When the rich win tax cuts, inequality grows. As sports become fiercer and richer, careers shorten and injuries abound. When executives are encouraged to compete for bonuses and promotions, it costs them friendships and creativity. An obsession with score-keeping constrains thinking and undermines the very innovation it hopes to spark. When pharmaceutical companies win patents on lookalike drugs, it costs us critical new medicines that never get developed. When food producers aim to dominate their markets with low prices, it costs us all in environmental and social degradation. And when the pressure to win exacerbates cheating and corruption, it costs us the legitimacy of our institutions and the credibility of our beliefs.

Over the last fifty years, we have leaned heavily on competition, hoping that it will solve our problems, motivate our children, inspire adults and reinvigorate companies and institutions. But we have shied away from the uncomfortable truth that our exaggerated veneration for competition has left us ill-equipped to solve the problems it has created. If we are to invent new ways to live and work together, we need high levels of trust and give-and-take: elements that competition so specifically and subtly corrodes.

As if in recognition of this, a rising generation seeks avidly for the tools and environments in which sharing, co-creation and trust are endemic and reinforced. And, increasingly, they are not disappointed. Evolutionary science has shown us that the human ability to collaborate and cooperate explains why we have survived to defy gravity and build monuments of lasting beauty and meaning – because we know how to work together. New models for sharing information, pooling resources, organizing complex projects and inventing new products abound, amply demonstrating that great work, inexhaustible innovation and passionate commitment amply and easily supplant exhausting rivalries. The wildly collaborative creative individuals and organizations in this book testify to the human capacity to cooperate, share, look across broad horizons and dig deep together. Our talent for coalitions, our ability to cooperate, even the creation of language itself – the ultimate tool for collaboration – testifies to an immense human capacity for solidarity.

Perhaps the long legacy of the Soviet Union explains the queasiness with which the subjects of collaboration, cooperation and altruism are approached to this day. Rather as Darwin feared killing God, we fear that any renunciation of competition must kill capitalism and return us to the corruption and cruelty of the Soviet experiment. Such rhetoric is, of course, historically inaccurate – the Soviet Union incited competition regularly and viciously in all walks of life. But the polarization implicit in that debate reflects the poverty of our win/lose mindset, blinding us to the greater opportunities and energies that lie elsewhere. We can find better ways to live, to work and to rebuild our failed institutions for the many, not just the few. All around us are examples we can and must learn from.

We are all competitive but we are not only competitive. No book, sermon, movement or political party will ever change the insatiable human appetite for status and distinction. But working together is human nature and around us, if we look carefully, are individuals and organizations that can show us the way. They know that growth, learning and creativity always depend on a vast array of people and ideas, freely shared and generously celebrated. They appreciate that fairness, safety and trust are essential to the unfettered exploration that generates new ideas. They don't accept that the only measure of success is the number of losers left in the dust. And, they entirely reject the idea that true achievement can be measured at any single moment in time. These trailblazers aren't driven by keeping score but are motivated instead by the belief that great work is done together, that efficiency is gained by trust and that safety opens the floodgates of the mind. They have everything to teach us – and sharing is what they do best.

When I started to explore these themes, the first response that greeted me was astonishment: you dare to question competition? What else is there? In the years that have passed, that reaction has shifted. Now, when I discuss my work, I see in people's faces and hear in their voices a sense of relief and hope. Yes, there is a better way to live and work. Yes, the alternatives are real, significant, practical and sustainable. There are forms of success that are better than winning. For all of us, there is a bigger prize.

PART ONE:
PERSONAL BEST

1. Oh, Brother!

'I want the first one!'

As Alice brings a plate of cakes, Harry stretches over to grab his piece. He's wound up, tense and excited. He's hungry, of course, but it's more than that. He doesn't just want cake. He wants to be first to get his cake and eat it.

We aren't in a poor home – there's no shortage of food. In this comfortable country house with sunny windows and a big open kitchen, there is more than enough warmth and light and cake to go round. Harry's parents, Alice and Paul, are kind, loving and calm. They're both lawyers; of the two, Alice had the more dazzling career until she stepped down to spend more time with her three boys.

And that's the clue. The tension, excitement, the slightly wired feeling in the room: it isn't about cake. It's about those three boys, each one of whom wants to come first, get most, be best.

Harry is eleven. He competes with Tom, eight, and Oliver, who is four. All three boys are handsome, boisterous, even charismatic in their, as yet, undeveloped enthusiasms. You can tell as you watch them that they're neither spoiled rotten nor do they want for anything. Growing up with plenty – of love, attention, stimulation, support and, yes, cake – has had its effect. The boys are bursting with potential that requires only time to unfurl. So they aren't competing because there's a shortage of anything. They're competing because they're human. And they compete all the time.

The next morning, as the sun starts to burn off the mist on the broad lawns that surround the house, Tom is up early making Ready Brek and getting ready to go for a swimming lesson.

'Where's the chocolate spread?' Harry asks.

His father, Paul, isn't sure but Harry knows for a fact that his mother bought some on Friday and it hasn't been opened yet. He conveys this information with the ferocity of a government minister at the dispatch box who won't brook dissent. His father duly finds the chocolate spread.

'You can't let him have that!' Tom protests.

'Yes he can!' Harry counters.

'You can't, Dad.' Tom is distraught. 'You can't let him have the chocolate spread. I'm going swimming. It will all be gone before I get back . . .'

Food isn't the only point of contention in the Hobbs's household. Footballs, TV time, Monopoly pieces, outings with Grandma, the place in front of the fire, bedtime: anything and everything can be fought over. It's exhausting for Alice because it never stops.

'If I give them each a sweet, there will be endless squabbling – a smartie is worth more than a wine gum. If I hand them each a biscuit, I just have two hands and the third one will always ask: where's mine? As if I'm not going to turn around and get the other biscuit. If for some reason, I don't give them a sweet, they'll argue about whose fault it is that there aren't any sweets today.'

Alice has invited me to observe her three boys because she recognizes how competitive they are. This makes her uncomfortable: such raw drive, the desire to win against the others so naked and unmediated. Like the rest of us, Alice understands the need for identity and territory to call one's own, but the open fight for it disrupts her family and unsettles her home.

It's also very draining. Every bedtime, they fight over something. When the boys aren't in school, contests, spats, conflagrations erupt with monotonous regularity and their mother recognizes that they are competing for her attention and approval, of which there can never be enough. The heat in the household invariably centres on Harry, who is handsome, tall with curly light-brown hair, has presence and exudes a sense of being top dog.

'Harry plays rugby at school,' his mother tells me. 'After a match, if he hasn't scored a try, he'll have a reason: he wasn't placed right, he wasn't given the chance. He won't ever say the other boy played better. Deep down inside, he cannot bear to say to himself: he scored the try because he's better than I am.'

Tom is smaller, quieter and feels like a deeper character altogether, as though he has knowledge that he's not sharing.

'Tom will watch Harry play rugby and say "he played well" or "that was a great kick" and he does it without any sense that it has cost him anything to say that. Generosity comes easily to him, but he won't put himself forward. He doesn't do his own PR. He's much quieter and he won't challenge.'

The youngest, Oliver, clearly loves being the baby of the family, in the safer spot because no one wants his position.

'Oliver just loves getting stuck in. He's only four, he knows he can't touch his brothers. But he's keen to show he can play the game, that he counts and that there's no reason he should be left out. But in the family pecking order, well, he's just above Rocket the dog.'

At school, Harry has to be – and invariably is – top of his class. He's good, his mother says, at marketing himself. His father, Paul, thinks he has the makings of a CEO or, perhaps, an MP.

'Harry has to be top dog; he has to be. He's very careful to ensure that everyone likes him,' Alice says. 'The teachers and the kids all like him because, of course, at school, they have no idea what a bully he is at home. Because he is a bully. He wants to make Tom feel bad. He can't be generous. He has to be the best. Whenever I praise Tom, you'll see him rise up and have to put him down.'

We are sitting in Alice's sitting room, lined with deep cream sofas; for the moment, the house is quiet. But Alice is on tenterhooks; she knows that moments like this don't last long and, just a few minutes later, something upstairs crashes to the floor, we hear howls of protest and somebody crying. With a weary sigh, Alice rises from the sofa and leaves to adjudicate.

Harry has to win. He needs his siblings to lose. You can see it in the way he carries himself, the way that he watches every move they make. Later in the day, when Alice tries to tell me what a strong swimmer Tom is, Harry stands in front of me, as though trying physically to block the words from reaching my ears.

Over the next two weeks, Alice kept a diary of her sons' interactions. It was relentless.

Wednesday the 12th. Tom has insisted on a trip to visit his grandparents alone because Harry has had several visits himself; there's an element of evening out the score.

Thursday the 13th. Oliver in a song and dance show at school. We told him how well he'd done. 'Tell the others,' he said, 'because they said it was going to be rubbish.'

Saturday the 15th. Major argument over rugby balls.

Sunday the 16th. Much arguing over small things; bickering and unsettled. Particular issue when Harry wanted to go fishing with Grandad and it's only safe for Grandad to look after one boy at a time. Tom very upset.

Monday the 17th. Huge fight over bathtime. Tom decidedly smug that he was 'getting away with it'.

Tuesday the 18th. Argument over a cake Oliver had been given at a birthday party. He had almost finished it (with brothers pleading for a piece at every mouthful) when a piece broke off, landed on the floor, whereupon the dog licked it. Harry then grabbed it – and ate it. Yuck! He was scolded by me, but the look on his face was telling me he thought it was worth it for the prize of a piece of unexpected cake, even if dog-licked. Tom, excluded from it all, with no doggy cake, went into meltdown.

Wednesday the 19th. Tom invited out to see the new *Johnny English* film. Harry was clearly envious and disappeared into the study for hours. He emerged triumphant, declaring he had worked out how to download films and was downloading, yes, *Johnny English 1*. Given our rubbish broadband speed, it took ages and then even longer to watch it back on the computer. This did not diminish his pleasure one bit; not sure if the film was any good, but he had succeeded in clawing back a piece of Tom's treat by undermining the novelty. Predictably, on Tom's return he announced, 'Well, I've seen *Johnny English 1* and everyone thinks that it's better.'

The diary goes on like this, day after day. It's exhausting to read and must have been enervating to live through. Earlier in the year, Harry had gone on a week-long school trip. The difference, Alice told me, had been absolute. The mood, temperature, conversations: everything in the family had been different. It was sad, she reflected, to be so happy when one of your children has gone.

What Alice and her husband have on their hands is a bad case of sibling rivalry. The phrase was first coined by psychologist

David M. Levy in 1941. That it took so long to name such a common phenomenon seems remarkable. Sibling rivalry kicks off the Bible, with the murder by Cain of Abel the first act of violence in a very violent book. In the ancient world, Acrisius and Proteus start their quarrel in the womb. Polynices and Eteocles, the sons of Oedipus, kill each other over Thebes; and Romulus and Remus, over the location of Rome. Shakespeare is replete with rivalrous siblings: *King Lear* pits sister against sister and brother against half-brother, *The Tempest* encapsulates a lifelong rivalry between Antonio and his brother Prospero, while *The Taming of the Shrew* draws comic steam from the pitched battle between amiable Bianca and the shrewish Katherine. Novelists from the Brontës and Jane Austen through to Saul Bellow and Jonathan Franzen have appreciated the energy and tension that the presence of brothers and sisters is bound to supply.

In contemporary life, the public and bitter feuds between Clement and Lucian Freud, Liam and Noel Gallagher, Peter and Christopher Hitchens, and Rufus and Martha Wainwright testify to the fact that neither fame nor success mollifies the urgent, primal need to come first. Even the most delicately presented rivalry, between David and Ed Miliband, ended with David feeling his only chance for success required him to leave politics and the country.

Sibling rivalry is a fundamental building block of stories and gossip because we recognize that its raw emotion is real and universal. From the moment that we are born, we compete for the resources of survival: attention, food, love, warmth and protection. For the newborn, securing the mother's (or caregiver's) undivided attention is an absolute biological imperative. Worldwide today, it's estimated that one out of every four children live in poverty.[1] Twenty-four million have no parents and every day 16,000 die from hunger. For all children, getting enough – attention, shelter, education, clothing or even cake – is a real and daily struggle.

Even in comfortable, secure families, infants are alert to the danger of anything that might distract or remove the love, attention and food that they need. As early as six months, we recognize that some threats are more serious than others: in one experiment, infants were found to be relatively unperturbed if their mother paid attention to a book but very unhappy when she interacted with a doll.[2]

But it is the birth of a sibling that provokes the most visceral reaction, for the newborn represents a far bigger challenge than any book or doll, a challenge no mother can deny. Judy Dunn is the doyenne of sibling relationships, having devoted nearly half a century to the observation and study of brothers and sisters in their families over long periods of time. She documented a 93 per cent increase in naughtiness after a sibling's birth, almost all of it designed to get attention.

'The upheaval of another baby coming into the family is *enormous*,' says Dunn. 'What is so interesting about watching siblings is that theirs is absolutely a no-holds-barred relationship. Most parents are in denial but, however desirable it may be to show your family as all cooperative, brothers and sisters let out their competitiveness very clearly. It just hangs out whenever you observe in a family.'

In the West, 80 per cent of us are siblings. That makes us either perpetrators, victims or, more likely, both. Violence – of emotion or action – is common. More than half of all children experience violence from a sibling in the course of just one year,[3] while, in the United States, a national study of family violence showed that 74 per cent of children had pushed or shoved a sibling, while 42 per cent had kicked, bitten or punched them. A study of British siblings showed that 54 per cent had been bullied, bullies or both. Name-calling and stealing are routine, as is violence in the defence of one's own property. Scientists in Canada who studied siblings two to four years old found that a fight of some kind broke out every 9.5 minutes,[4] a frequency that Alice Hobbs might find both familiar and reassuring: her squabbling boys are not unusual.

It is thought that sibling abuse (physical and emotional) exceeds parental abuse and is the most abusive relationship to be found in families.[5] So seriously does the National Crime Prevention Council take sibling rivalry that it provides advice to parents on how to manage conflict between their children.[6] We may love our brothers and sisters but we also hate them with a passion, and accounts of sibling rivalry are ubiquitous.

'I put my baby brother in the microwave and it might have worked except I couldn't get the door to shut.'

'I tried to get my baby sister to drink nail varnish remover. I put it in her bottle and mixed in milk – but it obviously tasted horrible, so she wouldn't drink it.'

'When we were having a bath, I pushed my brother under but he just fought like a tiger and kept coming up for air.'

'I threw my sister out of the window . . .'

Many siblings reminded me that the writer Alice Walker was blinded in one eye when her brother shot her with his BB gun; that they savoured this detail attested to their identification with Walker's experience. But had any of these been incidents of adult violence, we would take them very seriously. That they occur in childhood permits us to hope that they are transitory, that the kids will grow out of it, that love and generosity, self-control and fairness will overwhelm or mitigate such murderous feelings. We recognize infancy as the beginning of social understanding: the time and place where we learn to relate to others and to become the social beings on which our survival keenly depends.

Such strong emotions, however, rarely do what we might like them to do: simply evaporate. When they linger and fester, as they did throughout Diane Wilson's childhood, the legacy they leave is enormous.

'I was born the day before my older sister Beth's birthday. From her perspective, I stole her thunder!'

Diane Wilson got off to a bad start with her older sister and, looking back, it is clear that no one in the family knew what to do about it. Diane was the last of five children, born into a family of three boys and Beth. The older children had scarcely known their father, who had served in the army during the Second World War. Emotional and financial resources were thin on the ground and the rivalry and resentment between the two girls was fierce.

'My mother definitely played us off against each other. I was the good one, Beth was the difficult one. But this was never really talked about, it was just there, an undercurrent the whole time. My father just didn't get involved.'

Although the girls weren't physically violent to one another, the emotional violence between them was unmistakable and unforgettable. Beth's resentment of her younger, prettier sister was the background rumble of Diane's childhood: constant, unpleasant, dangerous and suppressed. Beth was very academic, which Diane was not; that made life at school for the two sisters tense and often humiliating. Beth would regularly chastise her sister for being such a failure and letting her down so badly.

'Even while we were at school, she used to wind me up. She knew just how to do it. When she was head girl, she would go out of her way to belittle me, yelling across the courtyard "Where's your beret?" There was just no way I was going to be academic the way that she was. Who would want to be?'

Knowing she could never match Beth's accomplishments, Diane turned instead to dance, for which she developed a real passion.

'I was keen on dance and, on one occasion, I remember Beth saying: dancing is a third-rate art – all you're doing is what someone else tells you to do. Mother's defence of me was: don't pick on her about that, it is the one thing she is any good at! Between the two of them ... My father by this time had had a stroke when I was ten. It was all very difficult.'

In a household of five children, open conflict wasn't encouraged and it's clear, in retrospect, that neither parent had the energy or the skills to mediate the intense rivalry between the two girls. An undercurrent of competitive tension was omnipresent, Diane says, but it was never allowed out into the open. Instead, confronted with her sister's unstoppable rivalry, Diane learned to do everything she could to stay out of the way.

'I used to read a lot of European literature – *The Idiot, Crime and Punishment* – but I would never read English writers. That was because Beth read English at Cambridge; that was her domain, so I stayed away from English fiction. Later on, people kept telling me I should do a degree; I thought I wasn't clever enough. I couldn't see my own intelligence. I didn't do a degree in order to avoid competing with her – I just wanted to stay out of her way.'

Neither girls found in their parents any kind of model of collaboration and their mother actively stoked the rivalry between them. Dance had been a way for Diane to escape into a world where her sister could not and would not follow her. But when physical problems brought her dancing to an end, she was left without any strong sense of her own identity. Instead, she developed a habit of self-subversion by which the mere idea of her sister defeated all her aspirations.

'I kept thinking: I don't need to be in competition with Beth so I don't need a degree. Everyone could see what was going on but me! As long as I didn't earn much money, didn't have any qualifications, didn't have a house, wasn't like her, I imagined she wouldn't envy me or attack me. She was so competitive that the only way not to be destroyed by her was to keep my head down. Delicate, vulnerable and a failure: that was how I distinguished myself from my sister.'

As we sat in Diane's warm house discussing events long past, the sense of anger, rage, confusion and fear was present and palpable. She was circumspect about where we could talk, not wanting the subject to infect other parts of her home. Like many people with painful sibling relationships, Diane is wary of re-entering territory that still has the power to frighten and depress her. A slim, attractive woman in her mid sixties, she leads a lively cultural and intellectual life now. But that has been hard won, pulled from the flames of a sibling relationship that always, it seemed, tried to make her fail.

Years of standoffs and silence would be interrupted by rapprochements and fresh starts that invariably ended badly. On one occasion, Diane was invited to stay with her sister – but then told to go out for dinner because guests were invited for whom she was not good enough company. It was as though the sisters were frozen at the moment of Diane's birth, spoiling Beth's birthday party and for ever stealing attention. As their mother aged and needed support, the battle between them revived with all the heat of infancy and Diane felt increasingly sidelined and abandoned.

Even the death of their mother, which might have brought about a truce, did nothing of the sort. By this time, the sisters were not speaking, and when Diane attended the funeral, she brought a friend for moral support. What she feared was not her grief, but her sister. At the reception afterwards, the sisters were never in the same room at the same time. They didn't see each other again for nearly twenty years and then they did not speak.

Competition stoked by her mother made rivalry the defining

characteristic of Diane's childhood and much of her adult life. And it wasn't just her relationship with her sister that was damaged; relating to women generally is problematic for her and she is still on her guard. If she gets close to anyone, she feels anxious and will start to defend herself – whether there's an attack or not.

'I don't know how to assert my own point of view,' she told me, 'while making room for others. It's taken me years to discover how to compromise without *being* compromised. The whole family dynamic has made it impossible for me to think of doing work that is really collaborative; fitting in feels too much like death.'

Only the support of friends and allies finally allowed Diane to complete her education and to start to feel that she has a life that is her own. Nevertheless, her struggle with – or against – her sister still feels very alive. I can't tell how far she's confiding in me because I've asked her to – and how far talking to me is just another way to strike back at her sister.

But I was grateful to Diane because, while so many people have quickly and eagerly told me stories of their rivalrous siblings, very few have wished to be interviewed on the subject. Clearly the feelings are too dangerous, packed with emotions that feel awkward, uncomfortable and sometimes shameful. In many cases, the rivalry is as intense in adulthood as in childhood, resolved only by both parties moving away from each other socially, professionally, even geographically. For a while, passions may seem to die down, only to be reignited at the moment, of a parent's death, when the task of dividing property often proves incendiary.

Diane's sister Beth clearly had to win, in matters small and large. Similarly, in the Hobbs family, Harry has a fierce need to be top dog and it's telling that, when he's away, the whole family is so placid. Both Harry and Beth, in their different ways, might be described as hyper-competitive, a characteristic described as an 'indiscriminant need by individuals to compete and win (and to avoid losing) at any cost as a means of maintaining or enhancing feelings of self-worth'[7]. Hyper-competitive people compete in inappropriate situations because every social encounter represents an opportunity for power, control or domination that can be either won or lost. Some researchers also regard this as an extreme form of individualism because personal advantage and narcissistic self-interest overwhelm all other concerns. Hyper-competitive people can feel successful only when others lose.

I recognize now that my father was hyper-competitive. The youngest and smallest of three boys, he was born into a poor Texas family where there was never enough of anything. He hated his brothers, left home as early as he could, rarely contacted them and didn't attend their funerals. He had grown up with a burning desire to get as far from home as possible. This served him well professionally but it also left him determined always to prove his superiority. If he met people whom he liked but who were less successful than he, his contempt shone through. Attracted to people who were more successful than he was, his sense of relative failure impeded any possible friendship. He was an adroit negotiator but a poor judge of when to stop: good at achieving his goals but graceless in victory. When negotiating complex agreements between oil companies and national governments, his ambition was not to secure a workable deal, he once told me, but to break his opponent's spine. Perhaps he was the only one to be surprised when his employer retired him at the earliest opportunity.

My father's competitiveness made him a bully. That stood me in very good stead in my own career, in which I encountered perhaps a disproportionate number of people rather like him: gifted, intelligent thugs. This wasn't industry-specific: they were as prevalent in broadcasting as in software development and venture capital. Many had a great deal of power, which was the chief reason people worked for them; no one would have done so by choice and most left at the earliest opportunity. Growing up around this kind of personality left me with a shrewd idea of how to deal with it: I was good at avoiding confrontation but canny when accepting it. But most of all it left me with a profound sense of waste: of talent undermined by its own aggression, and of a desire for human connection that was perpetually subverted by the need to triumph. I loved my father but I could see that he was trapped, isolated and ostracized by a drive he could not control.

He was also, as many hyper-competitive people are, attractive, even charismatic. Their energy and drive is dynamic and alluring, a siren song that lures others unaware onto the rocks of relationships that must fail. This makes their achievements often short-lived and always costly, in terms of damaged relationships, missed opportunities, lost connections. Because we can all readily think of high achievers who fit this profile, it's easy to imagine that hyper-competitive people are always successful, that their drive is some kind of guarantee that may be worth its high price. But we should beware ascertainment bias; what the world doesn't celebrate are the vast numbers of hyper-competitive people whose drive is what subverts them. I've met plenty of those too.

One in particular I'll call Tim, a brilliant BBC trainee with a double first from Oxford. His older brother had also got a double first from Oxford but had gone into the City. I was asked to oversee the production of Tim's first film, which I did with some difficulty as he made it very clear to me that no help was needed. He bridled at being a trainee and, although he was rapidly accepted as a peer, his need to prove himself made him spiky company. Assigned a gift of a subject and, as was usual in television at the time, a fantastic crew of prize-winning technicians, there was no reason for Tim not to succeed. Yet, when I came to view a rough-cut of his programme, I was shocked; it was a complete mess. Afterwards, the film editor explained the mystery. Listening to soundtrack recorded during the making of the show, it became clear that Tim would take suggestions and advice from no one but instead insisted on getting exactly what he had asked for. In the end, the seasoned crew stopped helping and submitted to his every direction. They stopped collaborating and started following orders.

After we re-shot and re-cut the film, I tried to explain to Tim what had gone wrong. He listened politely and then demurred. He had not, he said, gone into television to learn how to be nice. Many years later, I encountered him again. Still working in television, he had moved from company to company, each one originally enticed by his intelligence, each one eventually deciding that the costs of working with him were too high.

The problem with competitiveness like this is that it is fundamentally anti-social, requiring others to fail. Yet many social Darwinians, compelled by the visible successes they observe in highly competitive people, connect that drive with high levels of productivity and achievement. If only everyone, they argue, were so driven and determined to win, economic growth would skyrocket and vast human potential would be unleashed. Some parents – like my grandparents – studiously fuel their children's rivalry, hoping it will toughen them up for the real world. David and Ida Eisenhower brought their children up this way, as did Joseph Kennedy, Sr, who was famous for proclaiming that he wanted no losers in his family. 'Life is a fight,' one parent explained to me, 'and the sooner my kids get good at winning the fight, the better.'

Quite why the desire to make others fail should feel natural while the ability to play well with others does not is mysterious. Perhaps the sheer drama and excitement provoked by hyper-competitors feels more real, raw and authentic than more pro-social behaviour. But the problem with this crude misinterpretation of natural selection is not just that hyper-competitiveness is associated with all kinds of high costs and anti-social tendencies – bullying, narcissism and Machiavellianism – but that it is *not* associated with higher levels of success.[8] Becoming vicious in order to win is no guarantee of victory.

Why are some people hyper-competitive when others are not? For biologists, the prime suspect is testosterone. Everyone – men and women – is exposed to testosterone, in the womb, at adolescence and in adulthood, and most scientists believe that testosterone levels play a role in brain development. By adulthood, we each have a basal level of testosterone that stays fairly stable throughout our lives. Men with higher basal testosterone have been found to be less likely to marry, more likely to divorce and to achieve somewhat less in the way of education and income. Because testosterone is sometimes associated with aggression, it has been thought that higher basal levels might be correlated with a greater demand for dominance. But the voluminous studies on this topic have failed to prove a clear correlation.

What has emerged, however, are some intriguing details. When challenged, a man's testosterone levels will rise and they will rise again if he wins; it will fall if he loses. It may be that this creates a hormonal feedback loop in which those who need power get it – and are, therefore, more likely and more able to continue to demand power. This is not true for women, however, whose testosterone does not rise at a challenge.[9]

What is most striking about testosterone though is that it is implicated in poor judgement and weaker emotional intelligence. In one experiment, supervised by the renowned autism expert, Simon Baron-Cohen, testosterone was administered to women who were then asked to take a test that measured their ability to read people's faces. As the research team had anticipated, the testosterone impaired the women's ability to infer intention, emotions and other mental states, confirming the hypothesis that high testosterone levels negatively influence social intelligence.[10] Similar experiments that monitored naturally circulating testosterone similarly found that it appeared to counteract empathy.

Most intriguing of all was research looking at the relationship between testosterone and collaboration. This time, several pairs of volunteers were given testosterone orally while another group was given a placebo. Everyone was asked to work in pairs, watching a screen and anticipating at what moment a target would appear. At first, each participant had to reach their decisions independently; then they had to make their choices collaboratively. The researchers were pretty sure that the collaborative decision-making would be more accurate, which it was. But the question they really wanted to answer was: would testosterone improve or inhibit the quality of the collaboration?

What they found was that testosterone caused a marked decrease in the capability of the collaborative pairs. Primarily this was ascribed to an 'egocentricity bias': each participant was more likely to over-value their own opinion and to under-value the opinion of their partners. Raised testosterone levels, in effect, made each person more self-centred and much poorer at working with other people, with the result that they failed to capture the value of collaborating.[11]

We can see that there is a relationship between testosterone and high degrees of competitiveness but we don't know why some people have higher levels of testosterone than others. It sheds light on but doesn't fully explain the complexity of behaviour and real life outside of experiments. We won't – and shouldn't hope to – see the day when hormone testing is used in interviews or job recruiting. As complex as it is, the science is clear on one thing: biology alone can never account fully for the complex interaction of social and psychological processes that drive behaviour. Hormone levels on their own – before or after birth – can't explain personality and even the most neuro-chemically minded of researchers end up talking about the importance of parental attachment and of environment. There are simply too many other factors to consider – hundreds of other hormones for a start.[12] Temperament, pre-existing behaviours, social support and culture all play their role in a rich brew in which we can still only identify a few ingredients at a time. The fact that identical twins, raised in the same family, will develop different immune systems testifies to the complexity of the interplay between all of these factors. Most influential of all is experience: what happens to us and what we do.

Our brain's wiring is critically determined by the experiences that we have throughout life but much of the basic platform, we now can see, is laid down in early life. This was most vividly illustrated in a series of experiments in which young kittens had one eye sutured shut for the first three months of life. This was not deliberate cruelty; the goal was to ascertain how the parts of the brain responsible for visual cognition would develop. The results were striking: the part of the brain responsible for vision for the closed eye could not develop. Brain scans could identify clear, defined differences – big black blobs – which marked the areas where neural pathways had not grown. What's more important was that, after a certain age, they could not change. What had happened early in life was fixed. These were some of the first, dramatic experiments that demonstrated both the plasticity of the brain but also the degree to which it is minutely sculpted by experience.

Since that work, neuroscientists have been uncovering the stages in which those critical pathways of the human brain are laid down. What's clear is that connections that aren't used die off (as in the kittens) but connections that are richly stimulated wire together. This has been described by neuropsychiatrist Allan Schore as a 'use it or lose it situation. Cells that fire together wire together. Cells that do not, die together.' One of the conclusions he has drawn from his work is that, while too much stress may stop cells from developing, experiencing conflict *that can be and is resolved* may be how we develop the neural networks we need for collaboration.

The family is a learning environment, in which we are introduced to and learn to imagine the minds of others.[13] It can and should provide the safe environment where children's rivalrous feelings can emerge and be expressed as a way of learning about conflict. What matters isn't to eliminate the arguments and emotion but to create the safe place where they can be challenged, understood and resolved with love, by people who won't give up. That's what family dinners are for: not just the food fights but to learn the give and take, cut and thrust, of passionate debate.

Ezekiel Emanuel, today a medical ethicist at the University of Pennsylvania, wrote tellingly about growing up with his brothers Rahm (who grew up to be Chief of Staff in President Obama's administration) and Ari (a Hollywood agent and ostensibly the model for Ari Gold in television's *Entourage*). At the brothers' family meals, passion, solid information, honesty and argument were expected and respected. There were rules – no cruelty, no prejudice and no stupidity – but swearing was allowed. What Emanuel describes is common to the experience of many siblings who, looking back, say that their childhood rivalry made a profound contribution to their social competence, their emotional development and, ultimately, their parenting skills. Families are where they first experienced hatred – but also where they learned to deal with it.

Conflict is a critical part of brain development, of emotional and social learning. Children need to experience conflict – but also to have the positive experience of finding solutions to it: losing sometimes, winning other times, but always surviving it. And many siblings believe that expressing their rivalry in their youth makes them closer in adulthood. But hyper-competitive people may never have those experiences because they dominate too quickly; their submissive siblings (like Diane Wilson) never have those experiences because they get so good at avoiding the fight.

Experiments with families in which some parents were trained in mediation skills demonstrate that even very young children have immense capacity to learn how to resolve conflicts constructively and creatively. Parents without mediation training tended to intervene and adjudicate more; their children were more contentious, demanding and self-justifying. But in families where parents did have mediation training, the disputes were more severe but the children became better problem solvers and crafted more creative resolutions for themselves. In these families, parents helped but did not design the final outcomes because the children learned to do so for themselves – and they did it better. What the experiments illustrated was the profound capacity children have to learn from each other and from their parents the pro-social skills needed to collaborate and to integrate different interests, needs and perspectives.

The most creative response to sibling competition is deidentification, a term coined by psychologist Frances Schachter, who puzzled over why children in the same family, sharing 50 per cent of their DNA, were nonetheless so very different. Why is it, for example, that Harry must find an external explanation for any sports defeat when his brother Tom, in the same situation, can be so generous? After studying hundreds of sibling pairs, Schachter argued that brothers and sisters become different from each other as a way of mitigating their feelings of rivalry. She called this a 'Cain Complex' and saw that children – particularly those of the same gender and especially those born right after one another – would become different in order *not* to fight. Deidentification, according to Schachter, is a creative attempt at maintaining family harmony.

Frank Sulloway, a psychologist and historian of science, compares siblings to Darwin's finches from the Galapagos Islands that played such an important part in the development of evolutionary theory. All fourteen species of Darwin's finches derived from a single ancestor that colonized the islands some two million years ago. As such they were – and still are – a stunning example of just how rich and fast adaptation can be. Sulloway argues that human siblings similarly become increasingly dissimilar through learning what earns attention, resources, respect within the family environment.

'Strategies for dealing with sibling competition and for evoking sibling cooperation,' Sulloway wrote, 'are among the principal functional mechanisms that govern successful adaptation within family life.'[14]

Thus differences that start out as biology are made more extreme or moderate by experience and birth order. This is both a biological process, impacting the wiring in the brain ('neurosculpting') but also a strategy for protecting everyone in the family.

'The concept of niches,' Sulloway argues, 'derives from the field of ecology where it exemplifies how different species use available resources within their environments. Family niches may be conceptualized in a similar manner. Siblings compete with one another to secure physical, emotional and intellectual resources from their parents. Depending on differences in birth order, gender, physical traits and aspects of temperament, siblings create differing roles for themselves within the family system.'

Because we don't want to fight for territory, we claim some that isn't taken. In the quest for resources, Sulloway says that firstborns always have the easiest task. For a period of time, they have their parents exclusively to themselves and, however hard their parents strive in later life to be fair and equitable, they still seem to end up getting 10 per cent more care than laterborns. They typically will have an IQ that is, on average, three points higher than subsequent children.[15] With more attention and with no sibling rival, firstborns, says Sulloway, tend to be more closely affiliated with their parents' interests and attitudes. This makes them more conservative and defensive of a status quo that has served them, as incumbents, very well.[16]

Middle children invariably get less attention than the first or last.[17] Younger children are less likely to be vaccinated than their older siblings, with rates of vaccination declining 20–30 per cent with each successive child, an indicator perhaps of just how hard, even impossible, it is for even the best parents to be equitable.[18] Laterborns therefore, face a challenge; with the conservative 'position' taken, and in receipt of less care and attention, younger children have to fight harder for attention and resources. They haven't had exclusive attention from their parents, certain niches are already gone and, being smaller and less developed, they're able to do less. Their relative impotence forces them into more distinctive, attention-grabbing roles. They simply must diversify. And this often leads laterborns to be more receptive to, and supportive of new, radical, even revolutionary ideas. It may also force them into more collaborative roles, learning early that they are stronger through alliances than in isolation.

Sulloway has tested his theory against a vast amount of historical data, examining scientific revolutions from Copernicus to Newton and Darwin. In each case, he says, the new radical positions were adopted and promoted by the youngest, and the more conservative (even extremely conservative) ones by firstborns. He makes the same argument to explain the political fault lines of the French Revolution, with the firstborns adopting more conventional, moderate politics and the younger siblings promoting radical action. Bringing his research up to date, Sulloway also looked at the more prosaic example of baseball-playing brothers, where he identified the same trend. Analysing sibling pairs who had played in the major leagues through baseball's history, including Joe and Dom DiMaggio, and Cal and Billy Ripken, Sulloway found that it was the younger brother who more often tried to steal a base.[19]

The birth-order argument remains controversial but deidentification does not – and there are some striking examples of it, none more so than in the family of Ralph Nader, where the four children each decided to study a different part of the world: Shafeek took North America; Claire, the Middle East; Laura, Mexico and Latin America; while Ralph, the youngest, was left with China and the Far East; between them, they had the world covered. (Apparently they felt Europe didn't need any of them because it was so well taught in school.)[20] Similarly, the Kings of Leon is comprised of three brothers: Caleb Followill, who sings lead vocals; Nathan, who plays drums and percussion; Jared, who plays bass guitar; and cousin Matthew, who fills in vocals and guitar. The group is named after their grandfather and that sense of serving or honoring something bigger than any individual is key.

It's striking that sibling rivalry is such a well known phenomenon – it even has its own terminology – while the rich collaboration between brothers and sisters is less studied, even though it can prove so profoundly productive and creative. Many families develop both immensely gifted individuals *and* collaborators: the Wachowskis, who made *The Matrix* and *Cloud Atlas*; the Marriott brothers, who founded their eponymous hotel chain; sisters Klara and Johanna Söderberg, who created the group First Aid Kit; and sisters Este, Danielle and Alana Haim who formed the rock band Haim; the Bröntes; the Dimblebys; the Attenboroughs and many many more unknown but effective siblings testify to the capacity of families to produce energetic collaborators for whom success does not demand or produce dominance or exclusivity.

'From an early age, I think we all had some sense of a shared story,' Tony Bicât told me. 'Mother was centre of it. She created this household. The purpose of it was to provide my father with a place to work undisturbed. And because he was an artist, there was a sense that that was what we were all here for. There was this really strong sense that they worked together to create the home in which we all lived.'

Tony is the eldest of three siblings. Looking at all three today, it's clear that they're related. It isn't just the shared features: curly hair, warm deep-set eyes. They all have a calm, thoughtful pace to their language and an open and obvious sense of curiosity about each other and about the world. That all three children grew up to work in highly collaborative art forms – theatre, film and music – is scarcely surprising; they've been learning how to work with other people all their lives. Listening to each of them describe their childhoods, what's striking is that there's no struggle for dominance, and winning is not the issue. Tony, a filmmaker and playwright, knows that he was his mother's favourite – the others all agree – but nobody seems to mind very much, perhaps because each had their own niche.

'Tina and I played the piano and the violin,' Tony recalled. 'But when Nick arrived, it was just clear from an early age that – well – if he wasn't a prodigy, he was certainly very gifted. If there had been a contest, it would have been obvious that we couldn't compare – so there was no contest.'

'I'm the youngest in the family and I was never terribly good with language,' Nick Bicât recalled. 'But I could always win my older brother's respect with my stunts: throwing myself from the first-floor window or downstairs. Later on, of course, the music helped too.'

Today, Nick Bicât is an award-winning composer. He's written music for Hollywood movies, the London Chamber Orchestra, the Royal Shakespeare Company, Philip Ridley, David Hare, Howard Brenton, for TV versions of *A Christmas Carol* to the steamy melodrama *Lace*. His work couldn't exist without collaborators and he received deep early lessons in collaboration at home.

'Tony was the oldest and he knew more than me about just about everything. He was sharp and witty and perceptive. I wanted his approval, wanted him to like what I did, would want him to laugh. I wanted him to like my music.'

In between the two boys was their sister, Tina.

'Tony always had a story – that was his thing and he used us where appropriate,' Tina remembered. 'Nick was very musical and I made things: props and costumes. I made the pictures come alive. It was set quite early, how we played together. It was probably helped by the fact that we had a lot of space – a big garden – and, while there were grown-ups around, I don't remember them being with us. They were always there to step in and help us, if we needed it. But most of the time, we just got on with it.'

Tina has gone on to work as a designer with some of the world's most improvisatory and collaborative theatre groups – Punchdrunk, Ockham's Razor and Spiral. For the Bicâts, deidentification provided a rich early foundation because each child could bring something important and unique to the group. Each had their own niche and a unique capability that no one could take from them. That made participation safe. They don't describe a childhood free from conflict – money was always scarce and tensions abounded – but they learned early on, Tony says, to respect one another's territory and became very good at negotiating among themselves.

That capacity has continued throughout their lives. When their father died, the siblings convened to manage his art collection, a responsibility they discharge together to this day. In their professional lives, the Bicâts have sometimes collaborated with each other but more often with others. Each has had triumphs and failures but what has characterized their careers is a sense of freedom and of fairness, a sense of being both supported and independent.

This isn't about happy families as such. For the neurologist Robert Burton, the critical contribution that siblings make to early childhood is that they teach one fundamental life lesson that starts in the family but ultimately extends to all human relationships.

'You're not alone,' Burton told me, 'If you have a sibling, you aren't alone – in the sense that you aren't abandoned, isolated. But also you're not alone in the sense of Narcissus: there *is* more than just you in the world. And while this can feel terrible, it also contributes an important sense of camaraderie. It means learning the value of sacrifice, learning you can lose the argument and survive, you can express yourself and be original: those are all very necessary aspects of social understanding.'

For a long time, it has been so fashionable to see life as one long competition, from the cradle to the grave, that any other narrative has been dismissed as trivial, sentimental or irrelevant. This so puzzled and annoyed primatologist Frans de Waal that he has devoted a forty-year career to exploring how far competition dominates the lives and behaviours of our cousins: primarily chimpanzees and bonobos. Chimpanzees are of particular interest, he says, because they care intensely about power; it just isn't the only thing they care about. After a fight, they have elaborate rituals for reconciliation because they value relationships and appreciate that they need to be maintained. Chimps, bonobos, wolves, birds, hyenas and dolphins all learn to repair conflict and to reconcile differences, behaviours that, de Waal writes 'would be superfluous if social life were ruled entirely by domination and competition'.

Primates demonstrate clear awareness that they need help to accomplish their aims, that they can't do much singly. They're adept at building coalitions, mediating conflict and they show a distinct preference for pro-social choices. In one of his most famous experiments, de Waal showed that chimpanzees dislike unfairness and will, in some circumstances, reject rewards if they aren't shared equally. Even in the unlikely setting of a game-theory experiment, children and apes collaborate when they need each other. Many of de Waal's experiments have provoked outrage from economists who simply can't accept that competition and self-interest don't prevail. But his work has accumulated evidence showing that we have evolved behaviours to avoid the detrimental effects of extreme competition.

Diane Wilson and her sister, my father and his brothers, Tim the TV producer and all of the many siblings I've talked to who've confessed but avoided reliving the misery of sibling rivalry all testify to the impoverishment of lives ruled by competition. Unable to trust, needing always to win, seeing success only in the others' failures: these were habits taught early that, like the kittens' eyes, left a pattern of being and behaviour that could not be repaired. But the Naders, the Bicâts, the Wachowskis and all the millions of siblings who do move beyond competition find in each other a source of solidarity and definition.

Having equal capacity for collaboration and for competition, it depends on us, our families and the society we inhabit, which gets attention and reinforcement. In the last fifty years of Western culture, competition has proved the dominant, insistent trope with an ever-expanding library of books, tools, apps, classes, personal coaches and any number of score cards to make us bigger, tougher, meaner, more successful competitors. As though the entire culture has been caught up in a testosterone-fuelled feedback loop, we've been persuaded that if we aren't top dog, we must be underdogs; if we aren't winners, we're losers. What's striking in its absence is the equivalent effort to hone our collaborative gifts. We know they're in there – we just don't make much effort to refine them. Opting to compete rather than to collaborate is a choice, not an evolutionary inevitability, a choice that incurs high costs, not just for our family relationships but for the friendships, organizations, institutions and world that we create.

What does this mean for Harry Hobbs? Will his hyper-competitiveness abate with time, and the conflicts that exhaust his parents slowly but surely teach him how to be part of something bigger, and more meaningful than himself? It's hard to tell. Last year, Harry was encouraged to apply for, and won a place at Eton. 'No one in the family went there,' Alice told me. 'We have no connections; we just thought we'd give it a go. But when he learned he'd got in – that he'd "won" so to speak – there was a strange look on his face: what have I done?'

2. MAKING THE GRADE

Few tragedies can be more extensive than the stunting of
life, few injustices deeper than the denial of an opportunity
to strive or even to hope, by a limit imposed from without,
but falsely identified as lying within.

Stephen Jay Gould

Just off Kendall Square in Cambridge, Massachusetts stand three
office blocks, so newly refurbished that you can tell by looking
through the windows that they're only partially occupied. With
shiny steel and gleaming marble, they are just another piece in the
grand 3-D jigsaw that comprises the campus of MIT. In contrast to
the flashier buildings of Frank Gehry, Steven Holl and Fumihiko
Maki, 700 Technology Square stands out as a workhorse, the place
where hard problems get solved without fanfare.

Up on the third floor, Charles Shubert presides over a project
within the Office of Educational Innovation and Technology.
Shubert looks more like Father Christmas than a nerd: a large,
rotund man with a warm, benevolent gaze, he has a laidback
Midwestern style and very dry sense of humour. To say that he is
a master of understatement would understate just how droll he can
be. But appearances notwithstanding, Shubert and his team are
tackling tough challenges: how to take advantage of large-scale
computing systems and bioinformatics to advance the understanding of microbial ecology. It isn't just the science that's hard.
The simulations that Shubert and his team build use huge amounts
of processing power, multiple computer systems and a variety of
computing languages. Yet, the software must be accessible and

usable by cutting edge scientists whose research needs are far from simple to understand, never mind address. The layers of technical collaboration implicit in this work are legion: languages, disciplines, systems, infrastructure, knowledge levels and personalities all combine in various permutations, giving Shubert's projects maximal complexity.

But what's more remarkable than the sheer difficulty of these projects are the people responsible for producing them. It's not easy finding people who can effortlessly cross and translate between cutting edge biology and bleeding edge technology. Ivan Ceraj, who leads the project, is an economist from Croatia. He says that most of the scientists can't do computer programming at this level and most computer programmers can't do biology at this level. If you find people who do both, they can earn a lot more money elsewhere.

Key to the team are Shubert's 'finds': talents he unearthed in unlikely places and of whom he is inordinately proud. Like Shubert, Justin Riley comes from Missouri, and if you didn't know that, you might guess: a tall freckled man in his mid-twenties, his brown hair, sharp nose and relaxed gait convey the ease and informality of a farmer. But Riley is glad to have left Missouri; he just had no idea he would end up at MIT.

'I really struggled in math when I was thirteen, fourteen,' he told me. 'I'd get a C or a B if I was lucky. I was a nerdy kid and liked tinkering with things. But I had no idea about science or any sense it was something I'd want to do.'

In the early days of computing and with the advent of the Internet, Riley had fun breaking computers and fixing them. He taught himself how to build websites and earned a little money that way. After high school, he went to Missouri State University without any particularly fixed idea of what he would do. He was, he said, really just going through the motions of college.

'I had read about people connecting computers to do cool stuff. That aspect seemed a lot of fun,' he told me, laughing. 'In my spare time, I decided to check it out and ended up building a student project, HoToTo – a silly name meaning half bear, half man. My friends and I went to a warehouse auction selling off really old equipment – we were really just experimenting. Four or five of my buddies sat on the floor, took the computers apart, put them all together, blew a few circuits but got them going and installed Linux. It looked like a monster mounted on hardwood planks . . .'

One day, Shubert was home visiting his family in Missouri and decided to drop into MSU, where he knew the dean of sciences. In the corner of a computer lab, he spotted Riley and asked what he was up to. They talked for a while, Shubert wandered off and Riley gave him no more thought. The next day the dean told Riley how much Shubert had enjoyed the conversation; would it be all right to forward his contact information?

'I knew he was from MIT so of course I was interested!' Riley recalled. 'And over the course of the year, Charlie worked hard to get me here. I started work at MIT before I'd even finished my degree! Fortunately for me it turned out I love to programme, but before I came here, I had done very little. I was really worried about my qualifications; I knew very little scripting. I knew some loops and had played with writing in C, just working through a book. Chuck and Ivan threw me into the deep end with Java. Looking back, I'm actually still rather shocked that I got to come here! If I'd gone to the bathroom at the wrong time, I might never have met him, never got here.'

Shubert was thrilled with Riley's work, not just because it was excellent but because it validated something he'd always believed: that there's more talent in ordinary places than most people ever imagine or see. When he started looking for it, he found it. Riley's colleague is Sara Bonner; Shubert found her working as an administrative assistant and trying to finish college. She wasn't having a good time; a reputation for being argumentative earned her a fair amount of opprobrium from her peers.

'Then Charlie took me out for lunch and asked me if I'd like to be a software developer! I said: You realize I don't code – I've just done a few PERL scripts. But he said, no, he wanted to teach me and he had a grant that would let him do that, as long as I didn't mind minority money. I said I didn't mind any money as long as it was green.'

She later learned that Shubert had been watching her for a year; he was impressed by how hard she worked and how prepared she was to stand up for herself. Those were the qualities he sought.

Bonner says of herself that she liked to 'MacGyver' things – a term derived from a US television hero who could solve complex problems with everyday materials, mainly duct tape and a Swiss army knife. That combination of smart thinking and pragmatism was just what Shubert needed, and found, in Sara Bonner.

'It's hard for me to talk with grandeur about what I bring to the table until I go to conferences and talk to senior developers and I am just astounded by what they don't know. Charlie says I bring a special ability to be a user and a coder and to not feel uncomfortable disagreeing with him. Before I ask a question, I like to know the possible answers so I can be prepared for the conversation. So we have very thoughtful conversations here. We're not just poking each other back and forth; it isn't a contest.'

Justin and Sara weren't star competitors in the current education system; they weren't expert at, or even interested in, guessing the right answers but had retained the love of learning and exploration that Shubert prized. But nothing in their schooling suggested that they would, one day, be working at one of the world's most prestigious universities or that Justin would author a paper about software published in *Nature*. The competitive education system wasn't what got them to MIT. That they had the potential is clear now but what saved them, in the end, was luck. Imagine if Riley had gone to the bathroom at the wrong moment or if Bonner hadn't been argumentative. Charlie – a most unlikely fairy godfather – happened to notice them, happened to help them and happened to be in a position to change their lives. But, for most children, success hinges on being able to compete at every stage of their educational career. For their parents, failure is a constant, imminent and terrifying threat.

'What happens if the kids don't play the system? If your child goes to the wrong school, he will be scuttling coal somewhere,' Betsy Rapoport told me. 'They've been given a life diagram – go to the right school, then you will get the right job, the right amount of money and then you'll be happy and get promoted and move on straight up to the top!'

She's laughing but she's put two children through the New York state education system and now she coaches many more through the college application process. In the kids that she works with, and their parents, she sees the sense of emergency that characterizes their thinking about education as a permanent crisis.

'These kids have been competing since they were two! They start being coached and tutored at the age of three to get into kindergarten. *Kindergarten!* They have parents breathing down their necks, telling them that if they don't get into this nursery school, they won't get into the right elementary or middle school – then high school will be a disaster, their lives will be ruined. It starts young and it just gets more and more intense.'

Competition within UK schools may not start quite as early as in New York but parental anxiety and push are just as fierce. If education is competition and the stakes are so high, then you have to compete and you have to win, no matter what happens.

'In London, there is just a dreadful race for where your child should go – whether you're in the state or the private sector. It is just incredible,' Sue Anstruther told me.

'I knew one mother whose son puked when he was eleven, sitting the exam for Westminster Under. And the mother insisted on her son re-sitting the exam even though the school told her that, looking at what he had completed, the school wasn't going to be a good fit for him. At every single entrance exam my son sat, a child puked or burst into tears just because they felt under so much pressure.'

Both in the US and the UK, kids learn earlier and earlier that education is a high-stakes game: win and your life is assured; fail and you will never recover. Winning means getting into the right school, sitting the right exams, getting the right marks, making the right friends. These are lessons children pick up early and often and mostly from their parents.

Anstruther left a successful career at the BBC – at one point, she worked on *Dr Who* – to become a maths teacher. She's taught in state and private schools and the pressure she's seen parents putting on their children made Daleks look positively genteel.

'Many parents are enormously competitive about their children,' Sue Anstruther told me, with a mixture of horror and amusement. 'They talk about competitive friending – whether their kids are friends with the popular children, the kids of famous parents. And they're highly competitive about marking and exams. At parents' evenings, you'd have your mark book open and would try to hide it, but you'd see them lean over and try to see other kids' marks, wanting to judge their kids by the others. They were just like naughty schoolchildren themselves; they knew they shouldn't peek – but they still did it.'

Anxiety about the need to succeed has been running high for decades but the global economic crisis, together with high levels of youth unemployment, has turned fear into self-perpetuating hysteria. If well paid jobs are few, then a lustrous educational track record is crucial, with the risks of failure high and the costs of under-achievement deadly. As the Internet, robotics and globalization have eliminated entry-level jobs and, with them, chances of working your way to the top, a top-tier education appears the last guaranteed way to get ahead. No more the backroom-to-boardroom romance; now school, and school alone, is seen as making the difference between triumph and disaster.

Exams are the key. With their emphasis on standardized exams – starting at age five with the Early Years Foundation Stage profile, Key Stages one through three, then GCSEs, AS and A-levels, not forgetting for some Common Entrance, BTECs, HNCs, NVQs, music, drama, speech and dance exams – teachers, parents and children have all the objective tools and data they need to compete and compare. That's one of the consequences of standardized exams: everyone can see who's top – and who's not. Even though children develop at vastly differing rates, quite early they are firmly identified as academic or not, bright or not, high potential or low. It's because they know this that parents are so pushy, if not downright panic-stricken. They recognize that there's a snowball effect: that the good students will get taken more and more seriously, with the 'gifted and talented' being offered enrichment programmes and classes for academic high flyers, while the rest will get less and less. Children learn early whether it's worth their while even playing the game.

Streaming – or setting – is the first sign many kids get that they're not winners. Being in the bottom set may be intended to encourage them; in fact, it makes them, and their friends, and quite often their teachers, label them as 'not academic'. This is shorthand for 'loser', an assumption that the child just isn't very good at that subject and, by implication, never will be. What's alarming is how quickly that becomes comfortable.

An excellent education isn't, apparently, necessary for everyone. The ghost of the 11-plus, which bifurcated children into 'academic' and 'other' still hangs over British education. Those who were well served by grammar schools generalize from their individual experience and long for their return; those who were dumped into secondary moderns wonder whether the same bifurcation still occurs, just covertly. I've talked to countless teachers who argue that, well, some kids are going to be hairdressers so they really don't need to read Shakespeare. If you're going to be a bus driver, you won't need calculus. It reminds me of neighbours when I was growing up in London who wondered why my father was bothering to send me to university; as a girl, surely I'd just get married and settle down. Explicitly or implicitly, in Britain children are sorted as surely as Harry Potter was by the sorting hat at Hogwarts. Intrinsic to the whole idea of sorting is the notion that the innate talents of a child can be seen and served, that they're already there and that someone, somehow, can identify them. In Harry Potter, it's magic. In real life, it's competitive exams.

Some of these are high-status exams that will lead to university and professional qualifications, some are low-status exams that will identify the non-academic children. Ostensibly, it's an improvement from the grammar school/secondary modern – but not much. With one of the highest teenage school-dropout rates in the developed world, 20 per cent of British students have absorbed the message that, when you're bound to lose, there's no point competing. Forty per cent of sixteen-year-olds in Britain fail to get five 'good' GCSEs and one in six struggles with literacy. And that under-achievement can last a lifetime: OECD data in 2013 showed that only a quarter of adults had maths skills above the level of a ten-year-old while one in six adults could only just decipher sentences and read a paragraph of text. Thirty per cent of every *year* of sixteen-year-olds were deemed to have been failed by the education system.[1]

With such widespread under-achievement, what makes people imagine that competitive education – with schools in league tables, teachers paid by performance and students paid with results – is the answer? Because, under very defined conditions, it can increase motivation: competition has come to be used as the fallback moti-vator with which to address under-achievement. So competition cascades throughout education: children competing for places and exam results; teachers competing for exam results (which may impact pay); schools competing for their place on the league table; students competing for university places; and universities competing for their place on the league table. If children will run faster in a race, the argument runs, won't everyone study harder competing with one another? Isn't turning education into one giant multiathlon the key to bringing Olympian achievements to young minds?

The problem here isn't that you won't motivate sprinters with promises of medals; you will. But learning to think mathematically, to love words, to decode a map or design a good experiment: these are skills that require a different order of thinking and a different order of long-term motivation. And what we know from at least half a century of research into human motivation is that extrinsic rewards — rankings, prizes, grades — crowd out intrinsic drive. We can't, apparently, be deeply motivated by many things at once but only, really, by one. And hard, short-term rewards — money, medals, prizes — tend to crowd out the longer-term, self-generated drive.

This is so counter-intuitive that we persist in believing that the way to motivate kids (and adults) is to offer them rewards. The landmark experiment that suggested otherwise was conducted forty years ago by Edward Deci and Richard Ryan. Ever since their original work, different permutations of it have been tested and retested, without any significant challenge; the findings remain robust.

In the original experiment, a bunch of nursery school children were divided into three groups and given the opportunity to draw. The first group was promised a reward: if they drew, they'd win a certificate. The second group was told nothing — but was surprised by a certificate when it had finished drawing. The third group just drew and received nothing for its labours.

Two weeks later, the children were again confronted by paper and pens. Now the question was: which group would *want* to draw? The group that had initially been promised a reward was the least engaged: why should they draw when there was no certificate on offer?

Similar experiments have been conducted with different ages, tasks and rewards, in different industries and countries around the world, but the results don't vary. Grades, stars, certificates, money, trophies: 'virtually every type of expected tangible reward made contingent on task performance does, in fact, undermine intrinsic motivation.'[2]

As early as 1950, the eminent American psychologist Joy Paul Guilford had challenged his professional colleagues with a question: why is there so little correlation between education and creative productiveness?[3] Guilford made his name developing psychometric studies of intelligence, making a critical distinction between what he called convergent and divergent production. Convergent production, he argued, involved finding a single solution to a problem; by contrast, divergent thinking required surfacing as many solutions as possible. The first was fundamentally about following rules where the latter was inherently creative, imaginative and exploratory. At MIT, Sara Bonner was a classic divergent thinker: always seeking multiple solutions and exploring alternatives. This may have made her argumentative – she could see more solutions than many of her colleagues – but it is also exactly what made Charles Shubert so eager to recruit her. Yet, our educational systems specifically reward convergent thinking while inhibiting divergent critical and creative thinking.

When two psychologists, Teresa Amabile and Beth Hennessey, rose to Guilford's challenge, devoting decades of work to experiments that explored the connection between creativity and education, they concluded that there are five ways in which education can *kill* creativity: having children work for an expected reward; focusing pupils on an expected evaluation; deploying plenty of surveillance; setting up restricted choices; and creating competitive situations – all highly characteristic of the education systems we currently deploy.[4] We say we want motivated, creative students – but we opt for methods and structures known to undermine both. No wonder Yale graduate Alexandra Robbins compared high school to a game show: 'Education is no longer about a learning experience; it's a game of *Survivor* where kids are strategizing to work against each other and beat the system.'

As Education Secretary, Michael Gove argued that exam success makes kids happy: 'If we know tests are rigorous, and they require application to pass, then the experience of clearing a hurdle we once considered too high spurs us on to further endeavours and deeper learning.'[5] He bases this on the American cognitive scientist Daniel T. Willingham, who observed that kids enjoy learning if they experience 'the pleasurable rush that comes from successful thought'. But of course that rush of thinking isn't remotely the same as passing an exam; these are intellectually, emotionally and socially completely different experiences. In jumping from one to another, everything is lost in translation. Instead, once the exam pass becomes a commodity, especially surrounded with fear of failure, its capacity to inspire is profoundly circumscribed.

Moreover, as many politicians do, Gove generalized from his own experience of education. He was good at tests so he likes them and believes in them. But how students respond to the pressure of exams varies wildly and bears no relationship to capability. Instead, it appears that who loves exams and does well in them is significantly determined by our genes.

The COMT (catechol-O-methyl transferase) gene regulates the amount of dopamine in the pre-frontal cortex in the brain, where we make decisions, plan and resolve conflicts. One variant of COMT removes dopamine slowly; another variant does it fast. Dopamine levels increase with stress; enough helps you rise to the occasion but too much becomes overwhelming. So students with the slower variety of COMT typically find it easier to think if they are not under stress. Those with the faster variety may seem a little laid back but, under stress, they cope better. Some scientists distinguish between the two genetic stress responses as 'worriers' and 'warriors' but the key point about them is that they both excel – albeit in very different environments. Hence the paradox that hardworking students may fall apart in exams while the ones who never handed in their homework on time ace tests. What exams reveal most clearly is not intellectual or creative capacity – but a very great deal about how good you are at exams.[6]

The research into COMT was primarily conducted in Taiwan, which traditionally placed great emphasis on a single exam – the Basic Competency Test – taken by children when they are fourteen. In essence, this was their equivalent of the 11-plus. Applying their genetic insights to real-world testing confirmed the hypothesis that this kind of high-stakes test identified great exam takers but was less helpful in building or identifying intelligence. From 2014, Taiwan will no longer require the exam. Instead of sorting, educational policy now emphasizes raising attainment levels for everyone.

Of course, tests can check whether students are keeping up, how much they've retained, and what they still don't understand. But standardized testing associated with external rewards – be it stars, grades, medals or college places – turns learning from something that should be intrinsically satisfying into a transaction: do the work, get the grade. The product is prized over the process. With eyes so firmly focused on the external reward, the work itself loses meaning and joy. We produce expert exam takers when what we ought to develop is a bigger prize: the love of learning.

That may appear terribly sentimental but it really isn't. Apart from sounding worthy, what is the value of a love of learning? Why don't we just teach kids what they need to get jobs and get on with their lives? The problem is that no one knows what they will need. The world is changing too fast, industries come and go with such speed, that it is impossible to predict what the toolkit of the future will contain. Twenty years ago, it might have been reasonable to assume that knowing shorthand; how to run a printing press; or do electrical engineering; mastering the arcane information structure of the law; or being able to prototype packaging might have been important, but today those specific skills are redundant. Bosses type for themselves, newspapers are fast disappearing, no one uses typewriters, domestic appliances last for ever or get replaced cheaply, software is taking over the work of paralegals and 3-D printers will take care of your prototyping needs. Even doctors and lawyers face much of their work being replaced by machines. As the machinery for invention and manufacture gets cheaper and the software to run it gets easier, much old-fashioned expertise carries little kudos and even less job security.

In Dickens's *Hard Times*, the schoolmaster Thomas Gradgrind insists that facts, 'nothing but facts' are the fundamental and essential building blocks of education and a profitable economy. But facts don't have the currency they used to when everyone can look up anything on a phone. Moreover, many of the facts that today's researchers work with didn't even exist when they were in school; the Human Genome Project and the CERN Large Hadron Collider have revolutionized (and rendered obsolete) knowledge that a decade earlier looked essential. To survive in this new world, we cannot possibly expect children to leave school with all the skills or the knowledge they will need. So we have to aim for them to leave with a capacity and appetite for learning and divergent thinking that will stand them in good stead their whole lives.

This is what Justin Riley and Sara Bonner have – but it isn't what competitive exams deliver. Subtly, and often unintentionally, exams teach kids that there is a right answer that wins the reward. Everyone gets this message. While decrying exams and citing timetable pressures, teachers focus on teaching to the test and – implicitly or explicitly – encourage their students to learn to that test. Offered additional or mildly oblique supplementary material, what's the response? 'We don't need to know that, it's not in the test.'

You can't blame the kids; theirs is an intelligent, rational response to a structure where rewards drain motivation. And when teachers' pay derives, even in part, from exam results, they're caught in the same trap. At a time when we badly need to develop imagination, creativity and the intellectual initiative that generates new ideas, competitive testing is tailor-made to do just the opposite: cultivate a talent for playing safe, for second-guessing and ingraining a belief that there is such a thing as the right answer.

What exams do with magnificent clarity is deliver clear objective results so that schools can see who's top and who's bottom of the class. The vast array of exams we subject our children to does nothing in the way of intrinsic motivation but it does allow schools to identify winners and rank them.

'We rank kids behind the scenes,' Tim Meunier told me.

Meunier is the headmaster of Colet Court, which prepares boys for St Paul's, widely regarded as one of the top private schools in London. It nestles on the banks of the Thames, near where the annual Oxford/Cambridge boat race takes place. Walking to the school, I was struck by how many signs of exclusion I saw everywhere: locked-up parking spaces in front of a GP's surgery, gated driveways on Lonsdale Road, speakerphones, fences around gardens and churchyards. Barriers everywhere.

Along with Eton, St Paul's took itself out of the league tables a few years ago; Meunier said he thought they were unfair and didn't reflect the wide range of qualities that many good schools demonstrate. He's right – but he doesn't apply that same thinking to his own students.

'Somebody has to be bottom. We don't pretend that rankings are accurate, because statistically they are imperfect. But we want to know who's top and who's bottom. No other system would bring that to light.'

Meunier argues that the rankings are primarily for his management team, so that they can check no one is getting left behind. But he's a firm believer in winning and in prizes.

'We don't have this thing where there are no winners. I don't believe in that. At prize-giving too, we have prizes for improvement – recognizing those who pulled their socks up – but there aren't many of those. And there are prizes for being an overall good chap. But the main thrust is: if you win chemistry prize, it's because you came top. I would want it to be that way. I don't want my teachers choosing the one that is nicest or the most helpful.'

Meunier doesn't relish boys coming at the bottom but he may be a little naïve about just how secret his rankings are. Mothers at the school readily told me when their boys were top in a subject; they knew – and the chances are the other boys did too. That's unfortunate because the research shows that, while rankings may motivate the top two or three, they de-motivate everybody else. The price paid for a few motivated high achievers is the necessarily larger number of students who know they can't win.

But if rankings do very little for children, they do a great deal for parents. When, in the summer of 2013, Nick Clegg announced a new initiative to rank children at age eleven, much lip service was paid to the idea that this was no return to the bad old days of the 11-plus; it was just benchmarking to identify poorly performing schools. Naïve or disingenuous, the devil was in the detail. The percentile ranking would not be published – this was not, we were assured, designed to name and shame – but it would be shared with parents. The idea that, as such, it would remain private signalled only the isolation of policymakers from reality.

'The parents I worked with would have *loved* having class

rankings,' Sue Anstruther laughs, 'as long their children had been on top! But we didn't do it because the quarrels with the parents arguing the toss would have been unbearable. Any bloody exam I ever marked created rows about how there *must* have been something wrong with the marking system.

'From my own experience as a pupil, when we had rankings, it did me no good at all. I was doing fine anyway. But for others it really was a disaster. It's just too de-motivating for most of the children. Children, I think, are naturally competitive. You don't have to stoke that! They want to do well and if you engage and interest them – and don't frighten them – they will.'

St Paul's isn't alone in ranking their students. A number of British schools still do so, though they are all profoundly reluctant to discuss it. But formal class rankings are commonplace in the United States. Every student there has a running Grade Point Average (GPA) that makes it simple to rank students; some schools post the rankings on corridor walls. Even for the winners, there's a nasty social side-effect. Everyone knows that it is crowded at the top.

'My daughter was ranked number four in her class,' one New York mother told me. She didn't want her name, or her daughter's name, to be used but she did want their experience to be known.

'For most of high school, she'd been in the top five. And in her junior year, she was struggling with a math project, so she went to one of her classmates – also in the top five – and asked for some help on it.'

Her daughter took up the story. 'The top five are particularly conscious of each other. And it was weird because the three guys ahead of me were very math and sciency and I wasn't. I think they sometimes thought I couldn't be that smart. But anyway, I asked one of them to help me – and he wouldn't!' She paused for a second.

'He said his mother had told him not to, because it might jeopardize his ranking.'

American students are full of stories about key textbooks being hidden in school libraries, critical resources strangely going missing. What rankings do – naturally – is pit students against one another. How can they not? There's only so much room at the top – even in percentile rankings. As such, they teach exactly the wrong lesson for life: for me to win, you must lose. They turn every child into a competitor with every other child, just at the time in life when social understanding is developed. Positioning achievement as a solo activity is exceptionally poor preparation for working life, where almost all work is now done in groups. What skills are required for effective teamwork? Collaborative skills: the ability to look for and build on each other's strengths. But this isn't what rankings teach.

Whether by design or accident, the consequence of standardized testing is to facilitate comparison, stoke rivalries and enforce convergence and homogeneity. It may help policymakers benchmark, but it militates against the development of imagination, creativity and collaboration: all those gifts and talents avidly sought and so highly prized in adults.

The rare and inspirational teachers who model divergent thinking – the quest for multiple solutions – tend to stimulate creativity, but grades and competition do not. Critical to developing creativity anywhere is a climate of safety: the sense that intellectual exploration isn't dangerous and won't incur penalties, together with the confident appreciation that mistakes aren't catastrophes; they are how we learn. But extreme focus on exams, grades and rankings specifically undermines that security.

Deci and Ryan, the psychologists devoted to studying motivation, identified ways to increase intrinsic motivation: positive feedback that encourages the desire for a sense of competence, optimal (not impossible) challenges, freedom from demeaning evaluations and, critically, a sense of autonomy. People – young and old – feel intensely motivated when they feel they have some choice about when and how they work. The work becomes theirs. On a trivial level, this was demonstrated in industrial experiments in which the simple power to decide when to switch lights on and off made workers more productive. But, on a more sophisticated level, their work shows how important it is for students to feel that they are working for themselves, towards goals that they own: not their parents, not their teachers and not the state. That doesn't mean parents and teachers and schools can't help; their positive encouragement, guidance and unexpected rewards are invaluable.

But this is why rankings can't work. They deliver too many demeaning evaluations and present impossible challenges. And the competitive parents focused on rankings fundamentally undermine their children's sense of autonomy.

Competitive pressures and threats don't solve these problems because failure necessarily overwhelms success – the amount of negative feedback is always larger than the positive. Not everyone can win, be in the top 1 per cent or even 5 per cent. But just about everyone can absorb the lesson that they are bound to lose – which makes them increasingly less willing to try. 'In schools,' Deci and Ryan wrote, rather glumly, 'intrinsic motivation becomes weaker with each advancing grade.' The cost of rewarding the top 1 per cent is the steady de-motivation of the remaining 99.

For many kids, the competitive pressures they feel from school, from their parents and from their friends, simply become intolerable. So they look for help and find it in some peculiar and dangerous places. When Steven Roderick, a 24-year-old smart, gentle student started at the University of Massachusetts in Boston, he was dismayed to find himself getting Ds and felt he had to do something. He'd heard about Adderall, an amphetamine prescribed for Attention Deficit Hyperactivity Disorder (ADHD), and knew the drug was pretty easy to get. So he hoped that might be what he needed to get better grades.

'The first time I took it, I wrote a paper for an astronomy class that was out of this world. I could not believe it – I was so inspired it made me want to be a doctor!'

Adderall is a Class 2 controlled substance; its users can become dependent, needing higher and higher doses, and it has been compared to drugs used in sport: 'Adderall has become to college what steroids are to baseball: an illicit performance enhancer for a fiercely competitive environment.'[7]

'I went from Ds and Fs to straight As. But your brain adapts, you have to increase the dose, and by 2011 I was up to 45 milligrams. I started to feel Adderall was my best friend and my worst enemy at the same time.'

Because he couldn't sleep, Roderick was prescribed Ativan, a powerful sleeping pill. But then he got locked into one drug to focus and one drug to relax. His need for Adderall increased –

eventually he was taking 120 milligrams, would then come off it, take Ativan and sleep for days. His anxiety levels rocketed; the drop of a pin, he said, would make him spin round. Although he nearly completed his university course, ultimately he had to withdraw because he could not make it to enough classes.

'Look,' Roderick reflected, 'I am in a culture that constantly justifies the means to an end. So how do we persuade people not to take it? All you hear is how impossible it will be to get a job when you get out, and you are going more and more into debt, and you think without this I won't be top of the class.'

With the big external rewards dangled over their heads like the sword of Damocles, students like Roderick sacrifice all intrinsic engagement in their subjects. All they hear, from parents and policymakers, is about grades, university places, awards and prizes. So, naturally, that's what they focus on: the educational commodities needed to move on to the next stage of the contest. It's the product, not the process, that matters. And if you can't win the game, you may as well game the system.

At Stuyvesant High School in New York, academic achievement is social currency. With four Nobel laureates as alumni, the school has a terrific reputation for science, and it's a tough school to get into. But once there, students started to realize that everyone around them was pretty smart too; how could they compete? It was easier, and often tactically more astute, to cheat than to waste time on subjects they didn't care about or didn't intend to take beyond school. Kids were posting homework answers on Facebook, hiding formulae up their sleeves or photographing tests to email to their friends. The school is intensely competitive – its students aiming for Harvard, Yale, MIT – and failure is so unacceptable that winning at any cost seemed preferable. In a school newspaper survey, 80 per cent of students admitted to cheating.

'It becomes kind of a numbers game,' said Elias Weinraub, eighteen, who is now at Washington University in St Louis. 'It was kind of addictive, in a bad way, in a sick way.'[8]

One teacher began to see the same homework answers so often that she started to ask students to handwrite their work, hoping that manual labour might discourage them from copying off the Internet. The school has also had cases of students devising pencil-tapping codes and sending answers via cell phones. One survey of 40,000 American high school students found that 59 per cent had cheated in an exam; Rush Kidder at the Institute for Global Ethics estimated that, by the time they got to college, 95 per cent of students had cheated in one form or another. Sometimes they cheat to deliver better work; other tactics – hiding essential library books, removing notices from bulletin boards – are designed to make fellow students fail. If the grade is the goal, how much does it really matter how you get it?

Having obtained a goal by cheating, students don't necessarily kick the habit. At the beginning of 2013, Harvard College forced some students to leave after the largest cheating scandal in memory. 'Somewhat more than half' of a class of 279 had been asked to withdraw when a number of exam questions featured identical answers on a take-home exam – identical to the point of identical typographical errors. While many commentators expressed astonishment at finding cheating so prevalent in elite institutions, in reality this shouldn't be surprising at all. Having fought so hard to achieve positions within these schools, students are highly driven to preserve them. It is a chastening thought that, the more elite the school, the less the students might be driven to enjoy their education for its own sake. Thinking for oneself, straying from the defined and the predictable could feel like too great a risk with too much at stake. The tougher the competition, the greater the urge to deliver exactly what's wanted – even if doing so is pretty much the opposite of learning.

This phenomenon is not unique to Stuyvesant High School or Harvard or to America. As for British students, in 2010, grade-A coursework in all subjects was available on eBay and other 'paper mills' for as little as £1.50. As the system becomes discredited, even teachers sometimes aim to game the system, by bribing so-called troublemakers not to be around during school inspections or by being over-generous in their exam marking.[9] In the academic year 2009–10, over 17,000 incidents of cheating were recorded by British universities – up at least 50 per cent in four years – though many believe the true figure is higher, just undisclosed.[10] By now, cheating has become so widespread that administrators have had to turn to software to try to address their problem.

'It's ironic that technology – which has certainly made cheating easier – is also the best way to eradicate it,' Jason Chu told me. 'But the scale of the problem is immense and it's global.'

Chu works for Turnitin, which makes plagiarism-detection software that is used in 126 countries where coursework has to be checked to ensure that it hasn't been copied, wholesale or in pieces, from the 24 billion web pages, 300 million archived student papers and 120 million articles from 110,000 journals, periodicals and books that sit in the company's databases. The software is constantly being refreshed and updated, to block the new ruses students devise to find ways not to do the work. The good news is that, apparently, students have become better judges of high-quality sources to steal from; the bad news is that there are more 'cheat sites' aimed at secondary-school students than ever before. And they're getting better at covering their tracks.

'What we've found is, students try to circumvent our system,' Jason Chu told me. 'They will take a paper written in English and change the font or certain characters to Cyrillic – our algorithm can't identify Cyrillic – so we have to stay quick on our feet. We're wise to this. Or they will change some of the words into images and submit that. It all requires so much effort – they could just do the work!'

Chu started off his career as an academic; he believes passionately, he says, in critical thinking. And once kids have to submit their papers through Turnitin, he says, they learn quickly that they must think for themselves. They learn better how to think about and use original content and how to give credit where it's due. Although there's a utilitarian aspect to the business, what excites him about it is that it helps, in a strange way, to return education to its original purpose.

'It isn't that students don't know that plagiarism is morally wrong; they do – even if they think it is a victimless crime. But the real problem they have is that students are not thinking about the process. They are only ever just thinking about the results. We have perpetuated this, with our emphasis on assessment. We have told students that what they are "earning" is a grade. You do this: you get that. Their reward isn't doing the work. Their reward isn't thinking, or learning to think. It's the grade. It's all about the grade.'

Chu may be marketing software for a living but he brings to his work an intrinsic motivation that's hard to miss.

'The whole idea behind liberal education used to be about building moral integrity and character. That's all gone. It's a tremendous shift that has happened, that emphasis on results. It's just swept everything else aside.'

It's an enduring lesson. For several years, I taught a certificate course in entrepreneurship in Boston for MBA graduates. My students were at the end of a very long educational food chain. They'd successfully fought their way through high school, college and business school, in each case passing tests and doing everything that was expected of them. When they came to my course, they had chosen a programme that was entirely voluntary, using their own time and their own money. But at the outset, they all wanted to know how they would be graded.

I was astonished. I was teaching the students how to set up their own businesses – an activity for which grades could not be less relevant. True, many of the students, rather than founding a company, might go to work for a startup. But no investor or employer would ever ask what grades they got on the course. How could these ostensibly innovation-loving, risk-taking adults care about grades so much? Because that's what they had been trained to care about their entire lives. These were good students: obedient, compliant, well behaved, successful. They'd passed hundreds, thousands, of tests. Now, confronted by another hurdle, their only question was: what do I get? Twenty years of being graded, working for grades, judging themselves by whether they were better or worse than their colleagues was, by now, what they needed. When I told them I would automatically give them all As, they weren't pleased. They didn't just want to learn; they wanted their success assured by the relative failure of others.

Teaching international MBA and MSc students in Britain isn't so different. Much of their work depends on coursework and, well beyond the academic course of their programme, it is this that they find most challenging. One MSc course depends entirely on the quality of team collaboration – but invariably at least one team falls apart and fails completely because its members simply cannot work together. When I explain to them that a best-selling business book,

Give and Take, makes a persuasive case that the most successful people are the most generous, they don't believe me. And when I explain that it is written by Adam Grant, a professor from Wharton Business School, famous for being the meanest, toughest, most quantitative business school on earth, they're frankly incredulous. These students, like their American counterparts, have fully internalized the concept of success as a solo achievement that requires taking no prisoners.

While standardized testing was introduced originally to level the playing field, to be able to compare like with like and to motivate recalcitrant students, its pervasive legacy has turned out to be an epidemic of cheating and highly constrained, conformist thinking.

In Singapore, often pointed to as a beacon of competitive educational success, learning for rewards has more recently come to be identified not as a solution but as a huge educational problem.

'We don't think that kind of education will be useful for the future,' Dr Koh Thiam Seng confided in me.

Koh runs St Joseph's Institution, one of the oldest schools in Singapore. It's a traditional school, started by a Catholic priest in 1852. When I visited, the students were all in bright white uniforms, and the place is run with military efficiency. The school has 'O' levels and rankings and publishes its overall exam results. But while many commentators imagine Singapore's education to be run along extremely conservative, even old-fashioned lines, appearances (and stereotypes) can be deceptive. This traditional exterior masks some very radical thinking.

'The old kind of education just helped kids work to a formula,' Koh continued. 'But the problem is that once there is no formula, our kids are very weak. So we need to know when to change, when to adapt, when to realize the formula isn't working. That isn't what our current system does. Our top students can do it but we need our average to do that at a much higher volume. If the average guys are just working to the formula, we will be dead in no time. The world is changing just too fast. If we just prepare boys for exams, we have failed.

'Several years ago we were trying to move from exams as the sole criteria for success. So we went to New York for inspiration. To our horror, they'd gone in the other direction! They were trying to move to where we are and we are trying to move to where they are! Standardized tests won't solve this problem.'

The first day that I visited St Joseph's was an open day and I was taken all over the school. It was ninety degrees outside and bagpipes were playing but that wasn't all that surprised me. In the centre of the school, I came across science projects developed in collaboration with Harvard's ArtScience team. The idea of the projects is to realize breakthrough ideas in the space where arts, sciences, and engineering meet. Working in small groups, the students collaborate on 'seed ideas' all of which aim at a major need or opportunity in culture, industry, or humanitarian engagement. The core of these projects is that they are led and developed by students – autonomously – not by teachers.

'ArtScience provides a different context. The teachers see that the boys *are* capable of thinking. If you allow students to take ownership, they learn how to think creatively. You make a lot of mistakes and that is good learning.'

The challenge posed by these projects is that they don't offer, or aim at, correct answers. They aim to inculcate divergent thinking. Nobody knows whether a proposal will work or not so the students who work on them learn to endure high degrees of ambiguity.

'In this work, there's a lot of debate, rebuttal, disagreement. It is uncomfortable for us,' Koh conceded. 'But it's important. It's important to give people – students and teachers – safety, the leeway to make mistakes and not pay for it. You need students to challenge you to get innovation and creativity. So how to do that here? The only way the boys learn how to work well together is to do it, to learn how to have the arguments, how to stretch the question until they can find some answers. The ArtScience projects are hard and they're not traditional. So they are,' Koh started to laugh, 'they certainly are challenging.'

One year, the students wanted to raise funds for Myanmar. But they hit a snag: the Ministry of Education doesn't allow schools to raise money for foreign countries. So Koh told the students to figure out a way around their problem, which they did by finding a local mission that helps Myanmar. Only by making them solve their own problems, he insisted, will kids get the thinking skills the twenty-first century requires.

Koh describes himself as a maverick and says that what he is doing at St Joseph's is a very carefully managed experiment. He's gone carefully and slowly to dismantle some of the structures and expectations that, he believes, militate against collaboration and creativity. Of these, the most contentious was his determination to eradicate streaming.

'We used to have a talent class and a non-talent class. It was all academically banded. So then we mixed it up and we saw no drop in academic achievement. Nor were teachers unduly stressed teaching a variety of students. What we gained was self-esteem, the willingness to try and not give up.'

In most Singapore schools, all the top schools used to compete to take the top students who would go on to compete for government scholarships and eventually to become Permanent Secretaries. That isn't the world Koh is preparing his boys for.

'Traditionally, the top 3 per cent will go to Raffles Institution. We used to play in that league but now we don't want such a narrow band of students. So we don't play that game. Going forward we want the school to be more accessible to a wider range of students. Some of the boys here will go into government or end up running large organizations. But the kind of policy-making and decisions you make when you grow up will be different if you can appreciate that not everyone moves at your pace. If you go to a top school you're surrounded by top people and don't learn how to work with people not on your level.'

None of this experimentation means that the boys of St Joseph's Institution don't take their learning seriously; they do. But, along with knowledge, they're learning profound life skills.

'Many of the boys have no idea what they want in life yet. That's okay. I tell them that any scores just measure a point in time; they don't say who you are or how good you are.'

This isn't an abstract experiment for Koh; his son goes to the school, so the father has to practise what he preaches.

'He can't stand biology so he dropped it. There was a ruckus in the classroom: what signal are you trying to send? But that *is* the signal I am trying to send! Now he's enjoying himself. He has more free periods, he plays his guitar. He can make some of his own choices.'

Koh may be a maverick and his changes at St Joseph's may be an experiment. But he's grappling with a question that Singapore's government is watching avidly. When I met with the Minister of Education, Lawrence Wong, he readily acknowledged that grades and targets can't deliver the levels of creativity and collaboration that the country needs. Dr Koh's 'experiment' is important because the government sees that masses of rote learning, more tests, and submissive traditional teaching methods will not create a dynamic and adaptable workforce. A new approach 'Teach Less, Learn More' is trying to put more white space into the school timetables, to enhance art and music and to develop more curiosity and a love of play.[11] In a country that its own leaders describe as formal and wary of dissent, there is a refreshing recognition that the modern world needs adults who are fearless in exploration, comfortable with ambiguity and bold in taking risks – and that they won't be able to do any of that in later life if they never learned to do it in school.

Yet, panic-stricken by higher educational achievement elsewhere, what are we doing at home? More exams, harder exams, exams that penalize those whose spelling isn't perfect or whose punctuation is adrift. We say we want our schools to prepare children for the real world but we won't let them use computers or spellcheckers and we won't monitor their work as they go along. It's hard to conceive of the real-world environment in which two years' work is appraised, once and for all, in a few hours. In its enthusiasm for old style O-level-type exams, the British government seems to take pride in devising a system whose chief aim is a higher failure rate.

One of the most inspiring examples of great learning in recent years derived not from contests, prizes or exams but from a collaborative project pioneered by Devon schoolteachers, Dave Strudwick and Tina Rodwellyn, mentored by Beau Lotto, a neuroscientist who works with London's Science Museum. They were convinced that children *are* scientists: curious, investigative and full of good questions that they are capable of answering. Working with twenty-five 8–10-year-old students, they brainstormed questions about bees. Many of their first questions they had already had answered by research published in recent scientific journals; that's how good and relevant the questions were. But then the kids hit on a question that had not been answered yet: how did bees choose which flowers to go to for foraging? Was it colour or location that mattered most? 'Knowing that other animals are as smart as us means we can appreciate them more, which could also help us to help them,' the children reasoned.[12]

Working with their teachers and with Lotto, the children were encouraged to think of their experiment as a game, or a puzzle. So they designed and built a game of coloured Perspex circles and sugar water, which they put (together with a lot of bees) inside a Norman church near their school. It was designed to test whether it was the colour or the placement of the sugar water that most drew in the bees.

The children observed the bees in multiple conditions, recorded and analysed their results. They concluded that bees were very good at solving puzzles, that they could learn collaboratively and from their mistakes. They also succeeded in getting their experiment and its findings – written in their own language, not academese – published in a scientific journal, *Biology Letters*. This was the first ever peer-reviewed publication in which all twenty-five authors were primary school pupils who wrote in their own language (the paper begins with the words 'Once upon a time'.)

But perhaps most important of all, the children had learned to think like scientists and to enjoy it. There were no prizes but there was great learning, fun and a sense of accomplishment. 'Before doing these experiments we did not really think a lot about bees and how they are as smart as us,' the students wrote. 'We also did not think about the fact that without bees we would not survive, because bees keep the flowers going. So it is important to under-stand bees. We discovered how fun it was to train bees. This is also cool because you do not get to train bees everyday. We like bees. Science is cool and fun because you get to do stuff that no one has ever done before. (Bees – seem to – think!)'

The Blackawton bees project was provocative and inspiring because it showed the degree to which young children could do high-level reasoning and problem-solving without stress, without exams but for the sheer pleasure of thinking. It assumed that the children had the capacity and enthusiasm to learn, and created the conditions in which they could do so with a result that represented a huge intrinsic reward. I first heard about the project when one of the young students gave a presentation about it: she was confident, excited and proud. The experience had meant far more than any certificate, it had drawn in all the children and hadn't required any losers.

That is the kind of critical thinking which the PISA test is designed to capture. Every three years, a random assortment of 5,000 fifteen-year-olds gathers to do, yes, another round of exams. But these are different. The students can't pass or fail, they will never learn how they've done individually and there are no prizes. The PISA (the Programme for International Student Assessment) test attempts to benchmark educational achievement in 87 per cent of the world's economies.

PISA was the brainchild of Andreas Schleicher, an amiable OECD official who is far jollier than you might expect of a German statistician. He started to design PISA in 1997 when OECD countries clamoured for reliable insight into how well their respective educational systems performed. The test wasn't designed to audit knowledge but to gather data around students' ability to apply what they learned. Not one to set himself easy goals, Schleicher also wanted to ask students about their motivation, beliefs about themselves and learning strategies and to put some hard numbers around some of the most intractable questions in education: is there a relationship between spending and outcomes? How critical is class size? Are our schools adequately preparing young people for the challenges of adult life? Are some kinds of teaching and schools more effective than others? Does sorting work? What characterizes a successful educational system?[13]

The first exams took place in 2000. When the results were published a year later, the German government bayed for Schleicher's blood. The data he had collected was a severe blow to the national ego: for reading and literacy, Germany was below the OECD average; in a country that prided itself on equality, PISA showed that student achievement in Germany was more correlated with family socio-economic status than any other OECD country. Germany's tri-partite system, which ranked children and channeled them at

age ten into one of three types of secondary school effectively limited achievement. Sorting didn't work.

'Sorting doesn't work,' Schleicher said, smiling, when we met in
Edinburgh. He has personal experience of his statistically based
conclusion; as a child, he'd been told in no uncertain terms that he
'wasn't *gymnasium* material'. That was his first inkling that trying to
choose winners was counter-productive.

'Teachers routinely over estimate the influence of social background. That leads them to give up on too many children. There's
no trade-off between equity and excellence. None. The top-
performing school systems are the ones that do a better job of
educating *everybody*, not the ones that just try to choose or find the
few. The association between social disadvantage and low educational achievement is strong – but it is not inevitable.'

Schleicher was well protected by his employers, so he didn't lose
his job. But Germany wasn't the only country to be dismayed by
his findings. The United States, the richest country in the world,
was only average in literacy, below average in mathematics and science. The United Kingdom did somewhat better than that, coming
seventh in literacy, eighth in maths and fourth in scientific literacy.
Luxembourg, which ran the most expensive educational system,
lurked barely above the bottom of the list.

But amidst all the bad news were startling surprises. Chief
among these was Finland, which came first in reading, third in science and fourth in maths. In all the subsequent PISA tests, Finland
has remained the top-performing European nation. But those first
results were as surprising to the Finns as to the rest of the world.

'We really had no idea at all how well we were doing,' Pasi
Sahlberg told me. 'I'd like to be able to say that we'd worked it all
out. But that really isn't what happened.'

In the 1960s, 90 per cent of Finns had completed only seven to
nine years of schooling and university graduates were rare. A
widespread recognition that this posed a big risk to the nation as a
whole led to a remarkable series of reforms. Central to all of these
reforms was an unwavering commitment to the idea that education
had to serve the whole nation. This might seem obvious but it isn't.
Margaret Thatcher, for example, famously believed that 'nations
depend for their health, economically, culturally and psychologically,

upon the achievement of a comparatively small number of talented and determined people'.[14] If you believe that, then you want to identify those talented people early and develop them – in which case, competition early and often could work well to produce and promote the winners. But this, quite explicitly, is what the Finns rejected because they thought that the country could not afford to waste any of its human talent; the challenge of moving the small country swiftly from an agrarian to an industrial economy was too great. So the reformers demanded the active collaboration of *all* political parties together with the teaching organizations: education was simply too important to become a political football.

Today, Finnish students don't take any standardized tests until they are eighteen and, while they get written assessments, they don't get grades. That means teachers can't compare, or rank, students. Neither can the students themselves – or their parents. Finnish schools are not inspected; Sahlberg himself was Finland's last chief inspector of schools in the early 1990s, before politicians decided to eliminate the process. Without league tables or streaming, none of the data or tools a competitive person – parent or child – might need to compare schools or children is available.

'We invented Angry Birds – so it's not that Finns aren't competitive,' Sahlberg said, laughing. 'Our TV is as full of competitive games as England's – maybe more! But when it comes to education and the culture, there is really no room for trying to see education as a competition. Finnish parents define learning as developing the individual: sharing, helping, doing things together and being part of the community rather than trying to do better than your neighbour. So that's why we have no school rankings.'

Sahlberg started out teaching in Finnish schools; now he makes his living studying education around the world and trying to understand what has made the Finns' experiments work. What he won't accept is that his compatriots are in any way superior to the allure of contests.

'We can make a competition out of anything – for fun. But we just don't think it's the way to inspire a love of learning. We focused on equity and cooperation instead of choice and competition. What does high-stakes testing do? It narrows the way that children think, so it discourages risk-taking. It makes kids frightened – that's not good thinking – and it's boring!'

Sahlberg doesn't believe for one moment that it's anything uniquely Finnish – and he eagerly dismisses arguments that say the Finnish example is just anomalous.

'People say to me that, oh, it's easier in a small country – but Finland is the same size as Scotland, Connecticut or Massachusetts. They say it's ethnically homogenous but we have three native languages, 5 per cent foreign-born citizens and 10 per cent non-Finnish-speaking citizens. The diversification of Finnish society since the mid-1990s has been the fastest in Europe!

'Many people assume Finland has been able to perform so well because we make kids stay in school longer or have a lot of homework – so when I explain that school days are shorter compared to almost any others and that our kids don't do too much homework and there is little competition, many people do find it hard to understand.'

On the cold sunny morning that I visited the Aurora primary school in Espoo, I was expecting a gleaming new building, with shiny new equipment and lots of noise. That wasn't what I found. Instead, a small cluster of concrete buildings, a sparse playground. It looked a little bleak from the outside but inside the school was warm, quiet and calm. Students padded about the corridors in their socks while, in the staff room, teachers made coffee, read newspapers, did jigsaw puzzles. Marimekko mugs, a few computers, Angry Birds balloons, a mishmash of comfy chairs and quiet laughter filled the space. For a Monday morning, there was a lot of energy in the staff room.

Among the gathering teachers was Martti Helstrom, the school head. Grey-haired and sporting heavy glasses, he'd recently returned from a trip to Graceland, where he'd shot a movie about Elvis on his iPhone. I guessed that his green shirt, painted with a big black guitar, was a souvenir. As I sat drinking coffee, everyone smiled at me, Martti signed paperwork and we talked about his twenty-three years running the school.

'We are such a small country we can't afford to lose any child. So it's our job to understand the children, find out how they learn, where they're having difficulties. Everyone learns together but they learn at their own pace. They can stay as long as they need or move as fast as they want.

'The parents trust us for many reasons but, because we don't select who comes here, the school is not the enemy. It's very ethically demanding if you have power, so I think it's good we don't have power. Parents can choose which school they send their children to, but almost all of them just send them to the nearest one because they know we will look after their children. We won't let them fail. Of course, it helps that we have a great deal of autonomy, that we can organize the curriculum and the school day in the way we think best suits the children.'

Teachers in Finland command enormous respect; the job is one of the most admired and popular in the country; in opinion polls, being a teacher is rated more highly than being a doctor, architect or lawyer. All must have a master's degree and few cite salary as their incentive. They're sceptical of standardized tests, and many teachers say that if they lost the freedom to determine how they teach, if they were subjected to external inspection or performance-related pay, they would want to change jobs.

In the course of their training, the very first quality looked for in trainees is empathy: the warmth and understanding of their pupils determines whether they stay the course. When their training is complete, it is assumed that they will continue their own education – through further degrees and collaborative research that they carry out with their colleagues or with teachers from other schools. Funding for all of this professional development is planned to double by 2016.

Sahlberg calls standardization 'the enemy of creativity', but of course without standardized exams, the schools themselves cannot be ranked. Instead they are encouraged to work together through school improvement networks to share ideas and solve problems. That not only generates new projects; it also continues and expands every teacher's professional learning. And all headmasters teach.

'The teachers themselves are very against performance-related pay,' Hellstrom told me, 'because it destroys the idea of cooperation. And we don't need that kind of motivation. We need motivation – everyone does – but it must come from within. We think the main task of school is to create as many possibilities as possible for every child to succeed today. If you have that feeling of success you feel taller.'

Student achievement in Finland is assessed. Students get report cards but each school designs their own, so they aren't comparable across schools. Regular national assessments too are carried out, by sampling about 10 per cent of the school-age population. Individual schools can choose to take the same test and compare themselves against national benchmarks. But this is all voluntary and results aren't published. Without any high-stakes tests in Finland, very little influence from central government and no school inspections, teachers and schools can maintain their autonomy.

Later that day, I sat in on a class of 8–10-year-old pupils, watching a presentation about how rainbows occur. The classroom was filled by a piano, a fishtank and a model village the children had made for a school movie. Normally there are seventeen students in the class but a few were out with flu. As the presentation became rather intricate, a number of children stood on their chairs to get a better look. The teacher watched as she told me how hard it could be, sometimes, not to intervene.

'It's much better than a test; if you can explain something, then you understand it. We tried this, getting the children to explain how you convert fractions to decimals and I nearly lost my courage! But we persevered and after about twenty minutes they got it!'

A 75-minute 'siesta' in the middle of the day is when students can choose extra-curricular activities. One drama group played the game 'Park Bench' – but in English, for my benefit. They weren't angels – 'Get a life', 'Your mother's on fire' – but when the teacher had to leave the room, they organized themselves into a dance exercise.

Outside in the cold morning sunshine, a fierce football match was raging and I interrupted a young teacher who was reading.

'They are learning,' she said, 'but we also are learning. All the time. They have to learn about science and math and languages but we have to learn about them. Who they are, how they can do their best.'

'Don't you ever get frustrated, angry, disheartened?' I asked.

She laughed. 'Well, everyone has their bad days. But, you know, no, not really. If you love your students you just persevere. You know they can do it. You just have to learn how.'

Love isn't a word I'd heard used very often in schools but everyone I talked to at Espoo used it, sooner or later. So when I visited a high school I asked the head, Riitta Erkinjuntti, about it.

'Yes,' she said, 'why not? Love is a word you hear here also. The teachers know the students and trust them. When I discuss with them, even one who has behaved badly, I think: "you are so important to me, I am worried about you". You have to love your students.'

Her school – Meilahti in Helsinki – specializes in arts and design. Most of the high schools have specialisms and it is on this basis, not rankings, that students choose them. Design plays a significant role in the Finnish economy – not just Marimekko and Iittala but many Finnish designers have defined the look that we now call modern. From Meilahti, students will go either to university or to vocational schools. The system is designed to be porous so that students can move between the two – and continue to do so for as long as they want. During their time in high school, every student gets two hours a week of career guidance from a counsellor who will help them think through what their options are and where they want to go next.

'We believe in all the children,' Raila Pirinen says. She is both a career counsellor and teacher trainer. A warm enthusiastic woman, I stayed with her during the school holidays when she was still working quite cheerfully.

'The very best will get there but we don't want to lose anyone. If they need help, they get it for as long as they need it. We have a very strong desire not to produce anxiety among the children. You don't make good decisions when you are afraid. And we want them to make good decisions.'

The intrinsic motivation that the early reformers aimed at must have stuck because Finns continue in education for a very long time. Although education after the age of sixteen isn't compulsory, fully 93 per cent of Finns complete education sufficient to gain them entry to higher education and more than 50 per cent of Finns continue in some form of adult education.

'I see my students all the time – they never really leave me!'

Riitta Erkinjuntti said, laughing. 'Even after they've left, I'll see them in the city or they will come back for a visit. It's wonderful to learn about the jobs they're doing now, the amazing things they're learning about the new technologies, new ways of making things. They keep learning and I learn from them!'

Public opinion in Finland is opposed to ranking and league tables and, with the gap between Finnish high and low achievers the smallest in the world, parents seem quite content simply to send their children to the nearest school. Since many schools finish early in the afternoon, it means children can walk home and play.

'We trust the system because the teachers are good and they are very well educated,' Carita Orlando told me. 'It's better now, I think. When I went to school, it was less free and we were a little afraid of the teachers. But things are more relaxed now, and the children, they're pleased to learn.'

Orlando has two children – Eric, fourteen, and Erica, twelve – in the local school. We met one afternoon, after school, in their warm, comfortable modern home. Eric was upstairs, working on a server he had built; Erica was playing with a friend. The spring day was rather chilly, otherwise they'd have been outside. One of the great things about the school timetable, her parents told me, was that it was seasonally adjusted so the kids always had some out-door time when they got home.

As we started to discuss school systems, I had to explain what ranking was; the concept seemed weird to both parents and they couldn't understand what benefit it could bring. Like parents around the world, they both want to see their children do well in school but seemed bemused by the idea that one child's progress might have to come at a cost to other children. They're by no means unambitious, either for their children or themselves. Greg Orlando runs one of the bigger hotels in downtown Helsinki; Carita started and manages her own accounting firm but she also makes time to serve as a school governor.

The Finnish people aren't angels and their schools aren't perfect. Like other countries, they've experienced school shootings and there are always some kids – not many but some – who just don't make it. The impact of socio-economic backgrounds can't be erased but it's striking that this educational success story hasn't been achieved by making the school day or year longer, by increasing homework or by raising the numbers or thresholds of exams. And it hasn't created a competitive marketplace for schools or teachers or students. The corporatization of education – with its methodologies of bureaucracy, targets, inspections, benchmarking – has, so far, been studiously avoided, although it is regarded as a threat. But the fundamental reason, PISA's Andreas Schleicher says, that Finland (like Korea) does so well is because its schools educate everyone; they don't accept that for there to be winners, there must be losers.

'The goal of PISA,' Schleicher says, 'wasn't to create a competition between countries but to get the insight we needed to enable countries to improve. And many have done that: Korea, Shanghai, Poland, Singapore. Even Germany,' he added ruefully.

'And we have learned very basic lessons. We know now that money alone won't buy you great education; money explains only about 20 per cent of the outcome. We know that early streaming isn't associated anywhere with better overall performance, that the most successful systems aim at, and succeed in, raising achievement for everyone, not for the few. We know that there's no relationship between countries' educational attainment and performance-related pay as long as teachers are paid decently. And we know that no education system can ever exceed the quality of its teachers.'

Finnish employers are certainly satisfied. I spoke to recruiters and managers at accounting firms, hotels and high-tech businesses. If education is about creating a workforce, they weren't complaining. If they have any concerns, it is that their workers may be over-educated for some of the jobs they offer. But in a world that increasingly prizes intellectual over physical property, Finland is remarkably productive for such a tiny country. In 2005, Finland had the fourth most scientific publications per capita of the OECD countries, ahead of the US, UK and Germany, and was above average in number of patents per capita. Richard Florida, in 2011, gave Finland the top spot when it came to assessing the technological and innovative capacity of the world's leading nations.[15] The way to prepare pupils for a more competitive economy, Pasi Sahlberg argues, is to have less competition in their schools.

I thought there was one other important dynamic that I saw at work in the Finnish schools that I visited. I saw it in the Espoo classroom and the bright white Meilahti lunchroom where I ate alongside the teachers and the students. The meal was everything you'd expect of school food – wholesome but uninspiring. So it wasn't the food. It was a power dynamic.

Finnish teachers regard themselves as students. In every conversation I had with them, they discussed what *they* were learning, researching what they had yet to find out. Like the teachers in the Blackawton bees project, they exuded and shared their curiosity. Encouraged to continue their education, to collaborate on research and to invent improved teaching methods, they see themselves as students every bit as much as the children they teach. As a consequence, in their own minds and in the minds of the children they teach, they don't occupy a position of dominance, masters selectively handing down scraps of information to the deserving few. They can't imagine themselves as defensive gatekeepers, umpires or scorekeepers. Instead, they walk together with their pupils on a life-long journey in which they all continue to explore, make mistakes and learn.

That's what we all want for our children: a creative, courageous mindset whose capabilities long outlive the short seasons of exams and tests, that is resilient when making mistakes, ingenious in responding to the world's changes and generous in working alongside colleagues. We'd like to hope that it needn't depend on getting into the right school, trouncing friends, cheating, drugs or the sheer luck of not going to the bathroom at the wrong time. And we hope for a love of learning that lasts.

'My drive,' Justin Riley told me, 'isn't about school. I like building things, just the idea of starting from nothing and making something that's useful to other people. I want to do that over and over again – like a roller-coaster ride. Once you have that moment, you want another.'

3. The Morning After

Any competition junkie would have overdosed during the London Olympics. Every comparison, every statistic, every victory was used to draw meaningful conclusions about Britain, globalization, athleticism, nationality, ethnicity, history, geography, colour, design, weather and clothes. In the midst of a horrible summer and a hideous economy, good news abounded and it all had to mean something. Leading many of the euphoric headlines was a recurrent trope: haven't the girls done well? In 2012, 4,847 women had participated, 121 had taken medals and, of those, fully 77 were gold.

It was, to be sure, some kind of sea change, not just in Britain but around the world. After all, in 1908, male competitors had out-numbered females by 53 to 1. Forty years later, that was down to 10 to 1 but now women had just about achieved parity: of the 541 athletes, 262 were female and this was the first Olympics in which every participating team included women.

More remarkable than the numbers, though, were the victories. That the United States led the medal table didn't make anyone blink. What astounded those who chose to notice was this: US *women* topped the medal charts. For the first time in anyone's history, American women outperformed the rest of the world *and* they outperformed American *men*, winning fifty-eight medals to the men's forty-five *and* bringing home twenty-nine of the forty-six golds.

This was – and is – remarkable. After all, that's what a mountain of academic literature says. Experiment after experiment shows that women don't like to compete, that they perform worse under competitive conditions, that they won't volunteer for tournaments. Ancient stereotypes play into this perception: women are kinder, gentler, meeker, more sociable, more collaborative. Women stayed

back in the cave looking after offspring while their aggressive partners went out hunting and killing. Women lack testosterone, a
history of victory, blood lust, the killer instinct. Everything that
makes them so adorable – being nurturing, maternal, loving – is
also what makes them fail.

Heads of corporations looking at the level of female participation in the Olympics must have been baffled and confused. In their
world, the supposed lack of innate competitive drive has been used
to excuse the failure to get women into top jobs, top salaries, on
to the boards of companies. It isn't that women are less capable
(although some, like former Harvard president Larry Summers,[1]
would still have us think so), it's just that they lack the competitive
zeal to fight their way to the top.

The belief that women must be innately uncompetitive has
sparked some curious thinking. A flurry of experiments in the last
five years have attempted to match risk-taking with menstrual
cycles, trying to prove that women were only really competitive
once a month during their fertile phase. From an evolutionary perspective, this would make sense because the willingness to compete
would increase the probability of conception and quality of offspring.[2] Alas, double-blind randomized experiments pulled the rug
out from under that idea.[3]

When the Cambridge Centre for Gender Studies organized a
discussion of gender differences, they brought together some of
the world's leading academic authorities on the question: Deborah
Cameron, an expert on language and communication, Elizabeth
Spelke, who'd been appointed by Harvard to apply some real science
to Larry Summers's speculation, Simon Baron-Cohen, renowned
for his definition of autism as 'the male brain', and Robin Dunbar
the evolutionary biologist. Theirs was a serious and well informed
debate but most thought-provoking of all was their conclusion: the
men decided that yes, indeed, women were different. The female
scientists however, could not identify any fundamental cognitive or
developmental difference.

This might have been thought surprising but, in a way, it wasn't.
When examining competitiveness, the same dichotomy had also
appeared: female social scientists didn't see a significant difference
in competitiveness while male scientists did. A great deal of this

could be explained away by noting the often razor-thin margins of difference, by complicated experiment design or by subtle differences in what was measured. But amidst all the noise, one clear note started to resonate: women were less likely to choose a competitive reward structure. Given the option of being rewarded for work completed or being rewarded for how far they'd out-performed their peers, women more often chose to be rewarded for their work alone. Those that did choose to compete performed just as well as men, especially over time.[4] So it wasn't that women couldn't compete; they simply preferred not to.[5]

No, this couldn't be explained away by their caring, loving natures either. Linda Babcock – an academic who'd made her name proving that one reason women are underpaid is because they don't ask for more money – postulated that women might be deterred from negotiation not because they lacked competitiveness but because they believe they'll lose. And when she did the experiments, she discovered her hypothesis was right: women paid a higher social cost for initiating pay negotiations than men – but only in the eyes of men, who judged them more harshly. Attempting to negotiate for higher compensation had no effect on men's willingness to work with men, but it had a significant negative effect on men's willingness to work with women. So the desire not to attempt the competition of a salary negotiation might not represent anything more than world-weary realism. Maybe, Babcock's research dared to suggest, women didn't avoid competition because they were innately uncompetitive – but because they expected to lose. And they were right.

Into this fraught field waded a brave, imaginative and eclectic behavioural economist, Uri Gneezy. Gneezy is an Israeli-born academic with huge enthusiasm for hard problems and big questions. When we met one bright morning in California, he clearly had a big appetite – for breakfast, new ideas, learning about new industries. What makes his work so engaging is that he loves doing or watching experiments in the real world: how to price wine was one of his more entertaining forays. Though he's as easily sucked into game-theorizing as any of his peers, unlike many academic economists he brings to his findings a quality of real-world scrutiny that's rare and refreshing. One of his most widely cited papers – 'A

Fine is a Price' – dared to challenge the role that money plays in human motivation. Having taken the beating heart of finance into his hands, he was unlikely to be tentative when it came to gender wars. Instead he brought to them a uniquely grounded, genuinely curious mindset.

Reviewing all the literature around men and women's attitudes to risk and competition, he concluded that there were differences – though not as big and obvious as many people seemed to think – and that many, if not all, of them were socially determined. In many studies, the fact that women were more risk-averse than men was interpreted as a lack of competitive drive, but Gneezy wasn't so sure; perhaps, he speculated, they simply lacked confidence in their ability to win. Maybe competitiveness wasn't an innate, irrational drive; it might be a considered calculation, determined by environment and by culture.

He thought of a wild and wonderful way to test his theory. If competitiveness was socially determined, would women be more confident in matrilineal societies – places where women did hold power – than in patrilineal societies, where they traditionally lack power? It wasn't, of course, very easy to find a matrilineal society – the world has very few of them – but Gneezy located one: the Khasi in north-east India.[6] Here family life is organized around the grandmother. The youngest daughter never leaves home and eventually becomes the head of the household while older daughters set up their homes near by. Husbands come to join their wives' families, they have no property or authority and no social roles of real importance. By contrast, Gneezy also looked at the Masai of Tanzania, where wives are said to be less important to a man than his cattle and where, if asked how many children he has, a man won't count his daughters.

For Gneezy, this was a long way from Israel, where he grew up, or San Diego, where he now works. But, with characteristic aplomb, he designed an experiment that could be easily understood and carried out both by the matrilineal Khasi and the patrilineal Masai. It was important that the task should be easy to understand and not depend on any specialized talent or physical ability, so it involved nothing more complex than tossing a tennis ball into a bucket. Put into competing pairs, each team was asked whether they'd like to be rewarded per successful shot or by the number of shots by which they out-performed their opponents.

Neither culture proved especially gifted at the ball toss, hitting the bucket only about a quarter of the time. But the heart of the experiment was in these findings: in Tanzania, more Masai men than women chose to compete while, in India, more Khasi women chose to compete than men. Moreover, somewhat to Gneezy's surprise, the Indian women turned out to be more avid for competition than the African men. In other words, coming from a culture where they were accustomed to success and power, women were more willing to compete.

The experiment may be about tribes and peoples that seem very remote but the findings are realistic. It makes perfect sense to think that men and women are both competitive – but more likely to wish to compete in circumstances where they believe they can win. That women, in many corporate and political environments, don't put themselves forward isn't because they're biologically programmed to be decorative or weak; it's because they are shrewd judges of their chances of success. 'It is evident,' Gneezy mused, 'that while many well-performing females hurt themselves financially by shying away from competition, poorly performing males also hurt themselves by embracing it.'

At work, assessing the chances of winning can seem reasonably straightforward. In the pursuit of sex, love and marriage, however, it's much subtler.

'I always think that, to get a guy, I have to be drop-dead beautiful, a bit of a minx, clever – but not too clever,' Clare told me. She's a rising executive within an engineering firm: smart, accomplished and comfortable working with men all day long. But she's careful about how her competence comes across when she's out on a date.

'I want to be confident – I mean, I am confident, but you have to be careful not to come over too strong. If it's a first date, I guess you could say I'm cautious, watching the signals: just how much of me can the guy take the first night out?' She giggled nervously. 'It's really tricky because you want to impress the guy but you're careful not to make him feel small.'

When I asked single men what they did to attract women, a

similar element of gamesmanship surfaced. Rob is in his early thirties and works in the media. He has two brothers, both of whom are married with kids and he's conscious that his family is, as he says, just waiting for him to follow suit.

'I know my family expects me to bring home a gorgeous woman – because that's what my brothers did. So on the one hand I'm thinking: my wife-to-be has to be even better that my sisters-in-law. On the other hand, I'm also thinking: do I have what it takes to land a really fabulous woman? And it's really complicated these days because you have to have everything – it's exhausting! The body, the mind, the job, prospects, empathy, the . . . well, you know . . . everything.'

Rob's diffidence, he told me, wasn't just prudery. He didn't want to come across as too tactical, too pre-meditated. But he confessed that he did think about his dating life in competitive terms, where not only his brothers but all other men were his competitors. The writer and therapist Stanley Siegel is less bashful about the way this plays out.

'There isn't a man who hasn't compared the size of his penis to other men in the locker room or at the urinal, a sizing-up that leads to either a prideful smile or a sense of inadequacy,' Siegel wrote. 'It's the shame that's coined a catchphrase: "I'm a grower, not a shower." One handsome, straight, young man told me, "Men think about their penis at least ten times a day." How often have men worried if they are going to measure up, literally, when getting naked, with a new partner's previous lovers? Will a grin or a smirk greet the bared private part? And when it's two men about to have sex, isn't there always that moment of anxiety when they wonder whose dick is bigger?'[7]

Siegel's daughter Alyssa – also a therapist – agreed that size haunted many of her male clients. 'There's isn't a man with whom I've discussed this who hasn't measured his penis and then gone online to see how his size stands up against others. I think the insecurity comes from a deep sense of male competition that's inbred in our culture. Most men fear that they will not be able to attract and keep a mate. Will she fantasize about another man and leave me for someone better endowed?'[8]

In one year alone, the market for Viagra and Cialis in the United

States was worth nearly $4 billion. As Viagra goes off patent, pharmaceutical companies are rushing to develop testosterone treatments. Even though misuse of the hormone causes blood clots, tumours, infertility and liver damage, clinics offer testosterone treatments as a lifestyle option: one that may enhance a man's sexual mood and appeal.

Although these treatments have focused on men (and largely been developed by men) it's become clear that sexual appetite is no less important for women. Nor is this a recent phenomenon; after the sewing machine, fan, kettle and toaster, the fifth electrical appliance approved for domestic use in 1901 was the vibrator: fifteen years later, they were selling better than toasters.[9] Swathes of research into evolutionary biology and modern sexuality confirm that female sexual appetite is just as intense and women are just as prepared to spend very large amounts of money to attract a partner. In Britain, the breast-implant industry – despite recent horror stories – is worth £100 million a year. It's impossible to escape the vast numbers of models and celebrities whose breasts, hips, lips and faces have been augmented and decorated, all in pursuit of irresistible physical attractiveness.

Physical endowments, however, aren't always enough and what's missing on that front find substitutes in different assets. All of the men and women I interviewed about their search for a mate insisted, sometimes apologetically, that they would not take seriously a partner who didn't make a financial contribution. Unemployed actors, musicians and artists were regularly cited as ineligible. In China, this is even more overt; if a man cannot buy property, he will struggle to find a mate. In a society where men significantly outnumber women, men splash out on property to improve their prospects, but this just pushes prices up, making romance and housing an even higher-stakes game. Some observers have compared the property/partner chase in China to the peacock's plumage: an eye-catching but ungainly attraction that is a struggle to wield with aplomb.[10]

The idea of sex as a contest runs throughout human history and mythology, from Greek gods to Jane Austen to Bridget Jones. Men compete with other men whose physical, professional or financial assets may outweigh their own. Women compete with other

women whose intelligence, attractiveness or cunning may out-
manoeuvre them.

'A while ago, I was out with friends,' Clare told me, 'and there
was this guy – very handsome and single. He showed a certain
amount of interest and, over the course of the evening, we went to
another bar and then a club and I remember noticing that two
other girls kept tagging along. And I remember thinking: I am
going to put a stop to that. I'm not seeing them having that. It was
just a bit of fun but I was determined. I did find favour in this situation but it came with a certain amount of bitterness from the
other two. That was definitely a competition. I pretended to notice
nothing but did what was needed to win.'

She paused for a second with a rueful smile.

'If you're not winning, it feels despondent. I run from the front.
I like winning. If I think I'm not going to win, then I withdraw,
because I don't want to lose.'

According to psychologists David Buss and Cindy Meston,
women have sex for 237 different reasons. They haven't yet turned
their attention to men but the reasons they cite for women may not
be so very different: women have sex because they're bored, want
to get closer to God, to make their partner feel good, to punish a
partner who's hurt them, to impress their friends, hurt their
enemies, as a form of barter for gifts, to boost their self-confidence
or cure their headaches.[11] Sexual partners are often seen and even
described as trophies, prizes, belt notches. For many, winning an
attractive partner is a race that must be won in order to gain admission to the winner's circle.

Listening to young adults talk about the dating scene today is
both funny and sad. Clare and Rob, both in their early thirties,
work hard at their careers and at their social lives; both conceded
that success at work was a lot easier to manage and strangely less
stressful. The Saturday night ritual – going out on a date or with
a crowd of friends – felt like a requirement. Strategizing what to
wear, how to act, sizing up the prospects and the likelihood of success sounded like hard work. And assessing new opportunities was
a skill.

'For me, that's the hardest part,' Tom told me. 'You see someone
attractive and you want to get to know them but then the question

is: will they be interested in me? Sometimes, I have this game I play: how long will it take before she mentions a boyfriend – partner – fiancé – husband? The shortest it's ever taken? Twenty-five seconds! On some level, I guess I still feel like a fourteen-year-old on the edge of the school disco: you want to be part of the fun but you don't want to risk looking like an idiot.'

Tom's was a rueful not a hearty laugh. A handsome man with a good job in the media, he'd had his share of disappointments. And, like everyone else talking about the pleasure and pain of sexual competition, eventually he adopted the metaphor of markets.

'You listen for those cues, the references that say: I am not on the market. I'm taken. Spoken for. Reserved. You listen because you don't want to feel foolish and you also don't want to waste your time having a really long conversation with some girl who's going to waltz off the minute her guy walks through the door.'

'The market. That's what I hate – the idea of being in a cattle market. You see that at university immediately,' Mary said. A beautiful young woman, with long blonde hair and a steady, warm gaze, she recounted her experience at the University of Exeter with a mixture of hurt and disdain. The halls of residence commanded different prices: some, with the en-suite baths, double-bedded rooms and three-course meals, were a great deal more expensive than the cheaper and older accommodation she had chosen.

'People were definitely sizing each other up as potential partners. And I met a guy my first night. He was wearing a hoody advertising a ski resort I'd been to. So we got talking about skiing and, after ten or fifteen minutes, he asked me where I was living. When I told him which hall I was in, he just said "Nice to meet you" and walked away! I was quite shaky. I hadn't realized just how ruthlessly people were pairing up.'

Everyone I've talked to – from teenagers to retirees, gay and straight, married and single – describes with fear, loathing and humour the agonizing difficulty of competing for a partner. The fear of humiliation, private or public, is intense. The dreams of success are wild and often hopelessly unrealistic. Much of the time, everyone's pretending to have a lot more fun than they feel.

'Saturday night,' Penny groaned. 'That awful feeling: if you have somewhere to go, you have to spend what feels like the whole day getting ready. And if you don't have anywhere to go – God, you are such a failure. Maybe you've had a hard week, you'd really like to curl up, watch a DVD. But it feels so pathetic and doomed and you think: if I have one Saturday like this, I'll spend the rest of my life like this until I'm some crazy old woman found dead in bed with cats one day. So you hoik yourself up and you stick on the eyelashes and totter down the stairs in shoes you can barely stand up in because ...' She suddenly stopped. There was a long pause as the momentum of her description suddenly ran out of steam. 'I don't know why. I really don't know sometimes. Just – because.'

Penny works in a large accounting firm in London. She's well paid and one day expects to be made a partner in her firm. She has already far outstripped the professional success of her parents; her father was a schoolteacher and her mother looked after the family and did occasional supply teaching. Penny is proud of her achievements and her parents' pride in her. But she feels increasingly trapped by the feeling that somehow that's just not enough.

'It's not like being in accounting is the most sexy, romantic thing in the world.' She roars with laughter. 'I mean: "I work in accounting" isn't exactly the most lascivious opening gambit you've ever heard! So you almost feel you have to work the other side even harder: look, I have a sense of humour! Look, I can wear sexy shoes and tight skirts. If I take my glasses off, I'm really human!'

Disappointed and exhausted by too many fruitless Saturday nights, Penny turned to Internet dating. Here she hoped, she said, to 'cut to the chase' by working through the data to find the perfect match. Her friends had tried it and she hoped she would more quickly find a great companion.

'But guess what? It's all competitive online too! To be judged by a photo against all these other women ... it's a pretty fearsome experience. I'm not a conventionally attractive woman but all the others have the model pose down pat. And the men on the dating sites – some in morning suits, some at the top of a mountain looking fantastic, one in his cycle helmet after a triathlon. It's just very formulaic and quite intimidating.'

Clare, Rob and Penny have all had good relationships with different partners; they also all described themselves as 'still looking' and, when pressed, acknowledged that what they sought was someone they would marry. However much contraception, women's rights and sexual liberation may have separated sex and marriage, they still remain quite tightly coupled in the popular imagination. Helen Gurley Brown's 1962 shocker *Sex and the Single Girl*, while full of instruction for satisfying sex, nevertheless insisted that the whole point of premarital sex was to learn how to choose and become the perfect spouse. Reissued in 2004, Gurley still maintained that premarital sex was practise; it taught women both how to be great lovers and find sexual satisfaction, and how to discover what they liked and needed in a man. But marriage was always the end game.

That the wedding is the prize is a theme remorselessly trumpeted throughout popular media. Celebrity magazines are full of photo spreads documenting the great day, while drama as smart and insightful about women as *Sex and the City* still felt compelled to end the series with the protagonist safely married off to a rich and handsome man. Although the series had taken big risks in its portrayal of sex and female friendship, leaving Carrie Bradshaw single was somehow too radical a step to take.

Reality TV contests like *Take Me Out*, *Dinner Date*, *Girlfriends* and *The Millionaire Matchmaker* routinely position sex or weddings as the ultimate prize. In *The Bachelor*, muscle-bound men fly planes, wield power tools, race motorbikes, win triathlons, repair houses and love puppies, all as a way of proving that they have the physical, financial and emotional resources needed to be great providers and fathers. Those personal, physical and financial assets endow them with the right to choose from twenty-five gorgeous, available, seductive women for their 'perfect fairytale ending'. Reversing the format, *The Bachelorette* features beautiful, perfectly groomed, athletic, balletic and shopaholic women who are endlessly empathetic, sensitive and cunning, and get to choose their 'Prince Charming' from among twenty-five eager, determined and physically robust men. Success in these shows is simple: a proposal of marriage is the way you win. Although most of these relationships break up once the cameras disappear, the one that did result in a real wedding – series thirteen of *The Bachelor* – was broadcast on American television as though it were an event of national importance.

In Britain, we have no need for such artifice. The idea that a big, expensive wedding is the ultimate victory celebration is nowhere more explicit than in the over-heated narrative that accompanies all royal courtships. Never mind that, in the case of Princess Diana, the fairytale ending turned into a cautionary tale. When 'Waity Katie' successfully pursued and captured Prince William, she was publicly applauded for her strategic patience and duly rewarded with her prize wedding. The message these epic weddings send is not easily dismissed.

'When I was twenty-eight, I went out with a man and I absolutely loved him and he loved me and we decided to get married,' Eileen told me. 'This was me achieving what I wanted; it was absolutely all about the wedding. The minute we got engaged, my parents were thrilled and we all went into overdrive and it got bigger and bigger and bigger and he was absolutely horrified! And I was spectacularly jilted. It was a horrible experience, so public. You tell people you're getting married – and then you have to tell people you're not getting married. It took away a very romantic young girl's dream – being the chosen one – the perfect day. It felt like such a huge failure.'

Evolutionary biologists argue that all species are driven to reproduce and that, in our pursuit of sexual partners, we are simply doing what all living things do. Some go further, maintaining that when man was still polygamous, sexual contests were the origins of war. Monogamy, therefore, is the basis of a stable and civilized society. (This is why some politicians continue to believe that tax breaks for married couples – an ongoing cash prize – will confer some kind of social benefit.) But framing the pursuit of a sexual companion as a contest puts disproportionate emphasis on the prizes: the gorgeous partner and the big wedding.

Although it's too early to tell, it seems quite plausible that the same competitive narrative can frame gay marriages, too. All of the gay men and women I talked to insisted that the dating scene was not so very different. Some slept around a great deal, others settled down. That it was now safer to be open and honest about sexual orientation made the dating scene less dangerous and less secret. The demand for gay marriage was, first and foremost, a demand for equality: to have the legal rights and tax privileges enjoyed by heterosexual couples for decades. But that might also mean that gay weddings would come to attract the same climactic hysteria long associated with 'the big day'.

'I think that marriage is still seen as the goal of a lot of relationships in the LGBT community,' Cindy told me. 'To get that piece of paper. It is a status symbol and it gives you permission to exit the marketplace. Of course we don't know yet what the divorce rate will be. But it's certainly true that getting married, getting the certificate, is seen as an achievement.'

That weddings continue to be a big deal is clear from their price tag. The average cost of a wedding runs at between £18,000 and £22,000; average annual incomes are only slightly higher. As a consequence, a quarter of newlyweds start their married life encumbered by debt they've taken on to pay for the celebration. But they aren't thinking about the future; they're marking their victory.

'There's no doubt,' David told me, 'that I saw it as crossing the finishing line. I got married when I was forty-two and, on the one hand, it meant I was retiring from the race. That was a relief! On the other hand, I remember thinking all I could hear was the sound of doors closing. But I think there is this sense that you've won: landed the trophy wife and all that. I remember saying I'd waited so long because I was choosy, and there was some sense from my friends that, wow, I'd had a good innings, really played the field – and was still virile enough to land a prize! So yeah, it was kind of triumphant.'

'I think David was really proud of me,' Sarah recalled. 'I was ten years younger than he was and, in those days, very slim, very pretty. And I was proud of me because I'd really decided he was the one. I'd strategized and planned and made sure this time it worked. Because I'd had other boyfriends who hadn't worked out and I was determined this time it would.

'I remember on my hen night, sitting around with my girlfriends. Most of them were married, not all. But we got to talking about what our husbands, boyfriends earned – comparing salaries and prospects. And I sat there feeling very smug. It had been a chase and I had run it as carefully and as tactically as some people run marathons. So on the big day – the church, the dress – that was it. I'd won!'

Sarah and David's wedding pictures tell the same story: proud parents beaming alongside visibly triumphant bride and groom; you can almost hear the cheering. But now they both think that that was the problem.

'The day after the wedding was strange,' David recalled. 'It just felt like the morning after a big party. I woke up thinking I should feel different. But I didn't. A little hungover, maybe. But that's all.'

'I never really thought beyond it,' Sarah said. 'Get your guy. Get the babies. That's it. That's what I did. And then I was sitting at home thinking: now what? I'm young and I'm smart and I'm still pretty and what do I do now?'

It's easy to dismiss the emphasis on big weddings as a purely middle-class phenomenon, but it runs across classes, cultures and countries. But in the competition for a mate it isn't the only prize. In many communities where marriage is rarely thought of, the big prize is a baby. I saw this firsthand in a Nottingham community where many of the young women I met expected and hoped to have babies soon after leaving school. Girls as young as fourteen talked easily about how many babies they wanted and whether it would be better to have a girl first or a boy.

'You want your baby-father to be handsome,' Beth told me. 'Because you want a good-looking baby. You keep your eyes open and you definitely don't have sex with anyone who's ugly. Who'd want an ugly baby? So when I look at guys, that's what I'm looking for: someone really manly, strong. That way, I know I'll have a pretty baby.'

Beth's a pretty, young woman; she says her father was handsome, too. But he's not around anymore and that doesn't bother her because most of her friends don't have fathers at home, either. She's an energetic, resourceful young woman, bubbly and alert. Did she ever, I wonder, consider not having babies?

'I might. I might not. But you'd have to have a plan, something else you really were going to do. Otherwise, there's no jobs around here, what do you do? No job. No money. No baby – what a loser!'

For Beth and many of her friends, having a baby is a sign of reaching adulthood. For many of the men in her community, it's a sign of virility. Some boast of all the children they've conceived; their high score is a high score.

The problem with framing sexual conquest as a competition is not only that it is dehumanizing but that it focuses attention on the result, with little or no thought about what comes afterward. Like learning and exams, the immediate reward is more highly prized than the long-term process. While everyone's imagining the headline, the excitement and the drama, there's all too little thought about what comes afterwards. Cute, cuddly babies don't stay that way for long, all the excitement wears off and the hard work of raising children offers very few prizes. Similarly, after the big wedding day come the long years of life.

After their wedding, David and Sarah had two children and got a dog. David worked long hours as a management consultant and Sarah worked part-time in medicine. Like many couples before and since, they both struggled to balance work and family life. But the real issue between them became power.

'David earned at least twice what I did, he paid for all our vacations and he bought the house. So I felt I had to make it up somehow: doing the ironing and the cooking. After a while of course, I resented it. So what happened is, I just thought: I do the work here, it's my house. My kids. I just claimed the territory and thought: you have all the money? Well, at home, I have all the power. If David wouldn't contribute – then I'd make sure he couldn't contribute. So he was useless with the kids, never knew where anything was. He competed with money. I competed with competence. We definitely kept score.'

Life at home, they both acknowledge, became one long battle. They became 'champion bickerers' and routinely attempted to outperform one another. If David had a success at work, Sarah made him feel useless at home. If Sarah arranged a fantastic birthday party for one of their children, David complained about the bills he would have to pay. Looking back now, Sarah says she now realizes she had made it inevitable that he'd cheat.

'I wouldn't let him win at home so of course he had to win somewhere else. So he had an affair at work. I can't believe I didn't see it coming. Work was where he was successful. Of course that was his choice – he didn't have to do it. But I can see why he would.'

Sarah and David now live separately. When I asked David what role competition had played in the break-up of his marriage, he was thoughtful. At first he dismissed the idea but later in our conversation he came back to it.

'We are, I guess, both competitive people. I've always won. The affairs I've had – I guess you might call them conquests – in some ways they were just a continuation of my bachelor days. But I also think that, if I couldn't win at home – and Sarah, let's be quite clear about this, wasn't going to let me win – then I just took my game somewhere else.'

Adultery isn't uncommon. Although, understandably, it's hard to measure, academic research suggests that spouses spend a great deal of effort 'guarding their mates' and they do so because most have experienced what is called 'mate poaching'. Two of the leading 'benefits' are revenge and conquest.[12]

Emily Brown is a marriage therapist who sees in her consulting room what the infidelity psychologists study in their labs. What she sees is that poaching is almost always about power.

'Adultery is a form of competition,' she told me. 'It is a way of saying I am not getting enough of something – maybe sex, attention, love, success – so I can justify having an affair. If you bring that win/lose mindset into relationships it is devastating. The inability to admit to mistakes can be a problem, too. These small elements of competition just create a wedge that slowly pulls people apart. A lot of men still struggle if their wives are very successful. Not all, but a lot.'

That sexual contests are also power struggles is nowhere more luridly illustrated than in the relationship between the writer Ayn Rand and her acolyte Nathaniel Branden. Twenty-five years her junior, Branden was completely smitten when welcomed into Rand's circle of admirers and evangelists. (There's even a suggestion that his surname – which he changed from Blumenthal to Branden after meeting her – was an attempt to amplify his affiliation.) An avid devotee, Branden was initially excited and flattered by the prospect of an affair with Rand; as long as their respective spouses both knew and at least tacitly agreed, the relationship seemed entirely consistent with their belief that a moral life is the pursuit of rational self-interest. The unacknowledged sexual tension the affair introduced into their respective marriages even seemed to spice them up somewhat.

But it slowly became clear that what might have begun as a meeting (as Branden describes it) of minds and bodies is really a struggle by Rand to dominate all aspects of her young protégé's life. In order to maintain his allegiance to her, Branden must be unfaithful to his wife, cuckold Rand's husband, dedicate all his time, energy and thought to her work and lie to his friends and colleagues about a relationship Rand insisted be kept secret. In other words, he must subjugate himself entirely to the mind and body of Ayn Rand. At first this is exciting – she's famous and he is besotted by her ideology. But the relationship becomes an existential contest: who is more important? Whose ideas matter most? Who is the dominant actor in a tangled web of love, sex, business and money?

As Branden grows in age and confidence, his discomfort with her dominance, his subjugation and what he calls 'a life of lies and deception' becomes unbearable. Everything he gains – Rand's dedication to him of *Atlas Shrugged,* her permission to evangelize her work in an institution bearing his name – is a gift bestowed by her. When the competitive strains of the relationship blow it apart, they both compete for supporters, followers and copyrights. Rand sees everyone as an enemy or an ally. That the relationship was doomed by its own competitiveness is clear to Branden only much later in life.

'Competition corrupts the natural pleasure and joy of what we are doing. It takes the joy out of work, out of life, if you succumb to it. It is anti-life.'

Now in his eighties, looking like a snowy-haired Clint Eastwood, Branden still recalls his affiliation with Rand with some excitement. Her picture is on the wall of his Los Angeles study and he cites his memoir – *My Years with Ayn Rand* – as one of his favourite books. But he doesn't believe that her zealous belief in free markets appropriately relates to personal and sexual relationships.

'I competed with Ayn and her understanding of human psychology and that was a mistake. I wish I had handled it differently. She was too competitive, too narcissistic. I didn't see that then. You can't love someone and compete with them.'

He stopped and stared at me for a long time, piercing blue eyes watching intently for my response.

'It was a great adventure. She was a sorceress of reason. But reason isn't love. Love isn't winning an argument.'[13]

'I think it does depend a lot on whether there's some element of fairness in the relationship,' therapist Emily Brown told me. 'One couple I worked with, she was the big money earner and he was the financial treasurer of a church, earning very little. But they both really loved their jobs. And you are seeing this a lot more, where the woman is the major breadwinner. So it can work. But the couples I know where it does – they really work at it.'

In 40 per cent of American homes, women are now the major breadwinners;[14] in Britain, the figure is closer to 25 per cent. What makes these marriages work is the sense that they are working together on a shared project, what Glenda called 'the us'.

'My husband and I both work for "the us",' Glenda told me. 'That's why, if he makes a bed, I don't say thank you – because he hasn't done it for me. Maybe I think this way because I used to be a project manager. I might say "Good job!" because he's done it for us, he's done it for the household. We all benefit from the work that we all do.'

Glenda and her husband have a sense of a joint enterprise to which they both contribute the skills and income that they have. What's critical, she told me, is that both give their best. It is impossible to be treated as an equal at work if you aren't an equal at home – and that's measured not by income but by commitment.

In my own marriage, there have been times that my husband has been the sole breadwinner and other times when I've far out-earned him. We simply both agreed that we would do the work we loved and live on whatever it brought us. At home, we work hard – sometimes perhaps too hard – to be scrupulously fair in sharing childcare, chores and time to do what we want. Extra income doesn't buy extra privileges.

One of the advantages gay couples have, Cindy told me, was that you can't tell who is the major breadwinner and there are no traditional assumptions. When Cindy and her partner Beth first met, Beth had supported them both while Cindy started her business. When it thrived, Cindy became the major earner. The fact that no one knew and that nobody made assumptions was, she said, quite liberating.

'Nobody knows. And we don't care. We swap leads. That doesn't mean there's no anxiety attached to it – but there's a lot less social pressure about what the relationship looks like to other people. You can change places without a lot of social grief. In that sense, marriage shares a lot of properties of collaboration: you share the wings.'

After being, as she put it, 'spectacularly jilted', Eileen spent ten years living alone. But she still wanted to get married and have children. When she met Bill, they married quickly with a beautiful church service and 'a very homespun jolly reception' that, she says, put the wedding in its place. It wasn't the culmination of a race but the beginning of a lifelong project.

'The wedding is so powerful in our culture,' Eileen said. 'I still had vestiges of that but it's just one day and it's the beginning, not the end! The idea of the perfect day is so dangerous. But now I felt no obligation to turn up as a meringue! I wanted to turn up as myself – it must be terrifying for young men when this apparition turns up looking nothing like they have ever looked before!'

Both in their forties, Bill and Eileen had their first child a year after marrying and their second child two years later. Slowly they came to see their family as the ultimate collaboration: work that they shared and that meant that they had to find ways to live together.

'We came from very different backgrounds,' Bill said. 'I come from Salford, from quite a rough place where you have to defend yourself. And Eileen came from nice, leafy Buckinghamshire. My family, there's a lot of conflict, a lot of shouting. That doesn't happen in Eileen's family – they talk about their feelings a lot but they don't shout.'

Eileen felt she had to understand better where Bill was coming from, the kind of emotional language he was accustomed to. Bill had to learn that shouting and storming off weren't the only ways to resolve conflict. They both think that they had to change a great deal.

'I think it's about becoming a changed you. You're still who you are but you grow and change,' Bill told me. 'I'm not me anymore in the sense that I was when I was a teenager or in my twenties. But does that matter? I think the idea that people are fixed, that they don't change is just bizarre. Of course I've changed. That's what you do. It's not about growing older. It's about growing.'

'I agree,' Eileen said, 'though I think, for women, the loss of self in the early years is quite staggering. With two young kids, you do feel shoved to the edge of your own life. But then you work your way back again. Because of my family, I feel much more me, a richer version of myself.'

Eileen has continued to work as a journalist but Bill grew increasingly discontented with his work managing a local law firm. As his frustrations grew, the two of them decided to start a business together. The company makes and distributes savoury and sweet crumbles; Bill is the cook and Eileen – in between journalism assignments – does sales and marketing. They both say they really appreciate each other's abilities.

'The things Bill does, I can't do,' Eileen says. 'Incredibly organized, attention to detail. He has such a methodical approach to cooking – which is why he can do the work of two people. I could never do that!'

'People want to talk to Eileen and to buy from her,' Bill insists. 'Because of her journalism background, she's happy to cold-call. Selling is about understanding the other person and Eileen is good at that and I'm not.'

They don't always agree about everything. Both like to get their own way and experience the irritations most couples would find familiar: Bill spreads his work materials all over the house and Eileen doesn't load the dishwasher to Bill's satisfaction. What wins the day, they say, is who cares most.

'I do all the decorating because I care about it,' says Eileen. 'He trusts my judgement and doesn't care that much.'

'I can be quite bossy,' Bill admits. 'But in a lot of areas I cede my power to Eileen because I trust her and know she's good at so much. I'm less concerned because I know she wields power wisely.'

Theirs is a strikingly practical conversation. Both Bill and Eileen have each other's measure and they're highly committed to each other. Winning isn't on anyone's agenda. As good a marriage as theirs appears, however, it is increasingly a minority lifestyle. Today half of London's population between the ages of twenty and fifty-nine are single and fully one-third of British households have only one person living in them. Worldwide, Sweden tops the list with 47 per cent of households being singletons.

This new trend has led to significant hand-wringing on the part of politicians and sociologists. At the very least, it has provoked a housing crisis, with more people wanting their own space. But when author Eric Klinenberg set out to explore the causes and consequences of this unparalleled phenomenon, what he found was not a wasteland of lonely spinsters and misanthropic bachelors. For many, living alone was a cyclical condition, not a permanent one. Moreover, people living alone were socially more active than those who lived with each other; they created and enjoyed a thriving public culture.[15]

'When I was at school, I joined the National Youth Choir,' Carol told me. 'And the friends I've made there, I've kept throughout my life. And lots of them have got married and had kids. And I haven't. I've gone out with a lot of guys – I still do. But I think of my friends as my family. They're the people I turn to if I need something. And they're the people who contain all those memories of me over time.'

Carol stays at home on Saturday night when she wants to, goes out with friends or Internet-dates when she feels like it.

'My best friend, Rebecca, she and I have very similar taste in men and we have gone out with the same person, at different times! He was called Nigel and he had the biggest penis either of us had ever seen in our entire lives. And he had a girlfriend at home in Manchester and cheated on her with both of us. What's lovely is that he is long gone but we have this wonderful friendship. And we have never had any rivalry between us.'

Another singleton, Ben, says he does sometimes envy what he calls 'the power of two': joint mortgages, the ability to live in bigger houses in nicer areas because of two incomes. But he loves his independence and friendships and the time that he has to devote to them.

'I live on a very friendly street and I know everyone and everything about everyone. And it's great. My neighbour across the street, Sara, she's getting on a bit and I'll take her to her hospital appointments, call in on people if I haven't seen them for a while. I look after people on my street – and they look after me, feed my cats when I go away, water the garden. I have a much richer social life than any of the families here because I have the time to spend with people. And I like to think I'm part of the glue here, that makes the street a community.'

The singletons in Klinenberg's book, together with many I've known and interviewed, don't see sex as a prize or social life as a contest. Instead, they enjoy shifting between roles as friends, colleagues, godparents, uncles, aunts, nieces, nephews, neighbours. Changes in social mores together with reproductive technologies now mean that the choices people face are no longer binary: you can have children without getting married, without even having a partner. How we live, together or apart, with or without offspring, need not become a socially determined contest. It will, however, require very high degrees of social relatedness: people who are good at helping each other, sharing needs and burdens, asking for help and acknowledging mistakes.

Legally and technically, men and women, living alone or together, can have children now, with or without marriage and cohabitation. That may take some of the heat out of the social contest. But bringing up those children, to feel safe, secure and able to form relationships with the people around them, will always be an inherently social and shared act. As one single parent said to me, 'I'm on my own but I'm not alone. I have all these connections – to my son, his friends, their parents and teachers and his grandparents. And in a way, the more different we are, the harder it is to compare or compete. You need everyone to help.'

For all their lightness of touch, the so-called comedies of Jane Austen relate high-stakes contests in which failure was too terrible to think or write about. Characters without resources faced a catastrophic future, threatened with poverty, homelessness, desertion. Marriage and offspring felt like everything because they were everything. Modern reproductive technologies, accompanied by new social mores, have changed that. Individuals can live with or without marriage, with or without children, alone or together with partners of their own or the opposite sex. To some degree, this has lowered the stakes in what used to be a very high-stakes game indeed. There's more time to experiment and decide and there are more choices.

But the challenge of making and preserving connections, honing then teaching and inculcating the social skills required to be part of a wide, rich society has become greater than ever. Taught to compete at every turn is a poor beginning for young people at the outset of their social and sexual lives as the loosening of sexual, family and social structures puts greater pressure on individuals to build and maintain structures of their own. We've only just begun to think about what that means for young and old adults. What we do know is that this challenge confronts men and women everywhere. At work. At home. Equally.

4. Angry Birds

At the end of the nineteenth century, if you had been looking for a society characterized by competitiveness and social mobility, Norway would not have been your first choice. A stolidly conservative place, its greatest artist, Henrik Ibsen, so hated his country's stultifying conventions that he spent most of his productive life abroad, creating a new theatre aimed at exploding traditional ideas of hierarchy and dominance. In exile, Ibsen may have felt he wanted to be alone, but his homeland seethed with debate about social status, power and influence, and it was there that the subject found its first great analyst.

Thorleif Schjelderup-Ebbe was born in 1894 in Oslo (then known as Kristiania) to two successful and wealthy sculptors, Axel Emil Ebbe and Menga Schjelderup. As a child, he was talented, adored and spoiled. Educated at home by private tutors, every summer he and his parents would leave the city's heat for a country house some fifteen miles away. From the age of six, the boy occupied himself by making friends of the farmyard chickens, spending hours watching them, giving them names and avidly noting how they related to one another. When the family returned the following summer, he immediately recognized all of the older chickens and correctly identified the newcomers.

So engaged did the boy become that eventually he persuaded his mother, Menga, to buy him a dozen chickens of his own. In the winter, he would travel out to visit them; in the summer he would spend all day observing them. Thorleif had no interest in what they produced – eggs didn't matter to him. What captivated the boy was how they communicated. At the age of ten, he started to draw diagrams that accurately portrayed the status competition he was beginning to discern.

'He began to write down his discoveries about the hierarchy among them,' his son Dag later recalled. 'There were these triangles and, a strange thing, one of my father's laws, is this hierarchy: triangular, quadrangular, any kind of angle. Chicken A may be the master of B, and B may be the master of C, then you would think that A would be the master of C but by some quirk it's possible that C may be the master of A. It works in all kinds of rotations depending on when the chickens first met, how it happened then. Or if a chicken gets sick, it is reversed. He started to write that down.'[1]

This wasn't a childhood fancy and Schjelderup-Ebbe didn't grow out of it. He continued to monitor his chickens when he enrolled at the University of Oslo to study zoology and, in 1921, he published his thesis on hierarchies among flocks of hens. It is to Schjeldereup-Ebbe that we owe the phrase 'pecking order': *hackordnung*.

All of the chickens, Schjeldereup-Ebbe noted, wanted to be the first to eat. But the same one always succeeded; he called her 'the despot'. There was always only ever one despot and she pecked all the rest. In a flock of seven hens, three got to peck four others, one got to peck two, one got to peck one and a solitary hen got to peck no one. So the privilege of pecking and eating descended until the bottom hen got the least amount to eat and was, he wrote 'very nervous because of the number of pecks she received. I had the impression that she tired herself out in a constant attempt to avoid punishment and to get enough food. In contrast, the despot, who chased others from the food or the nest and who was never bothered by anybody, seemed to feel very well.'[2]

Pecking orders, as Schjelderup-Ebbe mapped them, were always vertical. Being at the top bestowed huge privileges – more food, more safety – and being at the bottom was perilous.

'A grave seriousness lies over the chicken yard and hens exhibit much anger and fear,' he observed. The pecking orders weren't stable and the chickens were never peaceful. Rebellions broke out and older chickens were particularly vulnerable. When new hens were introduced into the yard, incumbents invariably enjoyed an advantage and would fight to defend their primacy. They would also eat more than they needed to, consumption being a badge of power. But, at all times, every hen understood the social structure:

'There are no two hens in the same group that do not know exactly who is "over" and who is "under" ... The social structure is in the chicken's blood; it is exhibited by young animals when they grow up, regardless of whether or not they have been raised apart from the older chickens. In other words, the tendency to social structure is inherited rather than learned.'[3]

But while Schjelderup-Ebbe's analysis of social relations among chickens proved astute, his ability to understand the behaviour of humans proved, sadly, less successful. Initially taken under the wing of Kristine Bonnevie, the first woman professor in Norway, his mentor was, according to Schjelderup-Ebbe's son, 'very domineering, high in the hierarchy'. But the two scientists fell out when an article ridiculing Bonnevie was so well written that she concluded it must have come from Schjelderup-Ebbe. Deaf to his protestations of innocence (it later turned out to have been written by one of Norway's leading novelists), Bonnevie withdrew all support and cast her protégé out of the academic nest.

'You don't need the job,' he was told. 'You have money.'

But, like most scientists, money wasn't what Schjelderup-Ebbe wanted. He craved the respect of his peers and a position within the academic hierarchy. That was denied him by his Norwegian colleagues. Restless, he travelled all over Europe, publishing and teaching where he could. *'Fortgesetzte biologische Beobachtungen des Gallus domesticus'* – 'Biological observations of Gallus domesticus in its daily life' – was published in German in 1924 and would prove the seminal work in the study of social behaviour in animals. But that cut no ice with his Norwegian peers.

'They said, he has made a name for himself in Germany, he's not the kind of person we like here,' his son recalled. 'So they found a way of preventing him from getting his doctorate. It was most unfair.'

Schjelderup-Ebbe continued to cast his net wide, writing children's stories and poems, studying mathematics, chemistry, the intensity of fragrance in flowers and the difficulty of getting old seeds to germinate. Producing over 100 scientific works, he kept searching for his place in the academic hierarchy, but to no avail.

'In about 1955,' his son recalled, 'he got a letter from Konrad Lorenz and Lorenz said, your work has been a great influence on my work – my father was there before him! Then, in 1973, when the Nobel prize was given to three scientists (Konrad Lorenz, Karl von Frisch and Nikolaas Tinbergen) for their work in ethology, I said to him, you should have had this! After all, he invented the words "pecking order". My father is the one who discovered it.'

Throughout his childhood, Dag remembers his father keeping a scrapbook, cutting out and gluing clippings any time his work was reported. Having been passed over for recognition so often and so firmly, every mention and every professional membership was cherished. At his father's death, the books – ten volumes of them – were given to the university that refused to honour him. Poor Schjelderup-Ebbe: the man who had so keenly recognized and mapped hierarchies and power struggles never learned how to use his insights to his own advantage.

But his legacy was immense; not just the concept of pecking orders, as we apply it to this day, but the very idea that such structures can be made explicit and studied for their impact on social behaviour. Most of the time, like Schjelderup-Ebbe's chickens, we create and discern relative positioning implicitly – and we do so with surprising speed. Social hierarchies spontaneously emerge in children as young as two years old, along with the biological systems that process information about social ranking.[4] But the first person to map behaviour in humans with the same kind of rigour that Schjelderup-Ebbe brought to chickens was Harvard's Robert Freed Bales. He observed groups of people from behind one-way mirrors, trying to assess just how positions of dominance were determined. Just like the chickens, he noted that, while groups of people coming together for the first time may all start as equals, almost instantly there's 'a drift towards inequality of participation'. That drift starts to separate and segment people into roles and ranks and to define different social relationships in the group. Just as the incumbent hen is more likely to dominate than the newcomer, so, in a group discussion, the first person to speak is the one most likely to start building a reputation and a position of dominance. Other members of a group quickly start to adopt distinct roles or niches. One may become a specialist in advancing ideas, another a 'chronic objector'. Some are great at keeping the peace or releasing tension. Others gain respect while a few are just well liked. But in almost no time at all, everyone has a role and a rank. Usually, Bales concluded, the best liked contributor comes second or third in the hierarchy. 'It is not impossible,' he wrote, 'for the man ranked at the top in ideas also to be best liked, but apparently it is difficult.'[5]

Bales paid keen attention to the way that dialogue created hierarchy, but more recently it has become clear just how much social ranking occurs even before a word is spoken. Gaze and eye-line alone may assert dominance: those who look directly into your eyes before they speak and continue to do so after they've finished may, regardless of content, assume a more dominant position than those whose gaze moves on quickly. In experiments where all indicators of status were fastidiously removed, academic researchers found that all of their participants reached conclusions about relative rank before any conversation began.[6]

Body language communicates almost instantaneously and, for all our cognitive capacity, remains immensely influential even in circumstances where thinking should matter more than physique. In the hyper-competitive environment that is Harvard Business School, Amy Cuddy was well aware of a pecking order in her classroom; the despots stretched out in what she called a 'high power' pose, occupying a great deal of space. By contrast, others with a 'low power' pose would curl up, shrink into themselves, almost seem to disappear. She was pretty sure that these different poses weren't correlated to intelligence but she worried that they might start to correlate to grades. So she wondered whether changing body language alone could alter the confidence and contributions of the quieter students whom, she felt sure, had much to offer. Might it be possible, she asked herself, to 'fake it til you make it'?[7]

When she tried changing their postures, Cuddy found that there were too many circumstances in which conspicuous high-power poses were uncomfortable or inappropriate. So she tried something more subtle: if students adopted high-power body language *before* a critical social evaluation, might they still come across as more powerful? Cuddy designed an experiment in which, just before a simulated job interview, students would adopt high-power poses for just two minutes in private.

What she found was pretty remarkable. The students who

adopted physically powerful body language for just two minutes raised their levels of testosterone (the dominance hormone) by about 20 per cent, making them feel more powerful. Moreover their levels of cortisone (the stress hormone) fell by about 25 per cent, so that they experienced less stress. Objective observers of the simulated interviews – who did not know what they were looking for – assessed the 'high power' students as having more presence, being more compelling and more attractive.[8] Simply acting powerful, in private, was enough to convey status to strangers.

Our sensitivity to power and rank is immediate, unconscious and persistent. But just as influential as visual cues is the voice. At Kent State University, sociologist Stanford Gregory discovered that, below the audible frequencies in the human voice, there is (at around 0.5 kHz) a low hum that we all, quite unconsciously, discern. That hum conveys something about relative social status. Watching and listening to the sound waves of Larry King interviews, Gregory found that the more powerful the guest – George Bush, Elizabeth Taylor, Bill Clinton or Norman Schwarzkopf – the more King adapted his low hum to meet theirs. But when he interviewed less powerful guests – Garrison Keillor, Spike Lee or Dan Quayle – their lower status prompted them to adapt their voices to King's. The lower-frequency signal of the human voice, Gregory concluded, communicates much more than just pitch; it communicates power.[9]

He went on to test his research against nineteen televised American presidential debates. In each one, voice alone proved to be both an indicator of dominance and an accurate predictor of the popular vote.[10] Margaret Thatcher, of course, was famous for having dramatically lowered her voice when she became prime minister – a conscious effort to diminish her femininity. But what Gregory identified was the unconscious, virtually inaudible signals of status that we all receive and interpret.

We live in societies where rank and status are fluid and also where their symbols change over a lifetime. The competition for acceptance, attention and admiration is never more intense than during adolescence, when identity can feel fragile. A fascinating observational study of high school students mapped their pecking orders to try to identify whether social competition might be implicated in teenage smoking. When the researchers interviewed the kids, every one of them, without prompting, described which of their friends were on top, falling, moving up, in the middle, at the bottom, or cast out. Quite voluntarily, they described their social world as inherently vertical and they could 'recognise, differentiate and label their peers in terms of status, prestige and popularity'. From the information they received, the researchers could map the teenagers with the same diagrams and precision as Schjelderup-Ebbe had used for his chickens.[11]

Pecking order and smoking were closely linked. The largest group of smoking teenagers were the 'top' girls who, the researchers concluded, took up smoking because it made them stand out as self-confident and independent. But what was most intriguing about this study was its identification of where the stress levels were greatest. Being in the middle offered security; those girls were least susceptible to social pressures when it came to smoking. The positions in the pecking order that experienced extreme stress were at the top – afraid of losing the prime position – and the bottom – afraid of dropping out entirely.[12]

Competitive pressures manifest themselves in different ways in different eras. Smoking, promiscuity, intelligence, energy, violence, lethargy: all these behaviours have been fashionable at some time as young people strive for status and identity. This competition is pervasive and constant and can become addictive. In her brilliant memoir, *Wasted*, Marya Hornbacher described the social contests to be thin.

'Starving is the feminine thing to do these days, the way swooning was in Victorian times. My generation and the last one feign disinterest in food. We are "too busy" to eat, "too stressed" to eat. Not eating, in some ways, signifies that you have a life so full, that your busy-ness is so important, that food would be an imposition on your precious time. We claim a loss of appetite, a most-sacred aphysicality, superwomen who have conquered the feminine realm of the material and finally gained access to the masculine realm of the mind.'

When Hornbacher attended a boarding school for gifted, artistic teenagers, that she was (and is) a gifted writer was immediately obvious. But that talent was not enough to protect her from the need to compete for status within the intense community of the school.

'When you get to school,' she told me, 'everybody has talent and you are a fish among fish. On the talent front, you're trying to compete for a limited number of positions. As adolescents we took that at such a literal level. If I don't make it, I am *nothing*, so I have to make it. At the level of appearance and weight at Interlochen and Choate and Cranbrook and many British boarding schools, the girls are profoundly in competition with who can have the perfect body.'[13]

For Hornbacher, starving was what allowed her to rise in the pecking order; succumbing to temptation – eating – meant humiliation. Even when she ended up in hospital, what she calls 'competitive vanity' didn't stop; it escalated. Eating disorders, she told me, became a kind of endgame in which the most successful died.

'That is how you win. Being on units where people said: I had a heart attack when I was fourteen. Well, I had one when I was twelve. I watched a girl die. Well, I didn't die when I did that. I had liver failure and I was OK . . .'

Hornbacher was gifted, determined and lucky. She had true insight and, at some point, decided to live. She realized, she said, that starving to death was 'completely stupid and chicken–shittish of me'.

What makes Hornbacher remarkable isn't her anorexia but her insight. Eating disorders have the highest mortality rate of any mental illness. Five to ten per cent of anorexics die within ten years of contracting the disease; 18–20 per cent will be dead after twenty years and only 30–40 per cent ever fully recover. And this isn't just a girl thing; an increasing proportion of those suffering from food disorders – currently some 15 per cent – are male. Moreover, one unexpected consequence of other ethnicities acquiring more wealth and status is that now men and women of all races compete to lose weight. Eating disorders, once unknown in China, are now deemed to be at US levels.[14]

To Hornbacher, the cost of this social contest is two-fold. First, there is permanent physical damage: heart damage, an inability ever to have children. But she told me that the invisible damage was the way that extreme social competition concentrates so much energy and attention on the individual that it kills the ability to collaborate. With so much emphasis on self, thinking about, appreciating, connecting with anyone else became impossible. Competition imposed a form of tunnel vision that shrank her perspective and stunted not just her physical but her imaginative growth.

'At Interlochen, creativity was fundamentally disabled by competition. The competitive nature of the school deadened that collaborative spirit. There's an equation people make. If you are in a constant state of competition, you know how you'll win, how you'll get to the top of the tree. But you can't do anything else. There's no room, no capacity for anything, anyone else.'

Extreme competition, of the kind Hornbacher describes and experienced, is fundamentally anti-social. The desire to win rides roughshod over everyone and everything else. The problem with competing for status, Hornbacher says, is that it necessarily becomes addictive, driving you to greater and greater extremes, bigger and bigger risks. This is the dark side of empowerment: if you can be or do anything – if the game of life is yours to win or lose – then losing must be all your fault.

'The real world makes me feel impotent ... a computer malfunction, a sobbing child, a suddenly dead cellphone battery – the littlest hitch in daily living feels profoundly disempowering,' Ryan Van Cleave wrote. 'Playing *World of Warcraft* makes me feel god-like.'[15]

A gifted writer and a thoughtful teacher, Van Cleave conformed in no way to the cliché of the nerd or the anorak. Yet, he became addicted to computer games, sometimes spending up to sixty hours a week playing them. He had a dream job at an American university and a pregnant wife whom he loved. But nothing in his real world could possibly deliver the unalloyed sense of achievement he derived from computer games.

'Being a winner you have to have incredible self-esteem and I thought I was getting it through the game,' Van Cleave told me. 'Also that satisfaction – the OCD in all of us – of accomplishing a task. That feeling of completion and pleasure. The games are built so that the reward system continuously offers you carrots and better carrots so you feel like you are winning. And then there are leader boards so you have a public, worldwide arena for your achievements. People know who plays with the best group, who is best in the group; people are very aware of them. They're much clearer, much more absolute, than anything the real world delivers.'

The games and the status he won felt so rewarding that Van Cleave neglected his wife, his newborn child and his working relationships. The status of the virtual world felt infinitely more empowering than the havoc he was leaving behind 'IRL' (in real life.) The game gave him intrinsic rewards – I did better today than yesterday – and external rewards – everyone can see how great I am – in a way that the real world never could.

Van Cleave's addiction wasn't accidental. It was very deliberately cultivated, as all computer games are designed specifically to play on our hunger for rewards and status.

'For games designers, competitiveness is a crucial element. In single-player games, you want to be able to boast to your friends. In multi-player games, your score is where everyone can see it.'

Noah Falstein is an engaging enthusiast, a veteran of the games industry. Tall, balding with a small greying goatee and piercing brown eyes, he exudes intellect and critical thinking. Perhaps what's most surprising about him is his calm: he may build adrenalin-inducing software but quiet reflection is far more his own style. Falstein was one of the first employees at Lucasfilm Games, where he was instrumental in crafting many of the rules and language now standard in online and computer gaming.

'Addictive cycles are kind of dismaying,' he concedes. 'There's a fine line between pleasure and addiction in many things. Games are treading that line and we designers will confess that we look for ways to make games more addictive. It's one of those ethical dilemmas we have big discussions about.

'The games all have compulsion loops. It's a really disturbing term but we build them in and it makes games really good. We use a hill-climbing algorithm: Start with a low skill and challenge level and increase it gradually. If you increase too slowly, you wander into boredom; if you increase the skill level too fast, players give up. In games we draw it as a vibrato, a wavy line. You get a break and an extra challenge. Brain research suggests it works like physical training – glucose depletion and recovery. Don't give it every ten seconds – mix it up! Sometimes there will be big rewards after three hours. People become game widows. They're hanging on because they don't know when there just might be a big reward and they have to have it.'

In his quest for status, Van Cleave was as addicted to winning as Hornbacher had been to starving. After seven years of dedicated gaming, his wife threatened to leave, his kids hated him and his career hung by a thread. He had spent real money buying swords and armour for his avatar and used up irreplaceable time trying to secure esteem and success. With huge difficulty and discipline, he pulled himself back into real life, where he has stayed ever since, chastened and mildly in awe of how far he'd gone.

'I am deeply relieved to be out of it. Because there was no reason for it to end; you can play *World of Warcraft* for ever – and I think, at one stage, that's what I might have done, might have wanted to do! My wife had no confidence I'd ever be able to quit.'

What Van Cleave and Hornbacher both discovered, and nearly sacrificed their lives to, was the insatiability of status contests. Because the rewards are all relative, because there will always be someone who's done better, won more, achieved more. Satisfaction cannot but prove elusive. Social psychologists call this the hedonic treadmill and are quick to point out that it never makes people happy.

Running software companies during the Internet boom, I saw this played out on an epic scale. I watched with fascination as many people around me became suddenly very rich. At first their cars got newer, bigger and more expensive. Then they invariably moved house and often got a newer, younger wife. Yachts came next. Then, for the few, a plane. Then, a better plane. My own standard of living was improving fast too but what I came to understand (which I had not known before) was that there was no ceiling to this hierarchy. Status is always relative, not absolute.

'I can show you billionaires in their fifties who are still trading because they don't want to fall behind. They have a huge fear of losing day-to-day and they want to wake up every day feeling that they are going to win, just like any athlete.'

Michael Karp is the obsessive managing partner of Options Inc. Primarily an executive search firm, Karp's name was made advising banks and hedge funds on how much to pay their employees. When companies decide how to allocate their bonus pool, it's Karp they will call to find out what their competitors are paying.

Karp himself is insatiable: talking fast and furiously, glancing at his Blackberry, tuning into conversations outside in the hallway. As we sit in a glassed-in conference room full of hard edges – polished, green marble table, black leather chairs, glass doors – he was eager to describe the raw energy on which his business runs.

'Relativities – it's massive. Comparison with each other? Massive! That's why we are in business, because we know who makes more. That's what we do. We talk to people all the time. Where are you? What are you making? We have all that information. So when a client comes to us and wants to know what to pay – we can tell them how much more they're going to have to pay to get the people they want.'

On the day that we met (24 October 2012), the *Wall Street Journal* had just published a story about the top five hedge fund managers of 2012. Karp was excited; he knew them all and he knew just how they'd respond.

'Course they'll be thrilled – except the ones that aren't there, they'll be pissed! But I know those five, I know how they made their money; it's all sub-sub-prime! They're all watching each other. They all want to know: what's the other guy doing? How's he making his money?'

Karp pounds his hand into his fist and talks furiously. Next to him sits Jessica Lee, an elegant tall Asian American who analyses data from all over the world about pay and bonuses.

'Anything human is relative,' says Lee. 'As for pay, the curve is steeper. When I look at compensation for traders, before 2008 you would see the mid point and the average within the same range. Now a whole range isn't helpful anymore. Following the crisis, you have more losers and fewer winners.

'It is excruciating to go through what 4,000 people have earned and to silo them into specific categories so you can analyse and compare them,' says Lee. 'It's excruciating because you could be a senior vice-president at one bank and director level at another bank and so the titles may be different but still they are direct competitors. It's very labour-intensive.'

Lee perseveres with her excruciating work for two reasons. The data is a product – Options' annual report sells for $11,000 a copy. But by so meticulously picking through the data, Lee makes it possible to do side-by-side comparisons between individuals, organizations, responsibilities and productivity. When Options wants to recruit someone, they have more power in pay negotiations because they know exactly what everyone else is paid.

Options is not the only organization that collects data on compensation – there is a whole industry of compensation consultants – but it does so more comprehensively than most of its competitors. Karp does it compulsively.

'I have loads of competitors – Egon Zehnder, Spencer Stuart, all the big guys. They've all been around longer than I have, they're bigger than I am. But I never stop working. Today's Wednesday, I've already done two black-tie dinners this week. I have four more – and it's only October. November, December, big black-tie months. I'll talk to everyone, give everyone my card. We never stop. We're 24/7. That's how we get the data and that's how we win.'

What matters most about money – and the basis of Karp's hyperactive business – is relativities. Absolute amounts don't, in themselves, bestow status. For that, you have to be confident that you are getting more than the next guy. This is why pay becomes an insatiable issue: what matters isn't about getting enough but getting more.

'Transparency just inflamed competition,' Susan Rice told me. Managing director of Lloyds TSB, Scotland, she insisted that this had not been the intent – but now the information was available, it was hard to suppress.

'How do you know you're doing well? By doing better than someone else. It's a highly quantitative business so that's what marks you out: the numbers. It's tricky because the information shouldn't be secret, of course – but once it's public, the race is on.'

As though blind to the inflationary impact of transparency, in 2011 the High Pay Commission recommended more of it.[16] But this just heightened the insatiability of the high-paid. What mattered to them was not absolute numbers but relativities: being paid more than the next guy. Transparency merely accelerated a global bidding war, in which Michael Karp and his ilk were arms dealers and from which no one wanted to be the first to retreat.

Winning only delivers social status if it is visible to people who know how to read the signs. While a great deal of charitable giving may be altruistic, it isn't only altruistic. It is also as public a proclamation of status as any Rich List. Donors don't just want to give; most of them need to see their names are carved on the walls of buildings – which is why naming rights command such a huge price tag.

'I think that the honours system shouldn't be ignored in this context. That has been a powerful motivator for some people in the way they behaved. If they made huge amounts of money and could use the charitable side of the company – their ultimate aim was status, recognition, a peerage. It is a very powerful driver.'

I'll call the speaker Russell Stevens, because he doesn't want to be identified. A punctilious, mild-mannered man, he enjoyed a highly successful career in financial services. But after thirty years, he walked away, disgusted by widespread mis-selling of mortgages and insurance products to people who didn't need them and couldn't afford them. What drove such aggressive selling, he said, wasn't greed or anything to do with shareholders. From his vantage point, the desire for bigger and bigger profits was driven entirely by senior executives' desire for personal prestige and social status. If you made enough money and gave enough – visibly – to charity, then a peerage would surely follow.

'They were *all* honoured,' Stevens says of his former bosses. 'Status was a very powerful driver: gongs, titles meant an awful lot and I know it influenced the way my boss and all his colleagues operated. Certain charities we sponsored, certain meetings and facilities given to different organizations, quite significant amounts of money involved in that. And it worked! I'm not saying they didn't care about the cause – sometimes they did, sometimes they didn't. That's what lay behind a lot of bad moves: endowments, sub-prime, you name it. You have to generate the revenue to earn the status to get the visibility to get the gong. It only works if it is public – which is why none of this was ever anonymous, that wouldn't have served the purpose.'

Stevens is angry about an industry he used to be proud of, which he feels was hijacked by individuals who used companies entirely for their own ends. What drove them, he insists, wasn't ambition; they had no higher purpose or inspiring goal. They merely sought social dominance for themselves. Stevens is a gentle dissident, speaking without personal rancour or grievance. But the hunger for visible superiority, he felt, fundamentally hijacked entire companies and institutions.

Sir James Crosby, Sir Fred Goodwin, Lord Stevenson, Lord Browne: it is striking how the major business failures of the last ten years have come from corporations whose heads – and figureheads – were ennobled.

'More than money,' Stevens told me, 'people wanted to be part of the club. The Club, if you get my meaning. If you were in any sense an outsider, if you started to question activities, you rapidly became excluded. That is the most powerful part of competition – I don't want to be left behind.'

All social systems – be they organizations, industries or countries – have hierarchies, formal or informal, implicit or explicit and they may be very steep or relatively flat. Just how steep an organization is has come to be known as the Power-Distance Index.

This term was coined by a Dutch academic who studied organizations rather as an anthropologist might. For forty years, Geert Hofstede and, more recently, his son, were given the unique opportunity to study a vast multinational – IBM – to identify how the cultures of the organizations varied from country to country. Did behaviour and values really change from place to place and, if so, what characterized the differences? To be able to think about the work, Hofstede defined salient characteristics that showed how a culture worked. One of these was 'power-distance', which he used to describe the steepness of a hierarchy and the emotional distance between those who had power and those who did not. What Hofstede discerned was the imbalance in power relationships that Schjelderup-Ebbe and Robert Freed Bales had studied years earlier. But the Hofstedes sought not just to observe and diagram this but to measure it.

Today, you can follow their findings wherever you travel, using the handy Cultural GPS iPhone app; the higher the score, the steeper the pyramid.[17] The United States' power-distance rating is

40; the UK is rated at 35 and Canada at 39. Analysing countries like France (68), Russia (93), China (80) and Malaysia (104), Hofstede saw that in these societies, wealth, power, skills and status invariably went together. The powerful enjoyed great privilege and often came from the same families. Their societies were characterized by economic inequality (often bolstered by the tax system), and the exercise of power depended on social or financial dominance. In societies like this, you could predict that doctors would typically be treated as superiors by their patients and teachers would be regarded as gurus, handing knowledge down. Power-distance typified most working and personal relationships and corporate pecking orders typically mirrored the social hierarchies of the countries in which they were based.

'In the large-power-distance situation,' Hofstede wrote, 'superiors and subordinates consider each other as *existentially unequal* [my italics]; the hierarchical system is based on this existential inequality.' Leaders in these kinds of organizations are typically autocratic; when they do well, they're seen as good fathers. Visible power matters both to them and to their employees; their expensive cars confer vicarious status.

You can describe a great deal about a culture – of a company or a country – by observing the distance between the powerful and the powerless. The distance always carries a cost and, the greater the distance, the higher the social costs.

In the 1970s, when Michael Marmot conducted his famous studies of over 10,000 Whitehall civil servants, he showed that those at the bottom of pecking orders experienced the greatest stress and, with it, worse health outcomes. Men in the lowest grades of work – messengers, doorkeepers – had death rates three times higher than that of men in the highest grades. While some of this was subsequently explained by lifestyle choices – diet, smoking – those alone did not explain away more than one-third of their increased heart disease. Power-distance has a direct impact on their physiological and psychological wellbeing. Power protected the mighty in quite real, physical ways; distance left the powerless vulnerable and exposed to physical risk.

More recently, fMRI studies refined this work, confirming Marmot's finding that stress was worst at the bottom – but only in a stable hierarchy, which Whitehall was in the 1970s. But when, as recently, social systems become more volatile, subject to greater change and reorganization, then just like the teen girls, the stress concentrates at the bottom and the top. Dominant people fear losing position; subordinate people fear being cast out altogether.[18]

What's more, we all have a remarkably acute sense of where we stand. In studies that examined the relationship between socio-economic status, stress and health, participants were shown a ladder of ten rungs and asked to indicate where they placed themselves in society. Their *subjective* sense of where they stood turned out to be a better predictor of stress-related health outcomes than any objective data about them.[19]

This has clear costs as far as healthcare is concerned but it also has implications for our ability, individually or in organizations, to capture and use the productive creativity we are each capable of. Very steep hierarchies convey a severe, implicit and constant social threat: the shame of falling down or out. The pressure that these cultures exert on individuals makes it very difficult for them to think. And that is something we've known – or should have known – for over a hundred years.

Psychology rarely produces what it is confident enough to call laws. But in 1905, two scientists – Robert Yerkes and John Dodson – got together to study stress. Using what they called 'dancing mice' they put their subjects into a nest box wired with electricity. The box had two doors – one white and one black. Using a slight electric shock, could they teach the mice to discriminate between the two doors? Yes, they could; in fact their learning increased with the intensity of the shock.

But then came the second and more complex version of the experiment: would the same hold true when the mice had to discriminate between black and grey, a more subtle distinction? The results here resembled a bell curve. The mice learned well with a mild shock but far less efficiently with an intense shock. These findings, became known as the Yerkes–Dodson Law, which stated that stress can enhance learning on an easy task but it will impair learning on a more difficult task.

We've only recently begun to understand why Yerkes–Dodson has achieved the status of a law. Any complex task requires a lot from your brain: working memory, executive processing, decision-making, and divided attention. But stress specifically impairs the functioning of the pre-frontal cortex, where we do our thinking, and of the hippocampus, responsible for coordinating all the different mental activities required to solve a problem. So when we feel deeply threatened, we may have all the mental capacity we need, we just can't quite pull it all together.

The high stress of steep hierarchies makes it harder to think but also riskier to dissent. In most organizations, full of smart, informed people recruited and trained at great cost, the biggest problem is surfacing the knowledge that they have. Research into organizational silence shows that most executives have information, issues or concerns that they never voice: either through fear of retribution or a sense of hopelessness, that whatever they say won't make any difference. We've seen this repeatedly in scandals in the National Health Service, the BBC, the Catholic Church, parliament, banks and insurance companies: plenty of knowledge that no one dares articulate. The steeper the hierarchy, the harder it is to be heard, for knowledge to surface and for debate to take place. Instead, convergent thinking prevails, exacerbated by distance, fear and impotence.

The costs of steep hierarchies are, therefore, extremely high: not just worse health outcomes for individuals, but less creativity, innovation, productivity, even less credibility for the organization as a whole. But there is another cost, harder to see but critically important, and that is good, ethical judgement. Moral and ethical questions are, of course, particularly complex. We know that they are cognitively very expensive and that, when tired or distracted, ethical distinctions are some of the first to fail. So it isn't surprising to see that high power-distance environments, which are stressful and threatening, are associated with higher levels of corruption.

When Hofstede compared his data with Transparency International's Corruption Perception Index, what he found was that exporters from countries with a higher power-distance index paid more bribes. They not only had the power to do so but could be most comfortable that no one around them would protest or stop them. But what we also see, in all walks of life, from school to high finance, is that when people feel under competitive social stress, when their backs are against the wall, they are more likely to cheat. Hyper-competitive people in particular are associated with poor ethics because, for them, winning is so critical.[20] But in social systems where the difference between success and failure is acute, in steep hierarchies with maximum power at the top and none at the bottom, fixing the game can seem safer than playing it. And even those who might wish to change the game, find it impossible to be heard. Whistleblowers emerge from large, steep hierarchies where silence is pervasive; and speaking up, dangerous and rare.

As corruption is exposed in institution after institution – from schools to churches, sports organizations to financial services – we have to ask ourselves how far we have created the conditions in which this is bound to occur. Competitive social orders simultaneously make winning more important but riskier than ever before. The stakes go up but security disappears; stress increases and our ability to think declines. We find ourselves trapped in a compulsion loop of our own design: the more competitive a society, the steeper the hierarchy and the greater the inequality – which in turn makes the competition more fierce.

This problem of power goes some way towards explaining some of the aberrant behaviour observed in very powerful people: the sexual exploits of Dominique Strauss-Kahn, John Browne lying under oath, or Chris Huhne trying to get rid of his driving penalties. Power makes people feel more confident, more likely to view other people as a means to their own ends and more entitled: after all, as winners they deserve prizes. Academic research has further found that those with power are more likely to act in ways that disregard conventions, morals and the effects on others and is a predictor of sexual harassment because power disinhibits aggression.[21] In the same way that first-born siblings show less refined social understanding – because they can get attention without it – so more powerful people often demonstrate less social finesse because they think they don't need it. Status, pay and power create a sense of imperviousness, which is exactly what the Salz inquiry into Barclays Bank found: 'hiring the best talent in a highly competitive international market (and during a bubble period) ... pay contributed significantly to a sense among a few that they were somehow unaffected by the ordinary rules. A few investment bankers seemed to lose a sense of proportion and humility.'

After four decades of research, Hofstede has concluded that his power-distance index is becoming more polarized; steep hierarchies are getting more vertiginous as economic inequality has become more pronounced.[22]

'Increases in wealth may reduce power distances but only if and where they benefit an entire population,' Hofstede wrote in 2010. 'Since the last decade of the twentieth century, income distribution in some wealthy countries, led by the United States, has become more and more uneven: wealth increases have benefited dispro-portionally those who were very wealthy already. This has the opposite effect: it increases inequality in society, not only in eco-nomic terms but also in legal terms. This kind of wealth increase therefore also *increases* power distances.'[23]

While it's been recognized for a long time that both British and American government policy has led to a concentration of wealth at the top of the pecking order, the theoretical justification for that was that the wealth would trickle down. This, after all, seemed to be the gist of Adam Smith's argument that even though the rich were driven by self-interest, they were also 'led by an invisible hand to make nearly the same distribution of the necessaries of life, which would have been made, had the earth been divided into equal portions among all its inhabitants, and thus without intend-ing it, without knowing it, advance the interest of the society'.[24] On that basis it was argued that, if you cut taxes for the rich, they would spend the additional money they had and this would trickle down into society, creating jobs that would create more spending and thus generate growth, making everyone better off. With its ancient pedigree, trickle-down made intuitive sense, even if the term had been coined by a comedian, Will Rogers. The only problem with trickle-down economics was that it turned out not to be true.

When economists Thomas Piketty, Emmanuel Saez and Stefanie Stantcheva came to study the real numbers over a period of fifty years in eighteen OECD countries, they found that lower tax rates didn't promote growth, they created greater inequality. Allowing the rich to get richer was associated with greater income inequality, not faster growth. 'Lower top tax rates induces [sic] top earners to bargain more aggressively for higher pay.' Their gain wasn't everyone's gain, it was someone else's loss and, instead of growth, exacerbated inequality.[25]

The costs of this inequality, as Richard Wilkinson and Kate Pickett demonstrated in *The Spirit Level*, are pervasive and profound: poor mental and physical health, weaker communities, higher crime rates, increasing obesity, poorer educational achievement, weaker friendships and greater violence. Steep hierarchies and inequality break the social contract, separating those with rights from those with no power at all. What holds true for countries pertains to any unequal social group, whether it is corporations, charities, clubs or gangs. Extreme hierarchies – rich/poor, powerful/impotent – undermine and disable the social stability they purport to preserve. As competition widens the gulf between winners and losers, aberrations proliferate; smoking, anorexia, plastic surgery, lying, cheating, mis-selling, insider trading, corruption become the by-products of ferocious social competition.

But that competition isn't inevitable; not all societies are characterized by high power-distance. Hofstede also analysed countries characterized by low power-distance such as Finland (33), New Zealand (22) and Austria (11). In these societies, skills, wealth, power and status do not invariably go together. Power is based on expertise and the tax system is designed to reduce income differentials. Political and social power don't come from dominance but from the ability to secure the participation and collaboration of others.

In these societies, patients treat doctors as equals and students treat their teachers as equals. Education is seen as depending on two-way communication, and teachers expect to see initiatives coming from students. This is strikingly observable in the Finnish schools, where teachers and students alike are learners. Equally, in companies characterized by low power-distance, employees aren't afraid of their bosses; they are prepared to speak up, argue, acknowledge mistakes and typically prefer a more consultative style of decision-making. The emotional distance between managers and workers is far smaller. In organizations like this, smart leaders don't turn up in fancy new cars.

While high power-distance cultures have become more extreme, their low power-distance counterparts have become yet more gentle. Hofstede relishes a story about the King of Sweden being unable to pay for his goods in a store when he finds himself with a cheque book but without a cheque card or any identification. Only when citizens come to his rescue, using their coins to identify him, is the shopping assistant willing to accept his cheque, but not without first taking a note of his address. We may think that the association of wealth with status is inevitable but it isn't.

The power-distance spectrum that Hofstede analysed in such detail shows that human pecking orders aren't fixed; they reflect and enact particular values at a particular time. Our love affair with competition, the belief that contests will identify and elevate the best has produced a social structure that not only doesn't deliver prosperity but its opposites: volatility, stress, corruption.

But we don't have to live in the chicken yard. Many great projects work, not despite, but because there is no power structure; instead the energetic desire to make a great contribution is what drives work forward. Mike North is one such super-collaborator. By day, he works as the Chief Technology Officer of Nukotoys, which combines real-world toys, like playing cards, with computer games such as *Monsterland* and *Animal Planet*. For most people, that would be enough but Mike is a driven individual and he always looks for more ways to use and extend his knowledge. So he volunteered to work with Reallocate, a non-profit that brings together engineers to solve humanitarian problems.

'Engineers,' North told me, 'are the people who design and build the world; they want to create things and do good. But in the last few decades, if you are a good engineer, you get promoted and become a manager and you never do engineering again! And engineers really miss that. So they come into Reallocate to get back to hands-on work, creating something very tangible in a short amount of time. That's meaningful in a way that just being part of a corporate ladder isn't.'

At Reallocate, North was approached by a charity, MiracleFeet, helping children born with clubfeet. Could Reallocate's engineers help solve one of their problems?

'The kid in Nicaragua comes in to see the doctor,' North told me. 'He's eleven, he's travelled with his dad, and that meant riding a horse for three hours and a bus for six hours. When they see the doctor, he says you have to come in every week for six weeks. Well, that won't work! You need something he can take away, understand, and use by himself. You can't go in and impose technology; that never works.'

To solve the problem, North assembled a team of Reallocate engineers who set to work at TechShop, a public workshop open to anyone who wants to make something. When you join TechShop you don't just get access to great tools but to the rich wealth of the people who work alongside you. TechShop's founders believe passionately that inventors have to work openly together to learn from each other and grow. To North's project, TechShop brought Autodesk (which provided the team with prototyping software) and Objet (which has 3-D printers that are used to make product models). Without hierarchy or structure, everyone piled in to produce a foot brace for kids so easy to use that repeat visits to the doctor wouldn't be necessary. Sharing their tools and their ideas, the team could work their problem fast.

'The final, working Miracle Brace is a twentieth-generation product,' Mike told me. 'But that's why we needed help and why we had to have facilities like TechShop. The old big, corporate, hierarchical engineering model is too slow, too expensive, and it doesn't use the expertise of the people who are going to be living with the final product. Talk to people, understand what they want, prototype as fast as possible, get help and advice and insight from *everybody*! That's how you find your road.'

When they thought they were done, North travelled to Nicaragua to test the Miracle Brace on real children. And that was when he realized the power of his collaboration.

'It didn't all hit me until I was there and I had this magical moment,' North said. 'All these tools and people came together to help this person I never even knew existed. This is truly life-changing. You realize life is greater than your own.'

Most TechShop projects start with entrepreneurs who hope their ideas will spawn profitable companies. But everyone who wants to work there has to contribute to the open innovation that is so critical to its spirit. The machines are great – but the contributions of experienced designers, engineers and craftspeople make the difference.

In some ways, the physical creation of the Miracle Brace was the easy part: the talents of Reallocate, the facilities of TechShop, the resources of Autodesk, and Objet made that feasible. The hard part of any collaboration is getting everyone generously and selflessly to work together. With no power to make anyone do anything, how did he get his disparate team to work together so effectively? How had so many disciplines, working together voluntarily, managed to communicate well enough to make a product that actually worked for people they'd never met?

'Actually, I think it helps that you don't have any formal authority – no title, no status,' North insisted. 'Part of communicating as humans – that's what we're working on – is you have to be able to open up as a person.'

To do that, North runs a programme to help people learn how to design for developing countries. One part of the workshop teaches participants how to be clowns – more Cirque du Soleil, he says, than red noses. It may sound weird but the kind of communication you need is all about replacing power with humanity.

'That's what a clown workshop is,' North said. 'Open up, be vulnerable, draw in your audience so you can communicate on an emotional level. Drop the PowerPoint; be equals. Community, a sense of communication: that's everything.'

North is an inventive individual. He invented Reallocate, he was one of the inventors of the Miracle Brace – and he still has a full-time job making toys. But what strikes me most is how inventive he has been in his thinking about collaboration. Without a shared sense of language and risk, collaborative projects can descend into compromise, conflict or chaos. Developing instead a shared sense of vulnerability is a powerful starting point. Part of clowning around involves learning to communicate without status and without authority. It reduces distance so that sharing gets easier and differences – in disciplines and knowhow – become assets.

Belief in the power of collaboration underlies some of the most successful organizations in the world today: companies that depend on and develop the human capacity to create together. Hofstede always argued that an empowered workforce would require less supervision but even he might have underestimated just how far that could go. Crowdsourcing – the open call for all or any ideas to solve a problem – is used increasingly to tackle problems as wide-ranging as diabetes, software design and market research. Content platforms like QuoRa and Media allow people to publish mere drafts of ideas to test whether they're of any interest or value to others: unfettered feedback is the reward for sharing. Like TechShop but usually without face-to-face communication, crowdsourcing is all about tapping worldwide expertise that often lies buried deep down inside corporate pyramids, providing opportunities for brilliant ideas to surface regardless of title or power. The growth and success of crowdsourcing derives from the fundamental recognition that the best way to develop a new idea isn't by hanging on to it for credit – but sharing it in return for great feedback and contributions. The technology of crowdsourcing might be new but it answers to a deep human desire to help.

'The way you succeed here is by helping each other. That's really the key value: contribution.'

Sheona Barlow has worked for W. L. Gore in Dundee for twenty-six years, since she left school at the age of seventeen. She had a summer job as a receptionist but asked so many questions about everything that the plant leader suggested that she study electronic engineering. Eventually the company put her through four years of day release at the local college, then Open University modules toward an MSc in manufacturing and technology. Along the way, she had two children and worked on all kinds of different projects. What she didn't get was a title.

'At Gore,' she explained to me, 'it isn't really a pyramid. You work alongside your colleagues and communicate directly. You do your best for them; they do their best for you; everyone works hard. That's it. The most important thing you get isn't a title; it's the recognition and respect from your peers.'

Newcomers like Barlow get sponsors who show them around the organization and try them out in different teams until they find a project they want to work on – and people who want to work with them. The emphasis is on cooperation and autonomy, not rank. People like Barlow thrive because they're internally motivated – she clearly loves learning – and because they help their colleagues. Although Gore is a large, global company, with revenues of some three billion dollars, getting to know people isn't hard as each business unit is limited to a few hundred people. This is an organization deliberately designed to have the lowest possible power-distance.

When Bill Gore founded the business in 1958, his years of working for DuPont had persuaded him that he wanted to do things differently. He didn't want a hierarchy, he loathed bureaucracy and sought to create an organization built on trust and collaboration. He believed that people came to work each day to do a good job, that they wanted to do the right thing by themselves and by their peers – in other words, that they could be trusted.

The work at Dundee is the design and manufacturing of high-tech medical devices. Gore has a stellar track record for innovation, having registered over 2,000 patents for medical devices, polymer processing and electronics. Although they are famous for Gore-Tex® Fabrics, used to waterproof boots and fabrics, most of the revenue comes from inventing and manufacturing small numbers of highly complex, custom-designed products that often sit inside other gadgets. The Rover that landed on Mars contained cable assemblies and materials made by Gore; mobile phones, the black boxes in airplanes: all of these contain sophisticated technology invented and manufactured by Gore associates.

That the company is so remarkably innovative is ascribed to its culture. Everyone can take time to develop their own projects and ideas and to invite others to help them. This freedom is alluring; young associates are warned not to take on too much because what's most highly prized at Gore is each associate's ability to honour their commitments.

At Gore you have to share ideas early and widely. Just as Mike North did so effectively at Reallocate, instead of hanging on to a project in order to defend credit and power, at Gore you are encouraged to put your idea out where colleagues can see it, add to it, refine and challenge it. If the idea elicits no interest, that says a lot. If it provokes debate and discussion, that says even more. Whether or not people want to contribute to your idea depends a great deal on how much people like working with you, how generous and helpful you've been to others. None of that is about power in a formal hierarchy. One of the questions engineers with new ideas are asked is: who will want to celebrate with you?

Elixir guitar strings are a classic example of the Gore process at work. Dave Myers, a Gore associate working on cardiac implants, spent some of his time playing with PTFE, the long molecule that is the water-repellent in Gore-Tex. An avid cyclist, he wondered whether coating his bike spokes with PTFE would repel some of the water and grit that slowed him down. It did – but the market for cyclists eager to shave fractions of a second off their time wasn't big enough for a mainstream product. So Myers applied the same thinking to his other pastime: playing the guitar. What makes guitar strings go out of tune is the sweat and oils they absorb from the hands that play them. Might PTFE prove just as successful in repelling those? When he found that it did, Myers called a meeting and associates came to help him develop his new product idea. Such a large market existed for his innovation and it represented such an improvement over existing strings that it became an industry standard.

As Barlow showed me around the Dundee plant, the atmosphere was one of relaxed and quiet deliberation. This factory is as far from a black satanic mill as it is possible to get: spectacularly clean and full of concentration. The pool of work sits on shelves and it is up to each individual to get it done and move it through the system. Coordinators keep work flowing through and they check to ensure no one is struggling. It's easy to ask for help. On the wall is painted a quote from Bill Gore: 'Our success, our very survival, depends on having created a society, a family of teams.'

Leaders do exist at Gore but they aren't appointed; they emerge. A leader is defined as someone who calls a meeting – and people choose to turn up. Barlow became known as a leader because she was great to work with and was a terrific team builder. That capacity emerged naturally; Gore doesn't send people to business schools.

'Leading by example is key,' Barlow explains. 'We have had examples of leaders who've come in from other companies, from hierarchies and they think they can direct people and manage them and the associates say: I don't think so. If a leader thinks the position alone will make people follow, they're wrong. It's all about earning the respect and trust of your colleagues.'

One of the few titles in the company belongs to the chief executive. But even this appointment follows the same logic: to run the business, you must have earned the respect and support of the people around you. So when the previous CEO retired, associates were invited to nominate someone they would be willing to follow.

'We weren't given a list of names – we were free to choose anyone in the company,' Terri Kelly explained later. 'To my surprise, it was me.'

Kelly had been with the company all her working life. A mechanical engineer, she started out working on military fabrics. Like all the other associates, she initiated projects that gained traction – and others that never did. But she achieved the CEO role by earning the trust and respect of Gore associates over time. She is a leader only because people choose to follow her.

Key to these relationships is scale, the rule that says no business unit can be more than 200 people. This makes the relationships and commitments between associates close and personal. And while accountants might argue that this is inefficient, Kelly argues that the benefits it bestows – ease of communication, trust, reciprocity and innovation – easily outweighs any cost. And Gore has never had a single year of losses. This is a cash-rich company where, after three years, associates can become shareholders. After fifteen years, they may trade their shares in or continue to hold them. On retirement, associates get their cash value but shares in W. L. Gore don't leave the business.

When he designed his company this way, Bill Gore believed that people were innately collaborative and he was prepared to put his money where his mouth was. Fifty-five years later, it continues to be a powerhouse of innovation without having had to alter its remarkable culture. Competition and pecking orders don't explain its success – but their absence might.

Some of the most successful companies in the world deliberately and thoughtfully cultivate the flattest hierarchies they can. In some cases, this is because the founders believe that this drives higher levels of creativity and collaboration; in others the refusal of power is based on the recognition that there is always more knowledge and insight within an organization than at the top.

'I was just signing cheques one day and I thought: why am I

doing this? I didn't buy these things. I don't know why we needed them. Why do I have the power to do this? It's stupid.'

Chris Rufer is the founder and CEO of Morning Star, one of the largest producers of tomato-based products in the world. If you're eating ketchup or pasta sauce in the US, the chances are that you're consuming some of the billion pounds of diced tomatoes or tomato paste that comes out of Rufer's company every year. You won't notice that – Morning Star won't be on the bottle – and you won't find anything distinctive about the product. Except the way that it is made.

Rufer is a handsome man, even charismatic. But his own leadership was what bothered him. He thought long and hard about the process that ended with the cheque in front of him. Between needing something, getting it and paying for it, a lot of people, rules and authority intervened. Mulling over some of the core tenets of business – like 'the buck stops here' – Rufer decided it was all wrong. Instead of hierarchy and dominance, why didn't companies concentrate on two fundamental ideas: freedom and responsibility? Everyone who worked for him, Rufer thought, should have freedom to think about how to do their work and responsibility to figure it out with their colleagues.

'One day, Chris passed around a draft of some of the colleague principles, as he called them. About twenty-four of us sat around in a trailer and talked about it,' Doug Kirkpatrick recalled. 'We weren't quite sure what it would mean but I didn't see any downside to it. People should be closer to their own decisions. So we thought it was worth a try.'

Producing a billion pounds of tomato products through a decade in which prices have mostly been falling is difficult and risky. Nevertheless, Rufer introduced and the whole company has developed a process they call self-management, in which there isn't a hierarchy and there aren't employees. Instead, there are colleagues and colleague principles, chief among which are a responsibility to make things happen, an agreement to tolerate different values, taste, moods and methods, a commitment to direct communication and negotiation. But the two most profound guiding principles are: everyone must keep their commitments and no one can use force. No one has power *over* anyone else. Dominance is denied.

The Morning Star factory, a maze of pipes, turbines, pumps and valves roasting in the California sunshine, looks more like an oil refinery than a kitchen – and it's just about as dangerous. The roar and smell of the place is overwhelming as pristine hair-netted sorters pick out sticks, worms and rattlesnakes from the lorry loads of fresh produce delivered to the factory every day. Tomatoes are 95 per cent water, so every batch has to be cooked, evaporated and filtered at 212°F until it is a perfect 31 per cent solid, sterile enough to be stored outside for years. The lab where samples are tested for colour, pH and bostwick (how thick and viscous the paste is) looks like a pharmaceutical plant. Nothing moves quickly except the tomatoes on a conveyor belt; all the people are quiet and methodical, going about their business without bosses.

The air-conditioned control room monitors evaporators sitting outside in the hot sun. An array of screens allows a team of just three engineers to manage every stage of the process. Hans has been with Morning Star since 2002. A big, solid man – shaking hands with him feels like grabbing a brick. He is, his colleagues tell me, a top-notch mechanic; he's also (in his spare time) a taxidermist and children's clown.

'We have a lot of freedom here. We practise self-management like doctors practise medicine,' he tells me. 'That doesn't mean we get everything 100 per cent, it means we try to keep getting better.'

Previously, Hans worked in the Navy, where he liked the clarity that came with hierarchy. But at Morning Star what he enjoys is that everything *isn't* explicit.

'Here is fun because knowledge is the leader; you find the person with the most knowledge and, together, you make decisions. So you're always learning. In the Navy, everyone just took care of their one position. Here I man the plant. My colleagues man the plant. If there's a problem, everyone will run to it. Everyone is always learning, building their knowledge. We all just want to do what needs to be done better.'

Standing in beige overalls, one eye focused on computer screens behind him, Hans regales me with the details and nuances of producing such a vast quantity of tomato paste and the constant efforts to become ever more efficient.

'Every winter, we come up with new projects – ways to be more efficient, or to improve the machinery. We can bid for money for capital projects and then the people who know most, or will be most impacted, they decide if it's a good idea. If we have the money, then we vote on whether it's worth it.

'Today we're low on tons − trucking hasn't delivered so we've had to slow down. So we want to figure out how to make that smoother. We want to go fast − it's wasteful otherwise and we can't "ketchup"!' He's obviously made this joke many times but Hans's delight in talking about his work is palpable.

'We all do lots of psychometric tests − like Myers-Briggs − because we all want to understand how best to work with each other. You have to understand the next person to get along with them. I'm an ESTJ and everyone knows it. It's great because everyone learns how to deal with each other.'

Doug Kirkpatrick, who worked with Rufer in the early days of Morning Star, now runs the Self-Management Institute that attempts to explain and evangelize the learning that the company develops. He readily acknowledges that it can be hard for outsiders to understand how to navigate the company; without the titles of a formal hierarchy, buyers and vendors can find it difficult to know quite who does what.

'But what they find is that working with us is like working with a partner. We aren't out to screw them. We work the same way with our customers and vendors that we do with each other. We want everyone to be responsible, to hold to their commitments and to understand each others' needs.'

Kirkpatrick also concedes that this kind of low power-distance culture doesn't work for everyone.

'Some people have been hired who understand what we are doing at an intellectual level and they'll profess agreement. But at some point they decide "I can have my little island of hierarchy and I'm going to set myself up as king of the hill and work around this self-management stuff". But the culture just overwhelms them, because everyone here understands they don't have to be dictated to! So when that power play fails, that's the beginning of wisdom: that person either gets it or leaves. Nobody here can fire anyone − but anyone can request that someone leaves.'

When it comes to pay, the company doesn't benchmark against

its competition. Employing about 400 people, the average salary is more than $90,000 – and offers a wide range of benefits. But its chief attraction lies in the respect of your peers and the opportunity to learn.

'If you're living up to your colleague commitments,' Kirkpatrick says, 'you'll get a cost-of-living increase. If you think you've earned more because you've created some innovation or you can make a business case, there's a team that will consider it. Or projects you've come up with, you can come and talk about it. You are a self-managed independent businessperson here, so if you want something above and beyond, you can make the case.'

Kirkpatrick acknowledges that running a big complex factory with 400 people, high temperatures and significant danger isn't easy twenty-four hours a day. But it works. The team that mans the factory built the factory. They take pride in running it and improving it. And no one has a boss.

'I don't think anyone here feels that they work for Chris,' Kirkpatrick says. 'They work for each other, for the process, for the knowledge. It is a huge jugular paradigm shift. Especially if you are used to a command-and-control hierarchy. You have to relinquish that power intentionally.'

Reluctance to give up power is how Kirkpatrick explains the fact that, notwithstanding his evangelism, few companies have emulated Morning Star. Many are keen to learn but most lack the courage to abandon status and dominance. Not so Eileen Fisher who, over the last five years, has slowly but steadily handed over leadership and ownership of her clothing company to its employees. She has done so in part because she appreciates that doing so increases the company's value and ensures its longevity, but also because of a profound commitment to collaboration between every part of the business. The transition hasn't been without its challenges – fabric designers weren't used to talking to finance people and decision-making could be slow. But learning how to make space, accord respect and listen to one another is now how the company explains its exceptional success. In the fashion industry, characterized by big egos and power plays, this is remarkable – as is Fisher's regret now that she named the company after herself. After all, she told me, the company is really all the people who make it work.

At Valve games, new hires are given a handbook that, among other things, shows them how to move their desks from one part of the office to another. 'Welcome to Flatland' is how the handbook introduces the fact that 100 per cent of the work is self-directed. No bosses, no job descriptions, no hierarchy. Instead, everyone is encouraged to 'look for the most valuable work . . . At the end of a project, you may end up well outside what you thought was your core area of expertise.' The owners, producers and distributors of some of the top-selling computer games – *Half-Life*, *Portal* and *Dota* – the company aims to keep people productive and creative by giving them responsibility for everything they do. That includes choosing hours of work, with specific advice to try 'to maintain a sensible work–life balance and use your time in the office efficiently rather than working around the clock'.[26]

In South Africa, Paul Harris brings a fiercely egalitarian approach to one of the most highly regarded financial institutions in the country, FirstRand Bank. He does so because, like Gore and Rufer, he is convinced that the only way to get the best from people is to know what is really going on – something that's virtually impossible inside steep hierarchies. He's so committed to these principles that he wrote them down in what he told me was his management credo.

'I work *with* people; they do not work *for* me. I am obsessive about understanding market trends and the business and how we can improve it. Therefore I try to talk to anyone because everybody has something to offer if they are given a chance. My attitude is that "I have never learned anything from someone who agrees with me". So I welcome alternative views and new ideas. However crazy, because to get a good idea you must discard lots of bad ones. This way I harness the collective wisdom of the organization.

'I believe that the more power you give away the more you have, because when people are trusted and empowered they take ownership and will not let you down. I judge people by their ability and confidence to come up with new ideas. To express their views irrespective of whether they conform or not to conventional wisdom. Progress depends on new ideas and challenging the status quo. I judge management by their ability to harness the wisdom of people below them and thereby empower them. Not by the number of people they control but rather about the number they liberate.'

FirstRand is known across southern Africa as an innovator and a trusted resource. Harris believes its innovation derives directly from its people and a culture that demonstrates deep respect for every individual in it. As early as 2000, the bank introduced eBucks, an electronic payment system that brought buyers together, led the introduction of electronic banking and pioneered the use of cellphones for financial transfers in Africa. Yet when you talk to Harris, it is to the energy and enthusiasm of his people that he consistently pays tribute. What drove them, what drives him? The desire to do something better.

These are all big, complex, creative and successful businesses that have eliminated or reduced pecking orders in order to liberate the human capacity for creativity and innovation. Reinforcing the social bonds between people is how they flourish, eschewing the competitive forces that kill creativity and embracing those that enhance it: fairness, autonomy, freedom, debate. Their example challenges us to reject the extremely high costs of inequality and hierarchy, to see that they aren't a necessary evil but a cost imposed by people whose idea of winning requires unsustainably high levels of loss.

Escaping the stressful addiction of pecking-order competition isn't simple. There aren't as many companies like TechShop, Gore, Morning Star, Eileen Fisher and Nucor as there are people who would like to work in them. The economic crisis has left many people stranded in organizations in which they feel they have no choice but to compete to survive. And many manifest a form of Stockholm syndrome: having spent so long in these environments, they persuade themselves that they're great. After all, if you've got to the top through a highly competitive system, it's most unlikely you will find fault with it. Unlikely – but not impossible.

'Competitiveness was all the time in me,' Karl Rabeder recounted to me. 'I tried harder so all my employees had to try harder too.'

Rabeder is a tall, bird-like Austrian whom I met on a beautiful clear spring day in Mallorca. As we sat out in the sunshine, he told me the story of his childhood, brought up by a grandmother who always imagined that she would be free if she had more money, more land, more everything. He absorbed that lesson from her, he said, and it pervaded the gift business that he started to build in his twenties.

'I all the time compared myself with the maximum possible. All the things that I thought were possible I wanted to reach and get. It was more or less hopeless. Goals like doing in Germany what I did in Austria – a market ten times bigger – and then we could do the whole of Europe and then the US and then maybe buy a private jet! I asked myself the wrongest of all questions: what is possible? Not: what do I really want? Asking the question gives you a thousand answers and, following those, you lose yourself.'

Rabeder's business grew and grew. Was that, I asked him, because he had been a good boss?

'No. Because I did not really see my employees. I didn't see their personality. To be a good boss you have to realize what the work means to everyone. Sometimes I was hard on them, sometimes tolerant. I tried to turn them into copies of myself but I never knew who they were.'

When I first met Rabeder, I wondered whether he would be reluctant to talk about his past, the business that had made him wealthy. But he didn't mind at all, describing it like a foreign country that had been interesting to visit but even better to leave. He had, he told me, spent the first half of his life doing nothing but comparing himself, his company, his numbers to those around him, always checking where he stood in the pecking order. But that had never taught him to think for himself.

Eventually, Rabeder became so unhappy that he sold his company and in 2009 founded the non-profit organization MyMicroCredit, which aims to reduce poverty in South and Central America. In February 2010, he announced that he would donate his entire fortune, including the profits from all of his properties, his car, and his businesses, to his charities.

Today, Rabeder has homes nowhere. He rents a small flat in Mallorca and camper vans elsewhere. And he runs seminars for people who want, as he did, to escape the insatiable pursuit of status, rank and privilege. He is astonished, he says, at how many people languish in the same dilemma: desperate to escape the addiction of competition and to find the freedom they once imagined winning would bestow.

'I now live the maximum freedom I could find. I have friends around the world. A girlfriend. And my freedom. I always thought of myself as a bird who had decided to live a human life. And now I'm free, free as a bird!'

When visiting companies like TechShop, Gore, Morning Star and Eileen Fisher, I heard the same two words over and over again: trust and freedom. Being trusted gave people the opportunity to think for themselves, to make and learn from mistakes, to reach out for help. Trust was both what they got and what they gave. And freedom was the reward: not life on a beach or a week full of parties, but work enriched by others, the social capacity to connect to people without fear, intimidation or distance. They had escaped the chicken yard.

5. KEEPING SCORE

Nations have a sense of global pecking order every bit as fierce as individuals. So in 2000, when Sydney hosted the Olympic Games, the Australians found themselves the butt of many British jokes. Singled out for scorn was the design of the Games medals, which featured the Roman Colosseum. Didn't the ignorant Aussies know the difference between ancient Greece (where the Games were invented) and ancient Rome, where the famous arena stood? As imperious journalists mocked their hosts' lack of a classical education, they conveniently overlooked the fact that the medal design wasn't Australian and had been in use – without comment – since 1928.

To be sure, the design was anomalous. But that it had survived so long was no mere pedantic oversight. The great arena has long been the model for every Olympic stadium since the Games were revived in 1894. Its iconic shape resonates with tradition: throughout Western history, it was in places like this that spectators were entertained by competitors fighting for their lives.

Historians today still can't quite agree on the exact details of the entertainment displayed in the Colosseum; they don't even know whether a 'thumbs up' meant live – or die. The fragments of historical record that remain are centuries apart and don't add up to a single coherent explanation of how the building was used or why. Only one account of a gladiatorial fight survives, a poem by Martial in which the two combatants are so evenly matched that the crowd demands both be given honorable discharges.

What we do know is that Roman games were phenomenally expensive, both in financial cost and in lives lost. When the emperor Trajan celebrated his conquest of what is now Romania, he did so with 123 days of shows in which 11,000 animals were killed and 10,000 gladiators fought. Seating was in strict social pecking order, with the richest and most powerful at the front and the poor and disenfranchised high up at the back. Most exhibitions contained a political subtext; the slaying of crocodiles, for example, represented dominion over Egypt. Shows put on by aristocrats were straightforward attempts at popularity, not so far from the aims of politicians and corporate sponsors today. The Colosseum divided opinion; while attendance was usually high, not everyone approved of its spectacles. Seneca, in particular, found the slaughter pointless and corrupting.[1]

Lacking a conclusive account of the building has provided the perfect opportunity for writers of all ages to construct their own interpretations. Byron found the 'gladiators' bloody Circus' a noble wreck, Dickens was glad that it was ruined and Mark Twain mocked it as the birthplace of tawdry entertainment. Only Ridley Scott seems to have imagined it as a place of unbridled courage and outright heroism; for most people, the Colosseum is a daunting, deadly place where competition and entertainment met in a merciless exchange: win and live – or lose and die.

Perhaps the historical anomaly of the Olympic medal was overlooked for so long because the site reflected our ambivalence about intense physical competition for high stakes. To enthusiasts and romantics, elite sport represents the height of human achievement, a glorification of the body and a test of mental discipline. To spectators, it is showbiz: corporate entertainment or a day out for the family. For others, it represents cruelty, exploitation and suffering.

Olympic medals since 2004 are now historically more precise, if poetically less resonant. One side features the goddess Nike with the Panathinaiko Stadium, home to the first modern games in 1894; the obverse is left to the discretion of the host country. What can't be designed out of existence, however, is the huge cost that high-achieving athletes must pay to delight the public. What looks effortless isn't just effortful: like their Roman predecessors, the competitions of elite athletes requires that they put their lives on the line.

There was nothing brutal, grim or romantic about the University of Bath's sports training village. When I visited in the spring before the 2012 Olympics, its glass and steel felt more like an airport than a gladiatorial arena. With high ceilings bathed in sunshine and swarming with young, healthy, free citizens, the place hummed with energetic intent. Less athletic spectators could watch Olympic aspirants in training while more sociable undergraduates congregated at the cafe. The food on offer wasn't noticeably healthy but it was fuel.

Amidst the students and coaches sat a quiet young man, eating a sandwich and reading. When he looked up, it was his eyes that drew me in: so dark they seem to have no whites at all. He wasn't and didn't want to be the centre of attention; he was keeping himself to himself. This was Dai Greene, world hurdles champion and favourite for a medal in the 400-metres hurdles at the Olympics.

Greene is from Wales and he hadn't come to Bath for the architecture or because the university had a reputation for great social life. He was here to train.

'This is the highest track in the UK,' he told me. 'You can't beat it for wind and rain. If I can go through this, I can go through anything. I enjoy pushing myself. My mum says it is character-building. If I train in crap weather, I can run anywhere.'

With his quiet voice and lilting accent, there was nothing superfluous about Greene. At six foot one, he was lean, taut and self-contained. Born in Felinfoel near Swansea, he didn't know many people in Bath; his family and his girlfriend were both back home. He said everyone was 'friendly enough' but the truth was that he didn't have much time for friends. He was here to train six hours a day, six days a week. Nothing else counted.

'What gets me through training is to win medals.'

As a boy, Greene had wanted to be a footballer – his hero was Ryan Giggs – and he played for Swansea City at the age of thirteen. In his teens, he contracted Osgood-Schlatter disease, a painful condition caused by stress on the tendon attaching the quadriceps muscle in the thigh to the front of the tibia. The disease typically strikes during adolescent growth spurts but some studies maintain that half of its incidence is provoked by sporting activity.

But Greene loved sport, discovered he had a gift for hurdles and wanted to go to university, he said, 'to prolong the agony'. His first big success came in 2005 when he won silver at the European

Athletics Junior Championships, with a personal best of 51.14 seconds. The following year he qualified for the senior tournament but things started to go wrong: injuries and epilepsy caught up with him.

By now, Greene was so dedicated to his sport that rather than let disease get in the way, he decided to come off his epilepsy medication and try to control his condition through hard work, determination and a highly disciplined lifestyle. That wasn't an easy or obvious choice for a young man in his twenties but Greene was starting to develop a steely determination. In 2007, at the European Athletics U23 Championships, he took the gold medal with a new best − 49.58 seconds − despite an ankle injury.

'I had to switch my coach because my training was very one-dimensional and I kept breaking down,' he recalled. 'Then I moved to Bath but I still wasn't improving. It was a very dark time. You start to question what you're doing: Are injuries normal? Is everyone getting them? But all the injuries I had were because I was improving so fast − some elements just got left behind.'

But a year later, in 2009, he set a meet record and a personal best of 48.62 seconds and led the European rankings for the first time.

'When you watch the 400 hurdles, it looks pretty easy. The guys seem to take it in their stride − that's what the top guys do. But there are 150 strides that are all pre-planned and if I slow going into one stride, then I've lost two or three tenths of a second going in, two or three tenths going out. You have to make sure everything is spot on and you feel 100 per cent.[2]

'In athletics, you have got to train every day. When things are going well, you think it's easy. And I love pushing myself hard. I'll do an afternoon's training and be absolutely shattered. But I've gone through so much. There's nothing you can throw at me I can't handle.'

Greene's mother works as a care assistant in a primary school; his dad is a bricklayer. He says they work every day and the house is always clean; he's grown up in an atmosphere of quiet dedication. When he talks about them, or about his younger brothers still at home, they feel a long way away. When Greene talks about mental toughness, it doesn't feel as though the injuries are all that's on his mind.

Like every athlete, Greene has to balance events like the European Championships that bring prestige with the events that bring in money. Physically, no one can do everything in the calendar so athletes have to decide what matters more: prize money or medals. For Greene, there's no contest.

'I'm not motivated by money at all. In 2009, when I decided to come here, I was living off ten thousand pounds a year. It is nice to make money because it makes life easier but training comes first. For me, it's the titles and the medals. They are the highest accolades in sport.'

For Greene, competing isn't personal. He knows who his competitors are but he doesn't pay them much attention. If you look at other people, he thinks, you just get distracted and you don't want to give your competitors that edge or the mental support that could come from paying attention to them.

'There's only a few seconds – maybe just one second – between first and second place. So you can't give any sign of weakness. It's an intimate space, the call room. I remember one guy, before a race, talked about his flight getting in late and I thought: "you're just making yourself feel better, giving yourself excuses." Twenty minutes later, I beat him. You have to act invincible.'

It was impossible not to be moved by Greene: so many setbacks, so much discipline. Inside his calm understatement, there was so much going on: the determination to overcome his injuries, to control his epilepsy, to stick to the lonely, isolated regime – and to win at the Olympics. That determination filled his life. He focused so exclusively on the seconds and hundredths of seconds that determine the difference between winning and losing that nothing else seemed to exist for him. Every choice he made was defined by whether it contributed to, or detracted from, his goal. While the rest of us might watch our lives unfold day by day, Greene's life was something that wouldn't exist for him until he could look back on it.

'The Olympics are the ultimate because they are only once every four years and there aren't that many you can take part in in your lifetime. So you don't have many chances. To win one – you just imagine yourself winning on the podium listening to the national anthem. It must be the greatest feeling on earth!'

It must be, because the cost had already been high. Years of injuries. Years of solitude, running in the cold, the wind, the rain. Years of going home alone each night to watch television, go to bed, get back up and do more of the same. Years of nothing but thinking about time, the hundredths of a second, the tiny irreducible difference between success and failure.

In January 2012, Greene suffered another injury. It set back his training schedule but it didn't deter him. In July, he was made captain of the British Olympic athletics team after achieving a personal best – 47.84 – in a Diamond League race in Paris. After seven years of training, he had stripped 3.3 seconds from his time.

At the London 2012 Olympics, it was easy to imagine victory but watching the 400-metres hurdle race was agonizing. Greene had sacrificed so much to be there and hopes ran high, with constant references to Lord Burleigh, who'd last taken gold for Britain in 1928. As Greene stood poised in the blocks, he looked wound up tight – but suddenly tiny.

Just 14/100ths of a second – a time gone before you can say it – stood between Dai Greene and his Olympic medal. When the race finished, he panted on the ground, staring at the results board, willing the numbers to come right, grimacing when they did not. It was, everyone said, such a fast race. Finishing fourth meant no medal, no podium, no national anthem. Nothing. Only later, in tortuous interviews, praise for the victor. And plans for Rio in 2016.

'The records get faster every year because the training methods, the technology and the facilities just keep improving. In the next twenty years, you think the records must start to plateau – there must be a point where it stops – but they're still just going up and up. Faster and faster. And every year, there are so many more competitors . . .'

In the excitement and euphoria that surrounds the Olympic Games, it's easy to forget the simple fact that most participants lose. Out of the 10,820 athletes who took part in the London 2012 Games, only 962 – 8.8 per cent – took home a medal. Nine thousand eight hundred and fifty-eight athletes went home with nothing but memories, souvenirs, injuries and debt. Greene was one of the lucky ones. His training was funded by the Wells Sports

Foundation and because he's in a relatively high-profile sport, he received a great deal of attention and popular support. For most athletes in most sports, none of this is available.

Studying the world's top athletes, the US Track and Field Athletes Association concluded that 50 per cent of its top ten athletes earned less than $15,000 a year – derived from prize money, grants and sponsorship. That figure did not take into account any part-time job income but neither did it include the costs of agents' fees or health insurance. Sprinters and marathon runners stand to gain the most: world leaders with name recognition may get shoe contracts, appearance money, prize money and health insurance, all adding up to some $400,000 a year. But when you drop from runners with international name recognition to those who are only within the top fifteen in the world, those numbers halve. An American marathon runner in the top twenty to fifty might take home $25,000 in a year.

For the very top hurdlers with international name recognition, the earning potential can reach around $150,000 – while 50 per cent of those who are consistently top ten in the world earn between $30,000 and $100,000 before tax and agency fees. For jumps, throws and heptathlon, the numbers are lower still; and for race walking, there's really nothing.[3]

If your sport is more obscure – say, skeleton racing or the kayak slalom – there is little or no sponsorship available, only a training regime that, just like Greene's, requires total dedication and most of your time. For every Michael Phelps – a stupendous achiever in a globally popular sport – there are dozens of athletes dedicating just as much of their lives to a sport in which the earning potential of a lifetime career is negligible.

The Olympics, of course, are supposed to be about glory not money. But even the data from America for professional sports like baseball and football offer little to the vast majority of its players. In men's and women's basketball, there is just a 0.03 per cent chance of becoming a professional; in men's soccer just 0.04 per cent of players will turn pro. In football the rate is 0.08 per cent; and in baseball, with the most professional opportunities, only 0.6 per cent of high-school players will make a professional team. In no sport do the chances reach even 1 per cent.[4]

Darren Heitner used to be a sports agent but left the business, disillusioned by how hard it was for any but a few to make a real living. 'The promise seems so great but it's an illusion. It's common for most players not to make it to a major league. So minor league players are on a forty-man roster and they will make one to two thousand dollars a month – less than they might make, say, waiting tables. They do it because they imagine that they will get drafted into the majors – but 90 per cent of them will never have a day in the majors. So they have to survive on their signing bonuses.

'The average career in football is, maybe, 3.5 years; in other words, most players never make it to a second contract. In basket-ball the average career is about four years. There the contracts are for two years, with options on the next two years. So most of them don't make it to the second contract either. And the first contract isn't worth much money – especially after taxes and fees and all your costs.

'In baseball, players can be drafted out of high school. They're more valuable because they're younger and the teams hope they can develop them. So the kids sign on to a team with a six- or seven-figure signing bonus. Five, six, seven years down the line, when it doesn't work out, the organization doesn't value the player. He leaves and enters the real world with no qualifications, no real edu-cation, with nothing.'

In 2011 and 2012, the Knight Commission proposed reforms that were intended to protect players' education, either with stipends (which were rejected by most schools) or by linking teams' revenue shares to educational performance. These good intentions were subverted when a junior college offered such cheap and easy courses that just $400 and two weeks of easy study could earn athletes three full semester credits.[5] Heitner says that good agents will insist on contract clauses covering university tuition or a bonus for education so that the athlete has the chance of earning college credits in the off season. But plenty of players won't have the clause or won't commit much time to their schooling because they think they are the best – so they won't need a back-up plan. When you are entirely focused on winning, a plan 'B' isn't what you think about.

'These players grow up around enablers,' says Heitner. 'It starts with parents being gung-ho about their kids, telling them how great they are. Then they go to competitions at a very young age. They may really be the best in their local scene. Then their coaches tell them: "You're the best I've ever seen" – and they may be right! But it's not a local business, it's a global business. We've got great footballers coming into the game from Samoa! In baseball, so many of the major leaguers are from Venezuela, Japan, Dominican Republic. So it's a rude awakening when the competition expands to the rest of world and your talent isn't quite what you and your parents and your coach thought it was.'

Every competitive athlete will tell you that they are driven by love of the sport, not a desire to make money. But there are real costs to this passion: the time to learn, to study, to make friends, to have a life.

'At the age of fifteen, I was doing nine training sessions a week. Up every morning at five a.m., swimming four mornings a week, five evenings a week. My 'A' levels didn't turn out as I wanted – there was no time to do the work because I was at the pool whenever I wasn't at school. People thought I was insane but I just loved it.'

Erin Jeffries doesn't come from a sporty family but her parents supported her when, to their surprise, they discovered they had a daughter who was one of the fastest swimmers in England. Every morning, her mother Tish also got up at five and would drive ten miles to the university pool, sit and plan her working day while her daughter trained, then drive home and go to work. The regime was tough on both of them – and not just logistically.

'It was hard for her,' Tish recalled, 'to compete against her friends. There was one girl she was friends with and she could not beat her. Erin was the better swimmer but it was as though she couldn't risk the friendship. When the girl got ill and was off training – no problem winning the race. But when she came back, well, it was tricky. It's hard to want to beat your friends.'

'When I was training at Bath,' Erin remembered, 'I had no time for a social life. I didn't really form the friendships I might have if I had had the time. I was always swimming, training. I think it must have been quite annoying for the friends that I did have: that I was just never around.'

Erin looks like a swimmer: tall, lanky, alert. She swam long distances – 800, 1500 metres – because, she said, she had the
endurance not the speed. It wasn't inevitable that Erin would go to
Loughborough – she didn't quite have the 'A' levels to get in – but
her coach helped her and she won a coveted spot at the UK's leading sports university. The commute got shorter but the day was just
as intense.

'Monday, Wednesday, Friday: get up at 5, training 5.30–7.30,
back by 8, breakfast, lectures at 9, maybe three in a day. Lunch. My
day revolved around eating and swimming. Do work in the afternoon. Then training at 5 – land training, 2 hours swimming. The
other two days, training was just in the evening. Then Saturday sessions would be race pace. It was very competitive between all of us.
Sunday, a day off. Maybe I'd go out once every two weeks – not
as much as the others.

'When I won a race, it was the best feeling – doing a time you've
never done before. But when I lost a race, it was horrible, heart-
crushing. When you do a time off your best, when people like your
friends beat you, it's hard to see them afterwards. I didn't want to
talk to anyone. I was very emotional and I'd end up crying.'

Coming fifth in the country in the 400-metre medley, Erin
started to lose heart. Exhausted and frustrated, she started to realize how much she was missing: time with her friends, time to
study, time to think. Perhaps, she thought, if she were a sprinter she
wouldn't be so tired all the time – but she didn't have the build for
sprinting. As she talks about this time in her life, she is nearly in
tears, remembering the hope and frustration, the exhaustion and
the expectation.

'If I thought I'd make the Olympics, I would have continued.
But I'm sure I would have quit soon after that. The main thing is:
I wanted to get a decent degree. I wanted to feel that I could have
some kind of career afterwards. I wanted to have a life before it was
too late.'

In the middle of her third year, Erin stopped swimming. It was
an agonizing decision; while she was making it, she avoided her
friends, her coach, anyone who would try to persuade her one way
or the other. But now she feels she made the right decision, just in
the nick of time.

'Your whole life is centred around swimming. When that's taken away, you wonder: who am I? When I stopped swimming, I felt lost for a few months. But then I got a 2:1 – it was on the cusp – and I realized how close I'd come to not getting anything out of university. I was so glad I'd stopped and used the chance to study. I don't regret it now at all.'

Two of her friends persevered. Kate didn't make it to the Olympics and Rich, a friend since childhood, was 0.004 seconds off the qualifying time so he couldn't go either.

'It was a massive blow to his career, not making that tiny amount of time. Maybe he had had a bad night's sleep or been ill a week before. You could have trained for the last four years – and you just miss it. It's all for nothing.'

Erin doesn't swim anymore; she just can't enjoy it. Although it's hard for her to relive the extreme ups and downs of her swimming career, she's emphatically relieved that she stopped when she did. After graduating, she travelled all over the world – France, Switzerland, Australia – and although she worked everywhere she went, she said her real purpose was to retrieve the years of growing up that she had missed: the years when all her friends were building relationships and careers, partying, experimenting, learning who they were; she wanted to snatch that experience before it was too late.

What Erin was responding to – and acting on – is a well understood psychological phenomenon. The cognitive capacity of the human brain is quite constrained and there are hard limits to the amount of information we can process at any given time. Similarly, it appears that we can be motivated by one thing at a time, not by multiple aims. Assaulted by too much information, or too many motives, our brain acts like an editor, choosing what gets in and what gets left out. Extreme focus on a single goal creates tunnel vision that excludes anything extraneous to the goal. In true life-or-death circumstances, this is valuable. But the extreme focus that works well short term is impoverishing and depleting when it becomes a lifetime habit.

The logistical and intellectual demands of elite sports crowd out everything else, incurring a high cost well beyond any financial risk. Just when young people are exploring, finding out who they are and what they want from life, athletic competition represents an exclusive demand: sucking out every last bit of time, attention, energy, concentration, enthusiasm and leaving behind what can feel like a vacuum.

'You spend so many years working towards your particular goal to become an Olympic champion,' heptathlete Denise Lewis recalled. She had won gold at the Sydney Olympics – but the experience of winning wasn't what she had imagined.

'And when you achieve that, there is this sort of emptiness, this void. You just don't know what to do with yourself . . . There was just this: "what do I do now?" moment . . . You're back on your own in a bus travelling to the athletes' village. It's half past one at night and the world just seems a big place and you're just very much on your own.'

Retiring from sport at the age of thirty-three, Lewis had focused on her goals so long that she no longer knew who she was.

'I just felt like: who am I? What do I do? How will I call myself? The worst moment for me was when you have to fill out any form and you have to put your occupation. And I used to just tap my fingers thinking: what am I?'[6]

Andre Agassi says that sport stops you being who you are. He is rare among elite athletes, not just in being able to produce dazzling tennis but in writing an autobiography that goes far beyond the conventional lists of prizes and scores. His remarkable book, *Open*, tracks his agonizing journey before being allowed to be who he was – something that became possible only when, finally, he could stop playing tennis. What makes Agassi's book so unusual is his dawning sense of who he might be and his gradual recognition of the people, processes and vested interests that stopped him claiming his own identity. He comes to hate tennis because it gets in the way of his becoming who he is.

'Tennis is noncontact pugilism. It's violent, *mano a mano*, and the choice is as brutally simple as it is in any ring. Kill or be killed. Beat or take your beat-down. Tennis beatings are just deeper below the skin. They remind me of the old Vegas loan shark method of beating someone with a bag of oranges, because it leaves no outer bruises.'[7]

When, after the 2012 London Olympics, Sebastian Coe

brought out his memoir, *Running My Life*, critics were quick to point out how much personality was absent from the book. It wasn't just that the narrative was dull but that there were hardly any other people in it. His mother, her death, his wife, their divorce, his adultery: none of this gets much attention or provokes any insight. But Coe's story, banal as it might read, is not unusual. I spent most of one summer interviewing Olympic aspirants and one thing became monotonously clear: their absolute focus on their goal eliminated everything else in their lives. It wasn't just that they didn't have time for other things – friends, reflection, a social life. They didn't have the imaginative capacity left either. Such extreme focus – on scores, times, numbers, measurements – had made it impossible for them to think in other terms. That's the bruise you can't see.

The visible scars, of course, aren't trivial and Dai Greene's many injuries weren't unusual. While we might naturally associate sport with health and fitness, at the elite or professional level, it is more commonly connected to injury and long-term health problems. At the University of North Carolina, Frederick Mueller has been an enthusiastic sports coach but now he is the director of the National Center for Catastrophic Sport Injury Research.

'Before I started, we had lots of catastrophic injuries and a lot of rule changes were designed to prevent them. But recently the emphasis on winning has really taken over sport at all levels and that has created these problems. Nowadays, second place means you're a loser and that puts athletes and players under a lot of pressure.'

Mueller collates data on fatalities and serious injuries in all sports; his research has been instrumental in reducing death from head injuries and heat stroke in American football. Yearly reports show a rising concern about head injuries in soccer. But all the sports he studies – cross-country running, soccer, field hockey, water polo, basketball, swimming, wrestling, volleyball, gymnastics, skiing, ice hockey, pole vaulting, baseball, softball, lacrosse, track, tennis, rowing, horse-riding – are associated with fatalities, near fatalities and serious injuries. Most of these derive from the sport itself but some – heat stroke, and fatalities caused by trying to make weight in wrestling – are clearly caused by the drive just to win a spot on the team. These reports make for sobering reading as they list the deaths and catastrophic injuries caused by poor, often unqualified, coaching and a youthful desire to win.[8]

'You see parents fighting each other and coaches who have no training at all. And everyone wants to win! These kids don't have any time off and they're playing all the time and having minor injuries and overuse injuries and the parents are pushing that. Some of the injuries I've seen, the kids won't tell coaches if they're injured because they don't want to lose their spot, their scholarships – even parents are involved. With concussion, some of these kids will have problems for years afterwards.'

Concussion is now a fact of life in today's sport, with high-contact sports like boxing, soccer and American football proving most dangerous. During a single season of football, a professional American footballer will receive over a thousand blows to the head and male players face a 75 per cent chance of concussion. This isn't just the nature of the game; it is the direct result of wanting to win, with 78 per cent of concussions sustained during games – not practice. Mueller now compiles an annual survey of football injuries; in 2011, he found four fatalities directly caused by football and twelve indirect fatalities caused by heat stroke, blood clot and heart attack. In the NFL, offensive and defensive linemen have a 52 per cent greater risk of dying of heart disease than the general population. In part that is because linemen are getting bigger: in the 1920s, the average lineman was six foot tall and weighed 211 pounds. By 2011, the average was six foot eleven, weighing 310 pounds.

A recurrent problem for Mueller is that when players are injured, they won't stop but want to get back into the game. Rule changes are attempting to manage this – players suffering concussion must be cleared by an independent neurologist before returning to the field – but players often won't tell their coaches that they're experiencing signs of head trauma: loss of consciousness, visual disturbance, headache, memory loss. It is for that reason that he recommends that a physician be present at all games and practice sessions – something some teams can and do afford but many do not.[9] 'Without adult intervention in concussion management,' researchers wrote, 'youth sports can become a demolition derby.' And while it might be tempting to put this down to American hyper-competitiveness, the same journal found that, in the UK,

most football teams don't follow international guidelines on concussion and only half seem to be aware that they exist.[10]

Between 2011 and 2012, six retired NFL players committed suicide. After their deaths they were found to have been suffering
from a form of dementia called chronic traumatic encephalopathy
(CTE), a disease it is now thought derives from multiple concussions. One of these tragic cases, Dave Duerson, shot himself in the
chest so that his brain could be left intact for future study; he
bequeathed it to the Boston University School of Medicine. Since
then, the School has studied the brains of 35 football players and
found 34 of them to have had CTE. More recently it has become
possible to study the brains of players while they are still alive.
When researchers at UCLA did this, all five were found to be living
with CTE, whose symptoms include memory loss and depression.
It remains unknown whether the disease is specifically linked to
concussions or whether there are multiple aspects of football as a
whole that make it dangerous. Football, after all, as Michigan State
coach Duffy Daugherty once said, isn't a contact sport; it's a col-
lision sport. And that has led some observers to wonder if the game,
and the players' desire to win the game, isn't the heart of the problem.

'Calling the head-injury crisis a concussion crisis made it sound
as if it stemmed from how the game is played, not from the game
itself,' sportswriter Jonathan Mahler ruminated. 'It doesn't take a
concussion to damage the brain. The routine plays, the beautiful
plays, the most purely football plays – they all could be causing
brain damage, too. That's a reality nobody wants to acknowledge,
because if football's problem is indeed existential, if the game
doesn't *have* a crisis but *is* the crisis, the future of football is in more
peril than anyone thinks.'[11]

Three thousand eight hundred players or their families are now
suing the NFL over head injuries and for specifically promoting the
brutality of the game. Yet football is not the only sport characterized by serious injury and fatalities. Baseball has three to four deaths
every year. Soccer is the most common source of concussion for
female athletes, with a 50 per cent chance of concussion.[12] But,
after football, the most dangerous sport in America, says Mueller,
is cheerleading.

'Cheerleading accounts for more injuries than all other girl sports put together,' Mueller says. 'It is fiercely competitive. They start them really young, they travel all over the country and put in hours and hours in places that aren't safe with coaches who have no professional qualifications. And of course the more spectacular stunts – flips and twists twenty-five feet up in the air – are the riskiest.'

Laura Jackson was just fourteen when she went for her cheerleading try-out. Eager to win a spot on her high school team, she took a running start across the gym floor before launching herself into a flip. She can't remember what went wrong, only that she landed on her neck, turned blue and couldn't breathe. She had broken two vertebrae in her neck and the bones pinched her brain stem. Today, Laura is quadraplegic – and an active campaigner for cheerleading safety.

'Cheerleading has changed completely from what you might remember at school,' Mueller told me. 'It's a high-stakes sport now with a fiercely competitive organization. In many schools, it isn't considered a sport so there aren't any rules or regulations around how many hours you can practise. You get these kids working with coaches who have little training or awareness of the dangers. They do these tall pyramids, fantastic flips and the stunts are almost always performed on hard surfaces. So when they go wrong, the results are catastrophic.'

Over 30,000 American girls end up in emergency rooms every year with injuries sustained during cheerleading. The sport is not inherently dangerous; what makes it so damaging is the extreme to which the participants are being pushed – and pushing themselves – to win. Even athletics, fuelled by competitive drive, now carries dangers. Research out of the University of Leuven examined the heart muscles of triathletes and marathon runners after a race. While they expected to see hearts in peak condition, what they found instead was that the hearts had changed shape, with the function of the right ventricle (which pumps blood into the lungs) 'severely dysfunctional'. Some of the athletes recovered but some did not, with MRI scans showing signs of heart scarring. Although the sample size in the study was small, the medical director of the London Marathon, Sanjay Sharma, thought that it had to be taken seriously.

'My personal feeling is that extreme endurance exercise probably does cause damage to the heart in some athletes,' Sharma said.
'I don't believe that the human body is designed to exercise at full
stretch for as long as eleven hours a day, so damage to the heart is
not implausible. The potential for such projects is enormous considering the colossal increase in participation rates in endurance
events such as the marathon. The long term conclusions of the
authors may appear preposterous to some, but could prove to be
the retrospective "elephant in the room".'[13]

The promise and romance of money and glory drives athletes
hard. It always has. But now, the certain knowledge that for every
one of them that has a spot on a team, a place in the race, there are
hundreds more who would like to be there makes the competition
more intense. And as if that weren't stressful enough, the more
thoughtful contenders know that they don't have much time to
win. There's no time for second chances so you'd better make it
while you can.

Gymnasts have usually retired by the time they are twenty. Track
and field athletes typically retire in their thirties. A few players push
into their forties but, for the most part, sport is a young person's
game. That's one reason athletes are so focused; if they are going
to win, they don't have much time. Taking seven years to shave
three seconds off his time could make sense for Dai Greene if he
had all the time in the world – but he knows that he doesn't. His
whole life is run against the clock and the calendar.

Retirement, therefore, comes early to athletes and it comes as a
shock because, while sport may be a great metaphor for life, it isn't
very good training or preparation for it. Many athletes, in retirement, confront the vacuum that Denise Lewis so eloquently
described: they feel lost, without an identity, without a plan, and
without the structure, colleagues or social support that less competitive careers provide. They're retiring much earlier than their
contemporaries and are often depressed, disillusioned and
disoriented.

In a 2011 study of Olympians, a team of Swedish and Australian
researchers talked to medallists about their transition out of sport.
Thomas (none of the participants were identified), who had won
a medal in a combat sport, tried to become a coach. He found it

hard, he said, because it involved too much self-sacrifice to the interests of others; he had only ever thought of himself. Now he found, he said, that there was a difference between being a sportsman and being a person.

'If you quit and you retire from sport, you can't only think like this and you are not alone anymore, and it's not only going on success or that you win. You are living with other people and you have to socialize or whatever. It's a bit more complex.'

Finding an identity and learning to think about other people, Thomas said, was the hardest thing he'd ever done – much harder than winning his medal.

'You can win one time, two times. But one day it gets you. And that's one part of it that got me at the [second] Olympic Games ... What happens if you fight and you lose and you don't have the recognition? You commit suicide or what? You have to find something else.'

Michelle, who won in a team sport, suffered from depression and anxiety when she left sport to become a teacher.

'In [my sport] you would be training for some intricate little skill that you want to improve or perfect and you had constant goals and you had constant reassurances that you were doing the right thing.'

Michelle had spent her whole life as a perfectionist, aiming at measurable, short-term goals. But in teaching, perfection wasn't attainable, goals were ambiguous and there was never an absolute victory. Tunnel vision proved poor preparation for life's complexities.

Retiring professional athletes miss the extreme clarity of winning or losing. Scott Tinley, one of the finest triathletes in the world, continued to compete, he says, for far too long. On retirement, he felt lost, depressed, confused. He worked through his disorientation by interviewing over 200 fellow athletes about their transition to retirement. His book, he says, was written as a form of healing. Quoting baseball pitcher, Sandy Koufax, Tinley feels 'an athletic life is a self-liquidating life'.

Everyone missed the scoreboard, the applause. He cites statistics: the suicide rate among former NFL players is nearly six times the national average; the divorce rate for professional athletes after retirement is 60–70 per cent. And only the very lucky few have earned enough truly to retire. Most now had to reinvent themselves in a world that they don't know, for which they're often ill-equipped.[14]

'The careers are really short,' says former sports agent Darren Heitner. 'Many athletes go broke, not just because they're from poor backgrounds or don't spend wisely. You can't live your whole life on your signing bonus – even if you manage your money well. And with no education, it's really hard to find other opportunities. If you want to do TV and *Dancing with the Stars*, then you have to be a big name, have the right contacts, the right agent, the right relationships – the pool of athletes chosen is just so small. There's no way you can live off sports for the rest of your life. An Usain Bolt, a Peyton Manning maybe – these are profound exceptions. But very, very few can rest on their laurels for the rest of their lives.'

Time, for professional and elite athletes, is highly concentrated; so much depends on the short term – the minutes, days and weeks – that there's little room or time to look further ahead. The tunnel of their tunnel vision is strikingly short. Ironically, it is the extreme brevity of their careers that often makes athletes that much more determined to win and to win now. In 1984, a physician and biochemist named Robert Goldman asked 198 elite athletes a question: would they take an undetectable drug that guaranteed them a gold medal if they knew it would also kill them within five years? Fifty-two per cent said that they would. He repeated the survey every two years for the next decade and the results didn't budge. This came to be known as the Goldman dilemma.

In 2010, forty-eight professional American football players were asked similar questions: 'Is a good chance of playing in the NFL worth a decent chance of permanent brain damage?' 53.6 per cent said it was worth the risk. 'If a star player were concussed, would his colleagues want him back on the field? Half said that they would: 'When the adrenalin is pumping and it's Friday night, the selfishness comes back and I'd want him to come back.'[15]

In 2009, some bright Australian researchers asked themselves just how peculiar the dilemma was: perhaps we would *all* willingly make these kinds of trade-offs. They surveyed 250 people who were not elite athletes; of these, just two were willing to make the

Faustian pact. The study's authors concluded that athletes, to reach the elite level, 'must display a singular focus and desire to the exclusion of other life-affirming activity'.[16]

Many psychologists see the athlete's hyper-competitiveness and extreme focus as a form of masochism, in which physical pain helps to obliterate the psychological suffering of childhood trauma. Others see it as a form of narcissism: an unquenchable hunger for attention and applause. Rare is the athlete to whom victory is unimportant, who is playing the game for the sheer joy of it. The point of the game now is to win.

'The athletes themselves are paid to win and they like to win,' says Don Catlin, doyen of drug testing. 'They don't want to take drugs but the drugs work well so they have to decide: will I stay drug-free or not?'

Catlin virtually invented the drug-testing industry in the US in 1982. Working at Walter Reed Army Medical Center, he had developed tests for cocaine and street drugs. By the time he moved to UCLA, it had become clear that the United States would need a world class drugs-testing facility for the 1984 Los Angeles Olympics and Catlin was asked to start it.

'There was no anti-doping industry in the US at the time, none,' he recalled. 'Good funding was available so the department chair's eyes bulged! And I never really turned back. It was exciting.'

Although his job is to find ways to catch athletes cheating, Catlin has a lot of sympathy for the pressure they're under – and that they put themselves under.

'Life is tough for an athlete. It's rare for them to do well and most of them have no back-up plan. Olympic athletes aren't so well off; they'll make money if they win a gold medal and if they're in a high-profile sport, but not otherwise. Silver or bronze – it's nothing. They cut their education short, everything – school, friendships – is bypassed in favour of sport. They do the best they can but there's a lot riding on them.

'If you're Mark Spitz, that's OK – he won seven golds! Or in the old days, 10–20 years ago, if you were an East German, you might get a car, an apartment! Athletes don't know much about chemistry but the doctors and chemists and trainers – they know! The cost is so high, the athletes need to get a lot out. I admired those who stayed clean but it's really hard to fault those who do drugs: the winning margin is *so* close, and yet that tiny difference makes such a big difference to their lives.'

Catlin lives in the midst of a perpetual arms race. Every time he designs a reliable test for a new drug, a murky group of chemists, trainers and agents find a way around the test or invent a new performance-enhancing substance. It doesn't matter that many of these substances are life-threatening; the Goldman dilemma shows that the majority of athletes don't care. As the potential gains and the number of competitors both increase, the doping problem grows. The World Anti-Doping Agency, its American counterpart USADA, the Australian Crime Commission and the UK anti-doping agency all agree that the use of human growth hormone and peptides are on the increase and that testing is not keeping pace; although the agencies estimate that at least 14 per cent of athletes use banned substances, only 2 per cent are ever caught.[17] Nor is the problem confined to professional sports; because these substances are easy to get, amateur and sub-elite athletes are using them too.

Erythropoietin, one of a class of drugs more popularly known as EPO, is a case in point. Widely implicated in the now ruined career of cyclist Lance Armstrong, EPO is a dangerous drug. In 2008, a major review article reported that, when used to relieve anaemia after chemotherapy, it increased the risk of death. Other studies showed it was implicated in tumours and a 2010 study connected it to strokes and heart attacks.[18] By anyone's definition, this is a risky drug, especially when administered by individuals who may not have any interest in its long-term effects. Yet, Catlin says it remains the drug of choice – because it works. And you can easily buy it online.

For the goal-focused athlete, doping represents a horrible choice. It's often presented as a classic real-life example of game theory although, for the athletes concerned, it's no game at all. If everyone is doping, you can't win without drugs. If no one is doping, you improve your chances if you dope. The conditions under which not doping is the best strategy only exist when you can be completely confident that no one else is using a stimulant – and such conditions rarely arise. Many researchers in the field, looking at the numbers revealed by the Goldman dilemma, have concluded that doping is now endemic, infiltrating every sport and major event. And some athletes agree.

'Have I ever cheated in sport?' Will Carling, former England rugby captain wrote. 'Of course I have, in fact I am so sad I still do in order to beat my kids! How sad is that! But it is ingrained, not the cheating, but the need to win! And hence on a serious level, I look at these guys who have been exposed and wonder would I have been any different?'[19]

And it's all for us. Sport is big business, representing some 2 per cent of global GDP.[20] It's an entertainment business that draws crowds and headlines with bigger, faster, longer, more dramatic attractions. The races get longer, the games more fierce, the line-backers get bigger and the serves break new records. We don't want to think that tennis players may need to be shot through with cor-tisone just to get onto court for our entertainment. We don't want to consider that, as linebackers get bigger, their chances of heart disease increase. We like to imagine we are watching the triumph of the human spirit when, in fact, we are highly likely to be watch-ing the ingenuity of the criminal mind.

'It's not cheating if everybody's doing it,' was how Victor Conte explained it.[21]

In 2004, Conte was arrested for running the Bay Area Laboratory Co-Operative (BALCO), which supplied performance-enhancing drugs to top-flight Olympic athletes, boxers, cyclists, football and baseball players, some of the most famous names in American sport, including Major League baseball players Barry Bonds and Jason Giambi, and Olympian Marion Jones. The scan-dal plunged a stake through the heart of the idea that sports competition was fair, that it brought out the best in people and that it wisely and generously rewarded the virtuous and hard-working.

'The Olympic Games are a fraud,' Conte insisted. 'It's almost like: what I'm here to tell you right now is that not only is there no Santa Claus, but there's no Easter Bunny or Tooth Fairy either in the world of sport. I mean, the whole history of the Olympic Games is just full of corruption, cover up, performance-enhancing drug use. It's not what the world thinks it is.'

Conte had, he claimed, created the drug programme for Marion Jones that led to her five medals at the Sydney Olympics, that he'd done similar work for her then-husband, Tim Montgomery, enabling him to break the 100-metre world record. The BALCO scandal exposed how deeply steroids, EPO and supplements had penetrated American and Olympic sports. Conte felt 'his' athletes had no choice, that drug testers were always behind and that the athletes' desire to win was so strong that they didn't care about risk.

Victor Conte is a convicted criminal who spent four months in prison and four months under house arrest in 2006. The furore he caused led to new testing regimes in virtually every sport, keeping Don Catlin permanently busy.

'I thought it would be simple.' Catlin laughed. 'You find a drug, you just need to know its retention time and get a sample of it. I thought I could clean it up in about five years! I had no idea of the magnitude of the problem.'

As the problem grew, it became Catlin's lifelong passion. He was at the London 2012 Olympics, overseeing the testing lab there. As in Beijing, 4 per cent of athletes were caught doping but only 4,686 tests were administered so no one will ever know the full scale of illegal drug use. Nor is it clear how far anyone wants to know the truth. For the Olympic organizers, doping presents a dilemma: testing everyone is expensive and time-consuming and the more you do, the greater the risk of catching so many athletes that the Games might lose their romance.

'The challenge never stops,' says Catlin. 'Drugs with drugs inside. Masking drugs. Growth hormone is hard to detect. Genetic manipulation may prove impossible to detect. They're always trying to get ahead of our knowledge and understanding.'

The BALCO scandal came as an enormous shock to the American psyche. While President Bush used his State of the Union address to exhort lawmakers to expunge doping from American sport,[22] those directly involved in bringing perpetrators to justice recognized that something deeper than rhetoric was required. Travis Tygart was head of legal affairs at the United States Anti-Doping Agency when BALCO unfolded; its scale appalled him. He felt that it wasn't a case of a few athletes gone wrong but an entire ethos that had been corrupted. Cheating by doping, Tygart felt, was just the worst manifestation of the desire to win at all costs.

'All the athletes we caught,' Tygart told me, 'none ever felt good about cheating. They all knew it wasn't right and couldn't justify or live with it.'

Tygart grew up playing sports; as an adult, he coached school teams. But what he had loved when he was growing up had changed profoundly and he wanted to understand what had happened to sport. With that in mind, he commissioned *What Sport Means in America*, a sobering reflection on what competitive sports have become.

'The footprint of sport on society is large' the report found: three-fifths of adults were involved in some kind of sport and a quarter were actively involved. But cheating was also pervasive: one in five admitted to having bent or broken a rule, half knew someone who had broken a rule and, of those who had cheated, virtually all (96 per cent) cited knowing others who had done so. Sports volunteers, participants and fathers of children aged 8–17 had the highest rates of admitted rule bending or breaking.

Most striking of all was a contradiction. Americans *said* that what they cared about most in sport was fun, fair play, integrity, self-discipline, patience and a sense of community. What did they care about least? Winning and competitiveness.

But when asked what sport in fact rewarded, the answer was: winning and competitiveness. In other words, the idea of sport was great: games that could teach important life lessons. But the reality was completely different, teaching lessons yes – just all the wrong ones.

'We saw kids taking supplements,' Tygart recalled. 'Two day workouts and year-round seasons were becoming common. One parent of a fourteen-year-old inline roller skater – not even a money sport or an Olympic sport – his father had hired a trainer and put him on one of the most sophisticated programmes of human growth steroid that we'd come across. We talked to the kid: he was just doing what his dad told him to do. This was enlightening and eye-opening. It was the first time we saw the extent to which a parent would go. The parents were just so over-the-top win, win win. They weren't that far from pushing drugs – on their own kids!

'The culture gets more competitive and extreme. Win at all

costs! I'll do anything to get the scholarship. The erosion of family
dinners and vacations at the expense of driving kids to practice and
tournaments is just terrible. And it really made us think: what do
we want out of sports? Do we want an ethos that is all about winning at all costs, trampling the competition, breaking the rules? Or
do we want something more meaningful?'

The sense that sport had lost its way fuelled Tygart's mission to
clean it up. For over two years, in the face of three death threats,
he pursued the investigation into Lance Armstrong, doggedly accu-
mulating the evidence that finally stripped the cyclist of his Tour
de France medals and of his reputation.

Doping is the biggest, most visible sign of sport gone wrong. But
if winning is all that matters, then the huge costs of elite and professional sports – lost lives, shattered dreams, catastrophic injuries –
can seem acceptable. Just like commoditized education: if the
product, not the process, is all that matters, then the drugs and the
cheating are irrelevant. The problem, for Tygart, doesn't lie in the
sports themselves but in the society's idolization of winning athletes
and of athletic competition.

'We have so over-valued winning' Tygart concluded. 'We focus
too much on the minority. Does it make sense to focus exclusive
attention on a tiny group of winners? Common sense says no and
so does our research. When you focus exclusively on winning, that
overshadows all the other good attributes in taking part.'

It's important to recognize that Tygart is himself an avid sportsman. He loves sport – just not what it has become. And while it
would be comforting to think that this is just an American problem,
much in the UK demonstrates the same pattern. Two-thirds of
children say they feel pressure to cheat in sport because of a 'win-
at-all-costs' culture and more than a third said that they felt no
remorse when they did cheat.[23]

Stephen Baddeley, Director of Sport at the University of Bath
(where Dai Greene and many other Olympians trained), played
badminton at an elite level. But in the winter after the Games,
when asked to participate in a public debate – 'Would you let your
child be an elite athlete?' – he adopted the opposing position.

'I believe passionately in sport,' Baddeley told me. 'I wouldn't be
here if I didn't. But elite sports are different. They're bad for kids

physically. You have to push yourself to the limit and the body will break down – if it doesn't you aren't working hard enough. The research in badminton showed that 70 per cent of the under-16 squad had stress fractures in their back. That's bad for you. When you do sport you will lose. The good thing is that it teaches you to deal with failure. But teenagers, very few of them have the emotional resilience to deal with it, which is why you get lots of bad behaviour from teenagers in sport.'

Watching everyone from children to professionals at Bath's Training Village has given Baddeley a sharp perspective on the role that sport plays – or could play – in all our lives. Much of the problem, he says, starts with clubs that compete for talent at earlier and earlier ages.

'The clubs are competing against each other; they're picking kids early in order that they *not* go to other clubs. How do you pick out five-, six-, seven-year-old kids? Can you really say they're talented? It's ridiculous. But they get them to specialize – far, far too early. That's where the injuries come in. It isn't for the kids; you get tennis clubs picking kids just so they won't go into football . . .'

The very idea that some kids 'have it' while others don't offends Baddeley. Although he was talking specifically about sport, his views echo the teachers who believe that childhood should not be a moment when kids are sorted, but when their energies and enthusiasms find opportunities to unfurl.

'I avoid using the word "talent",' he tells me. 'Young people have potential and the idea that some eight-year-olds are more talented than others – I just reject it. Everyone's potential isn't the same – some are taller and that helps in basketball. But many more would have the same potential if they were just given the opportunity.'

The standard argument for paying so much attention (and money) to elite sports is that it will inspire the rest of us: that watching the Dai Greenes, Denise Lewises and Michael Phelpses of the world will send us all out onto running tracks and into swimming pools. That was supposed to be the justification for investing in the Olympics: the games would, as the tagline went, 'inspire a generation'. But, for three years, Baddeley worked for Sport England, charged with driving legacy participation, and he came to believe the legacy was a phantom.

'The legacy required an investment *before* the Games, to prepare for the demand. But that was never going to happen. I left in 2008 because I could see money being diverted out of Sport England to fund Olympic buildings like the pool and the velodrome.'

The games themselves absorbed the money needed to ensure a legacy, while lottery funding, on which much sports participation depends, was similarly siphoned off to ensure the games could take place.

'The Olympics set up a new lottery game specifically for the Games,' Baddeley continued. 'So the normal lottery income went down – so community sports were receiving less even *before* the recession and austerity hit. The legacy was never going to happen. You could see that even before the Games.'

A systematic review by the *British Medical Journal* found no evidence that the Olympics increases sports participation – and that was even before the government cut free swimming. A year after the Olympics, a report into their legacy was met with widespread derision while the House of Commons Education Select Committee warned that the severe lack of school facilities, qualified teachers and an over-emphasis on competition undermined sports participation. In the US, Tygart would love to imagine that the Olympics sent a nation onto the running track, but that isn't what he sees. In fact, the implication of USADA's research is that the emphasis on winning and winners is what sends people *out* of sport. Children feel such enormous pressure to win that, when they can't win, they quit.

'From a revenue standpoint,' he told me, 'capturing TV space for elite competition definitely draws viewers and revenue dollars. But we haven't seen any proof that that alone builds more participation in the grassroots level that leads to a lifetime involvement in sport.'

Trickle-down doesn't work in sport any more than it does in economics. Focusing resources, rewards and celebrity on the top few doesn't help anyone, maybe not even the athletes themselves. Using competition to identify the best and then using the best to inspire the rest turns out to be a great theory; it just doesn't work in practice. Instead, the message that is received says that sport is only about winning, and if you can't win, then you may as well not bother. Examining the 2000 Sydney Olympics, a study sadly concluded that the only pastime that was more popular after the games than before them was watching TV.[24]

Enthusiasts still believe in sport as a rich experience that teaches fairness, fun, the joys of community and collaboration. But the pastime has been hijacked by an obsession with competition, winners and winning. Could it ever be possible to get back to the original dream in which games were played, not fought? At USADA, Travis Tygart commissioned a second report to identify ways to repair the wreckage he saw all around him. If the problem wasn't sport *per se* but what sport had become – was there any chance that sport could regain its original and crucial playfulness?

Tygart's report, *True Sport*, talks a great deal about what sport could and should be, the values it ought to demonstrate. While bad sport provokes lying, cheating, violence, delinquency, alcohol and drug abuse, true sport could be a source of improved health, higher self-esteem, creativity and problem-solving; it could reduce the incidence of eating disorders, obesity, depression and suicide. Its eloquent plea to return play to games even suggests that healthy participation in sports can improve academic outcomes. But for that to happen, however, a lot has to change.

Parents and coaches have a big role to play. Just as Finnish schools do so well by challenging themselves to make all children succeed, so both Baddeley and Tygart believe that the central focus of sport should be on encouraging all children, not just the winners. Crucial to this change is 'to stop and remind ourselves that in sport, like so many other areas of life, experiences can be as important as outcomes'. In other words: the score is not the point. Kids drop out of sport because there's too much competition and not enough fun; the game isn't a game anymore. Winning needs to take a back seat – and stay there.

More important than early talent-spotting is the development of an intrinsic love of all sport. There is no relationship between early development and later success and, while most athletic directors saw specialization increasing, the report insists it is dangerous. Children who specialize too early risk the disappearance of their childhood, becoming 'socially handcuffed'. Athletes who specialize experience more pressure to succeed, have fewer meaningful social interactions and more overuse injuries. Ninety-eight per cent of athletes who specialize at an early age will never reach the highest level of sport; they're more likely to burn out. Instead, teachers and parents should encourage their kids to play many different sports and to develop a love of the game – not a need to win.

Coaches are vital role models and USADA is critical of how untrained and unqualified most school coaches are. They have the potential to inspire and develop young people – but lack emotional and physical expertise. Coaches themselves were self-critical, with 78 per cent of them identifying the inappropriate behaviour of coaches as the most serious problem facing sport today. Few coaches know enough about safety, physical development training or conditioning – while all feel huge pressure to win. The report argues strongly that coaches need professional training and qualification.

Parents need to change their game, too. 'When child athletes feel that their parents are supportive and positive and emphasize mastery and enjoyment, they are more likely to display concern for opponents and grace in losing. They also are less likely to trash talk or whine and complain about the coach or their playing time. Children of parents who create anxiety about failing and emphasize winning are more likely to engage in poor sport behaviors than children whose parents encourage enjoyment and self-mastery.' Some sports organizations have put in place codes of conduct – for parents.

Underneath *True Sport* runs a subtle but profound subtext. Sport articulates social and political values, in London and New York as surely as in ancient Rome. It is both an influence on, and a reflection of, who we are.

'In a climate in which corporate executives fabricate financial records, citizens evade taxes, professional athletes commit felonies or engage in immoral behavior, college football coaches are caught in recruiting scandals, colleges prefer students with athletic prowess over academic achievements, and university coaches are paid more than the president of the institution ... cheating and unethical behavior appear to pay off, or at least go unpunished in many cases. This breeds an environment in which only "chumps" play by the rules.

'If we let the desire to win run rampant and unchecked through sport, then we will continue to see the transgressions among athletes, coaches, and fans mount. If we cannot save sport from an obsession with extrinsic rewards, then where will our children turn to learn the lessons that true sport offers? And is our nation well served by a citizenry that learns to prize winning and extrinsic rewards at any cost as the values held most dear?'

After retiring from cricket, Mike Brearley, regarded as one of England's greatest cricket captains, trained and practised as a psychoanalyst. To many, this seemed a surprising leap but to Brearley himself, it was a perfect fit – and not just because cricket has always been regarded as the most cerebral of games.

'Sport gives you the licence to compete,' he told me, 'just as analysis gives you a licence to say what you think. We need those safe places that are set aside from the everyday business of life.'

As we sat in the warm, comfortable front room of his Chalk Farm house, surrounded not by sporting memorabilia but black-and-white Miró prints, Brearley was keen to explain that sport is not, should not be, the same as life. Its chief value is, or should be, its safe distance and difference *from* life.

'I have had one or two male patients for whom sport has been important. It allows inhibited people to show off their skills, to be flamboyant, allow disinhibition and create real engagement. People are really present to each other and it's very enlivening. At its best it is absolutely body to body, eyeball to eyeball, and a lot is revealed and allowed. But it is not quite life; it's to the side of life. This is what makes psychoanalysis and sport the same. They're both full on – but slightly "as if". You are not the patient's father or mother but "as if". That's an illusion that is allowed. It's through that artificiality that you can get to some of these things in life. But it isn't the same as life.'

Sport may not be the same as life but it has become a ubiquitous metaphor and mental model for success in all walks of life. And in just the same way that the gentle illusion of sport has become corrupted and distorted by competitiveness and winning, the same costs – tunnel vision, excess and cheating – can be seen in businesses that take modern sport as their mental model.

'I just wanted to win. It was just about me and my goal, nothing to do with anyone else. I was completely focused on my own strengths. I was there to win, that was my focus.'

Melody Hussaini sounds like an athlete but she isn't. She was a contender in the seventh series of *The Apprentice*. The programme makes much of the metaphorical connection between sports and business, with episodes often structured as races in which contestants have to clear hurdles. Challenges start as team sports but ultimately the game is all about soloists: the apprentices who can beat all their so-called colleagues to the prize. The overarching message of the show is that business is just like sport: vicious, antisocial, with one winner whose success is achieved only through the defeat of all competitors.

When she took part in the show, Hussaini displayed many of the characteristics of competitive athletes: tunnel vision, rigid determination, a focus on herself to the exclusion of others. The programme editors made much of the fact that, at the end of the first episode, she toasted herself; this became a recurrent theme throughout her appearance. She was both lauded for her drive and mocked for her inability to listen to others, use their talents or recognize their experience. Hussaini was eventually 'fired' because her determination to win had made her such a poor collaborator.

'I kept wanting everyone to know I deserved to win. A lot of that was edited to highlight my desire to win – but I did say those things, of course I did. I have a fighting spirit. When I was a child, I used to walk around saying: I am going to be successful. In life, you're competing with six billion people. You can't worry about everyone.'

Hussaini has fully absorbed the message that success is a solo, individual act, requiring a total focus on self. Even if she doesn't train for it as determinedly as Olympic aspirants, she has adopted their internal focus. When I drove to meet Hussaini outside Rugby, I couldn't find her house. I phoned for directions but she couldn't give them. She had, she said, always got home using her GPS. She had no idea where I was or what landmarks I might look for. Lacking the imaginative capacity to see what it might be like for someone *not* to know where she lived or how to get there, she was at a loss to describe her own surroundings.

A combination of maps, phone calls, Internet searches and my husband eventually got me to Hussaini's front door. Later, as we talked, she perched next to a muted television screen that covered one side of the sitting room. Although it was hard to talk as the gaudy images of *E!* flashed across the room, it never occurred to her to turn it off. What emerged was a bizarre, often contradictory collage of disconnected ambition.

'I would like to be on the top of the Rich List. I want it. But this can drive people to the point where they forget what they are trying to achieve. Competition for its own sake is a dangerous timewaster and a dangerous thing. It can breed pure greed. That's why I just focus on the destination.'

Hussaini runs a social enterprise aimed at giving young people the skills they need to abjure crime and to get into jobs. It seems a curious route to the Rich List. At the heart of Hussaini's drive, it seems, isn't a coherent project or a sense of how, meaningfully, she might connect with the world. All she wants, to the exclusion of all else, is to be a winner. Even if she can't decide what that means.

Hussaini has energy and intelligence. But it seems she can't connect with other people because she can't see them. Like many hyper-competitive people, her goals resist all connection to, or recognition of, the complexity and value of other people. To me, it seemed no accident that her business has no employees, only far-flung associates.

But Hussaini's idea of leadership isn't eccentric or even unusual. *The Apprentice* is predicated on the belief that success for one requires the defeat of everyone else and that business is just a matter of keeping score. After all, only one person can win this game show – and they can do so only by making everyone else lose. Entirely consistent with this image of success are the show's hosts, who position themselves as master manipulators and umpires. *The Apprentice* makes for hyperbolic entertainment, purveying an impoverished, decrepit image of business success as an act of short-term, quick-fix domination. And it's not alone. With their hyperactive commentators and scrolling stock prices, the TV shows and channels that focus on business now resemble nothing more than the sports programming on which they're based.

Just as the true value of sport has become corrupted and distorted, the application of the competitive sports metaphor to business and leadership has warped and misaligned individuals and organizations otherwise replete with talent and promise. The tunnel vision that athletes need to achieve their goals, the extreme focus displayed by Dai Greene, may work for well-defined and immediate goals achieved by individuals. But most of the work we do can't be defined by a single, momentary measure and, critically, requires imagination, mental flexibility and sustained creativity of a kind that the rigidity of tunnel vision specifically disables.

A competitive mindset may help you hit tomorrow's sales target or get through the week's call sheet but it's a terrible way to manage complex projects over the lifetime of a business. We know that vast business enterprises depend for their success on networks and systems of thousands of highly collaborative, interconnected creative people; rationally we recognize that one individual alone won't determine success or failure. But the absolute focus on self that athletic prowess requires – and that the former Olympians found so hard to shake off – stands completely at odds with the collective nature of business achievement. Nevertheless, the athletic image of leadership as an act of solo heroism has proved persistent and potent. Magazine covers sporting the rugged profiles of business leaders and the motivational life lessons of CEOs (strangely akin to athletes' memoirs) perpetuate the same trope: the heroic soloist can and will save the day, singlehanded. Ambitious organizations just need to pick winners.

Academic researchers have long puzzled over the myth of the CEO as heroic soloist. One study of 111 chief executives analysed photographs of the CEO in annual reports, the CEO's prominence in company press releases, use of the first person in interviews and overall compensation. They concluded that the more prominent the chief executive was by all these measures, the more dynamic and grandiose the company strategy, the larger the number and size of acquisitions and the more extreme and volatile the stock performance.[25] Outsize expectations of the leader put pressure on him (or, occasionally, her) to take more dramatic decisions and adopt a more hyperbolic profile.

Ambitious acquisitions offer a great shortcut to widespread publicity and applause (at least from those who stand to benefit.) They are, in the business world, what extravagant tries or runs are in sport: high-stakes manoeuvres that often end in injury and failure. Depending on whose research you credit, the failure rate for mergers and acquisitions lies between 50 and 80 per cent. But these moves persist because they make individual leaders look dynamic, decisive, tough and (when they're completed) victorious. That they are regularly written about as head-to-head contests between two hyper-competitive CEOs only sharpens their drama and enhances the charisma of the winner.

Tyco was a sure bet – once – because it was run by 'the most aggressive CEO in America'. GE, a vast multinational conglomerate, was apparently run by just one man: Jack Welch, author of *Winning*. BP, likewise, depended wholly on the genius and foresight of John Browne who, in his 'inspirational memoir from a visionary leader', drew up a chart that aligned columns of world events, BP events and events in Browne's own life as though they were all of comparable importance. Meanwhile, Paris-based Compagnie Générale des Eaux promised to transform itself from a successful water utility to a global media and entertainment business purely because of the towering will of just one man – Jean-Marie Messier. That the company had no relevant assets or capabilities, and the CEO no experience of the media business, didn't matter: heroic leadership alone would effect the transformation. Messier sometimes referred to himself as J6M. Four of the 'M's stood for *Moi-Même, Maître du Monde*: Me Myself, Master of the Universe. He was saying overtly what the rhetoric around leadership often suggests: that superheroes can do anything, win any race, clear any hurdle.

Like superstar athletes, they warrant extravagant pay and lavish surroundings. When Merrill Lynch CEO, John Thain had his office redecorated with its notorious $35,000 commode, or Tyco CEO Dennis Kozlowski boasted of his $15,000 dog umbrella, these props were not just pecking-order symbols: they were the just desserts of the heroes who singlehandedly guided their company's fates. Only when the businesses failed did they look extravagant; before that, they merely symbolized the faith that others had bestowed on their leaders.

We believe in stars. This belief in heroic leadership emerges every time a company hits a crisis. Instead of examining systemic issues, the cry goes out for a messiah who will, singlehandedly, compel transformation. Thus, in 2009, when America's car companies were in trouble, a 'car czar' was called in – Steve Rattner, a man with no background in the car industry. Rattner knew at once what needed to be done. Consulting Jack Welch and headhunters, he hired a new CEO for General Motors. Clearly, one man would turn around a vast, complex business. Being a heroic soloist himself, Rattner would know another one when he saw one: Ed Whitacre, former CEO of AT&T.

'His reputation was for toughness,' Rattner wrote about Whitacre. 'I remembered having once read a *Business Week* story that described him killing rattlesnakes on his Texas ranch (he would pin down the snake with a stick and crush its head with a rock). His flinty image was reinforced by his lean, six-foot-four frame, his full head of gray hair, and his laconic speech.'[26]

Although he'd never worked in a manufacturing business in his life, Whitacre got the job; clearly he had what every heroic soloist needs. Rattner writes admiringly of Whitacre's first meeting with his new team: '"I'm used to winning and have no intention of seeing that change at GM." The GM executives, unused to this sort of bluntness, were impressed, and so was I. It was superlative leadership as I had always imagined it.'

Whitacre went on to star in GM's television commercials; what the ailing business needed was for customers to see that it now had a dynamic leader. But, after ten months on the job, Whitacre lost interest and quit. He had, apparently, never wanted to stay a day longer than was needed and clearly killing snakes and appearing on television was all that was required for a complex turnaround. Bob Lutz, a renowned automotive veteran from Ford, Chrysler and GM, calls the story of Whitacre's triumph a 'fable'; crediting Whitacre with GM's revival was as accurate as 'crediting the rooster with making the sun come up'.[27]

The romance of the heroic soloist is seen nowhere so vividly as in the hagiography surrounding Steve Jobs. If you were to believe much of what's been written about him, you might imagine that Apple had little need of its large workforce: Jobs apparently did it all. The truth, as usual is more subtle: when Jobs had outstanding collaborators – Steve Wozniak at Apple, John Lasseter at Pixar, or

Jonathan Ive at Apple again – his businesses thrived. But when he was on his own at NeXT, without the creative conflict those brilliant peers offered him, his venture foundered.

It isn't that leaders don't have an impact; they do. The problem is that the leadership of any organization is infinitely more complex, subtle and contingent than any race or soccer match. Companies can't be saved with a single kick or by shaving a second off completion times. When we worship outstanding performers, we infantilize everyone else, conveying the message that everyone can – even should – be passive in the face of towering ability. In just the same way that focusing on elite athletes discourages sports participation, the focus on business leaders as winners conveys the dispiriting message that others don't count. Instead of galvanizing and surfacing the rich talent that always exists within these organizations, solo superheroes are expected singlehandedly to work miracles. That is, of course, why they fail.

Loaded with superhuman expectations, CEOs develop their own form of tunnel vision: working exorbitant hours to the exclusion of everything else in their lives. Jack Welch, running GE, wrote romantically about the long hours he kept and the weekends when he could go into the office and work with his team. John Browne, asking himself why he didn't retire earlier from BP (before his reputation was tarnished by a false witness statement) concluded that nothing outside BP was as exciting or as highly valued. When work excludes all other aspects of life, the reality checks, questions and discontinuities that we all need to test our thinking simply vanish; there's no time for them. Despite overwhelming evidence that long hours produce fatigue that clearly, and physically, damages our ability to think, heroic soloists imagine that their only chance of meeting outsize expectations is to work all the hours that they can stay awake. Like the athlete who ignores injuries, they're oblivious to the science that connects fatigue with biased judgement and rigid thinking.[28]

Corporate workouts incur their own injuries. Following up on Marmot's research into Whitehall civil servants Finnish researcher Marianna Virtanen examined the long-term impact of working very long hours and came to two startling conclusions: working eleven or more hours a day at least doubled the risk of depression.

And those working fifty-five hours a week or more began, in their middle years, to suffer cognitive loss – that is, their performance was poorer when tested for vocabulary, reasoning, information-processing, problem-solving, creativity and reaction times. This level of mild cognitive impairment in middle age also predicts earlier dementia and death.[29]

And, just as in elite sports, careers at the top are very short. Although no two studies can agree about the average tenure of chief executives, it currently hovers around five years and has been falling steadily. CEOs don't last long in the top spot not just because the expectations are too great and the business environment dauntingly complex. It is also because the mental model of leadership that derives from sporting success – the super athlete, the star player – lacks all the subtlety, complexity, collaboration and time that true achievement requires.

Nevertheless, when CEOs get the top job, many do just what elite athletes do: focus single-mindedly on the score. Share price becomes the single, simple measure by which winning or losing is defined. So pervasive and single-minded has the obsession with stock price become that most people now believe that every company has a legal obligation to prioritize stock price above all else. This is not true.

Lynn Stout, professor of corporate and business law at Cornell, is feisty and furious about the degree to which a wilful misunderstanding of the law has led boards and executives to succumb to what she calls the 'myth of shareholder value'. The law concerning corporate behaviour, she says, comes from one of three places: a company's charter, national law and case law. None of these, she argues, requires maximizing the share price as the over-riding responsibility of a company or its directors. Indeed, she says, most of our corporate problems can be traced back to this flawed idea.

The myth of shareholder value derives chiefly from neither lawyers nor business people but from economists – primarily Milton Friedman first and then William Meckling and Michael Jensen. Friedman argued that, because shareholders 'own' the corporation, the only 'social responsibility of business is to increase its profit'. That is not only a non-sequitur; legally, Stout argues, it is wildly inaccurate. Shareholders don't, legally, own a corporation:

it is an independent legal entity that owns itself. And directors are not 'under any *per se* duty to maximize shareholder value in the short term, even in the context of a takeover'. Case law – in this instance, *Air Products and Chemicals Inc. v. Airgas, Inc.*, – found that disinterested and informed directors can ignore today's stock price in favour of the long-term interests of a business.

When economist Michael Jensen and business school dean William Meckling, in the most widely cited article ever published in a business academic journal, proposed that executives be seen merely as agents of the shareholders, Stout found that the law did not agree with them. They had failed to capture the true economic structure of public companies, their purpose and stakeholders.

The problem is that they read the law wrong and they read business wrong. And if that weren't enough, there is a notable shortage of reliable results showing that shareholder primacy actually works better. In fact, there is plenty of evidence to the contrary, showing that companies whose governance requires more shareholder involvement actually do worse. The idea that corporations should be managed to maximize shareholder value has led to 'reforms' over the past two decades to give shareholders more influence over boards and to make managers more attentive to share price. The results are disappointing at best. Shareholders are suffering their worst investment returns since the Great Depression;[30] the population of publicly listed companies has declined by 40 per cent;[31] and the life expectancy of Fortune 500 firms has plunged from 75 years in the early twentieth century to only 15 years today.[32]

In her book, *The Shareholder Value Myth*, Stout argues that the myth has become so pervasive that, even though it isn't true, many CEOs and corporate directors believe it to be true. (So, strangely, do many corporate critics.) Most, when pressed, confess that they don't really know what the law requires so they assume the share price is how they are measured.[33]

Belief that shareholder value is a legal requirement gave rise to a second aberration, Stout says, which is the linking of executive pay to the share price. Although there is no evidence that performance-related pay delivers superior performance (and a lot of evidence to the contrary) many public companies have been eager to hold their executives to account by tying their remuneration to the company's stockmarket valuation. They may have hoped, in doing so, to counter increasing public disgust at high salaries and bonuses. But the effect of performance-related pay is to create tunnel vision of just the kind that athletes demonstrate, with absolute focus on short-term price goals often entirely at odds with an organization's long-term vitality.

A company's share price is, at best, a very weak indicator of its strength or value. Does anyone seriously believe that, in the course of a single day or week, despite no changes at all to its operations, a company genuinely becomes 1, 3, 5 per cent more valuable? Even Fischer Black, one of America's leading economists, conceded as much: 'the price is more than half of value and less than twice value' meaning a company valued at a hundred pounds might be worth anything between fifty and two hundred. It might also be on the brink of implosion – or explosive growth. None of this is revealed by its price.

The biggest damage done by the shareholder value myth is that it encourages what Lynn Stout calls 'fishing with dynamite': a preference for quick, brutal strategies that create a lot of value instantly – even if they wreck opportunities for the future. This, she argued, is what happened within BP, where pressure to cut costs led employees and contractors to ignore standard safety procedures. Many companies that cut jobs, training, research and development fish with dynamite, insofar as they're trying to make the numbers look great without any concern for the long-term health of the business or the environment in which it operates. Ornate tax-avoidance strategies similarly may save money during a CEO's brief tenure while destroying the company's long-term reputation.

Nevertheless, the allure of the stock price is that it represents a nice, simple score by which the CEO and the company directors can measure their own achievement. Stock price determines their place in the market just as visibly and publicly as if it were their seat in the Colosseum. Shareholders and pension funds, investing for the future, might want company leadership to consider the long-term health of a business but that isn't how CEOs are measured so it isn't what most focus on. The single metric of the stock price becomes so critical to a sense of status and success that managing it can become the company's core competence and the CEO's main focus.

Jack Welch, chief executive of GE from 1981 to 2001, for many years the champion of shareholder value, became highly expert at managing his numbers. In forty-one out of forty-six quarters, he hit his forecast to the *penny*, missing it five times by 2 cents and twice by 1 cent. The chances of these earnings not being 'managed' is statistically implausible. Similarly, Microsoft met or beat its market forecast for forty-one out of its first forty-two quarters, missing just once by a cent. This is what Roger Martin, dean of the Rotman School of Management in Toronto, calls 'gaming the game'.[34] To the degree that we conduct business as though it were sport, we must expect it to share the same aberrant behaviours.

Years after retiring from GE, Jack Welch changed his mind, declaring 'strictly speaking, shareholder value is the dumbest idea in the world'.[35] But, like many bad ideas, it has caught on, not least because it seems so simple. However, keeping score takes time and attention. It's impossible not to reflect that, while Microsoft was so busy becoming expert at this game, it failed to notice the emergence of the World Wide Web, or to develop serious technology for databases, computer games or mobile computing: all vast new areas of innovation. If the score is what matters, then, just like grades at school, the outcome is prized over and above the process required to achieve it. The score is all that counts.

On a daily basis, this is real and observable. When I ran companies for CMGI during a time in which its price was climbing steadily, there were days on which you knew how the stock market was doing without looking at a computer monitor: you could feel the adrenalin in the air, hear the excitement in the voices of employees who should have had their minds elsewhere. But just as you can't judge the long-term health of a football player by the number of points he scores, so you can't tell the long-term health of a company by its share price. CMGI crashed as fast as it had risen and it wasn't alone. Of the sixty companies eulogized in Jim Collins's *Good to Great*, which had been identified by their cumulative stockmarket returns, at least eleven have since gone from bad to worse. Scores don't tell you everything but, like the shadows on the wall of Plato's cave, they are easily mistaken for the real thing.

The compelling simplicity of the stock price distracts and detracts from the reality that is more complex and demands more effort.

But not all companies work this way. For many, success isn't about winning, because it can't be captured in a single score nor achieved by any one individual. The bigger prize is a creative activity that everyone can own.

'Profit is not the main driver, it is the result of what you do. No financial person will ever run this business because they bugger up more businesses than they ever help. If you were a cricket team and you were sending someone in to open bowling or batting, the last person you would send would be the scorer.'

Hugh Facey is as tough-minded an industrialist as you will find anywhere in the world. His manufacturing business, Gripple, has offices in Sheffield, São Paulo, New Delhi, Chicago and Strasbourg. The company makes a vast range of suspension devices, for hanging lights, heating components, fences, and pipes. A spinoff, Loadhog, produces weird and wonderful new packaging products. Both companies have won prizes around the world for innovation, design and engineering. Portly, grey-haired and with bushy eyebrows through which you can just discern sharp eyes, Facey describes himself, somewhat disingenuously, as a 'simple Yorkshireman'. But there's nothing simple about the way he thinks about business and leadership.

'I started my first business in 1989 and I sold it in 1992. And I thought at the time that it was wrong that I got all the benefit of the sale and not the staff – because they had grown the business with me. And I thought then that there just had to be a better way.'

Far from relishing the prospect of owning his company outright, reaping all the profit and the glory, Facey was determined that everyone who worked at his next business, Gripple, would own part of it. Over the years, he has adapted the company structure so that, now, everyone who works there, owns shares in it. Facey doesn't have an office; his desk sits alongside the rest of the staff in a wide, bright open space inside a red-brick Victorian gun-works factory. As Facey showed me around, he pointed proudly to slogans painted on the walls: empowering people, creativity, fun, energy.

'This was them, not me,' he insisted. 'The staff did all of this. They're the ones who have all the ideas. Business is about ideas, not about the bottom line. I find that the more we think about the ideas, the better the company does. And ideas don't come from accountants – scorers – they come from the people who make the products or the people who talk to the customers. You can only get ideas from people.'

At Gripple, 25 per cent of all sales come from products that did not exist four years earlier. Ninety-two per cent of their output is exported. The emphasis throughout the business is on innovation, creativity, problem-solving. Loadhog, the container business, was spun out of new ideas generated inside Gripple. The company also runs a small innovation lab where Facey and others in the company mentor and nurture young inventors from the local university. The long-term life of a business can never be guaranteed by a share price but only by the ability of the staff to invent new products that people need and want.

'We started making all our own wire rope a few years ago. All the gripples used rod rope to hang things – ducts, lights – but they were stiff and wires aren't. So we thought if we could make wire, it's more flexible, you can hang things diagonally. Turns out too that the carbon footprint is one-sixth of the rods. And now we don't have to depend on the Chinese.'

High levels of innovation don't mean the business never hits hard times; in 1996, everyone had to take a pay cut. The next year, though, everyone had an even larger pay increase. The point, says Facey, is to listen to people and to make them feel responsible for their work.

'Challenge everything. That's what we do here. We have no HR department and no buying department. They're all bullshit, they get in the way and don't let businesses run. If people own the business, why would they ever buy something not good for the business? We believe in letting our people get on and do it. There's one job description and it's the same for everyone: if the ball is falling, catch it. Same for me, same for everyone.'

When I asked if he ever had to fire people, Facey laughed.

'We never have any trouble recruiting; people have heard of us. If somebody joins and doesn't fit in, they usually just take themselves off because they're not happy here. What would the signs be? Turning up late. We have no time clocks but everyone knows what needs to be done and, if you weren't pulling your weight, weren't working hard – well – you just wouldn't fit in, would you?'

Facey is clear that the long-term prosperity of the business doesn't depend on his genius but on the commitment and creativity of every single staff owner. Every year, he has been giving away 5 per cent of his ownership in order that, ultimately, the company is owned by the people who work there. He has no ambition to be a heroic soloist; quite the reverse. Facey is passionate and committed when it comes to the power and potential of everyone else.

'Everyone here is always looking for the next idea, the problem we can solve. So we encourage people to come up with ideas. One was called a terralock. One of the US guys said there was a problem with the levees in New Orleans and Florida. So we designed something for them and now we have an order for a million dollars. We didn't have that product last year but now we're talking of it becoming a major product over the next two years. We are going to launch eighteen products this year. People should come to work and have fun; that's how you get ideas. Not just by keeping your eye on the boss and waiting to be told what to do.'

Contemplating retirement, Facey has restructured the company so that it can't be sold; it must, he insists, sink or swim, do or die. Success for Facey isn't about him. It isn't about the balance sheet. It isn't about defeating competitors, lavish acquisitions or dramatic exits. Gripple doesn't exist for any other reason but to invent great products that, in turn, generate jobs that last.

'I've no time for the big bonuses, the bonus culture. Here, when we do well, everyone's investment in the business is worth more; that's your bonus. And the better we do – the more we can do. That's a huge reward, too.'

Under its new structure, every owner within Gripple has one vote – 'me and the cleaner' according to Facey – and they will decide how the organization works. 'If they're going to bugger the business up, it's their own business,' he insists. 'The role of capital in this business is to be the servant of the members of this organization – the servant, not the master. That's the way it should be.'

Gripple is a flat, democratic organization – like Morning Star and Gore – but Facey has gone one step further in putting the future of the business wholly in the hands of those who work there.

He knows that employee ownership alone is not a panacea for all business ills and he has very clear views about the intricate details of organizational structure. What inspires him and the people he works with, however, isn't a life-or-death struggle against competitors but a lifelong contribution of human ingenuity to a community of colleagues whose lives are enhanced by work. It is a very different model from the cortisone-enhanced death throes of Andre Agassi's last tennis match; the extravagant and self-serving acquisitions of Jean-Marie Messier; or the intricate financial filigree of GE. Like many employee-owned firms, solvency and growth are the goals, not revenue numbers, not quarterly earnings. Proponents of these businesses argue that that is exactly what makes them so successful: focusing on meaningful improvement, not simplistic or arbitrary targets.

In the United States, half of all employees are involved in some form of employee ownership. In Britain, many companies (not just John Lewis) have some kind of employee distribution scheme. In his book, *Beyond the Corporation*, David Erdal sets out a compelling case that these companies are more productive, more creative and more responsive to a changing business environment than traditional corporations.[36] He didn't come to this conclusion at a desk but from direct, personal experience. Having inherited his family-owned printing firm, Tullis Russell, Erdal chose to turn the firm over to employee ownership, believing – and finding – that it would make the business stronger, more sustainable and better run. The young people in the firm became more committed to it and, contrary to some popular wisdom, the workforce was able and willing to make big, difficult changes in order to adapt to galvanic change within their industry. More of the world's most successful and global businesses are run this way than meet the eye: Zeiss, Huawei, Publix Super Markets, Arup.

'Forty per cent of our profit goes to every single member of staff. The rest goes to internal investment: more training, more R&D,' Terry Hill told me. 'We want to look over the horizon and see what's coming, in new technology, in new architecture. So we spend more on R&D than anyone in our field.'

Hill works for Arup, the global structural engineering firm responsible for some of the world's most complex and most cutting-edge buildings: the High Roller rollercoaster in Las Vegas, the National Aquatics Centre and the Bird's Nest buildings at the Beijing Olympics, the Marina Bay Sands resort in Singapore and the Millennium Bridge in London. The firm gets these assignments because they are always at the cutting edge of structural engineering; in 2013, they launched a microalgae façade in Berlin aimed at seeing whether algae could simultaneously shade and power a building. They're exploring biological bridges, detachable homes that can travel with you and the houses needed in 2050 when 75 per cent of the world's population will live in cities. This research, says Hill, is only feasible because the firm doesn't have shareholders, isn't in any kind of race, but is committed to just three things: excellence, honour in the way people treat each other and what he calls 'reasonable prosperity' – by which he means that anyone wanting to earn huge salaries can go elsewhere. The sheer complexity of their projects – and there may be as many as 10,000 under way at any one time – requires high levels of collaboration, something made possible only by equally high levels of trust. And that was engineered into the company through its ownership structure.

In 1970, when Ove Arup gave the firm to the staff, he effectively disinherited his children. He did so because he believed passionately in doing socially useful work in pursuit of quality and because he wanted people to join hands with others who thought likewise. Money, he argued, was a divisive not a unifying force – but with everyone an owner, that sense of mission would be shared in real and tangible ways every day.

'We don't waste time managing analysts' expectations, we don't have to mess with any of that,' Hill says with pride. 'We just build things. If anyone here is working on a problem they don't know how to solve, they can post a question on the intranet and, in twenty-four hours, they'll get an answer from someone somewhere in one of our offices who's solved that problem. We share knowledge and build trust: because we help each other and grow – personally, professionally, together. And most of our people – 75 per cent – stay so our growth is their growth. Even through the recession, there is not one year we have not grown.'

With 11,000 employees in forty-two countries, Arup's accumulated knowledge is immense. Asked to build riding stables for the Beijing Olympics, one Arup staff member needed help figuring out how to cope with 2,500 horses that would be jittery after being flown around the world. 'You can imagine the effluent!' Hill laughed. But it turned out that another Arup staff member had worked on the Jockey Club in New York and could pitch in. Why, Hill asked, wouldn't everyone help when they all stand to benefit from the firm's success?

Arup is a flat organization, designed not to create or worship superstars; Arup thought stars were manmade illusions that mystified thinking. Instead, he built a firm designed to succeed because in it every single person counts and becomes an owner from the day they start. If there is a pecking order it changes constantly: Hill was amazed, in his first year, when the person he had been working for on a Nigerian project later offered to work for him. But that flat structure builds trust – between staff and with clients: Arup is famous for never taking bribes; Hill says this greatly simplifies their worldwide business dealings. And because everyone is an owner, the chances of people staying silent are virtually nil: if anything, that everyone has a voice sometimes makes decision-making slower. But even that has advantages because choices that take a long time – like entering Japan – are also given a long time (ten years) to work. Most architectural firms last just one or two generations; Arup is in its fourth. It isn't aiming to cross a finishing line but to keep growing and learning and building.

In the US, half of all employees are involved in some form of employee ownership. Even private companies that started out wholly owned by their founders can change: after twenty-five years, Eileen Fisher has allocated 32.5 per cent of the clothing company she founded to her employees in the belief that this would make it more sustainable, collaborative and creative. So far, she says, nothing has proved her wrong.

My own experience of working in employee-owned firms is that they fundamentally change the way people in them think about their colleagues and about themselves. You need fewer rules; after all, if you own part of the company, you don't need anyone to tell you not to waste money or time. You don't require rewards to encourage you to support co-owners who are floundering and you don't need prizes to remind you that customers are critical. Above all, when anyone wins, everyone wins. The creativity of Silicon Valley can't entirely be ascribed to the fact that most employees own shares in their companies – venture capitalists or founders usually dominate decision-making – but, from my own experience, I know it changes the social contract: how people think and feel about the way they work together.

When everyone is an owner, the pecking order isn't a pyramid but a network. Because people relate to one another as peers, with equal passion and commitment, they bring the full richness of their differences to the problems and challenges they must confront. And if this provokes a lot of conflict, then, like siblings who must learn to mediate each others' needs, the organization gets very good at energetic collaboration.

To walk through the Gripple or Arup offices bears no relationship to spectator sports or to gaming the game. Instead, they hum with human creativity and energy of a kind no score can capture. Success in business or in life is not determined in a few seconds, minutes or even in a business quarter. We cannot measure progress in scores or tables or statistics. Life is both rich and confusing because it is full of ambiguity, change, uncertainty and ambivalence. It's very slick to talk about life as a game but, in our heart of hearts, we know that it is infinitely more complex, both more exciting and more boring, fleeting, persistently changeable, incriminating, forgiving – and long.

Back in Bath, 2013 got off to a good start for Dai Greene. He did well in early races and was running without injury. He's still focused and motivated, intent, he says, on capturing Kriss Akabusi's British 400m-hurdles record. He has support: Akabusi would like to see him succeed. He likes Greene, admires his discipline and wants the title to go to a worthy athlete. Akabusi himself is something of a rarity: a sportsman with a rewarding and happy retirement, running his own business and coaching executives. Of all the athletes I ever asked about winning, it was Akabusi whose answer has most remained with me.

'When you win, you have two feelings. In the moment, there is euphoria, a substantiation of what you've done, a getting-there. But after three or four hours, it's disappointing. Is that it? All over. The whole year geared to a race and it's done. The euphoria doesn't last longer than the drug-testing. You're getting your old man out, peeing in a bottle and it's back to reality. You start to wonder why you put yourself through all that and exposed yourself to losing. What I didn't know then – what I know now: you get much more joy down the road, like now. Getting joy out of life, that's a bigger prize now.'

PART TWO:
THE CASE OF THE
PURDUE CHICKENS

6. ONLY THE IMPRESARIOS SUCCEED

Winning at all costs comes at a price; collateral issues of rivalry, arrogance, selfishness and a lack of humility and generosity.

The Salz Report into Barclays Bank 2013

In the summer of 1951, *Harper's Magazine* gushed over 'an unrestrained, dramatic race involving a dozen of the largest American drug houses, several leading foreign pharmaceutical manufacturers, three governments and more research personnel than have worked on any medical problem since penicillin'.[1] What was all the excitement about? The prospect of manufacturing cortisone.

Cortisone is a steroid hormone that reduces pain and inflammation in muscles, joints and injuries. Today it is used to treat everything from eye disease to arthritis. It is what Andre Agassi injected during his final days on the tennis court. But, in 1951, cortisone wasn't easily available; it had to be extracted from cattle bile and cost $200 per gram (equivalent today to some $2,000). Everyone knew that this could be the miracle drug for arthritis and inflammatory disease. Movies showed helpless arthritics, after a single injection, bounding onto the dance floor and regaining their youth. Expense wasn't the only problem. Sourcing enough cattle bile required slaughterhouse animals in volumes no one could contemplate. So the race was on to find a way to produce cortisone artificially, at a price and on a scale that would enable it to fulfil its vast therapeutic and commercial promise.

The underdog in the race was Syntex, a tiny chemicals company in Mexico that pinned its hope on making cortisone from Mexican yams. Leading the effort was Carl Djerassi, a pioneering Viennese-born American scientist who had patented the world's first antihistamine. Djerassi was – and is – hyper-competitive.

'We were the underdog because we were tiny, because we were in Mexico,' Djerassi recalled. 'And we were up against the big guys – everyone wanted to synthesize cortisone. So yes, it was a race, everyone knew it was a race.'

Today, at the age of eighty-nine, Djerassi is as engaged and amused by the competitiveness of science as ever. With a mass of white hair and a white beard, he may look like an athletic Father Christmas but he is a mischievous and challenging interlocutor. Not for him the romance of science as the pure pursuit of thought; to him, it is, and always has been, a fierce contest.

The intensity of the race to synthesize cortisone wasn't just about making money. The challenge contained several particularly knotty chemistry problems. Anybody who solved them stood to earn what was, for scientists, more important than money: the accolades of their peers. That could only be achieved by being the first scientist to publish the solution to the problem in the *Journal of the American Chemical Society* (*JACS*). Establishing priority through publication was how the race would be won.

'Science,' Djerassi told me, 'is like the Olympics – but without silver or bronze. You come first or you are nowhere. We have to document the priority, that we got there first.

'Sure, there's joy in the discovery. But that's not why you're doing it. Let's take Hillary. He wanted to be first to climb Everest. If he'd only wanted it for the sake of doing it, he could have gone with a sherpa who had been sworn to secrecy, taken no photos and climbed down again, telling no one. That would be pure mountain-climbing. But that is not what he did. And that is not how we do science.'[2]

Djerassi's main competitors were led by Robert Burns Woodward, professor of organic chemistry at Harvard and blessed with a bigger team, more resources and superior infrastructure. In the days before overnight delivery and the Internet, being based in Mexico put Djerassi at a severe disadvantage. Scientific journals took weeks to arrive; he couldn't keep abreast of new research or new findings that could move his own work forward. So he persuaded a former classmate, who had just moved to Harvard, to phone through any research relevant to their work. Better still, he recruited a mole – nicknamed Flash – to spy on Woodward's progress.

By June 1951, Djerassi's team had succeeded: they had made and tested synthetic cortisone from yams. With mounting excitement, they rushed to write up their results and establish their priority. With no overnight delivery, they had to trust their precious manuscript to airmail delivery by propeller plane. Once it had gone, there was nothing to do but wait. With astonishing sangfroid, Djerassi went off to explore the pre-Columbian ruins at Palenque.

When he got back, an alarming telegram from Flash greeted him: 'Woodward finished cortisone Thursday. Writing note title *Total Synthesis of Cortisone*. Leaving nothing to imagination or intelligence of reader. Observed on his desk note quote tell Bliss, Gates says hold journal day or two unquote. Don't know importance of this. Arranged with Fieser publish same time. Suggest change your title.'[3]

Just a few weeks after Djerassi's success, the Harvard team too had reached the same goal. They wanted the publicity – and priority – too. The sentence about holding the journal referred to the date on which the news would be published – so whose account would appear first? Normally, every scientific article has to go through a lengthy review process – but the telegram implied that, in this case, review might be waived for the Harvard team. Djerassi didn't know if his own report had been accepted, was in the process of being reviewed or where he stood. Suddenly, being the underdog was not motivating but infuriating; just about everyone making the critical decisions about publication came from Harvard.

'It was impossible not to brood over the overpowering quasi-incestuous influence the Harvard chemical establishment had,' he later wrote. 'For a few days, a wave of paranoia overwhelmed us. Though a gringo chemist, I suddenly felt like a native Mexican – misused and discriminated against by Yankees up north. Even now, four decades after the event, I can still feel my adrenals respond.'[4]

In the end, four articles about the synthesis of cortisone appeared simultaneously in the August 1951 edition of *JACS*. But while Djerassi's report had arrived in the editors' office on 22 June,

Woodward's had not arrived until 9 July. Infuriated, Djerassi felt his competitors had 'gotten away with murder'. His only compensation was a huge picture in *Life* magazine, over which he gloated: it features him and his team, grouped around a giant yam.

'We were two weeks earlier!' Djerassi insists to this day. 'What difference does it make? To the world, to science, to patients? But we were first!'

Winning the race didn't turn out quite as Djerassi or the rest of the world expected: neither the Syntex nor the Harvard synthesis of cortisone was ever used on a single patient. While they had all been frantically competing with each other, two scientists working for the pharmaceutical company Upjohn had invented a simpler, cheaper solution.

What the race did achieve, however, was to put Syntex on the map as a company that knew how to synthesize hormones. And Djerassi's next project changed the world: synthesizing norethisterone, he made the first female contraceptive and is known, to this day, as the 'father of the pill'.

Djerassi is often charged with having precipitated a sexual revolution and divorcing sex from love. But within the scientific community, he is more controversial for the frankness with which he describes the competitiveness of science. Nearly into his tenth decade, he openly acknowledges that he is still competitive – '*very* competitive' he says – and insists that his colleagues are no different.

'Some scientists furiously deny this but that's just hypocritical bullshit,' Djerassi insists with relish. 'It's a mixture of poison and nourishment. Science can be most collegial and at the same time most brutally competitive. And your brutal competitors are your colleagues. You are dependent on them and compete with them – but brutally.'

Djerassi has been criticized by his fellow scientists for, as he says, washing their dirty linen in public. In several novels (which he calls science-in-fiction) he describes the often desperate, sometimes comic antics of scientists so intent on recognition, priority and prizes that they will perpetrate all kinds of deceit. Sexual infidelity, stealing, changing data, lying, Djerassi even has one character who changes her surname from Yardley to Ardley to ascend the alphabetical list of authors. *The Bourbaki Gambit* describes the per-petration of a scientific fraud to get revenge; the more memorable *Cantor's Dilemma* shows how far scientists will go to win a Nobel Prize. The books are clever and they're comic but Djerassi is quite outspoken about the degree to which the culture of science displays occupational deviance.

He is also more relaxed about it than many scientists. He has won his fame as father of the pill, secured his priority in synthe-sizing hormones and retired (albeit unwillingly) from Stanford. But for scientists still in the fray, the competitiveness of science is an increasing source of anxiety and alarm.

From an economic perspective, the world of science is a tour-nament structure: fostering intense competition by amplifying small differences in productivity (like two weeks) into large dif-ferences in recognition and reward. Tournaments turn everyone into competitors and, according to economic theory, this is sup-posed to bring out the best in individuals and force the best work to the surface. However, even economists now concede that tour-naments have perverse outcomes. These can be particularly costly in an activity like science where collaboration is critical.

'We had two groups of scientists both looking for a particular gene for rheumatoid arthritis. One group was in the US and the other was in Sweden. And they were in a race! They found all the families and generations of families that had the gene but they had a problem: each team's group was too small to be statistically important. Neither team could generate sufficiently meaningful data. Their competition had divided the field into two parts, nei-ther of which was large enough to count. They both had to have the numbers!'

Vijay Kuchroo almost giggles with the perversity of the situation he describes. The Samuel L. Wasserstrom Professor of Neurology at Harvard's Medical School, he has seen this scenario more times than he likes to remember: great science, immensely clever scien-tists, stymied and stalled by their professional rivalry.

'They had to share their data or no one would have anything with any validity,' Kuchroo tells me, still astonished by the stale-mate. 'In the end, my colleague David Hafler brought them together. He said he should get the Nobel Prize for this – not for science, but for peace: it was so difficult to get these groups to work together!'

As we sit amidst the sprawling and lavish buildings that constitute Harvard's medical establishment, Kuchroo thinks intently about the role that competition plays in science. Now in his fifties with a mass of salt-and-pepper hair, he brings to his work the same youthful enthusiasm I first saw twenty years ago. He's known to work all hours, to be relentless in thinking and re-thinking problems, and while that could make him sound like a bully or a bore, he's neither. Immensely well liked and highly regarded, Kuchroo has a personal gentleness in his manner that belies formidable focus.

'Science, you know: it sounds so abstract. Much of what we do is so abstract. But it is also terribly personal. It's not about a product or an institution. It's *you*. It's *your* name on the paper, it's *your* work. A lot of scientists take it so personally and – in extreme cases – you get suicides when people turn out to be wrong. It's just very, very personal.'

Kuchroo recognizes that such intense identification with work has its benefits but lately he has been more concerned with the problems it provokes.

'The problem of credit – who gets the credit for the work – is very difficult. Everyone wants the credit and that can make people very solitary and very competitive.'

Kuchroo isn't just talking about ego. Credit, to an academic scientist, is the currency of progress. Research has to get published in order to gain recognition. Every published article builds a scientist's professional résumé, and the number of times that it is cited by other scientists indicates the importance of the author's contribution to science. A steep pecking order of professional journals determines prestige: publication in high-impact journals like *Nature* or *Science* can make a scientist's name or even, in China, earn the authors a house. It is customary for most scientific papers to credit multiple authors, with the first-named author having done the most work and, often, the last-named author being the sponsor and supervisor. But too many authors will diminish everyone's lustre so the competition for authorship is critical; careers can depend on it.

'If you have ten post-docs,' Kuchroo says, 'some may be disproportionately the backbone of the lab. They provide the ideas, open discussions and they should get credit – but this is often not the case. It is the person who sees what the idea could be and brings it to fruition that really matters but often the authors in the middle may have been the backbone of that idea.'

Kuchroo worries about this because having a lab full of rivalrous scientists is profoundly counter-productive. He has seen that in his own lab.

'Five or six years ago, I had a lab filled with some of the best people I ever had. But they had no common purpose. You could see it: the tissue-culture room was trashed. No one cared! No one talked to one another. Everyone was working hard but they weren't producing anything. Competition really was taking its toll.'

Part of the problem was that everyone seemed to feel they had to behave like masters of the universe – even the ones who didn't honestly feel that way about themselves. Kuchroo recognized that a few motivational speeches would change nothing and that ratcheting up the competition was likely to make things worse. Instead, to unlock the creativity his lab was losing, Kuchroo took an unusual step. He employed a psychologist, Kerstin Lagerström, from the Karolinska Institute.

'Vijay had told his group that I was coming and we were going to work together on team development,' Lagerström recalls. 'I'd say that 60 per cent were eager to work with me, 20 per cent were just wondering what it was all about and 20 per cent didn't turn up.

'That some didn't turn up – I'm used to that. But to ignore it was telling. One of them – he was thinking that talking about a team was rubbish: "I will make my science and I have no need of a team." Some of them had other priorities, thinking: "why spend time on this? I'm too busy. My time is expensive." Some of them were curious and frightened. What would happen? You could hear that.'

Her affiliation with the Karolinska Institute, Lagerström told me, helped her to get the scientists' attention; the Institute's committee awards the Nobel Prize for medicine. That commanded respect even from Harvard researchers. But what struck Lagerström most of all was that everyone who turned up seemed to work as individuals, deciding their own timetable and priorities. She also felt there were far too many egos in the room.

Lagerström asked the group to consider three animals: lions, owls and St Bernard dogs. Which one, she asked the lab members, do you feel like? With a corner of the room designated for each animal, she asked the scientists to go and stand with their fellow animals. And she watched as they observed each other: how many in this corner, how few in that.

'There are men there thinking about being lions who are not. You put them in three corners. They can see: my god, in this team we have too many lions. We have just two dogs. What does it mean? And all these owls are standing about. Everyone stopped for a second.'

Lagerström asked each group to explore the characteristics of their animal, their positive and negative attributes and then to present their animal to the others. All the time, she watched as the scientists collaborated, discussed and puzzled over the exercise.

'So they are talking about the animals all the time. After ninety minutes like this, they are so in these animals, they can talk about them. But they think they aren't talking about themselves. We have all these animals in this room and every animal is necessary for this team.'

Getting the scientists to discuss how the animals related to one another defused personal tensions and released a deeper conversation about how collaboration works. But then Lagerström asked each of them to fill out a questionnaire about their own working habits. Suddenly sharp contradictions emerged: how people imagined themselves was strikingly at odds with the way that they really worked. They thought they were leaders or collaborators but, for the most part, they all worked as soloists.

When the group broke for dinner, Lagerström was aware of some of them phoning their missing colleagues to tell them that something important was happening, that they should turn up the next day.

Over the two days that she spent with them, Lagerström helped the scientists to see two important things: first, that their behaviour in the lab got in the way of the very achievements they sought. They might imagine themselves to be collaborative but, in fact, most were isolated and uncommunicative. Second, they came to see that a productive working environment needed all three animals. Lions, she explained, defend the group and bring out the best in people. Owls do most of the thinking and the work. The St Bernards are more interested in other people than themselves; they are the glue of the group but become despondent and passive if there isn't enough action. The group only works when all three can contribute fully.

'The message from me,' Lagerström continued, 'was that *everyone* has to think about how they can improve their communication with everyone else. Everyone needs to get feedback so that the team can become better. And everyone – not just the leader – needs to take responsibility for that.' Collaboration is just that: co-labour.

For Kuchroo, the experience revealed that collaboration had to be designed, not assumed. He had, he told me, hired too many owls who thought they were lions – meaning he had hired a lot of young scientists who wanted to be superstars and thought that the way to achieve star status was to act like prima donnas. But this was futile because, if they couldn't or wouldn't share, they could achieve nothing. And he needed to have more than one lion in the lab because that would foment debate, which would encourage everyone to speak up.

'The scientific discipline requires collaboration,' Lagerström observes. 'But the system rewards soloists. And they think it's productive but, for science as a whole, it's just the opposite.'

Although many scientists have told me privately that this is a bigger problem in the United States, it is not unique to Harvard or to American scientists. Dame Linda Partridge has devoted her professional life to working on the science of ageing, with labs at University College London and the Max Planck Institute in Germany and, in both places, the problem of soloists is rife.

'We had a young Russian scientist working here,' she told me when we met at her London lab. 'Very good, very smart but with, I'd say, big sibling-rivalry issues. She absolutely cannot compromise, cannot negotiate. She has to win. She just can't work with other people. We sat her down one day and said: "Look, by doing this, you lose. Your colleagues will never help you." But she can't get it. During the Soviet period, the authorities deliberately created very high levels of competition within the scientific institutes. It's quite ingrained in the culture.'

When I related Lagerström's story about lions, owls and St Bernards, Partridge's eyes lit up with recognition.

'In Cologne, I ended up with a lab full of owls and they drove me mad,' she told me. 'I don't normally get really angry but I got as close to exploding as ever. A real failure to engage. They were boring, introspective, just tedious. And they contributed nothing to the general good. Some of them thought they were being German – a German phenotype! They didn't ask questions and imagined that they were working to a good standard because they were careful and meticulous. But the problem with this kind of behaviour is that it won't produce investigators – they can't do the more playful side of things to be a fully functional scientists. And we didn't have any St Bernards, no one saying "Thank God It's Friday". If we had outings, it was an organizational effort not a fun effort. It was just a pile of owls.'

Partridge is the least owl-like person you can imagine. Vivacious, attractive and full of energy, she exudes enthusiasm for her work and for fellow scientists. But her pile of owls proved maddening. Apart from her personal frustration, what, I asked her, was the cost?

'Poor productivity. To get a project through, you have to engage with other people and with me! They just failed to get the best out of each other. They weren't proactive about reading or sharing the literature, pooling their knowledge. They should know more about a project than I do! So now, I try not to bring them in, the owls. I have brought in a potential lion. He's winding them up – which is part of the point. He will clash with the most dominant male and that won't hurt. With any luck, it will encourage the rest to pitch in.'

It's hard to imagine anyone with more zest and talent for collaboration than Partridge. That she works this way is in part a personal preference. But her approach is also bolstered by her conviction that sharing the lead generates the intellectual vitality that sustains scientific work across generations.

'I want to push my collaborators into greater prominence. I am them! Without them, I wouldn't be me. To let other people take over the lead in programmes is so hard. If you don't give people the job to grow into, they won't. And it can be extremely frustrating because the funding authorities often fail to realize how many people you need to produce the work. So we can make a team bid but then I'll get asked to lead the project. I don't want to – I want others to get the chance so that they can stretch and grow. But the funders want insurance so they want me. They don't seem to see that the only real insurance is talent – lots of it – so you spread the risk. Solo leadership is a real blind spot in science.'

This isn't just a matter of personalities. Many institutions are predicated on the belief that competition will surface the best talent and that combining the top talent will produce the strongest, most high-achieving teams, departments, organizations. They often cite the theory of natural selection to explain why this must work. Since nature is constantly selecting the best for breeding, thus creating resilient, productive species, surely what great teams need is to combine talents honed and selected by competition. This interpretation of Darwin is more than a little simplistic and, when applied to teams, throws up significant problems.

William Muir teaches and researches population genetics and he wanted to understand, in practice, how natural selection really plays out in groups. Perhaps because he works at Purdue University (with its agricultural associations), he chose to explore this by investigating how to breed the most productive chickens.

Chickens have always lived in flocks and, in the egg industry, they're typically kept in groups of nine to twelve. Seeking to increase egg production – the marker of a successful flock – Muir designed an experiment. In the first instance, he simply identified the most productive groups of hens and observed them as they bred freely. Then, as a contrast, he selected the most productive individual hens and used them to breed the next generation of hens. What, he wanted to know, would prove the most productive method: the free flocks or the super-hens?

After six generations, Muir compared results. The free flocks were still full of plump, fully feathered hens and egg production had increased dramatically over the course of the experiment. But the second group, supposedly a super-group of hens, were shockers. After six generations, only three hens were left; the other six had been murdered. The three survivors were nearly bare of feathers, having plucked each other mercilessly.

When the evolutionary biologist David Sloan Wilson reported

this experiment to some of his colleagues, showing slides of the ragged super-hens, a professor exclaimed, 'That slide describes my department! I have *names* for those three chickens!' It turned out that her department had adopted the policy of promoting individual high-achievers purely for their individual accomplishments and the results had proved just as catastrophic as Muir's.[5]

Just as Kuchroo had discovered with his lab, collecting outstanding soloists doesn't yield highly productive systems. So tournaments that foster internal competition in order to identify and reward those soloists can work – they'll find talent – but they won't foster an environment conducive to highly creative, imaginative work.

Over a decade, the tournament, which has always been the model for scientific achievement, has become strikingly more cutthroat. In part this is because there are more scientists than ever. While governments demand ever more science graduates, the truth is that the scientists we already have struggle to earn a living in a vocation they love. The competition for resources militates against the collaborative relationships that original science depends upon.

'Throughout most of its history,' writes David Goodstein, vice-provost at Caltech, 'science was constrained only by the limits of its participants' imagination and creativity. In the past few decades, however, that state of affairs has changed dramatically . . . What had been a purely intellectual competition has become an intense struggle for scarce resources.'[6]

Every principal investigator who runs a lab produces, on average, at least ten PhD graduates who must then find a post-doc position before qualifying to run their own lab. But nowhere are scientific budgets increasing by that order of magnitude. The chances, therefore, of getting a position and funding for research recede even as recruitment increases. So perverse is this system that one professor has referred to biomedical research as 'a Ponzi scheme' claiming that 'we are selling our incoming graduate students a bill of goods'.[7]

Principal investigators have no interest in this changing; the more post-docs they can get (and the cheaper) the more work they can generate. An over-supply of post-docs makes them pretty cheap and there is no evidence that earning a PhD will increase your lifelong earning capacity. The cost in money and time means that young scientists will never catch up financially with their non-scientific peers.

'There's a lot of dead bodies, out of my lab anyway,' one scientist acknowledged.[8] 'There are going to be kids that aren't going to make it. I know they're not going to make it, but I'm going to lie to them. I'm going to say, "Well, you might get a PhD." And I know that their chances are probably one in three.'

Science is inherently and necessarily a collaborative and accretive act. Every new finding builds on earlier work; hence Newton's famous statement 'If I have seen further, it is because I have stood on the shoulders of giants'. Each discovery, large or small, positive or negative, opens up avenues for subsequent exploration or shuts off dead ends. On a formal level, that's what the scientific journals that so haunted Djerassi are all about: not just staking a claim to priority but disseminating the information required to enable other scientists to take the next step. On an informal level, discussion, debate, the exchange of knowledge and mistakes allow everyone to do more considered work and to avoid duplicating errors. That is how science, as a system is supposed to work.

But it all falls apart when the sharing stops. That's why Kuchroo was so concerned by the behaviour in his lab: without discussion, work won't progress. Scientists are haunted by the fear of being scooped, of finding that work they've invested years in has been duplicated elsewhere and published first. That fear makes them stop doing the one thing that makes science productive: talking to one another. Fear generates silence, which stops creative work in its tracks. In 1966, 50 per cent of 1,042 scientists said they felt safe talking about their research; by 1998 that number had fallen to just 14 per cent. 'Secrecy,' the researchers wrote, 'is strongly predicted by scientific competition' (measured as concern over having one's research results anticipated).[9]

'I'm always wary of submitting grants to study sections,' one scientist acknowledged, 'because it's not unknown for them to take your ideas, kill your grant, and then take and do it. And I think all of us have either had that happen to them or know somebody who had that happen to them.'[10]

What should be a collaborative, open endeavour atrophies in the face of competition, isolating both scientists and their work that could be improved if shared and challenged by colleagues. Scientific conferences, which are supposed to be a maelstrom of collaboration, have instead become a standoff of defensive, rivalrous researchers more afraid of being scooped than being discovered.

'I presented my dissertation to an international conference,' one scientist recalled, 'and the topic was on ethical decision-making by nurses. A number of famous nurse-ethicists came up and asked if they could have a copy of my paper, which wasn't published yet . . . And I talked to my post-doc group and our mentor, and they said, "You're not going to send it, are you? . . . You're a fool if you do."'

'I presented posters for an academy meeting,' another scientist confided. 'And then a few months later, I saw an article almost the same. And I said, "What's going on?" So I look at the time the paper was submitted. It's almost the same time, you know? I don't like to say anything, but it was almost identical.'

'And you thought they were just taking pictures,' his colleague commented.[11]

The over-supply of ambitious science graduates has produced 'a crisis of expectation' in which a legion of ambitious young scientists considers all peers and potential collaborators as rivals. And, as Vijay Kuchroo identified, that has consequences scientists now call 'normal misbehaviour': secrecy, sabotage, data 'cooking' and culling.

Secrecy easily morphs into misrepresentation when scientists feel that the only way to protect their work is not to share their findings in full. In the rush to publish and establish priority, crucial details are omitted so that fellow scientists can see what you've done – but will not quite be able to emulate or challenge it. At its worst, data-editing can change the picture completely. One scientist reported being asked to 'shave' the last two data points off her results since they seemed to undermine the impact of her conclusions. But without the full data, scientists could not understand or build on her work.

Under enormous pressure to claim credit, to win research grants and get tenure, scientists regularly talk about gaming the system: promising more than they know they can deliver, eking out results into three papers where one would be more coherent, cutting corners in the rush to publication. The process of peer review, by which research reports are vetted by colleagues, has come in for increasing scrutiny and criticism because getting published is so critical to a scientist's career and reputation. Just as Djerassi feared that his Harvard competitors might be shown favouritism, so today scientists anticipate that the work they submit to peer-reviewed journals may be rejected or intentionally stalled by reviewers who are also their rivals. The same fears apply to grant applications. It isn't uncommon for grant reviewers to dismiss areas of research, arguing that it is unfruitful, in the hope of doing the work themselves.

This 'normal misbehaviour' isn't new. In the days before science brought any financial or institutional rewards, journals were created specifically in order to establish priority; that was the only prestige science had to offer. But the promise of status introduced a motive for fixing the game. Writing in 1830 on the '*Decline of Science in England*' Charles Babbage identified forms of scientific misconducts that he called the 'trimming, and cooking' of data. He also lamented the prevalence of pleasers: scientists so ambitious to be elected to the Royal Society that they always conformed to prevailing views, never risking argument or debate. Since Babbage's time, however, pressures on scientists have increased, not just because of the over-abundance of scientists but also because of what has come to be known as the Matthew effect.

The name, coined by sociologist Keith Stanovich, refers to the Biblical quotation: 'For unto every one that hath shall be given, and he shall have abundance: but from him that hath not shall be taken away even that which he hath.'[12] As applied to real life, it means that winners tend to attract more benefits to themselves, thus perpetually putting themselves in a stronger position to win yet more. Just as in sports, where a few gold medallists get the commercial endorsements, professional sponsorships, top coaches and premium facilities, and the rest fight over scraps, in science, the Matthew effect is seen to reward the top scientists with well paid secure jobs, excellent facilities and more post-docs than they can handle. They will also find it easier to get their research funded and published and are routinely asked to discuss their work at conferences around the world. Meanwhile, the rest must compete furiously for marginal visibility and scraps of funding for research that is under-resourced. In some countries, it is even government policy to focus on so-called centres of excellence, leaving the rest to die by the roadside. The problem with the Matthew effect in science isn't that it is unfair; even scientists themselves don't seem too perturbed by issues of justice. What bothers them is that it doesn't generate great science.

Science is both accretive, incremental and, to some degree, random. That is to say it requires large amounts of quite small insights to produce a transformative event. Very small insights can be disproportionately important because, without them, the next step can't be made. But you don't know what those small bits will be and you particularly don't know where they will come from. One classic example of this is the invention of polymerase chain reaction (PCR) by Kary Mullis, a scientist described to me variously as a 'surfer pothead', and a 'combative but competent chemist'; he describes himself as 'a generalist with a chemical prejudice'.

In 1983, Mullis was working for Cetus Corporation, a young biotech company in Emeryville, California. He described his work – duplicating DNA – as repetitive, slow and boring. DNA was hard to study because it is so long and thin that even mild shearing forces break it at random points. So if the DNA is removed from 1,000 identical cells, you will get 1,000 copies of any given gene, but each copy will be on a DNA fragment of differing length. That lack of uniformity made it hard to study on any meaningful scale.

Driving to his weekend cabin one Friday night, contemplating an experiment that he knew wouldn't work, Mullis had an idea that he thought could radically improve DNA duplication.

'For the next few weeks I described the idea to anyone who would listen,' he wrote later. 'No one had heard of its ever being tried; no one saw any good reason why it would not work; and yet no one was particularly enthusiastic about it. In the past, people had generally thought my ideas about DNA were off the wall, and sometimes after a few days I had agreed with them. But this time I knew I was on to something.'[13]

He was indeed on to something. Mullis's invention of the

polymerase chain reaction (PCR) is widely credited with having made possible the revolution in genetics that followed and in 1993 he won the Nobel Prize for his work. But no one would have picked out Mullis as a high-achieving scientist to back. He didn't have a raft of publications to his name or a famous sponsor and he wasn't working in an elite scientific institution. And much of the scientific understanding that was required for PCR had been lying around for years.

Stories like this in science (and there are many) acquire a semi-mythological status because they illustrate the degree to which you can't pick, or plan, winners. 'Identifying the top 10 percent,' wrote one journal, 'is impossible without a crystal ball or time machine.'[14]

That is what makes the Matthew effect dangerous. If it were possible to pick winners, concentrating resources on them might make sense. But, since you can't, the concentration of resources on the few – any few – reduces diversity and productivity and amplifies risk. Science relies on having many eggs in a very broad array of baskets. But the Matthew effect in science reduces the baskets, the eggs – and the surviving chickens. It also creates a very steep pecking order.

The imbalance pertaining to individuals affects institutions also; Djerassi's paranoia about Harvard wasn't unwarranted. With a handful of organizations attracting the laureates and the lion's share of funding and therefore the pick of young talent, the likelihood of knowing journal editors and peer reviewers increases. And that matters because at *Science*, for example, just one-fifth of submissions make it through an initial assessment and, of those, only a quarter make it on to publication.[15] The editors of those journals wield exceptional power as gatekeepers, and scientists look for any edge they can find.

Djerassi was lucky to get his article not just published – but read. In 1968, researchers estimated that about half of 1 per cent of the articles in chemistry journals were read by any chemist. That means, of course, that the top-tier journals – *Science, Nature, Cell, Chemistry Review* – have a disproportionate impact; they become the journals everyone must read. That, in turn, ensures that the most significant work is sent to them, giving them and their editors the power of an intellectual oligarchy. The articles they publish are the most read and become the most frequently cited – causing them to be read yet more. Thus a few powerful journals gain more power while the rest dwindle.

This has a profound effect on the richness of the scientific system as a whole – because discoveries cannot make an impact if no one knows about them. Only work that is perceived matters. So the cost of unread articles is not just the career or ego of the young scientist; it is the impoverishment of the scientific community as a whole.

I've never met a scientist who, when asked about a Matthew effect in science, did not immediately confirm its ubiquity, to the detriment of science overall. Young scientists see how the game is played and their knowledge can be corrosive. Every colleague is a rival; every collaboration poses a threat. Confronted by the stark realities of modern science, every researcher competes in the race to become a publishing star.

At the turn of the millennium, one such star was Jan Hendrik Schön. A shy, German physicist working at Bell Labs, he had just turned thirty when he started to attract attention. He'd had a shaky start after arriving in America; like many a young scientist, he worried about job security, his data wasn't good enough to publish and he was on a short-term internship. But then his data began to improve. Working on ways to turn non-conductive plastics into semi-conductors or even super-conductors, Schön's research held immense promise for computing, for laser technology and for nanotechnology. One Princeton scientist said that Schön's work 'defeated chemistry'.[16]

Schön was a classic owl: shy, retiring and more inclined to work alone than in a large research group. For visa reasons, he had to keep returning to the German lab where he'd done his PhD and where he continued some of his research. So, although an avid basketball player and affable sportsman, his work was mostly solitary. That didn't hurt his reputation; if anything, his isolation enhanced it. Schön was said to have 'magic hands' and, although he had the occasional collaborator, much of his behaviour reinforced the mystique of the brilliant young loner.

He was working at Bell Labs at a particularly stressful time. Between the 1950s and 1970s, the lab had had the reputation for being the most fertile lab that had ever existed, producing seven Nobel laureates and credited with the invention of the transistor, the laser, information theory, UNIX and the C++ computer language. But, by the time Schön arrived, the lab was owned by Lucent, whose share price was falling. Senior managers felt under pressure to cut costs and to generate big wins that would prove the relevance of its research and justify the lab's continued existence. Schön's work fitted the bill: brilliant science with immediate technology applications. And every one of Schön's papers, published in *Nature* and in *Science*, increased the lab's intellectual prestige.

Celebrated in MIT's 'Innovators Under 35' Schön was credited with having produced 'single-molecule transistors whose electrical performance is comparable to that of today's best silicon devices but which are hundreds of times smaller ... Schön's clever design established Bell Labs as a leader in the race. But Schön is not interested in simply reinventing the transistor ... He also helped devise the first electrically driven organic laser, which could mean cheaper optoelectronic devices. The soft-spoken Schön recalls being "very surprised" by how well his molecular transistors worked. But it won't be a surprise if Schön helps transform microelectronics.'[17]

When Schön's mentor, Bertram Batlogg, was due to move to Switzerland, Schön asked a colleague whether he should follow. No, said the friend, he should stay put. If he moved with his mentor, Batlogg would get too much of the credit; 'Hendrik, you're the star.'[18]

In the two years that followed, Schön published paper after paper. The scientific world was agog. Bell Labs was thrilled with their superstar, while the leading scientific journals competed so fiercely for the privilege of publishing his new work that they reduced the time they took reviewing it.[19]

As Eugenie Samuel Reich recalls in *Plastic Fantastic*, Schön's work was so exciting that physicists around the world sought to reproduce his effects in order to understand them. To do so, they had to be able to replicate his experiments. When they couldn't, they blamed themselves, assuming that their techniques were inadequate, their materials sub-par or their equipment faulty. When Joe Orenstein at Berkeley tried and failed to get Schön's results, he said he felt 'like a clumsy oaf'.[20]

At the University of Minnesota, Allen Goldman, one of the world's leading authorities on superconductivity, and one of his post-docs, Anand Bhattacharya, hoped to surpass Schön's discoveries. After trying for nearly a year to reproduce Schön's results, they got nowhere. Bhattacharya wrote to Schön, asking for help; he hadn't written sooner, he said, because Schön was such a star. Schön answered their questions but still nothing worked. The post-doc grew increasingly frustrated as work that was supposed to last just two or three years stretched to five.

At the University of Delft, Ruth de Boer's PhD research, based on Schön's findings, seemed to get nowhere too. Nearly in tears, she considered quitting. In Florida and in Japan, scientists had the same experience. No one published anything because negative results aren't deemed to be findings – and no scientist wanted to broadcast failure. 'Just because you don't understand the science,' one investigator commented, 'doesn't mean it's wrong.'[21]

By 2001, Schön was on a 'publishing rampage'; he was listed as an author on average every eight days[22] – and speculation abounded that he would win the Nobel Prize. As Schön became more famous, he also became more isolated, preferring to eat alone or to hang out with German-speaking researchers working in areas different from his own. Any criticism of Schön's work was dismissed as competitive jealousy.

Superconductivity and nanotechnology were becoming such hot topics that *Science* started publishing some of Schön's work on *Science Express*, a website designed to fast-track new scientific discoveries. But as the publications accumulated, so did the questions. The data looked too smooth; there wasn't enough noise – random data that didn't fit. And many of the effects that he described even Schön himself couldn't explain.

By the beginning of 2002, Schön was pestered by mounting questions prompted by his work; his colleagues tried to persuade him to publish more detail so that other scientists could replicate his findings. He couldn't. But while some members of the scientific community were sceptical about his ferocious productivity, just as many were dazzled by the new scientific celebrity. During a talk at Princeton, he was challenged by professor of physics Lydia Sohn but she soon fell silent, feeling no sympathy in the room. As she left, another faculty member asked her pointedly how many papers *she* had published in *Science* or *Nature* recently. Schön and his colleagues 'were golden people, you couldn't say anything', was how Cornell's Paul McEuen described them.

But the sheer volume of Schön's work aroused McEuen's suspicions. On 9 May 2002 he worked through the night comparing Schön's data in different papers. Over and over again, even though Schön claimed to be using different materials, the data were identical. 'This stuff is fake,' McEuen concluded the next morning. Too many of the graphs were too similar; there wasn't enough noise or mess to prove that different experiments had generated their own results.

For at least four years, Schön had been doing science backwards: identifying what it was that scientists hoped to find and generating the data that looked as though he had found it. An investigation into his work found him guilty of using the data set from one experiment for numerous papers and to have plotted his graphs from mathematical equations, not actual results. Twenty-eight of Schön's papers have now been retracted. His PhD was revoked, his prizes rescinded and the German Research Foundation banned him from German science for eight years. That ban has now expired.[23]

Had Schön falsified his data purely because of the competitive pressures he felt to produce? According to Eugenie Samuel Reich, who researched Schön's story, he is such a pleaser that Schön would explain anything the way you wanted to hear it. What was the case, however, was that Schön fully appreciated the competitive pressures around him to produce big news in high volume. Likewise, Bell Labs wanted, and needed, the acclaim Schön brought them; it strengthened their position in the scientific and financial marketplace. *Science* and *Nature* competed for his stunning papers, each one seeking to be the first to publish them. The scientists who knew first hand that the experiments could not be replicated – well, they didn't want to tell anyone they had failed. Everywhere Schön looked he saw competition and succumbed to it.

Schön's was one of the most daring and extreme frauds in scientific history. But it is not an isolated incident. Scott S. Reuben, an anaesthesiologist working at Baystate Medical Center in

Springfield, Massachusetts, is said to have fabricated results in twenty-one papers going back to 1996. His research appeared to provide support for multimodal analgesia: the use of nonsteroidal anti-inflammatory drugs and neuropathic agents in place of opioids for pain relief. All of his scientific papers have now been retracted. Andrew Wakefield's work, linking autism with the MMR vaccine, has been disproved and retracted but not before persuading 40 per cent of parents to abjure vaccines, thus reducing herd immunity and setting the scene for a measles epidemic in Swansea in the spring of 2013. And Wakefield's work still lingers in the minds of many parents and autism activists in a way than can never be retracted. But perhaps the most daring of frauds was that perpetrated by Korea's Hwang Woo-suk, who claimed to have cloned human embryonic stem cells.

Nor is scientific fraud limited to the so-called 'hard' sciences; the social sciences too have had their scandals. The most notorious of these involved Diederik Stapel, a Dutch social psychologist who attracted attention when he seemed to prove that eating meat made people more selfish and that white people were more likely to discriminate against black people when they met in messy environments. *Science* had trumpeted that Stapel's work had profound policy implications and he was made dean of the School of Social and Behavioural Sciences at the University of Tilburg. But suspicion was aroused when he wouldn't let students participate in his research or dissect his data. Stapel's data was too perfect and he had, it turned out, developed a habit of sharing only the results that confirmed his hypotheses, fatally distorting the bigger picture. Eventually, fifty-five of Stapel's journal articles were retracted. Talking with remorse about what he'd done, Stapel cited competition as a reason – not an excuse: 'There are scarce resources, you need grants, you need money ... I am a salesman. It's like a circus.'[24]

One widely shared characteristic of fraudsters is that they are almost always pleasers: good at intuiting what's wanted and delivering it. Their work reinforces stereotypes and expectation; far from being original or creative, they can see what will make them successful and just take short cuts to get there. They don't need to be original thinkers; they flourish in highly competitive environments precisely because success is so clearly defined, hot topics are so obvious and because (as in sports) the focus is on outcomes, not experience or learning.

Schön, Reuben, Stapel and many other scientific frauds point to a larger trend in science, which is the alarming – and increasing – rate at which research papers are withdrawn when they prove to be fraudulent, unreliable, incomplete or inaccurate. In October 2011, *Nature* reported that retractions had increased tenfold over the past decade – while the number of published articles had increased by just 44 per cent.[25] Most scientists believe that this retraction rate represents only the tip of the iceberg when it comes to faulty, rushed, misleading work.[26]

Papers are withdrawn either because they are found to contain mistakes (73 per cent) or because they are fraudulent (26 per cent). Although plagiarism is a concern, fabrication – making up the data – proved a bigger one.[27] Online, retracted articles can be withdrawn or identified as having been withdrawn. But, in print, that can't happen – so faulty work can have a long afterlife: one study showed that retracted research was still being cited twenty-four years later.[28]

Retractions are symptomatic of the intense competitive pressure to produce – too much, too fast – that all scientists experience today. With too few jobs, low pay and the severe bifurcation of scientific talent into winners and losers, the pure love of science for its own sake is easily abandoned. In one study, 17 per cent of postdoctoral fellows acknowledged that they were willing to 'select or omit data to improve their results'. And 81 per cent were willing to select, omit or fabricate data to win a grant or to publish a paper.[29] You could call this science's Goldman effect: if the reward is great enough, the risk seems worth taking.

The rising rate of retractions, of course, represents a huge cost: wasted resources, wasted time and wasted opportunity. For every experiment that is done, each post-doc that is hired, others are rejected or never even attempted. The time and effort that so many gifted scientists spent trying to replicate Schön's work wasn't just wasted; it was unavailable for work that might have proved authentically productive.

Ferric Fang, professor of medicine at the University of Washington, sees the growing rate of retraction and fraud as indicative of the dysfunction of competition in science more generally.

His argument isn't theoretical. As the editor of *Infection and Immunity*, Fang confronted scientific misconduct first hand when one of his authors, Naoki Mori, was found to have manipulated data and images. Fang was so disturbed by the experience that he launched his own research project to identify how widespread the problem was becoming.

'We have found,' he told me, 'that the more important the journal, the higher the number of retractions. But you get all kinds of other dysfunction: old work pawned off as new and a strong skew to positive findings. In science, we are rewarding people only if they find a positive result and that's the wrong incentive. There are countries where you get huge cash rewards if you get published in *Science* or *Nature*. You get rock star status! If competition could be ratcheted down, if there were more jobs so scientists were not so desperate, things would be better. The degree of competition dictates the severity of the problem.'

These aren't abstract problems for Fang. He is careful about the kinds of personalities he recruits into his own lab and tried hard to model the collaboration he feels is essential to productive science.

'I've become a lot more sensitive to recruiting collegial people. I tend to blab the minute the experiment is done! I *want* to get feedback and I share unpublished data because it pays off: my colleagues point out things I hadn't seen. Science is a community endeavour and it's crazy when we take individual credit.'

Fang readily acknowledges that he can withstand being scooped – as he has been – because he's well established now. But, for the younger generation, he says, excessive competition is demoralizing, destructive and counter-productive. Anxiety over the future, he says, is at an all-time high.[30]

'There is a very real risk that we will lose a generation of scientists. As older scientists hold on longer because their retirement plans aren't as healthy as they had expected, I see young people bailing or choosing other options entirely. So many young people have no prospects – nothing attractive to retreat to. We could accommodate a larger scientific workforce but it would need a very different structure.'

The tournament of science has generated a vast array of perverse outcomes: secrecy, sabotage, the Matthew effect, fraud, fabrication, plagiarism, a rising rate of retractions – all of which undermine public faith in and support for science. If the collegiality and transparency on which science fundamentally depends is being destroyed by too many scientists chasing too little funding, I asked Fang, wouldn't science be better with fewer scientists? If there is such over-supply, why do governments keep calling for more science graduates?

'My sense is that science has evolved into a more aggressive, business-like activity where scientists see themselves as small businesses competing in a zero-sum game for credit and funding. Science is a team sport but the rewards are individual. This is a big disconnect and a huge obstacle to career paths. If funds were given to institutions instead of to individuals, then we might be able to organize things differently, have career paths and mid-level scientists. But no one wants to make a first move because they all compete with one another.'

The fundamental cost to science of head-to-head competition is trust. Young researchers, competing for jobs and funding, don't trust their colleagues enough to collaborate with them. Established scientists don't always trust each other's motives. The desire to establish priority erodes a sense of common purpose. The pressures of time, money and ego corrode the integrity of work that, if it can't be trusted, undermines public respect and understanding for science at the very moment we need it most.

Many of the most pressing issues we face today – climate change, antibiotic-resistant diseases, the immense challenge of feeding a population of eight billion and more – need the richest array of scientific solutions the world can provide. But the competitive ethos that has infiltrated the scientific community – even been encouraged by some – fundamentally disables the skills, talent, enthusiasm and creativity on which we all depend.

'We have big problems right now that science can solve,' Fang insists. 'But if you look at the needs of society and the relative number of people doing high-quality science,' Fang told me, 'just 0.1 per cent of the population is an active scientist and that's not enough! The US spends twice as much *on beer* as it spends on research and development, and funding is at its lowest point since the 1960s.'

We badly need the learning, discoveries, therapies and inventions that science has to offer but, in our blind love affair with competition, we have introduced structures, values and incentives that undermine the very creativity we seek.

You might think that the business world would know better; after all, it's often to the commercial world that policymakers look for ideas of better management and structural reform. But much of the competition in science has been imported from the business world, where executives don't know the story of the Purdue chickens and many imagine themselves social Darwinians, convinced that the struggle for survival is the best way, even the only way, to generate commercial fitness.

'We used to have these internal pitches,' Joe told me, 'where we'd be put into different teams. The idea was that we'd compete to design the best concept, tagline, whatever. It was a shootout, the most dysfunctional thing I've ever seen. Teams would steal briefing materials, they'd go into databases, remove crucial information and never put it back. At first I thought: this is a game. They can't mean it! But they did mean it. And it wasn't fun.'

Joe worked for one of the largest ad agencies in New York. Now a freelance creative, he doesn't want his full name disclosed because he still works in the industry. But he can't stand working in any one company for too long, he says, because the dog-eat-dog cultures are so vicious. At his last agency, Joe headed up a business unit that, like all the others, was responsible for its own profit-and-loss account. His unit's profitability determined his bonus and his place within the corporate pecking order. That, he said, had all kinds of perverse consequences.

'I had a really talented designer working for me,' he recalled. 'But her forte was animation and I didn't have any animation work. One of the other teams had a great animation job and I tried to get her involved in it. But the guy leading that team thought that, if he gave it to her, she'd be off of my books and my team would look more profitable. Well, he didn't want that, did he? So he wouldn't take her – so she left. The next time we wanted to pitch a big animated campaign, we didn't have the talent we needed.'

Internal competition of this kind has just the same effect in advertising and other industries as in science: no trust, no sharing, plenty of sabotage.

'A few years back, I was in a team pitching for new business,' Joe told me, shaking his head. 'And the same agency had four teams, all in the same company, pitching against each other. It got so we had to take our materials home with us at night – because otherwise they'd go missing or – oops – someone spilled their coffee on a big display. Just ludicrous stuff. We communicated via private email accounts so we couldn't be hacked! I had to check that everything charged to my accounts was actually my business – because other business units used to try to move their costs into mine. It was mad! All within the same company . . .'

For Joe, his profit-and-loss accounts and his position within the corporate pecking order were the means of keeping score and fostering internal competition. For highly competitive people, the clarity of that score and the possibility of a clear win makes work more exciting. From the first time Brad Ruderman walked onto the trading floor at Lehman Brothers, he was hooked.

'I saw a situation I couldn't believe,' he told me, 'So competitive as to boggle the mind! Energetic people just knocking the cover off the ball: energy, activity, just the most amazing scene to behold.'

Ruderman couldn't wait to join in and, after a friend introduced him to the managing director, he started to work his way up. It was quickly obvious to him – and to everyone – how the game worked.

'We're all on commission,' he explained, 'and, every day of the week, our prior day's commission would be posted on the window of the managing director's office. So every day you walk into work, your net income is posted for everyone to see. If that doesn't foster competition for someone who is already competitive, what would? Of course, that's what it's for. For someone like me, if you're not up there somewhere near the top, it's a disaster. You have to do something because otherwise, well, you're nothing.'

Earning anything less than $100,000 a month, Ruderman explained, made him a loser. But if he had made $140,000 in July, then anything less than $120,000 in August made him a loser too. So every month, he needed more and more to stay in the game. This wasn't, he hastened to assure me, because of what the money could buy. It was because the money identified him publicly as a winner or a loser.

'It wasn't greed,' he told me. 'I didn't need anything. It wasn't about stuff. It was about my personal scoreboard with everyone else. Sometimes, there'd be three days left in the month and I hadn't hit last month's target, so I'd push the envelope to do something not always in the best interests of my client. I lost all morals, all ethics.'[31]

The business-as-sport metaphor plays its part, with many sales organizations using these kinds of scoreboards to motivate their teams. At HBOS, on Saturday mornings, if salespeople had met their targets, they would be presented with cash. Had they failed, they would be presented with a cabbage. The ritual public humiliation, firmly segregating winners from losers, was supposed to be motivating. Instead, it was implicated in the widespread mis-selling of mortgages and insurance. Likewise, when Anthony Salz reviewed what had gone wrong at Barclays Bank, where mis-selling and interest rate manipulation had flourished, he found at the heart of the dysfunctional bank a culture that employees described as 'winning at all costs'. The glory of being a winner and the shame of being a loser were both so extreme that no one dared buck the system. The word used least often to describe the bank's culture was courage.

The American clothes store, The Limited, used to run sales meetings at which high achievers sat at the front, with lower earners stuck at the back – just like at the Roman Colosseum. They called the strategy Winning at Retail – or WAR, for short. What they, and Lehman Brothers, and other firms using these kinds of humiliating techniques don't seem to acknowledge is that these 'wars' create casualties: in Ruderman's case, it was his clients and his own internal sense of right and wrong. His frantic desire to compete caused him, as he later recognized, to abandon his moral compass and to chase success at any cost. The same could be said, on an epic scale, of Barclays, HBOS and many other financial institutions now paying billions in compensation for mis-selling.

Because human beings are competitive, when we are put into these tournaments, our first response is to try to win. The most obvious way many people try to do this is by working harder – which is, of course, why the tournaments are created in the first place: companies are trying to motivate the workforce to be more productive. Longer hours become another kind of arms race, both for attention – face time – and the hoped-for productivity that more hours will generate. The problem is that it backfires. Over 100 years of research into productivity has shown that, after about forty hours a week, when we work longer, we make more mistakes – and the extra time goes to cleaning them up, the mess we made.

'We see it here in England and in the US, but if you really want to see long hours,' Jim Brady told me, 'go to Hong Kong.'

Brady worked in financial services in Asia – Hong Kong and Singapore – for years. He loved the people and the work, he says, but he didn't love the way it got done.

'We were working quite ridiculous hours – being at your boss's beck and call at two a.m., at seven a.m. Emails in the middle of the night, followed by more emails: why haven't you answered me yet? It would make headlines in the paper here if we worked people like this. This is quite senior people being treated like that. They try to raise the issue when they feel safe – but only on the understanding that nothing will happen. It's hours, it's language, it's huge targets. You can only drive people that hard for so long. Then they crack up, they have heart attacks, they leave or they make – and this certainly happened – they make very big mistakes. But there's this sense that, if we don't run, all day, every day, someone, some competitor, will be on our tail.'

Juliet Schor, in *The Overworked American*, estimated that, as Americans worked longer, they slept less, losing 60–90 minutes of sleep every night. The accumulated sleep debt doesn't just make people feel bad; it also makes them perform badly. As the brain becomes steadily more fatigued, it starts to siphon off energy (in the form of glucose) from the parietal and occipital lobes to the thalamus. The reason for this is efficiency: the thalamus is what keeps you awake. But the parietal and occipital lobes give you capacity to think. Thus the harder you have to struggle to stay alert, the less able you are to do the creative, imaginative thinking that modern work most requires. So the harder we compete to stay in the game, the worse we get at playing it.[32]

For genuine creativity and collaboration to flourish inside organizations, the people who work there need to be rested, alert and able to trust one another. But notwithstanding the physical and ethical costs implicit in pitting employees against one another, many large corporations take internal competition one step further, formalizing it into forced rankings: a process by which all employees are placed in a strict pecking order so that the bottom 10 or 15 per cent can be eliminated. The system was made famous by Jack Welch at GE where, every year, the workforce was forced into ranks of the top 20 per cent, the middle 70 per cent and the bottom 10 percent – who could be let go. Welch argued that the system was kind because it gave the bottom ranks plenty of warning that they were failing.

In various permutations, the same concept is still applied, by some estimates, in half of the Fortune 500 companies. AIG divides people into five ranks; GlaxoSmithKline, into four; Lending Tree, into three. Advocates of forced ranking argue that the system rewards outstanding performers. But what none of these companies seems to appreciate is that forced ranking creates levels of competitiveness and distrust between individuals that makes the system uncreative. Lions, owls and St Bernards can have just as fierce a standoff in an office as in a lab.

Puzzling over the curious failure of Microsoft to develop any truly innovative technologies for over a decade, the writer Kurt Eichenwald found that every single employee he interviewed cited 'stack ranking' (the company's version of forced ranking) as the most destructive process inside the company, driving out untold numbers of bright people.

'It leads to employees focusing on competing with each other rather than competing with other companies,' a former software developer told Eichenwald.

Top-notch developers did not want to work with other strong performers because doing so would risk their ranking. As a consequence, jobs were secure to the degree that people surrounded themselves with pleasers who would never pose a challenge or a threat. By putting all of its employees in a constant state of threat, Microsoft didn't inspire ambition for excellence but a prevailing desire for safety.

'People do everything they can to stay out of the bottom bucket,' one Microsoft engineer said. 'People will openly sabotage other people's efforts. One of the most valuable things I learned was to give the appearance of being courteous while witholding just enough information from colleagues to ensure they didn't get ahead of me on the rankings.'

Eichenwald's descriptions of the horse-trading that characterizes Microsoft's ranking process are eerily reminiscent of the same process at Enron, where it was called 'rank and yank'. Managers retreated into conference rooms, pulled down the blinds, and started to write up employees' names on white boards or post-it notes. Then the trading began: I'll let you keep Jane, if I can keep Kevin. Because a certain percentage had to fail, much depended on office politics, fitting in and not standing out. This kind of popularity contest is a recipe for obedience and conformity: the opposites of innovation.

When, at the end of 2013, Microsoft announced plans finally to abandon its employee ranking system, it did so to try to create 'One Microsoft', tacitly acknowledging the divisive impact these systems always incur. Forced rankings are a particularly perverse form of motivation because they destroy one of our most profound motives for working, which is the desire to belong to a group. Humans are inherently social; we can do very little alone and crave the safety and sense of connectedness that social relations provide. Maslow ranked the need for 'love and belongingness' in the middle of his hierarchy, testifying to our intrinsically social nature. Yet formalized evaluation tournaments threaten our relationships with all co-workers, atomizing the society of the workplace until it's everyone for themself.

Competing to work the longest hours would be bad enough but the various permutations of forced rankings generate a persistent sense of threat: always under evaluation, individuals fear ostracism. What we now know about brain function suggests that this is cognitively exhausting. The brain has quite hard limits to its capacity, and energy used for one activity is unavailable for others. When we feel threatened, our brain's amygdala, constantly scanning the horizon for danger, generates fear and anxiety, sapping energy from the prefrontal cortex, the part of the brain we most need for planning and decision-making. Working under a persistent sense of threat therefore carries a cognitive cost, as fear drains our capacity to think and learn.

Yet every company says that it wants and needs creativity and innovation. These are often correlated with risk-taking; you have to be willing to tolerate a great deal of ambiguity and danger to realize an idea that no one has tried or seen before. So some businesses will set out specifically to recruit people who demonstrate a high tolerance of risk. Intel has done this for years. But, once inside the corporation, something strange seems to happen: risk tolerance declines, even vanishes. Intel has long puzzled over this problem, little imagining that its ranking system – called Focal – may have much to do with it. But many of the people I spoke to within Intel, some of whom had worked with the company for ten or twenty years, didn't find this phenomenon puzzling at all. No one, they said, wanted to risk their standing in the rankings.

'If I'm getting arbitrarily ranked by my peers – of course I'm going to stop taking risks!' Jackie Witt told me. 'The system wasn't based on achievements, knowledge, skills: it's based on whether people like you! People that are likable aren't always the most productive or creative.

'You know the Intel mantra, Andy Grove's slogan: Only the paranoid survive. Well sure, they *survive*. But paranoia isn't a great state to do creative thinking. So what you found at Intel was that easy, compliant people moved up. People were paranoid enough to make everyone their friend – but that's where the energy went! I worked with someone there who was a risk taker and she was not moving up. She was very productive, not necessarily well liked but hugely effective. But she was stuck indefinitely at the middle third. But I thought her work was outstanding, original and driven. But of course, she just left.'

Witt is a seasoned project manager, highly accustomed to competitive multi-disciplinary teams. Her very calm, thoughtful approach to complex projects has led her through Intel, Toyota, Genentech, Apple, Fujitsu, even through subsidiaries of GE. She says that much of her work resembles mediation: getting combative teams to listen to and take each other seriously. There's sibling rivalry aplenty, she says, and when there's a charismatic CEO, it's worse because everyone is vying for attention and credit.

'Turf wars. Toxic people. This kind of dysfunction can be very disheartening,' she said. 'It costs people jobs, bonuses, mental health. A lot of people don't feel they can walk away, so they stay feeling abused, angry, frustrated. And they didn't start that way. They started out hoping to do a really wonderful job.

'The other thing about forced rankings is that – however frequently they're done (in some companies it is every six months) they're very present. They absolutely make you concentrate on the here-and-now. How am I doing *today*? You can't and you don't think about the long term. Why would you? If you don't do well today, there won't be any long term. So the kind of sustained thinking, horizon-gazing, imaginative speculation you need to be truly creative – it doesn't even cross your mind. You are always focused on the present threat.'

Witt approaches turf wars and toxic people with knowing bemusement. But they came as a shock to Cathy O'Neil, a young Harvard data scientist, known online as mathbabe. In 2007, she left academic mathematics to work at one of Wall Street's most secretive hedge funds, D. E. Shaw.

'When I was being recruited,' she says, laughing, 'I didn't know they were specifically looking for competitive people. I was interviewed by person after person all asking me math puzzles. And I kept answering them because I'm a mathematician and I love math! I think they interpreted my facility as smugness and that impressed them. But I wasn't nervous because I didn't care that much. I just got through by sheer luck and love of subject.'

When she started work, however, she was amazed by the culture she discovered.

'People didn't talk to each other! You couldn't ask for help. I was told – *explicitly* – not to ask for help. Why? Because nobody wanted to be seen helping anyone else. There were some nice people there but, if you really insisted, the only way you could ask a question was online – so that, if someone decided to help you, nobody else would find out!

'There was a foosball table. You thought, when you saw it, that that might be kinda fun. But it was not there for fun. It was there so everyone could compete with each other, show off to each other. My feeling was that they got competitive people because they wanted everyone to stay in line and to define their self-worth through their banking achievement. Everyone had to acquiesce to the bonus.'

D. E. Shaw was famous for attracting the brightest people it could find; former Harvard president Larry Summers (the same man who questioned women's innate ability) had worked there for a $100,000 a week. O'Neil knew her colleagues were brilliant; that wasn't in doubt. But they did not want to share anything. This made meetings quite peculiar.

'In a group meeting, you couldn't say what you were thinking. People had ideas, of course. But they'd never tell you what they were because they might be thinking of starting their own fund. And if they articulated their idea, then that would be owned by D. E. Shaw and they'd end up in competition with their own idea! So if you had a good idea, the one thing you absolutely had to do was shut up. You didn't want anyone to steal your idea – or to steal it and outperform you. So you had these meetings, with plenty of super-smart people around the table: all saying nothing.'

If scientists don't share because they seek priority, financiers don't share because they want credit – and the money that comes with it. A new person working in an old fund didn't dare contribute a fresh idea because that wouldn't attract any credit or bonus – because the fund was already in production. So you wanted to save your bright ideas for a new fund; that was the only way to get all the credit. Or it might be worth even more if you left and set up on your own. In the meantime, you'd better just keep your thoughts to yourself.

'There was just so much scheming and strategizing about how to turn proprietary ideas into money. You'd have to have special trust with a specific person to be able to collaborate. Basically everyone was just your rival. Every other person constituted a threat. It was very unpleasant. I think of myself pretty much as an alpha female and I'm more than capable of looking after myself but this was pretty intense. It was very repressed. The atmosphere of secrecy – the idea that anything of value had to be *hidden* – it was just very repressive.'

O'Neil ultimately left D. E. Shaw, returning to academia and to advise Occupy Wall Street on better economic models than the ones she watched collapse all around her. But she insisted, contrary to much public commentary, the business models she'd seen in action *had worked*. The financial crisis came about because those business models had delivered – but only to the advantage of their designers, not to the benefit of anyone else. The economic crisis was just, writ large, what she'd seen at the hedge fund: a tournament that disproportionately favoured a few.

Competition, she concluded from her experience, always provided a motive for gaming the system. It didn't promote excellence. It didn't generate great thinking because great ideas couldn't spread. And it militated against anyone taking responsibility when the system broke.

'When it's each man (or woman) for himself, then who cares about the system? Nobody! As long as I'm okay, I'm okay. I'm a winner. You're not? Too bad.'

Competition puts value on secrets, encourages a lack of transparency, the hoarding of information, and discourages the desire to share or to collaborate. As such, it can become criminogenic: producing environments that inspire or even normalize criminal behaviour. No wonder academic studies found that highly competitive people were more likely to be drawn into insider trading, which seeks to make money from private knowledge.[33]

The secrecy has two profound consequences. It creates a Matthew effect: making those who have information richer and those without the information poorer. This is visibly demonstrated in the crime of insider trading, where those who have information gain more money, more power and thus more access to information. And that, in turn, makes the winners feel sublimely independent from, and not responsible for, the system as a whole.

That can be seen in the raft of insider trading cases brought since the financial crisis. But perhaps more profoundly, the disconnectedness of the solo winner is most visible in the choices made by traders who, as early as 2005, started to glean the consequences of sub-prime mortgages and the explosive derivatives market. To them, this was the ultimate big secret. And so, instead of warning that the house might be on fire, they placed big bets on it burning down. Hedge fund traders like John Paulson, Michael Burry and Eugene Xu felt no responsibility for the system as long as they could figure out how to use it to be winners. In the race to establish the intellectual priority of their cunning, this was too good a chance to miss. Those who gain most from the tournament have the least interest in repairing it.

Scientists don't give up easily; tackling hard problems is what they do for a living. At the Weizmann Institute of Science in Israel, the molecular biologist Uri Alon struggles daily with the challenge of creating a productive lab in a scientific culture that militates against collaboration. At times, his experience in science has been so bad that he couldn't shave, couldn't get out of bed in the morning. Being scooped filled him with shame; getting stalled or lost in a project was crippling. But he also loved science so much that he felt that there had to be a better way of doing it. How could he counteract the destructiveness of competition with levels of engagement and motivation that would be more creative? What would the motivations and processes be that could change the dog-eat-dog culture? He found some of his answers in improvisational theatre.

Alon doesn't come across as a natural performer. In person, he's introverted and intensely serious. But the process of doing improv changed the way that he thought about and did science.

'Unlike science, in improvisation theatre they tell you what will happen when you get on stage: you will fail miserably. You'll get stuck. But what happens *when* you're stuck is different. First, you expect it to happen because everyone tells you it will happen. And then, everyone shows you a lot of solidarity. They've been there, too. You aren't a loser – you're one of them.

'I also learned from improv theatre how to have a conversation that opens up new ideas. The central principle of improv is to say "Yes and . . ." – to agree and build. So if one actor says "Here's a pool of water" and the other says "No, that's just the stage" then the idea is over, it's dead. It's called blocking. But if instead, "Here's a pool of water!" "Yes, let's jump in! Look – there's a whale." "Let's grab its tail. It's taking us to the moon . . ." That way you unlock hidden creativity by building on each other's ideas.'

In science, competition promotes blocking but in Alon's lab, 'Yes and . . .' prevails. This has two consequences: it broadens everyone's thinking, making them more responsive to each other and opening up new ideas. Students feel supported and encouraged to

persevere. 'Yes and . . .' also creates a climate of safety: the sense that thinking can be wide-ranging and risky. Instead of competitive stress narrowing focus and imagination, solidarity and encouragement enlarge human creativity.

Creating an environment in which students expect to fail, but fail safely, made Alon's lab very creative. He and his students made surprising and important discoveries on the interface between physics and biology, about general principles of how biological systems like the body are designed. A rich emotional environment of risk-taking, support and creativity put the lab on the map.

Alon can't protect himself or his students from being scooped. But what he can do is mitigate the fear and shame that accompanies it. He's even written a song about the experience, 'Scoop, scoop'[34], which he sings, with his colleagues, any time one of them is scooped. I've seen him do this on stage too and the impact is striking. Alon isn't a dazzling singer or guitarist – but that's the point. He's willing to be fallible and vulnerable in the service of supporting, encouraging and motivating the people around him. If the price you pay for sharing is that you sometimes look a little ridiculous, it doesn't matter. What matters is being creative and the encouragement that provides to others.

Alon's a well-published, highly regarded scientist. But one of his most widely cited publications isn't about biology; it's about managing motivated teams. It was published in *Cell* but is relevant to any walk of life. In it, he comes to three conclusions: Productivity is a function of enough autonomy to feel free, responsible and proud. Threats decrease that sense of freedom and obstruct the support that every creative person needs; Social connectedness is, in itself, motivating. In his weekly two-hour lab meetings, Alon carefully sets aside the first half hour to talk about anything *except* science: birthdays, the news, vacations. Then, when a paper is presented by a member of his lab, the group is given a role to play, as imaginary referees or brainstormers. The goal, he says, is to teach every member of the lab that they are there for each other.

But most important of all, Alon insists that the route to great innovation or discoveries lies through failure, what he calls 'the cloud': the part of the process when things go wrong and you lose direction. Second-guessers never make it to the cloud because they play safe, which is why they achieve little. But truly creative people find themselves in the cloud routinely because they're exploring new territory. If, when you're in the cloud, you think about winning and losing, you stay stuck. Fear shuts down your imagination and ability to think broadly. But when Alon's students come to him and say 'Uri, I'm in the cloud', his response is: 'Great! That means you're close to something important.' That's when he shows the student most support, encouragement and solidarity.

The reason competition is so detrimental to creative work is because it severs the link between people who could help, and because it insists on framing everything as success or failure. The motivation to avoid failure represses the courage needed for exploration. But time and again, talking to people who have led a life full of innovation, creativity and achievement, what I've found is that their abilities come, not despite failure, but because of it. The founders of Twitter came up with the idea for the micro-blogging site only after their attempts at audio-blogging failed to take off. Even box-office-busting directors like Steven Spielberg, James Cameron and Robert Zemeckis have made flops. Alon's now highly influential thinking about science came from thinking and talking to others not about their successes but about the shared experience of being stuck. Had he concealed his sense of confusion – like the scientists who couldn't replicate Jan Hendrik Schön's results – he would never have been able to motivate himself or all the people around him.

Critical to everything Alon discusses is trust: the feeling that it is safe to explore and to make mistakes. Mistakes, after all, are how we all learn: how we learned to walk and talk, how we experiment and discard what doesn't work in the process of finding what does. Intense competition makes people afraid to make mistakes – and even more reluctant to share them. And that's dangerous.

'If you can't talk about mistakes, you learn nothing. If anything, it just convinces you that you're perfect – which is really dangerous,' David Ring told me.

One of America's leading orthopaedic surgeons, he has become as famous for his openness about errors as for his skill in the operating theatre. On one occasion, he operated on a woman who needed treatment for trigger finger, a condition in which a finger gets locked rigidly into position. But Ring failed to operate for that condition; by mistake, he operated for carpal tunnel syndrome.

He immediately told the patient what had happened and did the correct operation the same day. But what startled his colleagues was that he wrote and published an article, describing how the mistake occurred. Instead of hoping no one would learn about the error, he analysed, publicly, everything that had gone wrong: surgeons had been running late so stress was high; the nurse had marked the correct arm but not the incision site; the operating room had been changed so the nurse who prepared the patient wasn't present and the nursing team changed during the procedure. Documenting the series of errors led to improvements in the system that stopped them happening again. David Ring, previously known as a good doctor, came to be described as a great man.

Ring now argues that the way to make hospitals safer isn't to compete for perfection but to create a climate of safety where errors can be openly acknowledged and swiftly fixed. And he's a major leader in a movement to eradicate blame and celebrate improvement. The more people could own up to errors, the faster they could get fixed. In hospitals around the world, the greater the climate of safety to acknowledge mistakes, the fewer get made – because each one, treated as learning, has allowed the organization as a whole to improve. Ring says that medicine has learned a lot about the value of mistakes from the aviation industry where everyone, at any level, is encouraged to speak up about the smallest slip. Of course, as he pointed out, in an airplane, everyone really is in it together.

Where competition isolates people, pitting them against one another, we can all do better, more creative work acknowledging how much, in fact, we need one another. Alon's lab is more productive because its members support each other through the cloud. Ring's hospital is safer because he doesn't think he's perfect. The excellence of the work derives from networks of support and improvement in which every contribution counts.

'Everyone was royalty.' That's the way John Abele describes the rich collection of physicians, surgeons and scientists who helped him build Boston Scientific into one of the world's leading medical-device companies. In sharp contrast to the scientists who jockey for position or the CEOs who tell their stories as heroic soloists, Abele describes his business largely by telling other people's stories. Disruptive technology may have been what made the company rich but Abele is quite confident – in fact, positively evangelical – that the business derived from its talent for collaboration.

'A lot of people think collaboration is soft,' Abele told me. 'It's a paradox. In order to gain control, you have to cede control. You have to recruit some of the people who maybe don't want to see you succeed. It's fraught with contradiction. This kind of collaboration isn't soft at all – it's very, very hard.'

Critical to Boston Scientific's early success was development of a balloon catheter that could enlarge narrow or blocked arteries without surgery. The device had been pioneered by a junior physician, Andreas Gruentzig, who built early prototypes in his kitchen, using a razor, tubing and adhesive. Gruentzig was passionate, curious and clever but perhaps his greatest – and least predictable – advantage was that he had little personal or professional power.

For years, Gruentzig practiced on dogs and corpses but of course the time came when he had to try his device on living humans. To do so, he needed the help and support of surgeons, the very people whose work his device would disrupt. According to Abele, who loves celebrating Gruentzig's achievements, it was the young doctor's modesty and curiosity that won him allies.

'Instead of proclaiming that his ideas were revolutionary breakthroughs that would change medicine, Andreas referred to them as incremental advances. He was always the first to point out the deficiencies in the tools he pioneered and was constantly on the lookout for signs that they were flawed. People responded in part because of Andreas's unusual willingness to share credit for whatever was achieved.'

In 1976, at an annual meeting of the American Heart Association, Gruentzig started to introduce his device to surgeons. They became so intrigued by his ideas that they all wanted to come and see his work for themselves in Switzerland. Demand grew so great that he had to use another new technology – video conferencing – to accommodate everyone. What he wanted most of all, and what drew in so much interest, wasn't his desire to show off his device but his passion to get ideas from his expert audience. Critical to this process, says Abele, was that Gruentzig didn't think of his device as 'his' and he didn't see the surgeon community as out-siders. In the project to find a way to clear arteries without surgery, everyone was equal – including Gruentzig himself. Everyone was royalty.

Intense interest in his device meant that, as well as his innova-tive catheter, Gruentzig pioneered one of the world's first live demonstration courses – a practice now standard in medicine around the world. He did so in order to share every detail of his technology because he wanted the surgeons to understand it, share their doubts, concerns, ideas, recognizing that that was his best way to improve the device. In addition – as if two breakthrough ideas weren't enough – he created a voluntary registry of the cases that he and his colleagues treated, in order to track results and share data. The very fact that everyone had access to each other's pro-cedures put them on their mettle to do their best work.

'It's no exaggeration,' Abele later wrote, 'to say that the rapid sharing of experience and techniques enabled by the registry saved many lives and prevented untold complications ... And when it came time to publish papers, Andreas and his closest collaborators made sure to spread the intellectual wealth.'[35]

Gruentzig was just the opposite of the scientists in Kuchroo's labs; he made headway, sharing lavishly, by refusing to posture or jockey for position. His pioneering product wasn't developed for a non-profit but for a commercial business; the fact that money was to be made from it did not impede the sharing – of knowledge, insight, data and experience – that contributed so critically to its success. Nor were Gruentzig's collaborators saintly and selfless; Abele describes them as having big personalities, ample ego and terrific self-confidence. Moreover, they were all rivals and most were far more established and successful than the inventor himself. That Gruentzig had no power – to compel their attention, to demand their time, or to tell them what to do – lay at the heart of their fruitful collaboration. There was no power-distance problem because Gruentzig didn't have or seek power. What he did was inspire others to join his quest for a breakthrough procedure. He spoke to physicians' highest aims and to their professional pride and never presumed to have all the answers. His big contribution lay in keeping everyone's trust levels high.

'All the divas think they are best,' Abele told me wryly. 'But what you really need are impresario skills: not putting yourself at the centre of the picture but bringing everyone in. I see a lot of people define collaboration as individuals and institutions working together for a common goal. No, that's not enough. In great collaborative leadership, the job is to tweak the environment so that the sum is greater than the individuals who are contributing. This is a very different category of leadership and it may involve sacrifices. People laugh and joke and think collaboration is some kind of feel-good enterprise and, I'm sorry, in those situations the achievement is never greater than the sum of the parts.'

That the talents of collaboration are so elusive may not be because they're rare but because they're rarely taught or celebrated. Our educational systems focus relentlessly on solo achievement. In a survey of 1,824 university students given a series of mock job descriptions, any that mentioned teamwork or collaboration were specifically rejected. The students didn't want to be collaborators – they wanted to be stars. Employers were even discouraged from mentioning teamwork in job ads if they wanted to attract high-achievers.[36]

The sports world celebrates and overpays individual athletes and, even within team sports, habitually attributes success to individual star players or coaches. Apeing the entertainment industry, which monotonously find the easiest marketing strategy is to turn a soloist into a brand, young people beginning their careers are told that they too must be brands to sell themselves effectively in an increasingly terrifying job market.

The cult of celebrity invariably portrays outstanding performers as superstar soloists. Worse still, the myth of the selfish, misbehaving soloist is rampant in entertainment. Ask aspiring young artists, in music, film, theatre, dance or painting and they will recite for you the huge egos and trashed hotel rooms that denote success. They don't know the lamentable fate of William Muir's super-chickens either and, as surely as the young, uncommunicative Harvard scientists, they've come to believe, as one young musician insisted to me, 'it's the assholes who succeed'.

This is all highly misleading. Not just because the bulk of all work today is done in teams and we badly need people who can do this with skill and passion. But, even about the entertainment industry alone, it's simply wrong. One of the distinguishing features of the 'idols' produced by talent contests is how swiftly their glory is extinguished. The most successful artists depend on a dense skein of collaborative relationships, richly knitted and fastidiously maintained. Nobody does great work alone and no one survives very long if they aren't good at working with others.

Nowhere is this more obvious than in the music industry. In 2012, when Adele's album, *21*, won six Grammy awards and became the fourth biggest-selling album of all time, it was easy for the press to express astonishment and delight at the brilliance of one young woman. The truth was far more interesting.

That one album used the services of over 100 musicians, producers, arrangers and engineers. If you were to add in the design and marketing executives behind the album, that number could double. The brand may focus on the individual but the operation itself depends fully on making all the contributors work together.

'Adele is a brilliant collaborator. She wouldn't be able to do what she does if she weren't also fantastically good at working with other great people,' according to producer Jim Abbiss.

Abbiss has worked with Adele since, as an unknown young singer, she brought out her first album, *19*, in 2008. He has a long and distinguished track record working with artists as diverse as the Arctic Monkeys, Björk, Massive Attack and the Kooks. Both as an engineer and a musician, he has spent a great deal of time in recording studios seeing how music comes together.

'Although the technology in music today means you *could* in theory do it all yourself – nobody does! And nobody does because it is always better – always – as a collaboration. Whether it's a whole ton of people like *21* or just a few people, the music gets better.'

If the music industry has a reputation for slick and aggressive self-promoters, Abbiss doesn't fit the image. Thick-set and wearing a plaid shirt, he looks more like a builder than a musician. He's keenly alert to the people around him and curious about places and ideas he hasn't encountered before, demonstrating many of the qualities that John Abele so admired in scientists: passionate curiosity, modest confidence and mild obsession. He describes his job with marked understatement – he serves his artists, he is just a sounding board – and you rapidly sense that he contributes to a production only what it needs: tough love at times, reassurance at others. He demonstrates a genuine curiosity about other people, listens very carefully and works hard to progress an idea, even in a conversation.

'Adele is very open and giving so it's hard not to like her. That helps. Of course, she can also write fantastic melodies and songs and sing better than most people on the planet so she can afford to be generous! But she genuinely likes people who can make the work better. She doesn't have any arrogance or worries about that.'

Adele's commitment to the song is, according to Abbiss, what makes her a great collaborator. She'll embrace what makes it better and reject what doesn't. Dominance doesn't come into it.

'We worked on a song together for her first album, *19*. This was a cover of Bob Dylan's 'Make You Feel My Love'. I thought it needed strings and suggested a string quartet. Adele had never worked with a string quartet before and wasn't sure how to use it. So I called in Rosie Danvers.'

'I just got a call,' Danvers recalled. 'Jim said, "Can you bring in your quartet and do some work with this singer, Adele?" I didn't know her – no one did. Jim said there was no need to do anything in advance, just turn up with the quartet. And I thought: just turn up? I was upset because every project I do – I want to do it to the best of my ability. I wasn't going to chance it. I wanted it to be fucking brilliant!'

Rosie Danvers is a classically trained cellist. She found session playing unsatisfying so she created her string quartet 'Wired Strings' in the hope of building richer collaborations with a wider array of musicians. Hers was a relatively new idea and this unexpected opportunity with an unknown talent wasn't an obvious winner. But that didn't matter. It was in her nature, she told me, to give of her best. Eight months pregnant, she listened to the demo and set to work. The singer had, she thought, a 'notably good voice'. That just made Rosie work harder. Two days later in the studio everyone met for the first time.

'So Rosie played us excerpts and Adele would say what she

thought: she liked this, didn't like this,' Abbiss recalled. 'Everyone had to be quick and confident to adapt – and everybody was. Bear in mind, at this point, there isn't any money, which means there isn't any time. But in the space of three hours, everyone changed a lot of what they'd come in with and we got great performances from everyone. The whole mood was: the best idea wins. It's not about you or her or me. The best idea wins.'

As Abbiss and Danvers separately related the story, they both beamed, laughed and smiled: clearly, this had been a great experience for everyone. Studio sessions are expensive and often stressful but, for each of them, these three hours had been relaxed, productive, creative. Danvers left the session feeling that she had achieved everything she'd hoped for when she'd formed her quartet.

'We all just left the session pumped! You're creating something *together*. It is just so much more fulfilling. Second-guessing is boring. But this time, everybody contributed. And everybody loved it!'

The reference to second-guessing is telling. Truly successful artists with staying power aren't choosing between deviant behaviour on the one hand, and obsequious compliance on the other. They're developing the skills, nuance, empathy and intelligence required for complex collaboration. Danvers wasn't passive in her collaboration; she wasn't waiting for a moment of solo glory (like Kuchroo's sullen scientists) nor did she look for alibis in case she wasn't successful. A fully mature collaborator, Danvers took responsibility for the quality of her contribution. Not surprisingly, she's gone on to work with Adele both in live shows and on the award winning album *21:* listen to 'Set Fire to the Rain' and that's Danvers and her quartet you will hear giving the song its distinctive sound. She's also brought the quartet to work with artists as diverse as Beyoncé, Jay-Z, Emeli Sandé, Kanye West, Lana del Rey and Paul Weller. Almost always the brief is vague, invariably there's little time but always she's determined to bring her best and to knit together the contributions that everyone brings to the work.

'I don't want any competitiveness in my sessions. In a traditional orchestra, the leader sits at the front and then there's a pecking order all the way back. Forget that: everyone sits where they want.

We all have to pull together, I need everyone's feedback. People like that. It gives them responsibility for the whole. It's more than just turning up. I want everyone to go away feeling they've given their best. It isn't about being chummy. It's about creating something together.'

Just as in science, who gets the credit is, Abbiss says, always an issue. Credit impacts royalties so there's more than ego at stake. But the best artists tend to be those who can appreciate the contributors who've made their work so good.

'It's important to be fair about credit,' Abbiss explained. 'Because sometimes the smallest thing can make such a huge difference. Generosity lies at the heart of collaboration, I think. And it's striking that the artists who have real staying power ... they're all great collaborators. They know they need other people and they welcome them and they're generous in the credit they give.'

Everyone I've spoken to in the business appreciates that no great music is made alone. Reluctant to name names, every producer I spoke to could identify the bands that had talent but lacked staying power because they behaved like divas. Many hadn't started that way; media hype and celebrity branding had turned many artists' heads, sending them down an acute trajectory from prima donna to has-been. But the artists with sustained, meaningful careers continue to be provoked, stimulated, inspired by fellow artists. They don't create in a vacuum.

This is not, of course, the message conveyed by the numerous talent contests around the world, where the focus is all on solo winners, finding the single individuals whom record labels can market and then easily replace. Music schools aiming at producing genuine musicians for a lifelong career hate these tournaments and most musicians do too. Too much focus on personality and packaging, and the music, they say, gets lost. It was impossible to have this conversation with classical musicians without, sooner or later, one name coming up repeatedly.

'Lang Lang,' one musician groaned. Actually, they all groaned – and refused to be named. But the cause of their discomfort was always the same.

'He simply doesn't listen,' one horn player told me. 'It is an incredible thing to say about a musician. Perhaps the worst thing that you *can* say. But he doesn't listen. He is so focused on being the top dog, the centre of attention, that he really has no idea what else is going on inside the music. So of course, when he ignores us, we ignore him. The concerts are just awful. I'm amazed we don't get booed.'

Although he's far too polite to name names, it's Lang Lang who hovers over my conversation about music with the pianist Fou Ts'ong. Widely regarded today as one of the world's greatest living pianists, Fou Ts'ong won his fair share of competitions during the course of his seventy-year career. But the competitive nature of music, he says, has changed.

'This competition culture is very detrimental because it is producing performances that may be technically dazzling but are very, very unmusical. Technically there are thousands who can play the most demanding works. So they feel that they have to do something to make themselves special. But they don't need to; the composer is special enough. The performance is supposed to be about the music, not about the performer.'

With his focus on Chopin, many of Fou Ts'ong's concerts are solo affairs. Doesn't that mean that he is, after all, the centre of attention? How does a soloist collaborate?

'But that is what you must do!' he insists. 'When I am playing, I am always playing *with* the composer. That is the important one. It is never about me. It has to be about the music. My god is the composer. I am always there only to try to communicate what the composer wants, so I am working, really, I am working for him, with him.'

On large orchestral works, like a piano concerto, Fou Ts'ong always learns the entire score, not merely the piano part. It would not, he told me, occur to him to work any other way.

'I have to have a concept of the whole piece, otherwise how do I know what the piano is doing? Anybody who is a real musician always has the whole thing in his head, not just his part. Very often there are these days a lot of pianists with brilliant fingers but they concentrate too much on the piano part and you cannot play the music that way. I try to teach my students to learn the score and ask good questions. The greater the composer the more complex and varied their text. That's what I call the right approach.'

Whenever I talked to orchestral players about the tension between soloists and orchestra, Fou Ts'ong was regularly hailed as an exemplar: a brilliant, perfectionist musician who tuned in fully and completely to every single player. For him, any other approach is anti-music because players who do not work with each other also don't collaborate with the composer and thus create nothing original.

'No matter how much I know the score,' Fou Ts'ong insists, 'I always find something new, often very subtle. To try to discover the composer, to keep asking questions – that is the greatest originality.'

The one place in the world where you might still expect the deliberate cultivation of star soloists is the Royal Academy of Dramatic Art, famous for the many remarkable actors it has trained: Richard Attenborough, Peter O'Toole, Glenda Jackson, Alan Bates, Anthony Hopkins, June Whitfield, Alan Rickman, Fiona Shaw, Adrian Lester, Imelda Staunton, Ben Whishaw, Sophie Okonedo and many more. But, even here, director Edward Kemp is looking for skills and talent that go well beyond individual excellence.

'A lot of the students who apply imagine that acting is all about them. It's part of celebrity culture,' Kemp told me. 'But that's not what we're looking for. We spend days with audition candidates because we want to see how they work with one another, how each young actor keys into what they're being offered by everyone else on stage. It's about what they reflect and respond, not just about what they do individually. Many don't understand that and come to give their big performance. But they don't do well. Not here, not anywhere really.'

Just as music producers see that collaborative musicians enjoy longer careers, RADA's teachers recognize that actors who both give and get a lot from each other have richer, more substantial opportunities. Over the years that I've served as a Council member for the academy, we have periodically worried that students applied in large numbers imagining that beauty and presence would be enough. But what the profession wanted and rewarded were actors highly attuned to one another, who brought experience of life that enabled them to read, interpret and send signals with subtlety and understanding.

As I watched auditions for the 2013 class of student actors, the range of styles, age, size, body shapes, accents and approaches was remarkable. But talking with the tutors, I came to see what they were looking for: a rich (and sometimes mysterious) blend of experience – this is my contribution – with responsiveness: what I offer you is tempered and mediated by what I get from you. One candidate, Dino Keljalic, was a Serbian refugee who had fled first to Holland, then to Norway, where he'd trained as a doctor but then decided that he had to give acting a try. Tall, muscular, with dark curly hair and a sharp black beard, he undoubtedly had physical presence but this wasn't what made him compelling.

'What's remarkable about Dino,' Kemp reflected, 'is that you can see that he brings understanding of other people to the actors he shares the stage with. He's engaged by them, interested in them. That's what it's about: what happens *between* people.'

Earlier, Kemp had told me that identifying artists with true potential was always difficult, not least because no one can predict how life will change them. He told me a story about an oboist at a neighbouring music school whose career had stalled. Thinking she lacked the ability to forge a career as a professional player, her tutor recommended that she consider other options. She had an idea for a website business so, while continuing her musical training, she set up her company. It flourished and she did well. But what amazed and delighted her tutor was that her music dramatically improved.

'That's what makes this such a tough business,' Kemp concluded. 'You imagine the way to get better is to hammer away at it for hours. But it's more oblique than that. You can't do great creative work if you don't have a life to bring to it – and to the people you work with. It's about responding to other people. If it's all about you – then it's not really interesting.'

In recent years, a wellspring of innovation in modern theatre has come from new collaborative companies of artists – actors, writers, designers, musicians, puppeteers – who devise work together. The Canadian director, Robert Lepage, speaks openly about how he creates his plays: bringing, he says, nothing but his ability to listen to what his collaborators contribute. Choreographer, Twyla Tharp attributes huge successes in her career to her collaboration with audiences. When you try to unpick who did what in many of these theatre groups – Punchdrunk, Kneehigh, Handspring, Complicite – you find yourself in the middle of a maze with no centre. It isn't that everyone is doing each other's work – each brings unique expertise and discipline – but the cross-reactivity is so dense that it becomes impossible to map. None of this is possible where someone is trying to win.

Groups like this flourish by finding and developing outstanding partners. Many work together for years because finding the right blend of people who appreciate the challenge of working together can be so rewarding – but also so difficult. The impresarios and producers who understand how to blend talents, cultivate and nurture the participants they depend on: a flourishing flock of chickens is hard to construct and requires years of trust, mistakes, shared failure and shared success. Ask any CEO what their biggest worry is and they'll say: the people. Not because they can't find great people – but because the competitive mindset of almost everyone they recruit militates against their being great team members. Companies know that they derive greater creativity and innovation from teamwork – but what, they wonder, makes a great team?

To answer that question required collaboration too. A team of researchers from Carnegie Mellon University and MIT started with individual intelligence tests that show that there is such a thing as 'general cognitive ability'; in other words, if you're good at one thing, you're very likely to be pretty good at other things. And that general cognitive ability is a reliable predictor of a wide range of outcomes, including success at work, even life expectancy. But was there, the research team wondered, a group equivalent: a way of distinguishing very able teams? – And, if so, what were their characteristics?

They brought together sixty-three participants and set them an architectural design test. When the volunteers worked on the project alone, their general intelligence turned out to be a good predictor of their performance. Next, they were put into groups – but here it turned out that neither the average general intelligence of the group members overall *nor* the intelligence of the single smartest group member proved a good predictor of performance. You couldn't design great teams just using the maths of intelligence tests. Moreover, factors such as group cohesion, motivation and satisfaction didn't seem to explain the high-achieving groups either.

What made the crucial difference were three things. First, there seemed to be a strong correlation between group achievement and social sensitivity. This was measured by the 'Reading the Mind in the Eyes' test (the same one that measured empathy loss in the testosterone experiments). The groups whose members were better at reading faces, that were more responsive to one another, turned out to be more productive. Second, the under-achieving teams had a few members who dominated the conversation – divas, soloists, owls. But the teams in which every member made a more equal contribution performed better. Finally, the teams that had more women did better, too.

What the research concluded was that it might be easier to raise the intelligence of a group than an individual. You don't need to add super-brainy people – that would just give you the problem of the Purdue chickens. But you do need to find team members who contribute their best but don't dominate, who are alert and responsive to everyone in the group and eager to hear what they bring. You also need to have enough women.

Collaboration matters because we know we do better work, find more ideas and craft more solutions when we work collectively. It's hard because so little in our culture trains, rewards or even seems to notice great collaboration. Yet Uri Alon, David Ring, Adele, Fou Ts'ong, the inventions of Boston Scientific, of Punchdrunk and the productivity nurtured so carefully now within Vijay Kuchroo's lab all testify to our innate capacity to do phenomenal work together. That talent lies within us, naturally, always, inherent. What we need is to build the structures and processes, the habits and relationships that draw it out and make it grow.

On the fourth Thursday of each November, Americans sit down to Thanksgiving dinner. Almost every table will sport a roast turkey and, alongside it, a dish of cranberry sauce. One of my earliest childhood memories features a sparkling pressed-glass plate holding the translucent red log of cranberry jelly. Every year, we would carefully extract it so that it emerged intact like a glistening, wobbly jewel, rimmed by the indentations of the can that had held it.

Ocean Spray cranberry sauce is one of America's most iconic products: sold to sixty-two million homes and made from a hard, bitter berry that grows only in North America. Like Thanksgiving itself, the cranberry represents the triumph of creativity and daring over adversity. But the story of Ocean Spray, the company responsible for the fruit's ubiquity, challenges many of America's most ideological notions of competition.

The cranberry sauce of my childhood was first invented by Marcus Urann, a Maine lawyer who had invested heavily in cranberry bogs. The berry is one of just three indigenous North American fruits (Concord grapes and blueberries were the others) and had first been cultivated on Cape Cod.[37] Observing that the sandy winds of the Massachusetts Bay helped the vines to flourish, farmers in the 1820s started to layer their bogs with sand in order to produce a crop large and reliable enough to market. In the 1890s, Urann started buying up bogs but he found that he was producing more fruit than he could sell. Since the berries didn't keep very well, he looked for a way to use up the surplus and is credited with being the first farmer to can cranberry sauce. Although many jokes are made of this rare example of a lawyer's creative pragmatism, his example was swiftly copied until Urann found himself in head-to-head competition with two other farmers: Elizabeth Lee and A. D. Makepeace. At this point, Urann did something even more creative: instead of competing with them, he invited them to join forces with him.

The name Ocean Spray was Urann's but the company was run by all three farmers along the Rochdale Principles: the governing ideas, pioneered in the 1840s, that led to the creation of the cooperative movement in the UK. Central to Ocean Spray was the idea that farmers owned the business together, and that the goal of the organization was to preserve the value of their farms and the crops they produced. Instead of competing to become the biggest or most powerful, each farmer would help the others by sharing resources and knowhow to expand and enrich the market for them all.

From its inception until his death in 1963, Urann operated as General Manager with Makepeace as treasurer; fundamental to the business throughout its history was the principle that the growers were the owners and ultimate managers of the business. Urann's legal expertise turned out to be particularly helpful. By cooperating with his erstwhile competitors, the new company attracted the attention of the Department of Justice. Urann and his colleagues reached an agreement according to which they agreed not to run the company on competitive principles: the goal was not to eliminate other cranberry growers, merely to co-market and co-develop new products. A depression in agricultural prices during the First World War generated widespread support for farmers and in 1922, the Capper-Volstead Act gave cooperatives like Urann's additional protection for their organizational structure. They weren't combining in order to fix prices, but to develop and co-market their goods.

The sauce business thrived, as did the cranberry farms. The 1960s and 1970s saw an explosion in product innovation, with the creation of bottled cranberry juice cocktail and its many extensions: Cranapple, Cranprune, Crangrape. Global sales took off after research in the *Journal of the American Medical Association* showed that cranberry juice reduced urinary tract infections.[38] Subsequent research indicated that proanthocyanidins in the berries prevents plaque formation and periodontal disease, while regular, long-term consumption of the juice can kill *Helicobacter pylori*, which causes ulcers and stomach cancer.

That the bitter little fruit had miraculous health-giving properties was, of course, sheer good luck, unknown and unforeseen by Urann and his confederates. But the way they chose to run their business was their own deliberate design and choice. Putting cooperation at the heart of the company has had consequences for every aspect of its success.

'We now have 750 farmer owners and I work for them,' asserts CEO Randy Papadellis. 'I sometimes think of myself as the Chief Alignment Officer because that's what I spend all my time doing: keeping everyone's interests aligned.'

Those 750 farmers elect thirteen board members, who hire the chief executive. Votes are proportional to a farm's size and there has, on occasion, been some tension between the big farmers and the smaller farmers. But the alignment that Papadellis talks about is firmly focused on building and protecting the long-term profitability of every single farm, large or small.

'We don't work for faceless shareholders,' COO Ken Romanzi insists. 'We work for third-, fourth-, fifth-generation cranberry farmers who want to keep value in their farms healthy. We know them personally; they're our neighbours. And that produces incredible pride in this company: that we aren't just making and selling "stuff": we are using all the creativity we can find to develop and protect the farms, the traditions and the people that depend on them.'

Romanzi isn't a romantic. Before coming to Ocean Spray, he worked for Frito-Lay, where his claim to fame was the launch of jalapeno Fritos. His philosophy then, he said, was that if a product stood still, you just had to put cheese on it. But since Papadellis recruited him, Romanzi has become a vocal champion for the co-op and the farmers whom it serves.

'We promise the farmers that we will take all of their crop, that nothing will be wasted and that we will get the highest possible value for it that we can. We do that by building the Ocean Spray brand and by creating great new products. But then there's this night job we have. We start talking about crop supply, fruit supply, what form the fruit is in. And they can see they do even better if we work on those products together.

'You wouldn't have any of those ideas or discussions if you worked for Coke or Pepsi. You would just beat up on your procurement people to get the lowest price. But we procure from our owners so we aren't trying to drive their prices down but to drive our product values up. This isn't about winners or losers, about top dogs or under dogs.'

Every year, the company's profits are paid as dividends to the owners, who decide how much executives get paid. Papadellis laughs when I ask him about his pay. He's not, he says, paid like the CEO of Pepsi or in the market for yachts or precious gems. But 'I'm paid well enough. The board has done well by all the employees because we do well by them.'

'Until you're in it you don't realize the difference the ownership makes,' Stu Gallagher tells me. His office is full of antique cranberry scoops and spectacular photographs of gleaming red bogs. 'I live around these farmers every day. They are my neighbours and I've coached their kids' sports teams. The whole business is just part of the fabric of your life. You don't feel like that at Nestlé where I used to work. When we go into a new country, we aren't just another faceless American corporate giant; we have a story to tell that people around the world appreciate.

'The time horizon is endless: the children's children. If that was a private-equity company, they're looking at three years. At a public company it's a quarter. It makes my job more satisfying, meeting three or four hundred owners, the grower, the spouse, the kid, the grandchildren: they all come to our annual meetings.'

Three times a year, the executive team hits the road to share news about the business and hear about the crop. This is when farmers who might otherwise be competitors share ideas about how to tackle issues like water shortages, environmental regulation or plant diseases. Ocean Spray's agricultural staff provides everyone with more scientific research than any one farmer could afford. Instead of vying to outdo one another, they share experience from region to region.

At Boston Scientific, John Abele believed that true collaboration was characterized by passionate curiosity, modest confidence and mild obsession. He would be right at home in Ocean Spray's product development, where dedication to the cranberry borders on the religious. Kathy Reilly has spent fifteen years at Ocean Spray, living, breathing, dreaming cranberries.

'Growers come up with great product ideas,' Reilly recalled. 'I was at our annual grower meeting and one of the growers had made their own pressed berry bars – sweet and dried berries pressed together with sauce and sugar – and said their kids love them. It was one of the best things I'd ever tasted. One grower made a salsa. So, now, we have a berry bar in the works and we make a fruit salsa. We can't use all their ideas but we test just about everything that comes our way.'

Working in a sprawling colonial mansion surrounded by cranberry bogs gives the company a relaxed and comfortable atmosphere. This shouldn't be mistaken as laid-back. Every executive I met at Ocean Spray was keenly aware of their responsibility to the owners and to the farms. But I also found an appreciation that creativity and innovation derive from the careful nurturing of relationships and a commitment to the long term. No one can call a meeting before nine a.m., during lunch or after four p.m. In the summer, everyone finishes at lunchtime on Fridays. And no one takes vacation during the harvest.

'It doesn't work without trust,' says Papadellis. 'That trust requires constant communication. Repeated communication. There's a lot of give and take. You can't just focus on a few because the structure requires that everyone counts. I report to the biggest farmers, the smallest farmers and everyone in between. We have to make sure that, at no point, is anyone left behind.'

Papadellis knows from bitter experience that his task isn't simple. He came into the company in 2000 as COO and immediately confronted a crisis. The farmers couldn't agree on the company's direction so the board kept getting thrown out and, in its own turmoil, firing chief executives. The source of so much conflict was an opportunity to sell the business to Pepsi.

'They made a very big play for the company – flying in on corporate jets, making videos about us with Britney Spears, trying to show what a big deal they could do with us. But I thought there was nothing they could do that we couldn't do ourselves. And that keeping the business as a co-op would keep the farmers themselves in a much stronger position. They would never have to compete for the management's attention.'

In what Papadellis laughingly calls 'a resounding 50.8 per cent vote' the farmers decided to keep the co-op. The real heroes, he says, were the 49.2 per cent who agreed to support the management plan: 'They gave us the space to execute and it worked.' Conflict subsided as all the farmers agreed to give Papadellis's plans a chance. Fundamentally, he concludes, for all the turmoil of the turnaround, the co-op structure had worked. It didn't mean there wasn't conflict, but it made everyone appreciate that any solution had to deliver not for the few but for everyone.

The experience of keeping so many stakeholders firmly connected hasn't just made the business creative and profitable. It has also taught everyone at Ocean Spray to become nimble collaborators. The company has strategic partners everywhere, with Nestlé in the US, Gerber in Europe, Heinz in Australia. Working for years in a company where no one person, department, group or investor can be the superstar has imbued Ocean Spray with the habit of sharing that underpins its success: $2 billion revenue in 2012 and a compounded growth rate, over the last decade, of 5 per cent per year. The company simply couldn't achieve this if it tried to sort farmers into winners and losers or if Papadellis and his team lost sight of the good of the whole. It is engineered to avoid surplus and waste. There can't be any picking of winners and there's no incentive for lying or fraud. The very structure of the business makes a Matthew effect not just impossible but undesirable. For anyone to win, everyone has to win.

That the company focuses on the long term isn't, of course, only a function of its structure. The cranberry business runs, necessarily, on a long cycle – it can take up to five years and $60,000 per acre to create a new, productive bog – and that militates against short-term thinking. But so too does the design of a company where 75 per cent of owners must agree before any change can be made to the ownership structure.

Cooperatives – worker-owned but not worker-managed – are widespread in agriculture, though not (as we'll see) as widespread as they could, and perhaps should, be. And not all co-ops have proved wholly resistant to the siren call of Wall Street. Diamond Walnut Growers started as a co-op at the same time as Ocean Spray but went public in 2005, since when it has been riddled with accounting issues.

On the other hand, in every country and in every industry, cooperatives are among some of the world's most successful businesses, employing over a billion people. The world's largest cooperative, Mondragon, runs banks, schools and universities. It also manufactures computer chips, sheet metal, bicycles and washing machines, as well as operating business consulting services and retail outlets. The seventh-largest company in Spain, the co-op has proved strikingly resilient throughout the country's economic turmoil. In 2012, the *Financial Times* awarded it a 'Boldness in Business' prize for driving change; sixty years after it was started, the company's business structure was deemed innovative and inspiring.

The success of Mondragon has worked to the benefit of the entire Basque region of Spain, where it is based. But the Emilia-Romagna region of Italy may be an even more striking example of the social and economic power of cooperatives. Eight thousand co-ops are based here, employing three out of every four people and generating a GDP per capita that is 30 per cent above the national average. People within the co-ops don't just work together; the co-ops cooperate with each other. To make clothing, one co-op may specialize in cutting, one in dyeing and another in embroidery, and by working together they can protect the expertise for which the region has become famous. The same cluster model applies to world-famous products like Ferrari, Lamborghini and parmesan cheese.[39]

In the United Kingdom, 13.5 million people belong to 6,000 co-ops, which are responsible for turnover of £35 billion. Since the economic crisis, they have significantly outperformed the economy as a whole, growing by 19.6 per cent since 2008 while the economy overall has shrunk by 1.7 per cent.[40] And it's striking that the Co-operative Bank, which had, after the banking scandals, picked up millions of new customers, came unstuck when it adopted strategies identical to its traditional competitors.

While there are a host of differences between co-ops little and large around the world, they all derive from the fundamental aim of creating business structures in which the Matthew effect is impossible or irrelevant, where success is focused on the many not the few, and where everyone has both a stake and a responsibility. They are structured specifically to eliminate the perverse incentives of head-to-head tournament competition. This does not make them uncompetitive in the sense that they cannot make their way in the world. It does make them uncompetitive in the sense that nobody's success requires the failure of their colleagues. They operate with a promise, not a threat.

For Randy Papadellis, who worked for global, publicly traded packaged-goods companies before going to Ocean Spray, what strikes him as remarkable about the co-op structure isn't so much its historic legacy as its profound fit for the future.

'I think we may be where other firms need to get to. We have a longer horizon, not focused on quarterly returns but on passing on to the next generation. We are tied into a much longer-term view than most companies. We take a more holistic view where we are committed to making sure that everyone we work with – everyone – benefits. No one gets left out. We all win or no one wins. And that's not just us, our generations, but the generations of the future.'

In South Carver, Massachusetts, the 2012 cranberry harvest was particularly fine. Over several warm days in October, Gary Garretson watched with paternal pride as aquatic harvesters roamed across the water of his flooded bog. He'd made these machines himself: floating watercraft with what look like egg-beaters at the prow, gentling stirring the water to shake the berries off the vine. As they floated to the top, the pond took on a brilliant red sheen and large wooden brooms brushed them towards the shore.

'It's been fabulous. I think we are the perfect model, from the 5-acre grower to the 2,000-acre grower, we are all under the same umbrella. I can't fathom anyone who thinks that entering into a contractual agreement with big producers will be more beneficial than dealing with their brethren collectively over time. Pooling my money and my fruit with other growers, we increased the marketing ability and opportunities for success for my farm.'

With his sprightly white walrus moustache, Garretson stands watching as his fruit accumulates on the water. His fleece sports the logo for his farm; his chest-high waders are labelled Ocean Spray. He clearly feels no contradiction between the two.

'Here you are all treated the same whether large or small. Everyone at Ocean Spray is just top notch – they have our best interests at heart. It is difficult to get 750 people to agree on anything – it is a real challenge to be doing that. But as messy as it can be, it is the fairest and the best deal for farmers and our success is their success.'

In their different ways, Ocean Spray, Mozilla, W. L. Gore, Morning Star, TechShop, Eileen Fisher, Gripple and the huge range of cooperatives and employee-owned firms around the world represent paradigms of successful collaboration. They demonstrate that our instincts and talents to work together are just as strong and more productive than the competitive instincts that pit us against each another. In addition, these companies are notable for being strikingly well run by chief executives who are not lavishly rewarded and whose names and faces are not broadcast across the media. The success of these organizations is systemic, not heroic.

The most creative teams, labs, groups and companies all represent, in miniature, societies that energetically develop trust and respect between people. Their strength and energy comes not from picking winners but from providing a broad base of support for everyone to grow, give and connect. Just as Finnish education is determined to help every single student, creative teams find courage in working with colleagues who offer generous support, challenge, insight and human connection. In place of the tight focus on competitive goals that narrows thinking, constrains imagination and infuses work with fear, people are creative when they can stand tall, scan the widest horizon and dare to explore.

PART THREE:
THE BUSINESS OF WINNING

7. CLONE WARS

While many young engineers aspire to retirement at forty, Andy Hildebrand got his wish. He had spent eighteen years working on signal processing in the oil industry. Sending sound waves down below the earth's surface produced reflections which could, when correlated correctly, map what the waves hit and where. For companies like Exxon, this was a critical tool for identifying oil reserves. That the stakes were high taught Hildebrand an invaluable lesson.

'It really gave me a sense of quality that is very demanding,' he told me. 'Coming from the oil industry, where people are going to spend maybe 300 million, 600 million dollars drilling wells – you can't afford software that fails. So I have this mentality that software just shouldn't fail.'

Free to pursue his dreams at the age of forty, Hildebrand took himself off to study music composition at Rice University. He wanted to write music for symphony orchestras but it's tough to find full orchestras ready and willing to try out a neophyte's student compositions so Hildebrand started playing with synthesizers. His software expertise came into play, of course.

'At the time, synth playing was onerous because of limited memory which meant that you could only do loops. So I reprocessed the synth so that you couldn't hear the repeats. A friend said a lot of people needed that – you could make money doing it but I knew there wasn't a lot of money in music. I was just having fun.'

Hildebrand gives the impression of someone for whom having fun is a pretty serious motivator. Bearded, relaxed and unpretentious, he has a talent for dabbling – and for listening.

'So I'd already sold a couple of pieces of software and one day I was having lunch with my sales rep. And his wife was with us and he happened to mention that it would be really nice if I could write something that would make it sound like she sang in tune. It was a pretty awkward moment; everyone just looked down at their food. But I knew right away how you'd solve that problem. I just didn't think anyone would be interested.'

In 1997, Hildebrand didn't have anything new to take to a trade show so, hearkening back to the lunchtime conversation, he decided he'd write the software for the sales rep's wife. No focus groups, no market research. Just having fun.

'They ripped it out of my hands!' he remembers with a laugh. 'I had a demo booth and I'd pick an out-of-tune vocal and, in real time, it would be in tune. People were astounded. Not that it hadn't been done before; others had tried and failed because the software didn't work well enough. I guess there weren't a lot of well-educated signal processing experts in the music industry! But this did work well. That's why it was a big hit – because you couldn't tell, it sounded natural and there were no glitches.'

'Dr Andy' as he's now known in the trade, had created Auto-Tune, the world's best-selling audio plug-in, which can shift the pitch of a sung note without changing the timing of the perform-ance. That means music producers can eliminate bad, fluffed or wrong notes; it also means that they can change voices overall. Auto-Tune makes it possible for singers to produce recordings that are pitch perfect without costly and exhausting retakes. If you think that your favourite singers have miraculously flawless voices, it isn't a miracle; it's Dr Andy's software.

Almost every Top 40 single played on the radio uses Auto-Tune. It sprang to fame in Cher's best-selling song 'Believe'; it gave Kanye West's 'Heartbreak' its plangent tone and has been used by artists as varied as The Black Eyed Peas, Bon Iver, Miley Cyrus, Eminem, Jamie Foxx, Faith Hill, Wyclef Jean, Kid Rock and Billy Joel. Many performers are quite cagey about whether they use it or not, pre-ferring to sustain their myth of perfection. Because, ever since its debut, Auto-Tune has been considered by many music lovers to be a form of cheating.

Hildebrand himself is jovially unconcerned by these accusations. Being able to correct the odd duff note radically altered the eco-nomics of recording as it now required fewer takes and less perfectionism. And using Auto-Tune, he says, is no different from his wife using make-up to look her best, or using Photoshop to eliminate red eye in photographs. Sure, some people go further and use it to erase the vocal equivalents of lines, crow's feet and double chins, but who cares? If the music gets better, surely that's what it's all about. In the digital age, music is an industry characterized by artifice and Auto-Tune is just one of the many tools it uses.

Nevertheless, and much to Hildebrand's delight, Auto-Tune soon became a *cause célèbre*. Nothing sparked comment, or sales, more than Jay-Z's song 'Death of Auto-Tune', which suggested that Auto-Tune ripped the heart out of music, replacing it with all that was phoney and crass.

The indie pop quartet Death Cab for Cutie took the debate one step further by sporting blue ribbons at the Grammys as their protest against the banal uniformity that Auto-Tune produced. The flaws and idiosyncracies of the human voice, they insisted, were what gave it character and shouldn't be airbrushed out of existence. The most meaningful argument against the plug-in, however, came from R&B artist Ne-Yo, who endorsed its utility – but also felt it was being misused.

'Auto-Tune was meant to be a safety net,' he argued. 'You sing and sing and sing and you don't want to blow your throat out trying to do the same note a thousand different times. So you sing it a few good times and you let the Auto-Tune catch whatever notes fall out. It's not supposed to be wings; you're not supposed to strap it on your back and jump off the building. Not: I can't sing at all so let's turn Auto-Tune all the way up so that I just sound like Willie the Robot. That's whacked, that's terrible. It takes all the character out of your voice. You hear it on the radio and you go: who is that? Because you have no idea because everybody sounds the same.'[1]

In theory, one of the chief virtues of competition is that it is supposed to motivate people to be creative so that the marketplace is replete with a wide variety of products: something for everyone. The desire to be better, do better and beat the other guys should drive everyone into work determined to invent fabulous new goods and services that will attract customers and lower prices. Consumers should benefit because they have more to choose from – for less.

But this new technology allowed anybody and everybody to populate the airwaves with music that was virtually indistinguishable. It didn't make music better, it made it all the same. Reality TV stars like Kim Kardashian, Heidi Montag, Michaele Salahi, Angelina Pivarnick and even the desperately unmusical Rebecca Black could aspire to musical careers of sorts, only because of Auto-Tune; singers like Ke$ha, Amelia Lily and Cheryl Cole don't even seem to try to differentiate themselves from each other. Even Andy Hildebrand, who vigorously defends his plug-in, accepts that it has changed people's idea of what music is.

'People never heard the mistakes before,' he says. 'Lots of people didn't sing in tune at all – think of Marilyn Monroe singing "Happy Birthday" to JFK! But, now, you cannot possibly sing out of tune. You just won't get away with it. So it has changed how people listen and what they expect to hear.'

People have become accustomed to flawless, homogenous music and so, mostly, that's what they get. The problem is that what used to make each singer unique has now, increasingly, been carefully and fastidiously removed. No wonder Auto-Tune is sometimes called audio botox.

Although the problem may be exacerbated by software, it isn't, at heart, a technology problem. The theory may be that competition drives creativity but the reality is that it produces clones. Because creativity and innovation are hard – why bother? It's so much easier to spot a success and then just copy it. That's one of the themes in Charlie Kaufman's brilliant film *Adaptation*, in which the protagonist, played by Nicholas Cage, accosts screenwriting guru Robert McKee (as impersonated by the actor Brian Cox). McKee's book *Story* and the non-stop seminars that he conducts around the world aim to teach anyone and everyone how to write a Hollywood filmscript. There's a formula (largely derived from Aristotle), a method (every scene must have a beat) and some standard tricks. In the movie, Nicholas Cage's character only succeeds when producing a script that cleaves limpet-like to the tired rules of the McKee system.

McKee isn't the only formula-hawker; Syd Field will tell writers pretty much what needs to go on every page, while *Save the Cat!* – 'the last book on screenwriting you'll ever need' – tells you

'how to make your story like everything else out there only different'. Aspiring writers lap these up.

In *Adaptation*, this kind of thinking is a joke; in real life, it's tedious. Kate Leys is one of Britain's leading script-development editors. She has worked on some of the most successful British films of recent years – *Four Weddings and a Funeral*, *Trainspotting*, *The Girl with the Pearl Earring* – and with a wide range of writers and producers, from veterans who are too well known to admit their debt to her, to aspirants just starting out.

'Success breeds clones. That's exactly what happens. People making commissioning decisions default to clones. They want replicants! And we in the audience feel this happening; it feels like everyone is making the same decisions.'

It would be hard to find anyone with a more wry sense of humour about the film business. But somehow, Leys has resisted the cynicism that pervades the business and continues to marvel at its ability to throw up insanely bad copycat ideas.

'I was once sent a script called *Four Funerals and a Wedding!*' Leys roars with laughter. 'You do think: bless your heart, to have misunderstood so profoundly makes you almost endearing. It does happen!'

Even politicians fall into the trap, as when David Cameron solemnly urged British producers to make more movies like *The King's Speech*. In fact, what audiences want is not just more of the same but fresh, creative works that respond to and reflect their moods, times, preoccupations. And these keep changing.

'When I worked at Film4,' Leys recalled, 'I remember coming into work after the Labour election landslide and looking at the slate in front of us and we were all thinking: the world has changed; we need to rethink this stuff. What worked yesterday won't work tomorrow. The *only* way to stack the odds is to see it as a risk. If you want to play safe, decision-making becomes conservative and becomes cloning. But you have to stand on quite a distant hill to see that happening.'

Few decision-making executives in the film industry last long enough to gain that perspective, the average tenure of a studio head of production being just eighteen months.[2] So, while smart, imaginative, creative people might like to take risks, they rarely seize the opportunity to do so. In part, Leys says, this is because too much money is on the table.

'Studio film execs are looking for exactly the same thing you or I would be looking for. They want original, offbeat, quirky stuff; strong voices, great stories, big ideas. It's what they do with those scripts when they get them that goes wrong. Creativity is about risk, and very large amounts of money are about *not* risk. So the moment the spend is agreed, everyone around the money begins to panic. A whole lot of people start to ask questions, like: is it really, really going to work? Will people really, really get this? Is it definitely good? Shall we change it a bit? Shall we take out this weird bit, and that risqué bit, and the very bleak ending? It can bland itself out in a matter of weeks. And then it reverts to formula.'

But of course sometimes the idea wasn't even fresh to begin with. Hence two *Anchorman* movies, three *Spider-Man* movies, five *Pirates of the Caribbean*, six *Resident Evils*, seven *Star Wars*, eleven *Star Treks*, twelve *Friday the 13th*s and a peculiar rash of penguin movies: *Happy Feet* and *Happy Feet Two*, *Mr. Popper's Penguins*, *March of the Penguins*, *The Pebble and the Penguin* and *Surf's Up*. The film business may be competitive but it's alarmingly easy to go to a multiplex with twenty-four screens and find nothing you want to see.

In their quest for a sure thing, many executives have been persuaded that their safest option isn't to make decisions at all – but to use algorithms instead. The premise behind Epagogix software is that enough data derived from previous box-office successes creates the capability to predict the next ones. The software can rate explosions, violence, plot turns, love scenes, car chases and quirky characters. Of course, with the technology comes the same problem that Auto-Tune provoked: tested using the same tools, the movies all turn out strikingly similar products. In the summer of 2013, many consumers couldn't remember which explosive blockbusters they'd seen and which they'd missed. Box-office returns were down, perhaps because, if you'd seen one movie, you felt you'd seen all the rest.

You might expect that the relatively lower costs of television would make a wider range of creativity more feasible. But you'd be sorely mistaken.

'Why does BBC One have three medical drama series running *all year*?' asks Archie Tait. 'When you add up *Casualty* (fifty-two weeks of the year), *Holby City* and *Doctors*, that's a massive chunk of the drama budget gone, right there. So there's very little room or budget for manoeuvre or for taking risks.'

A seasoned television executive, Tait has worked on dozens of TV dramas and drama series. The economics of production, he argued, require that any viable company have a recurring series of some kind – in his case it was *Morse* – to cover the overheads of the business. Only once that was secure was there any chance of doing something different. One of Tait's most memorable productions, *Chimera*, caused shock and amazement when it appeared to kill off every single one of its characters in the opening episode. So radical a departure from format, he says, just wouldn't be feasible now.

'Greg Dyke – who broadcast it – loved it! But now a broadcaster would say that was a slap in the face to the audience. Because broadcasters want to ingratiate themselves with audiences and not surprise them. In part, that's because they're all using the same market research that asks people what they want – and they can only answer with what they know. Most people have no other way to articulate their desires.'

What Tait calls the 'Downton effect' explains the sudden ubiquity of costume drama from *The Bletchley Circle* and *Spies of Warsaw* to *Parade's End*, and *Blandings*, which Tate describes as 'the broad comic *Downton*'. Producers and broadcasters copy style but they don't really rise to the challenge when they see something extraordinary.

'Take *Mad Men*. It may make broadcasters think setting things in the 1950s is okay now but all they do is produce something like *The Hour*, which is a soap in *Mad Men*'s clothing. It has none of the ambition that *Mad Men* has in taking on big and deep psychological issues, national ideas about how people think and behave. We just copy the way it looks.'

The ubiquity of formats – cooking shows, bakery programmes, reality TV and talent contests – is partly explained by the degree to which broadcasters spot a success and then just copy it. It's cheaper to keep an audience than build a new one so as long as a programme gets viewers, it's economical to renew. I was involved in commissioning the first series of *MasterChef* for the BBC in 1988; I was incredulous, on returning to the UK thirteen years later, to find it still on our television screens.

Formats persist because of the structure of the industry itself. The independent producers of these shows are usually paid only just what they cost to make – sometimes even less. The only way that they, and their companies, can make a profit and stay in business is to sell the format around the world. Simon Cowell's production company, Syco, can make as much (or more) money by selling the format for his talent contests than from the shows themselves. The same goes for shows like *The Renovation Game, I Hate My Body, Jeopardy!, I'm a Celebrity . . ., Big Brother, Who Wants to Be a Millionaire?* and *Secrets of Shoplifters*. Once an audience is established for the shows, it's easier for schedulers and cheaper for producers to keep them running, around the world, indefinitely. There is no financial mileage in producing something fresh and original that can't be endlessly repackaged and resold. But when I asked Tait whether this could ever produce (or find) another Dennis Potter, he replied with, first, a stunned silence – perhaps he was amazed anyone remembered – and then a loud guffaw.

'No sequel! No format! No franchise! Are you kidding? I show *The Singing Detective* or *Pennies from Heaven* to students and their jaws drop. They have never seen anything like it!'

Tait concedes that some identical programming can emerge coincidentally from a shared sense of the zeitgeist. Two series about department stores, *The Paradise* and *Mr Selfridge*, came out too closely together to have copied one another. Just as scientists around the world may suddenly feel the time is ripe to solve a particular problem, and Alexander Graham Bell and Elisha Gray filed patents for the telephone on the same day, so TV producers may separately identify and pursue projects that feel like they will touch a nerve. But they are very much more likely to do so if they come roughly from the same kinds of backgrounds.

In the 1980s, when I was working for the BBC, Margaret Thatcher deregulated British television. Channel 4 was given over to independent producers, while ITV and the BBC were forced to source 25 per cent of its output from them. In an awkward and temporary alliance, the libertarian right hoped to create a free market for production businesses that would disrupt the BBC, while the multicultural left dreamed that a more open industry would attract a more diverse range of people, from different backgrounds, ethnicities, with varied tastes and life experiences. The 'cosy duopoly' of the BBC and ITV, mostly staffed by Oxbridge graduates, would be shattered and all kinds of exciting new talent would rush in to service an open market.

That wasn't what happened. Although for a brief period a thousand small production houses bloomed, populated by writers, artists, psychologists, journalists and social workers, over time the businesses consolidated and the same kinds of people with remarkably uniform tastes rose to the top.

We should not be so surprised by this. Our brains have a distinct preference for the familiar. The human brain is lazy; rather than process information afresh with each encounter, it prefers to look for matches, indicators of a known quantity not requiring scrutiny. This is a highly efficient shortcut but it has a catch. What is most familiar to us – is us. So we prioritize and feel better about people like ourselves, books like those we've already read, music we've already heard. There's simply less neurological demand exerted by those things roughly similar to what we already know – so they make us feel safer and more secure. This is the neurological foundation of bias.[3]

Romantically, this affinity bias explains why there's an overwhelming statistical likelihood that people marry others who have roughly the same height, body shape, age, hair colour, eye colour and background. It's why we settle in neighbourhoods mostly populated with people like ourselves who have kids more likely to attend the schools we choose for our own children. We aren't comprehensively homogenous but we are neurologically biased in favour of those very like ourselves. So we can't be terribly surprised when film and TV companies of similar people make strikingly similar choices. Creativity requires divergence but ostensibly creative industries embrace convergence with a vengeance.

Competition has given consumers years' worth of highly formulaic detective stories, medical dramas, game shows, talent contests and reality TV programmes and endless musical wallpaper. But maybe it doesn't matter; it's just entertainment. Yet the same patterns endlessly repeat themselves in other competitive arenas. Political campaigns, working from the same or similar market research, target the same voters and ignore the rest, even though a democracy is supposed to engage everyone. Once Apple brought out its iPhone, every other telephone manufacturer scrambled to come up with something similar – some so similar they got sued. When the iPad came out, the same pattern repeated itself with quick copies that, like HP's TouchPad, were almost as swiftly withdrawn because they had absolutely nothing new, additional or better to offer.

Nowhere is this cloning compulsion more expensive than in the development of new drugs. While pharmaceutical companies endlessly complain about the high cost of producing new drugs, the truth is that, despite increasing research and development spending by 12.3 per cent every year since 1970, these businesses aren't any more innovative now than they were fifty years ago.[4] Despite flurries of mergers, acquisitions, de-mergers and restructurings, the rate of production of new drugs has proved surprisingly constant, creating what everyone both in the industry, and in the world of academic science, regards as a profound innovation problem. This is because the drug companies concentrate on 'me-too' drugs.

A me-too drug duplicates the action of an existing drug but some minor alteration allows it to be marketed as though it were a completely new therapy. So Tagamet (cimetidine), Zantac (ranitidine), Pepcid (famotidine) and Axid (nizatidine) are all brand names for histamine H2-receptor antagonists, which means that they all treat peptic ulcers in fundamentally the same way. Any new drug that comes out – think particularly of Viagra or Prozac – is invariably followed by a clone that is different enough to need FDA approval, a patent and to be marketed as though it were different – while bestowing virtually no therapeutic improvement whatsoever. The goal of these drugs is often to circumvent patent expiration or to cash in on a new market pioneered by a competitor. There is no requirement that the 'new' treatment be different, only that it prove superior to a placebo.

Omeprazole was a heartburn drug produced by AstraZeneca and which, in 2002, was about to lose its patent. Generating some $5 billion a year, such a loss prompted a great deal of so-called innovation, leading in 2001 to the introduction of esomeprazole, one of the best-selling drugs in both the US and UK. The two drugs were basically the same, with the marginal difference that the molecular structure of the newer drug is a mirror-image of the old one. Complex molecules can exist in left- and right-handed forms and all that AstraZeneca did was swap a right-handed pill for a left-handed one. There was one big difference though: the new pill was more expensive. Ten times more expensive.[5]

Classic economic theory argues that not only will competition offer more choice – but that competition will also bring the price down. But that doesn't seem to be the impact of the me-too drugs. Research suggests that drugs described by the FDA as having 'little or no therapeutic gain' enter the market at the same price as the old drug in the US and at about twice the price in some other markets. Other studies of anti-arthritic pain-relievers showed exactly what shouldn't happen: efficacy was *negatively* correlated with price – but toxicity was positively correlated with price. The more expensive clones were less effective and more dangerous.[6] The stomach ulcer treatment Tagamet went *up* in price when its clone, Zantac, entered the market; and both drugs continued to go up in price when more clones – Pepcid and Axid – came in too.[7]

Price isn't the only problem. As always in competitive environments, sharing and trust are predictable casualties. That pharmaceutical companies work on drugs that are so similar means that they fiercely guard the data collected about clinical trials. Competition is always the reason given why they can't publish this material – they don't want to give anything away to their rivals. Were they not racing neck and neck down exactly the same narrow alleyway, of course, this would not be such an easy excuse and the open publication of data would make for significant improvements in patient safety. Instead the industry has become notorious for its reluctance to share any data, good or bad, that might leave patients, doctors and funding institutions wiser and safer.

Moreover, while the differences between these drugs may be minuscule, they still take time, attention and research resources. And while the drug companies are loath to release data about how much they spend and where, public data on the number of subjects in clinical tests suggests that fully 80 per cent of R&D spending goes on products that do not offer any significant therapeutic improvement.[8] Selling more clones, instead of finding new treatments, represents a gigantic opportunity cost: time, effort, imagination, creativity and scientific knowhow devoted to me-too drugs that make no impact on human health.[9] At the same time, the pipeline for new antibiotics is running dry, a problem so severe that Britain's Chief Medical Officer, Dame Sally Davies, has asked that it be tabled as a national emergency. Arguing that this danger represents a greater threat than terrorism, she maintained that "If we don't take action, then we may all be back in an almost nineteenth-century environment where infections kill us as a result of routine operations.'

While drug companies just try to copy each other, failing to lead the innovation the world needs, they also studiously avoid work on so-called 'orphan diseases': conditions whose sufferers aren't numerous enough to constitute a major market. Since each orphan disease afflicts a small number of people, you might think they didn't really matter. But when you add all these diseases together, they afflict one out of every ten people. Copycat drugs don't discriminate: they fail big markets and small ones alike.

'Our priorities are tilted by marketplace imperatives,' Bill Gates told the Royal Academy of Engineering, surprised to discover a 'flaw in the pure capitalistic approach'. In humanitarian terms a malaria vaccine is the biggest need but it gets virtually no funding.

From a doctor's perspective, this presents two problems: for some diseases there are no drugs at all while, for others, there are too many and telling them apart is incredibly time-consuming. When patients come in asking for the new clone that they've seen promoted on TV and in magazines, doctors feel a responsibility to proffer an informed response. Trying to make sense of an ever more crowded marketplace of approved and off-label treatments is complicated, eats up time and increases the costs of medical treatment overall.

Copying the competition isn't just uncreative; it can also create a sense of comfort that's misplaced. The mortgage market, prior to the bank bust of 2008, was full of people – home buyers, realtors and lenders – copying what they saw around them. Social competition meant consumers didn't want to be left out – after all, if your neighbour made money buying and flipping houses, you didn't want to be left at the bottom of the pecking order with nothing. Market competition meant all the estate agents and lenders felt the need to pile into a heated market; failing to do so would mean a loss of market share, perhaps a drop in share price, even the loss of a peerage. The competitive desire not to be left out overwhelmed many financiers' rational concerns.

'By 2003,' Michael Sarnoff told me, 'sub-prime lenders were multiplying and everyone knew the loans were just stupid: [lending] to people with terrible credit, no income, occupancy fraud, income fraud . . . They all started throwing wood on the fire in the form of additional lending so you could lend to anybody, to a dead person! The amount of crime in the mortgage industry was just incredible.'

Sarnoff is a staid, sane Midwesterner who worked – and still works – as a chief credit officer at a large Midwest bank. Even after all this time, he's outraged by what his industry has done. But he's also more prepared than many to explain just why no one stopped it.

'Sub-prime was about ripping off poor people,' he told me. 'But here's the thing: to function as a business, we have to employ a sales force. And it was hard to recruit salespeople. There was no way on earth that we could hire, let alone retain, a single good salesperson if we weren't prepared to let them sell sub-prime. They stood to make huge commissions off these deals – of course they wanted to sell them! So what were we supposed to do? Sit on our principles and watch as every salesperson we had walked out the door? To stay competitive, we had to let them sell sub-prime.'

What Sarnoff experienced first hand – the competitive pressure to offer salespeople whatever they wanted to sell, no matter how stupid – was replicated right through the food chain. At Countrywide, official company policy declared that any loan a competitor offered, the company would match; it didn't matter if it was reckless or extravagant. Ratings agencies, fighting over business (and all using the same software), didn't want to turn anything down because they'd lose clients to their competitors. Investment banks, packaging up collateralized debt obligations, didn't want to bring too much scrutiny to bear or they'd lose customers. In the heat of an inflamed market, nobody kept a cool head.

That the economic crisis has proved so profound is in part because so much risk was exacerbated by the replication of the same products, the same kinds of debt, in the same kinds of institutions. Classic economic theory turned out to be wrong: a competitive market had not diversified risk but concentrated it. Competition hadn't produced variety but encouraged everyone to do the same thing. When the market crashed, there were no safe havens to run to.

As the markets are increasingly dominated by algorithms, the chances of this kind of amplification only increases. Not only are similar (if not identical) pieces of software used to conduct trading, but analysis of markets may turn out to be more uniform than you might expect. Thanks to algorithms, future news outlets don't need journalists anymore. Narrative Science, a Chicago software company, can take market data, analyse it, structure it and turn it into an article complete with illustrations and graphs. It looks like, but doesn't quite feel like, the real thing. If you've read a story lately that came out of Chicago with no byline, chances are it wasn't written by a person but by a machine. The inherent danger of this model lies in the fact that all of the analysis proceeds from certain assumptions about how markets work, producing a feedback loop that amplifies what it analyses. People reading the articles draw conclusions that lead to trades that produce data that is analysed according to the same instruction that leads to more trades . . . and so on, theoretically for ever. Instead of a functional market in which a wide cross-section of styles, assumptions and attitudes balance one another, algorithms keep doubling down on the same old beliefs, leeching diversity out of the system.

The importance of diversity is easily seen in nature. Right now, the British landscape is being devastated by Chalara dieback, a disease affecting ash trees. In Denmark, the fungal disease has already killed up to 90 per cent of ash trees and experts expect the same impact here. What makes the disease so catastrophic is our lack of biodiversity: most of our ash trees are the same species. Safety and resilience require diversity – but that's just what our landscape and our business environment lack.

Why innovate when you can copy? The irony is, of course, that it feels less risky following the leader than being the leader – even though, as it turns out, it isn't. Convergence feels safer than divergence: people imagine there is safety in numbers. So, after the heady days of sub-prime mortgage and credit default swaps ended with a crash in 2008, many investors were left wandering around a market that felt like a ghost town. Until they stumbled upon a dark corner of the derivatives market that they'd mostly overlooked: the commodities futures market.

This market invested in the future price of food. Before 1999, only those actively involved in growing, producing or selling food products – farmers, millers and companies like Kraft and Nestlé – were allowed, by law, to make big investments in coffee, cocoa, wheat, soybeans, beef and chicken. Goldman Sachs created a derivative that tracked twenty-four raw ingredients – the Goldman Sachs Commodity Index – but mortgages and debt were so much more attractive as investment vehicles that commodity prices stayed relatively stable. In 1999, the law changed; now anyone could take very large positions in commodity markets. So when the tech bubble burst in 2000, suddenly real food looked a lot more interesting than virtual companies, and the commodity index funds attracted a fifty-fold increase in investment.

That was nothing, however, compared to what happened in 2008. With most markets moribund, real food – something people absolutely had to have, where demand was tightly coupled to a growing global population – looked immensely attractive. According to the Congressional testimony of institutional investor Michael Masters, in the first fifty-two trading days of 2008, commodity speculators 'flooded' the markets with $55 billion: an increase in the dollar value of outstanding futures contracts of more than a billion dollars a day. By July, this reached $318 billion.

Fred Kaufman, who has tirelessly researched this new bubble, describes the commodity market as a 'sparkling new casino' and everyone wanted a place at the table.[10] Academics started to publish articles about the new market, and financial publications soon scented which way the wind was blowing. The *Financial Times*, *Global Pensions*, the *Journal of Finance*, the *Journal of Portfolio Management*, the *Journal of Derivatives*, all analysed, dissected and fuelled the new trend. 'You had people who had no clue what commodities were all about suddenly buying commodities,' one

Department of Agriculture analyst told Kaufman, but that didn't matter to the brokers. Everybody wanted a part of the new me-too investment vehicle.

These clones didn't bring prices down. 'The more the price of food commodities increases,' Kaufman wrote, 'the more money pours into the sector and the higher the prices rise.' Desperate to find a place that could deliver the kinds of returns they all remembered from the go-go days of the building boom, speculators who had no interest in agriculture, or food at all, piled in, outnumbering the true investors four to one.

Commentators noticed food prices going up but blamed the phenomenon on China (wanting more protein) or the world's growing population. Others said that the price of wheat had skyrocketed because so much had been given over to ethanol production. They were all wrong. Prices weren't rising because real people wanted to eat more or because they wanted to burn greener fuel. A herd of money managers was piling into the same derivatives. Barclays, Deutsche Bank, Pimco, JPMorgan Chase, AIG, all wanted the same products and the same returns.

As food prices started to rise, the New England Complex Systems Institute started mapping their correlations to increasing civil unrest around the world. The result was alarming; it wasn't just British and American households that were feeling the pinch. 'Despite the many possible contributing factors, the timing of violent protests in North Africa and the Middle East in 2011 as well as earlier riots in 2008 coincides with large peaks in global food prices. These observations suggest that protests may reflect not only long-standing political failings of governments, but also the sudden desperate straits of vulnerable populations. If food prices remain high, there is likely to be persistent and increasing global social disruption.'[11]

As Kaufman criss-crossed the world talking to governments, investors, analysts and farmers about the consequences of food derivatives, he grew increasingly furious and distraught.

'The 1936 Agriculture Act limited the degree to which people not working in the industry could invest in it. But, once commodities were deregulated, it opened the door to people treating food as if it weren't food. Derivatives are a classic virtuality – an imaginary construct derived from something else. So food derivatives – which do have a real impact on what real people can afford to eat – became an investment vehicle. Just like mortgage-backed securities made people forget that they represented real homes for real people, food derivatives make people forget they're having an impact on real food prices. But with food it's even more important than your home; it's a matter of life and death. But not for investors. They just think it's virtual food!'

Food, Kaufman realized, had become financialized just as our homes had been. The more people invested in it, the bigger the bubble grew, the more people wanted in. Only this time the endgame didn't make people homeless, it left people hungry.

'If Wall Street concocted a scheme whereby investors bought large amounts of pharmaceutical drugs and medical devices in order to profit from the resulting increase in price, making these essential items unaffordable to sick and dying people, society would be justly outraged,' Michael Masters testified to Congress. 'Why is there not outrage over the fact that Americans must pay drastically more to feed their families?'[12] And why, he might have continued, do we turn a blind eye to the fact that what hurts Americans can kill those who live in less affluent parts of the world?

That the market for food has become so explosive an issue and so dangerous for the world is significantly a function of the concentration of investment in the commodity derivatives. If only one or two institutions or traders were interested in it, we might deride their values but not be threatened by their choices. But with all the major financial institutions – including pension funds – looking for returns off the back of farmers and those seeking to be fed, it seems unlikely that there is anyone in the world who won't feel the impact of this demand shock.

Kaufman doesn't believe this market can be fixed. It's a classic bubble and bubbles come about when everyone competes by doing the same thing. Like many people disgusted by the role that derivatives played in the economic crisis, Kaufman joins the chorus clamouring for more transparency in what remains, to this day, a dark market. Although economists like Alan Greenspan argued that unregulated derivatives markets were safer because of their relative freedom from restraints, their extreme opacity and propensity for disaster proves such confidence ideological and obtuse.

In 2013, as part of the larger attempt to repair their reputation after the scandal surrounding LIBOR (London Interbank Offered Rate) manipulation, Barclays Bank decided it would no longer invest in food derivatives. Whether this was a tacit recognition that doing so was wrong, or a more tactical sense that the market had peaked, no one would say. And while Fred Kaufman was delighted by Barclays' exit, he still argued that the original law, restricting investment in agriculture to those primarily involved in producing food should be reinstated and that the position limits, destroyed in the 1990s, needed to be brought back. In other words, regulation – reverting to old rules – is the only way to curtail the human appetite for imitation.

For pharmaceutical companies, for whom imitation proves so lucrative and yet so stunningly uncreative, the antidotes may be harder to find. Over the last fifty years, these businesses have got bigger and they're now spending in excess of $70 billion a year on R&D, but still they have not improved their ability to innovate. Many industry veterans argue that this is because they have become too big and sclerotic. That, at least, is Jean-Pierre Garnier's excuse – and he should know, having run GlaxoSmithKline for eight years.

'The leaders of major corporations including pharmaceuticals have incorrectly assumed that R&D was scalable, could be industrialized and could be driven by detailed metrics and automation. The grand result: a loss of personal accountability, transparency and the passion of scientists in discovery and development.'

In his own business, Garnier tried hard to restructure research to make it more productive, with questionable results. He hoped that smaller groups would make pharmaceutical research more akin to academic work and inspire the same qualities of dedication and commitment. But, to this day, the company's best-selling drugs remain glucocorticoids, the steroids beloved of athletes. What Garnier faced, and all pharmaceutical companies have to face, is the question implicit in their business: do they exist to maximize shareholder return (which is certainly what Garnier believed) or to discover and develop new medicines? Many in medical research dismiss as nothing more than a myth the idea that drug companies can be both investor-owned businesses and unbiased research and education institutions. Given that a genuinely new drug has such a high chance of failure, costs at least a billion dollars and takes, on average, twelve years to develop, the incompatibility between the two goals becomes obvious. To be prepared to be genuinely innovative requires a gamble on the scale few CEOs will contemplate or survive – at least not while their eyes are firmly focused on the share price.

Some chemists are taking matters into their own hands, quite literally. Lee Cronin has pioneered the use of 3D printers to produce new molecules and treatments for disease. His dream – and it isn't yet a reality – is to do for drug discovery what Apple has done for music: create an open network where anyone and everyone can publish their discoveries and share them.[13] Why shouldn't we, he asks, be able to download and print our own therapies? Whether this is a brilliant theoretical question or turns out to be a profound disrupter of me-too drug development remains to be seen.

What Cronin and others argue, however, is that technology ought to make the kind of innovation drug companies eschew easier and cheaper. After all, it's done that for almost every other industry – why not pharmaceuticals? It is in that context that industry thinkers have turned to open-source development as a possible alternative to corporate research. Software products like the Firefox web browser, Thunderbird email client and Popcorn online video editor are all created by developers who collaborate online for free. Much of the Internet was built like this and some of it continues to be. The reward for participants is the recognition and respect of their peers, combined with the excitement of cutting-edge software development and the knowledge of having contributed to something great. Many engineers contribute in their spare time or are encouraged by their employers to do so because building cool tools is how they develop their expertise.

Diagnosed with a brain tumour, the Italian artist Salvatore Iacanesi hoped to crowd-source his treatment when he hacked and then published all of his medical records online, asking for help and advice from strangers. Receiving over 500,000 responses was, he said, overwhelming; he had to ask his respondents for help organizing and tagging the contributions. Approaching the problem in this way was not, he insisted, anti-medicine or anti-doctor; surgeons removed his tumour. But he believed this was the best way to surface a broad range of knowledge – and to feel more human. The chief benefit of open-source development is that it combines such a divergent (often global) cross-section of people and thinking styles. That they are working for their own delight and generosity elicits more engagement and imagination. Unlike many research executives, open-source developers aren't clocking in, following orders, playing politics. They're doing what they love, to delight peers they respect. Often buried under the steep hierarchies that characterize large organizations, they express their expertise and their humanity by making their contribution.

The quest for new drugs has led to the pioneering of a particular kind of public-private partnership, modelled on open-source software development. One example is the Medicines for Malaria Venture, which posts its challenges, reviews submissions and then selects which project will be funded. Research is outsourced to a network of some 300 scientists at forty institutions, some of which are universities but may also include drug companies and research institutions. At each stage, findings are reviewed and then continued or concluded. Critical to these partnerships is the determination to focus on neglected diseases; they do not exist to create yet more me-too drugs but to confront some of the biggest medical challenges in the world. They've been able to function on lean budgets and to attract a rich cross-section of participants and funding sources.

These partnerships seem more agile, more creative and willing to take on more risk than large pharmaceutical companies. They also move faster and attract a far wider array of people, from doctors with firsthand clinical knowledge of a disease to those with pure academic training. That diversity alone promises higher degrees of creative thinking. But it's too early to tell whether this new ecology of drug development will prove more than a fig leaf behind which the drug companies can hide. They are, at least, a creative attempt to escape the hypnotic attraction of imitation.

That software developers turned to software to develop more software doesn't seem as far a stretch. In 1998, Mozilla was launched as an open platform for software development, specifically

aimed at giving users more choice and greater innovation. The
Mozilla browser – Firefox – had merged the work of 10,000 contributors, has been downloaded over three billion times and is used
on every continent on earth – even Antarctica. The browser pioneered features (like 'Do Not Track') aimed at giving users more
control of their data. When Mozilla launched their mobile phone
operating system, that this was not just another me-too product was
fundamental: 'We're not trying to get in the middle of an operating system fight,' CEO Gary Kovacs insisted. 'What we are trying
to do is be the catalyst to drive more development around the open
web.' Existing phone systems didn't allow users to switch platforms:
if you bought your apps on Apple, they wouldn't go with you
when you moved to Android. But Mozilla's new Firefox OS does
make this possible. The goal, says Kovacs, isn't to steal market
share – but to provoke other companies into giving users the freedom they want.[14]

Mozilla's products are built by developers working all over the
world, from favelas to mansions. But human interaction still matters. Every year Mozilla brings a thousand of its star and developing
engineers together at MozFest. New technology may have made it
possible to work without ever meeting face to face but it hasn't yet
erased our desire to do so. Many of the world's most innovative
businesses work the old-fashioned way: putting people in a building together and watching the sparks fly. For Adam Lowry and Eric
Ryan, the heart of innovation is always human.

'You don't want to outsource your soul! Innovation is completely the heart and soul of everything we do so we all do it, we
all do it together – and we all need each other for it to work.'

Lowry is the most unlikely of detergent mavens. A tall, handsome advertising veteran, he set up Method with his schoolfriend
Eric, because they'd always wanted to work together. Early in 2000,
they couldn't help but notice that everyone was spending more
time and money on their homes than ever before – yet they
cleaned those homes with products that were toxic, stank and were
so ugly they had to be hidden in cupboards. This made no sense.
Why not invent products that were beautiful enough to be left on
display, made from ingredients that smelled great and respected
both the planet and the home? Lowry and Ryan's determination

to forge ahead didn't depend on an absence of competition, far from it: they had only to go into any supermarket to see the ferocious odds stacked against them. But their innovative new business was grounded in an awareness of the way that people, values and lifestyles were changing.

That these two handsome young men wanted to make domestic cleaning products had much going against it. Not just Procter & Gamble, Unilever and a host of multinational behemoths. In a market besotted by virtual businesses like Pets.com and Google, they were proposing a physical product, sold in bricks-and-mortar stores. The men had just $45,000 each, no background in product manufacture and few contacts. What they did have was a burning sense of mission, a belief that jobs should offer people more than just a salary. They weren't interested in motivating people with competition; they thought playing to human altruism – the opposite of competition – would prove more creative and long-lasting.

'Most of us want to know our work creates something positive in the world. If you are in business, you want to feel you're doing something more than just paying the rent. We wanted to build a company with new products, to create work that made people feel they were contributing to something important. Altruism is very motivating.'

'It's not,' Lowry told me, 'that I'm not a competitive person. I went to the Olympics as an alternate for the US sailing team in 2000! But I'm a big believer in not letting the competition – any competition – tell me what to do. I'm completely focused on sustainability. Eric's completely – obsessively – into beautiful design. The most sustainable product without beautiful representation won't fly here. And the most beautiful product that contains toxins, well, that's just shallow.'

After founding the business, the two men hired a CEO whose primary job is to operate the business. They made that choice because they didn't want to jockey for position and neither of them wanted to veer away from their core expertise. Wanting neither power nor the distance that came with it, they didn't believe they could get anyone else to collaborate if they didn't do so too. But just as fundamental as what goes on inside the business is their insistence that what goes on outside matters too.

'We don't steal from our competitors because we don't want what they make. Because they're always doing the old thing and we don't want to end up being like them. I'd rather get my inspiration from the world of art or architecture or walking down the street or talking to people. It's far more rewarding, exciting, inspiring. It's the only way you redefine the game. You put things together in a new way.'

This isn't just rhetoric. One of the first Method products signalled just how audacious and serious the two men were: a condensed laundry detergent.

'We knew that making things small was better for the environment: fewer trucks on the road making fewer journeys,' Ryan recalled. 'So we made small the big idea: we concentrated the detergent three times, which also made it easier to handle and less cumbersome to take home. It was a huge hit. So then Unilever got permission to do Small & Mighty. Then WalMart, P&G, everybody copied it. Warehouse and distribution costs came down. Today, anywhere you go, all the detergents are concentrated. We changed the norm. So our next goal is to change it again.'

Because their competitors instantly copied Method's first innovation, the company had to provide another. Lowry was at pains to point out that this wasn't less risky for the small company but more so. Method had far more at stake: their very existence.

'If you look at P&G, Tide detergent is a $2 billion brand and they make $100 billion. We are nowhere near those revenues! The point is: innovation is riskier for us than for P&G. And yet we take the risk and they don't. We do it from a philosophy that gets us out of bed every morning. It is something we believe in very deeply: radical step-change innovation.'

But wasn't it, I asked them, intensely annoying to find their creativity so instantly and flagrantly copied?

'That's the way you change the world. It showed we were right! It showed we were on to something. We get copied all the time. It just means we have to be really good at coming up with new ideas.'

Betting the whole business on innovation has meant that Lowry and Ryan have had to think hard about how to provoke and sustain it. They put the company headquarters in the centre of San

Francisco, because they want it not to be isolated but to be in and of the world. Zoning laws mean that they are strictly controlled in the substances they can pour down their drains – but that's fine because they're committed to non-toxic substances anyway. The offices are sparkling white – they're very serious about being clean – and the primacy of design is visible everywhere. In the conference room where we met, the walls were emblazoned with a quote from the film *American Beauty*: 'I don't think there's anything worse than being ordinary.'

'We made a very deliberate decision not to outsource anything except hard manufacturing. So we have vertically integrated all aspects of product development. We have chemical engineers here, packaging designers, ad designers, everyone is here. The traditional way to do this kind of business is to use lots of outside agencies. We don't do that. For us it is an imperative that everyone and everything we need is right here so that we can predictably create things that are innovative.'

You only have to look around at the way Method employees are seated to see there's very little hierarchy here. Ryan sits next to customer support, because he wants to absorb the questions or complaints that customers call about. Information flows fast at Method because it sparks ideas. The walls are covered in continuous whiteboards: these 'wiki walls' in hallways and around workplaces map a new product's development or dead end. Anyone can add a comment, a thought, an inspiration. Key to the quality of collaboration needed by the company are a few ground rules: assume goodwill. Ask questions. Communicate directly ('you can't do anything new via email'). And, just as in Uri Alon's lab, be supportive: 'Yes and . . .' replaces 'Yes but . . .'

Prototypes are everywhere: soap dispensers, dishwasher tablets, wood-polish bottles, products that made it and more that did not. In the corner, a 3D printer whirrs away, slowly accreting the layers of plastic that will model a body wash container. This is not just trendy; design is central to the strategic positioning of the business – beautiful containers were what earned the products shelfspace in Target and Waitrose. But design thinking lies at the heart of the way the company works and succeeds.

'Design thinking,' Ryan explains, 'is about creating new choices that didn't exist before. It's holistic. It's not about line extensions or market research or copying the other guys. Most companies use agencies because they don't have (or want) the creativity they need. But that is what we are all about. So we mix everyone up here so we hear each other, pay attention to each other. Everywhere you see what people are working on – and you think about it, add to it. It's fundamental that we're all in a design loop of failing and learning and getting better.'

Research and development at Method isn't off on its own, in a different corner or floor of the building. It's at the centre of the action, where everyone can see what's being worked on. The purpose of all the displays is to provoke ideas and cross-fertilization. Just as at W. L. Gore, sharing ideas openly and uncompetitively is how they get better.

'It's important that everyone talks about the object, not about "my idea",' Adam tells me. 'We put stuff up on the walls so people talk about the design. We put whiteboards everywhere so all our work is visible without politics or territory. In design you learn that ideas are currency but you have to let go of them quickly so that they can grow. Design thinkers don't copy, they create.'

The advantage of keeping everything inhouse is that it allows the company to move fast. A good idea can be prototyped quickly, held, touched, passed around, sniffed or prodded, poured or pinched. As much energy goes into fragrance design as into figuring out the most efficient and greenest way to ship products half-way across the world. No discipline at Method is pursued without some element of design thinking because everyone is highly committed to finding new and better ways to do business. Ryan and Lowry both came from families that had worked in the automotive industry. Growing up, they'd seen that industry dying on its feet because of its failure to innovate and it has left them both with a passion for creating a company that is, as Eric said, 'one giant continuous brainstorm'.

'We've built a business that is fantastically innovative in organic green chemistry. We win prizes for our bottle design. People send love letters to our detergent! We have redefined the game. But there is *still* category management.'

The bane of Method's existence is what's known as the category captain. Most major supermarkets don't have or want to have buyers for every kind of product they sell. Instead, in every category – like detergent – they appoint representatives and these are usually executives from the major suppliers, like Unilever or P&G. Those companies recommend to the supermarkets which products to stock; not surprisingly, they typically prefer their own.

'So the category – the trade – has a huge incentive *against* innovation,' Lowry explains. 'We often get in the back door because we're loss leaders: people come to the store just to get our products. So we have a direct relationship with the retailer. That means we have to develop and maintain really wonderful relationships with our retailers and serve them fantastically well. We have to think about our customers in a different way.'

Nevertheless, a few years ago, having seen the growing appeal of Method products and losing out to them in several categories, the major manufacturers started to fight back. Internally, some even developed teams with the mission 'Kill Method'. Lowry and Ryan were not daunted.

'Everyone launched their green varieties – a million of them. Went in, said: you have this Method stuff but here's our offering and they aren't spending a million dollars on advertising and we will spend a hundred million – so we want that space. It was dirty. But we just have to be very focused on the kinds of products we want to create, the companies we want to work with. And we can tell we're successful because people still keep trying to copy us!'

There is a school of thought that argues that there is no absolute innovation, that every new thing is a combination of old things. The idea that weak artists borrow and great artists steal is variously attributed to T. S. Eliot, Pablo Picasso and Steve Jobs. More recently the filmmaker Kirby Ferguson has argued that 'everything is a remix' and he's done a brilliant job identifying the many weird and wonderful sources of music, imagery and language that have been borrowed to create work we all imagined was entirely original.[15] Led Zeppelin's 'Stairway to Heaven' is a remarkably un-transformed version of a song, 'Taurus', by the group Spirit, with whom Led Zeppelin had earlier toured. The first Apple computer was famously a remix of technologies pioneered by Xerox PARC (and later re-interpreted by Microsoft.) Henry Ford didn't invent the assembly line or the automobile and Gutenberg didn't invent movable type. All of these inventions derived from bringing together elements that had previously been disconnected. That kind of innovation isn't driven by competition but by creativity and an engagement with the world that says the time is right.

Lowry and Ryan agree, arguing that many of their own innovations are simply tremendous mash-ups. That the company has variously been described as the Herman Miller or the Aveda of home cleaning captures their debt to values and thinking in other industries. But in their determination – despite provocation – to keep coming up with new formulations and ideas, they show the degree to which cloning, or genuine innovation, is a choice. Individuals and companies don't have to copy, they aren't forced to imitate or to join the herd. They could, can, do better.

In his enthusiasm to demolish some of the more romantic and unhelpful myths around innovation, Ferguson almost – but not quite – argues that originality isn't all it's cracked up to be. His is a compelling post-modern argument, wittily and forensically assembled and he's clearly right that much of what we enjoy borrows (often heavily) from other sources. But while imitation might be how we learn, it isn't all we can do. The TB patient resistant to every known antibiotic, or the Somali farmer trying to feed her family, isn't impressed by market share nor enraptured by the marketing millions spent to capture minute percentages of old business. From the discovery of the poliovirus to the reinvention of the humble laundry detergent, true innovators testify to the immense human gift for creativity and perseverance, sparked not by competition but the sheer conviction that copying is a cop-out but solving problems and helping people is human.

8. SUPERSIZE EVERYTHING

> People say to you: 'I know a place where you can get more.' It's very hard to say, 'No, thank you, I'm happier with less.' Hard to say that. People start thinking you must be stupid.
>
> *David Hare,* The Power of Yes

On 19 September 1928, construction began on the Chrysler Building in New York City. Walter Chrysler, founder of the eponymous car company, had decided that, as his sons would probably settle in New York, they needed something to be responsible for. (His two daughters, apparently, had no such needs.) As the sons of one of the richest men in America, their requirements were pretty special.

'They wanted to work and so the idea of putting up a building was born,' Chrysler later recalled. 'Something that I had seen in Paris recurred to me. I said to the architects: "Make this building higher than the Eiffel Tower."'[1]

A year after construction started, Wall Street crashed. But Chrysler persevered: his building had to be big. Not just big, the biggest. With the Bank of Manhattan under construction on Wall Street, the race was on to build the world's tallest skyscraper. When his rival topped out at 927 feet, it looked as though Chrysler had lost by just two feet. But his architect, William Van Alen, had secretly assembled a spire in the fire shaft and, just a few weeks later, its twenty-seven tons were hoisted into place, giving the art-deco tower its full 1,048 feet – thus surpassing its New York rival and the Eiffel Tower too.

Chrysler's triumph was shortlived. Three months after the Crash, in defiance of economics and gravity, John Jakob Raskob and Pierre du Pont began construction on the Empire State Building. The two men had made their fortunes together at DuPont and General Motors and they did nothing by halves. Finished in just one year and forty-five days, the building was on time and under budget; the Depression had brought down its labour costs. But at 1,250 feet, its record as the world's tallest building would endure for forty years.

It's easy to dismiss the passion for size as simply the indulged idiosyncracy of crazed tycoons. But the desire to build big is ancient: the Aztecs with their great stairs, the temples of southern India, the cathedrals of Europe all make a statement about their builders and their culture by the confident mass of their presence. Skyscrapers are just the modern manifestation of an ancient feeling. 'It's about power,' the architect Philip Johnson wrote. 'Power and domination. All those words we don't use anymore, but the feelings are still in the human breast, and they have got to find expression.'

Although he was perfectly content to design skyscrapers – most notably the ATT building in New York, the Williams Tower in Houston and the two leaning towers of Madrid's Puerta de Europa – Johnson recognized that they served no real economic purpose. 'Our commercial skyscrapers are the result of the pushing and shoving of the competitive commercial world. There is no relationship between their size, their cost and their utility. In the commercial world, the skyscraper came into existence because we didn't have any religion to express. But it was an expression, not the result of economic needs. It was an expression that wanted to reach to heaven.'[2] The size was the message.

But even if, as Johnson argues, power and dominance serve no meaningful purpose, they always incur costs. In biology, the cost can be painfully visible. During courtship, the argus cock pheasant spreads his large secondary wing feathers, which are decorated with beautiful eye spots; the bigger they are, the more they stimulate the female. And the longer the feathers, the more progeny the cock will produce. So the more beautiful cocks produce more descendants. That should be a competitive advantage. But the evolution of the argus pheasant has run itself into a blind alley because the most gorgeous cock has feathers so huge and unwieldy that they may cause him to be eaten by a predator, because he can't fly away fast enough. Oskar Heinroth, the teacher of Konrad Lorenz, commented: 'Next to the wings of the argus pheasant, the hectic life of western civilized man is the most stupid product of intra-specific selection!'

In architecture between 1995 and 2005, the allure of size ran into an equally blind alley with the rise of 'starchitects' and the huge blockbusting constructions that made their names. Big public commissions had long been decided by competition but now these became big, showy and controversial affairs that turned architects into brands. The contests were no longer about architectural firms but about celebrity designers. A plethora of new prize events sprang up, destabilizing careers and demanding bigger, flashier trophy buildings. America's Pritzker Prize (first won by Philip Johnson) had long been considered the Nobel Prize of architecture, it's $100,000 award signifying the 'supreme genius' of the architectural world. But European institutions were keen to enter the game and update their image. The Stirling Prize, the Aga Khan Award, the Mies van der Rohe Award, France's Grand Prix national de l'architecture and the Deutsche Architekturpreis all fuelled the new breathless rhetoric.

After building the Guggenheim in Bilbao, starchitect Frank Gehry was assailed by requests from individuals and institutions who wanted to 'have a Gehry' – a clone to show that they, too, had arrived. They didn't want anything very different, just more of the same big showy buildings with which to compete for tourists and renown. Renzo Piano, Daniel Libeskind, Norman Foster, Zaha Hadid: all the starchitects were begged to design not just buildings that fulfilled a human or social need but iconic structures that shouted out who had built and paid for them. It was, said architecture critic Miles Glendinning, the perfect marriage of big capital and big buildings.

'The rhetoricians of architecture's capitalist revolution talk happily of architecture as an exercise in "branding and advertising". For them, the task of architects is not to make the world a better place, but "to become tough, Machiavellian businessmen", driven by "hyper-rationality" in their incessant pursuit of market advantage.'[3]

Architecture's most influential critic, Charles Jencks, wrote that the world of architecture was now one of 'dog-eat-dog competition, requiring competitive capitalist training in how to get the job and keep it. At any one time, there are four isms, five trends, 100 architects who are competing on a world level.' And their job, he said, was to 'find out what makes a good iconic building and why'. Sooner or later everyone writing about architecture cited Howard Roark: the heroic protagonist and emblem of extreme individualism of Ayn Rand's *The Fountainhead*. Like Roark, every architect now had to tell an heroic career story and to articulate a unique, radically individualistic style that proclaimed itself with volume. You just couldn't win with smaller, subtler buildings, and winning was what architecture was now all about.

One of the many architects caught up in the whirlwind was Richard Meier, who won the competition to design a new Getty museum in Los Angeles. Nothing about the project was small. Costing nearly a billion dollars, the site required slicing the top off a mountain to create the perfect position for a vast swathe of white stone. Sixteen thousand tons of travertine marble were shipped from Italy to cover the 1.2 million square feet edifice. The model of the structure was so gigantic it could not fit into the museum's own lift system.

As the building neared completion, even the board that had commissioned it started to baulk at its daunting Aristotelian absolutism. It was, commented one member of the museum board, 'all but overpowering'; but that was its point. Meier proved that height wasn't needed to create a building of stunning dominance that left its spectators feeling small. The board had got what it asked for but, for many, it was a shock. Late in the day, and over Meier's head, they brought in another artist – Robert Irwin – to design a garden around the building to soften its edges and humanize its tone. Meier saw the garden as his competitor, siphoning off attention and impact from his powerful signature design, and he fought Irwin at every stage. When the site was finally opened, huge debate swirled around which was more remarkable – the building or the gardens. What nobody talked about was the art collection the museum was commissioned to showcase.

The fact that training to be an architect is the single most expensive education in the world, with very low starting salaries, and that there is an over-supply of trained graduates, made it more urgent for practitioners to enter competitions and win them with huge shiny buildings that brought attention, glamour and notoriety. But Miles Glendinning argues that even starchitects started to grow wary – and weary – of this passion for the big and the loud.

'There certainly was,' he told me, 'big pressure to make big noisy buildings. But architects are quite subtle people and around 2005 they started to feel pretty uncomfortable with some of this. There was a feeling that it was immoral, in bad taste, to do these extravagant buildings. That it was no longer so interesting. All that titanium and those big, computer-generated curves.

'You saw influential architects – Rem Koolhaas for example, has excellent antennae – try frantically to distance themselves from it. Renzo Piano started trying to find a more ecological, more refined language. But of course, we're still stuck with Piano's Shard; in architecture, you always have the situation that the building starts to go out of fashion even while it's being built. Time moves on, leaving the building behind.'

The problem with starchitects wasn't just that their big showy buildings had unfortunate side effects: the reflection from London's Walkie-Talkie melted cars, the Los Angeles Disney Concert Hall blinded drivers and the Vdara Hotel's pool deck singed hair and melted plastic. At the times that these grandiose constructions were designed, what wasn't being addressed was how to house ordinary citizens in affordable houses whose energy consumption wouldn't bankrupt them or exhaust the earth's resources.

The age of austerity, Glendinning says, hasn't produced an aesthetic of austerity; in the West, architects are left feeling quite confused. They had learned to compete but the visual vocabulary of size they'd created to do so didn't lead anywhere. In the context of the economic crash, these huge, expensive buildings suddenly looked irrelevant and crass, oblivious to the inequality they came to symbolize. Renzo Piano's Shard may be the biggest building in western Europe but it's hard to see what other role it plays in the London landscape. Once you proved you could build very big, very strange shapes, there was nowhere left to go. The buildings famous

for being big were, finally, only big, often overpowering their purpose, their environment and the people who came to see them.

The pursuit of size for its own sake exerts a magical allure; bigger is better. The super-sized Big Mac meal, the Big Gulp slurpee, the armour-plated Hummer and the hyper-caffeinated energy drink are all expected to outperform their mundane rivals. The fantasy of more is that size makes you invincible and growth is its own reward. But the obsession with size always incurs costs, compromises and sacrifices obscured by sheer grandiosity.

In churches, bigger has long come to imply supremacy. The 10,000 panes of glass in Philip Johnson's Crystal Cathedral near Garden Grove, California stand isolated among big box stores and petrol stations. Acres of parking lots were designed to facilitate massive crowds; if the church itself overflowed, you could sit in your car (just as in old-fashioned drive-in fast food joints) and listen as services were relayed through loudspeakers hanging from trees. But the site proved so costly that, in 2010, the Crystal Cathedral Ministries filed for bankruptcy and the buildings were sold to the Catholic Church. The lesson learned by all the independent churches was specific; size does matter but it's safer to measure it in followers.

There's fierce competition to address the spiritual hunger that is one hallmark of modern American life. Scientology, Islam, Buddhism and Pentecostal churches argue about which is the fastest-growing religion but none questions that they are all expanding rapidly. Sermoncentral.com ranks American churches by attendance numbers. Topping the list is Joel Osteen's Lakewood Church in Houston, Texas with over 43,000 worshippers every weekend. Those numbers count – and they're watched avidly.

'In late 1999, we had a core attendance of 6,000 that came every Sunday,' Steve Austin told me. A former probate lawyer, he is now the senior director responsible for pastoral care and Christian education at Lakewood. As we sit talking in his windowless office, surrounded by standard-issue faux-wood furniture and filing cabinets, he could be reciting the metrics of any business.

'Our TV viewership is ten million weekly and growing. But because we broadcast in over 150 nations, it is almost impossible to quantify how many people come to hear our message. We have one million people tapping our website every month. Joel has 1.2 million Facebook followers and about 800,000 Twitter followers.'

Six months after I met with Austin, those numbers had doubled. Austin was pleased with the attendance numbers but still worrying that the Church's website content wasn't as successful as that offered by online rival Joyce Meyer.

'We still have a way to go to improve our online offering and infrastructure. But who knows exactly how many people Joel touches? People read his books, listen to his tapes, watch the TV. He is the number-one evangelist in the world today, bringing the lost into the kingdom of God.'

Austin was the first of many people I spoke to who compared Lakewood's pastor, Joel Osteen, to WalMart founder, Sam Walton. They were both, he said, self-effacing but had a true sense of where they'd come from and where they were going. That sense of mission, I was told, drove spectacular growth.

'It was a rocket!' Austin says with enthusiasm and nostalgia. 'It was very much driven by that Jim Collins book, *Good to Great*. That helped us a lot. The most stressful part was moving here, to this campus and having to beef up the infrastructure of volunteers and personnel and putting systems in place to handle explosive growth. So when people came they would have a positive experience the minute they're in the door. That requires infrastructure.'

Lakewood can afford infrastructure. While the big earners for the church are Osteen's best-selling books and recordings (his first book, *Your Best Life Now*, has sold over four million copies), worshippers are expected to tithe – that is, to commit 10 per cent of their income – to the Church. Attendance and revenue, therefore, grow together, generating a total estimated at between $77 million and $100 million a year. There's competition for that income and Lakewood has proved astute at capturing and keeping it.

On the day that I visited, the infrastructure worked magnificently. Driving down Highway 59, I expected to spot the church easily, by its size or its crowds. Instead, I drove right past. The building – a former sports arena – is lost amidst the mirrored towers and marble monoliths of corporate America. Only the logo of a flame indicates the country's largest church: no spire, no steeple, no cross, only a long line of American flags. And as for traffic, so many policemen are out directing drivers that there isn't a hint of grid-lock. All the parking garages, used to service the surrounding office blocks in the week, are fully available at weekends to churchgoers, who turn up in their thousands and walk – or are bussed – to the main event.

Once inside, ferocious air conditioning assails the senses. This is familiar territory: the slowly curving outer corridor that rings the circular arena. It could be Wembley or the O2 arena (where Osteen has also preached). An army of stewards point the way to available seats. It's quite a hike; along the way, signs point to rooms for chil-dren's services, crèches, bookstalls, toilets, escalators and seminar rooms.

At the Houston tourist bureau, I'd been told that Lakewood Church is the city's number-one visitor attraction. The sheer size of the church is what draws ever more people to it. No one is too young or too old for Lakewood; while the main services are addressed to adults, kids can go off in their age groups to play areas and Sunday school lessons in facilities decorated by former Disney designers. The main goal, I was told, is to make the kids want to come back and bring their parents.

I am directed into the arena by a steward who opens a door, ush-ering me to the top of a steep staircase flanked by people standing up, arms aloft, palms up in prayer. On both sides of the stage, two huge rockeries and waterfalls; next to them a pair of choir lofts with twelve rows of purple seats holds singers on either side of the stage. In the centre of the stage, a vast, golden globe spins slowly. Absent are any religious symbols – no cross or crucifix, image of God or Jesus can be seen. Giant screens show musicians and celebrants while projecting lyrics so that everyone can sing along: 'Nothing is impossible.'

The audience, or congregation, is strikingly multicultural: black, white, Hispanic, Asian, native American. Most are middle-aged, well dressed and look affluent. No one acknowledges or speaks to me as I find my seat. Many hold Bibles and almost all are standing in a state that looks, but does not feel, like ecstasy. The auditorium is vast and strangely impersonal, too large for any real connection between pastors and congregation. Had you arrived with any anxiety about being swept away by emotion and rhetoric, you would quickly relax.

> Nothing in this world can satisfy
> Jesus, you're the cup that's by my side.

Like the production values, the musicianship is technically perfect: Israel Houghton, winner of four Grammy awards, has two gold albums to his name. Steve Crawford and Da'dra Crawford Greathouse are leading lights in the world of gospel music. Every one-hour service comprises roughly forty minutes of music and, when it's done, the stage sinks out of sight and is given over to twenty minutes of speech from Joel or Victoria Osteen.

Before each speech, the congregation is exhorted to hold up their bibles and repeat together, 'This is my Bible. I am what it says I am. I have what it says I have. I can do what it says I can do. Today I will be taught the word of God. I boldly confess my mind is alert, my heart is receptive. I will never be the same. In Jesus' name. God bless you.' Then they sit and listen.

Physically, Joel Osteen is the most unlikely of preachers. A slight figure with huge white teeth, he seems startled to find himself on stage in front of 7,000 people. Legend has it that, before his father died, he had never preached in public and never imagined he would be any good at it. But forced to fill in after his father had a heart attack, he discovered an immense gift. Immaculately dressed in suit and shiny tie, brown curly hair perfectly in place, his tiny eyes try to make up with brightness what they lack in size. With his long, narrow, slightly lopsided face, Osteen works hard to connect with the audience in front of him and the one he knows is watching on television. Cameras on the end of long cranes move in for their close-up; like motivational speakers the world over, he likes to kick off with a joke.

'I like to start with something funny. I heard about this 85-year-old man. He was out fishing one day and he heard a voice saying, "Pick me up!" He looked around, didn't see anything, thought he was dreaming. He heard it again and he looked down and he saw a frog. He said in amazement, "Are you talking to me?" The frog said, "Yes, pick me up and kiss me and I will turn into a beautiful bride." The man quickly picked him up and put him in his front pocket. The frog said, "Hey, what are you doing? I said, kiss me and I'll turn into a beautiful bride." The man said, "No thanks. At my age, I'd rather have a talking frog.'"

Osteen says that writing his weekly sermon is the single most important task of his week. He has perfected the art of communicating to a vast multicultural audience from the widest variety of backgrounds in language simple enough for everyone to understand. Pacing the vast empty stage, he speaks, beaming, without autocue or notes.

'You've been framed. God has put a boundary around your life. Nothing can penetrate your frame that God would not allow. Trouble, sickness, accidents: they can't just randomly happen. The frame is set. You don't have to worry about your future; there is a frame around your health, a frame around your children. A frame around your finances. It's a boundary set by the creator of the universe.'

His audience loves him. As I watch the people to either side of me, they're rapt, bibles open on their laps, grinning at the funny stories, intent upon the rising tide of repeated phrases.

'You can run as much as you want but the good news is that you will never run out of your frame. You will keep bumping up against it again and again. It will always push you back towards your divine destiny ... You are ruined for living a defeated, mediocre, compromising life. God's calling is on you. You can go your own way but God has a way of getting you back on course. God has put a frame that you can't penetrate. The enemy can't penetrate. Drugs can't penetrate. The wrong people can't penetrate.

'Some of you think that you are too far gone, you've made too many mistakes. People tell me often, "Joel, I'm just not a religious person." Listen. None of that matters. All that matters is the creator has put a frame around your life.'

Replete with anecdotes about cars and kids, Osteen bounces between Bible stories and more mundane lessons from daily life. He talks eagerly about his mother, who sits in the front row, and about his wife, Victoria who is almost as accomplished a speaker. The two of them look as though they stepped out of the cast of *Dallas*: polished, groomed and brimming with health. Their story –

the gawky boy who became the world-famous, wealthy preacher with the beautiful wife, gorgeous kids, massive house – smoothly implies that, if the American dream can come true for the Osteens, it can come true for everyone who listens to them. Everything about this service – and there are several throughout the day – is technologically proficient and efficient. It has to be. To attract this many people and send them away satisfied demands the highest production values.

'Never get stuck in a rut but keep growing ... We get a vision of increase. We know you reward those who believe in you. God doesn't want to see your kids in rags. God doesn't want you to suffer but to see you succeed.'

Osteen is deliberately, insistently ordinary: no fancy language, no difficult ideas, no complexity, no anxiety, no problems. His message is relentlessly upbeat: you are good, God will look after you, everything will be all right. Only believe.

The service features little in the way of prayer and Osteen's theme is only faintly religious. He will cite scripture and recount stories from the Bible but hardcore Christianity is neither his style nor his mission. He preaches family values but accepts that families come in all shapes and sizes; everyone sins but is forgiven. Pressed hard by friends and critics alike to pronounce on the subject of homosexuality, he ducked and dodged until he came up with the formulation that homosexuality is a sin – the Bible says so, according to Osteen – but we are all sinners and can expect forgiveness. At a time when one part of America campaigned for gay marriage while another wanted gays locked up in concentration camps to prevent breeding, Osteen's was an astutely noncommittal position.

'I don't believe homosexuality is God's best for a person's life. I mean: sin means to miss the mark.'[4]

Pressed by Piers Morgan on CNN to explain the problem of evil, he did not, he said, know enough about Hitler's childhood background to comment. He has no view on capital punishment, even though his home state executes more offenders than any other in America. And following the Newtown school shooting, in which twenty children died, he felt it was not his responsibility to take a stand for or against gun control.

'I really don't, because political issues divide us. I'm trying to reach as many people as possible. There are good people on both sides of the aisle, and I don't know what the best answer there is either, but I just try to guide them and give them hope in this time of need.'[5]

To keep growing, Osteen must adroitly remain non-committal, ambiguous and bland. He can't be for or against gun control, for or against the shooter of Gabrielle Giffords, for or against homosexual rights. Saying nothing is the price Osteen pays for leading the biggest Church in America. It would be wrong to call Osteen's language Orwellian – he does not use words in ways that are opposite to their meaning. Instead, he is supremely skilled at using words to evade meaning. Careful to avoid throwing fuel on the fire of American partisanship, he also does nothing to put it out.

Apart from tithing, Osteen can't tell his followers what to do; taking any position would alienate someone. If he wants to keep his numbers growing, all that is left for him is to flatter his followers – and this he does lavishly. If Osteen believes anything, it is that his millions of followers are all terrific. What he aims to do is just what his broadcast tagline says: 'Discover the champion in you.'

'You are someone to be celebrated. You are talented. You are smart. You are attractive. There's something great about you ... Listen, God breathed his life into you. You have royal blood flowing through your veins. He crowns you with his honour and favour. You have to put your shoulders back. Hold your head up high. Walk confidently. Talk confidently. Think confidently. Act confidently. People are going to treat you the way you present yourself.'[6]

Osteen's only message is that, if you believe in yourself, your dreams will come true. It's as simple as that. But the problem with this message is that it is unlikely to be true. High self-esteem may be the *outcome* of hard work, discipline and success; it isn't the cause. Although the self-esteem movement has long argued the connection between high self-esteem and achievement, when the veteran social scientist Roy Baumeister reviewed the scientific literature, that wasn't what he found. Lab studies did not show that efforts to boost self-esteem led to improved performance. Looking specifically at school performance, it was clear that, while those who did well felt better about themselves, the reverse was not true: merely encouraging students to feel confident didn't make them do any better in tests. The self-esteem movement, started by Ayn Rand's former lover Nathaniel Branden, had promised much but delivered nothing.

That finding was reinforced by the work of Carol Dweck, who has shown that blanket praise for children – you're so smart, you're so talented – far from motivating them to work hard, encourages them to believe they're innately so brilliant that they need not work at all.[7] Far more effective than self-esteem are self-control, self-discipline, perseverance. Confidence, on the other hand, may suggest you don't need those things at all; you are already 'someone to be celebrated'.

What boosting self-esteem may very well do, however, is develop narcissists: people who look upon themselves as fundamentally special, entitled, unique. According to psychologist Jean Twenge, we are living through an epidemic of narcissism, represented by a generation of children who imagine that thinking positive thoughts *alone* will make good things happen. Citing numerous studies of college students, she shows that narcissistic traits rose as fast as obesity from the 1980s to the present day.

'Our country's focus on self-admiration has certainly been successful in raising Americans' opinions of themselves,' Twenge writes. 'Self-esteem is at an all-time high in most groups, with more than 80 per cent of recent college students scoring higher in general self-esteem than the average 1960s college student. Middle school students, often the focus of self-esteem-boosting efforts, have skyrocketed in self-esteem, with 93 per cent of late 2000s tweens scoring higher than the average eleven to thirteen year old did in 1980.'[8]

Many people insist that the world is now so competitive that you have to feel great about yourself, or at least act as if you do – 'Walk confidently. Talk confidently' – if you want to compete. But the problem with this behaviour is that it separates feeling good from *doing* good. This, Twenge argues, has created a nation of phonies.

'We have phony rich people (with interest-only mortgages and piles of debt), phony beauty (with plastic surgery and cosmetic procedures), phony athletes (with performance-enhancing drugs), phony celebrities (via reality TV and YouTube), phony genius students (with grade inflation), a phony national economy (with $11 trillion of government debt), phony feelings of being special among children (with parenting and education focused on self-esteem) and phony friends (with the social networking explosion).'[9]

Promoting self-esteem, as Joel Osteen so relentlessly does, may make his Church grow but it won't make his followers work better or smarter. In one experiment, psychologist Don Forsyth and his team at Richmond University took two groups of college kids and, to one group, sent a weekly email containing a practice question. To the second group, they sent a weekly practice question but with it came messages reminding them of the importance of confidence, encouraging them to keep theirs up: 'Bottom line: Hold your head – and your self-esteem – high.'[10]

The students who had been encouraged to boost their self-esteem 'showed a substantial drop in grades ... Feelings of unrealistic optimism,' the researchers concluded, 'can lead to complacency rather than active coping. Indeed, weak students may maintain self-esteem best by withdrawing effort and minimize the degree to which their self-esteem is contingent on good grades.'

The self-esteem that Osteen sells to his congregation won't deliver. The idea that feeling good alone will solve anything turns out to be neither true, nor the "truth". But flattering his audience is an effective way for Lakewood to boost attendance and revenue; it is both cause and consequence of being big. Because the warm glow of self-esteem quickly fades, like an addict you must go back for more.

Whether Lakewood is riding the rising tide of narcissism or contributing to it, the Church's lust for growth necessarily corrodes its message. After the service, as Joel and his wife Victoria stood in a reception line, shaking hands with visitors, I went behind the scenes to meet with Donald Iloff, Lakewood Church's Chief Strategist. We sat in what felt like the sitting room of a giant: huge chairs and sofas, empty tables and fake book spines created the illusion of a home that was really a corporate reception area.

Iloff is a seasoned campaigner. He used to work in Washington as a lobbyist; at one point, he told me, he had Enron as a client. A friend of Lee Atwater's, he was closely involved in Texas politics and the Bush/Quayle campaign in 1992 but there is nothing he takes more pride in than the achievements of Lakewood Church.

'Never in the history of the United States has there been a Church this big! But you know,' Iloff demurred, 'we don't really go by numbers. We know our TV audience numbers. We're the number-one podcaster and always in the top ten worldwide. We're the third-biggest influencer on Twitter – we crushed Lady Gaga because we had more retweets and mentions.'

To my ears, Iloff, just like Steve Austin before him, sounded like any corporate executive regaling me with his quarterly results. He is, after all, media-savvy and highly accustomed to monitoring his numbers.

'But we don't have size goals. We don't sit down and say: these are the numbers we want to hit this year. We're really wanting something else. You know, if corporate executives were to look at what they do as spreading influence, they'd think about their models differently. Does Intel influence? It does. Does Apple influence the world? It does. That's how we think about growth. Are we influencing our community? How can we create the most influence? That's Joel's goal.'

So how, I asked him, could he see that influence growing?

'We see growth everywhere. It doesn't matter about the economy. We keep growing – and growing all over the world.'

But for an organization that purports to provide some kind of moral leadership, the example Iloff proffered to illustrate Lakewood's growing influence was puzzling.

'A few years back, we were talking to the president of Liberia. The president! And he is saying he really wants Joel to come to Liberia. They see our TV show but he wants us to come in person. He's a huge fan. They made a huge effort to try to get us there. Things like that show us our influence is growing all the time.'

As he's proudly telling me this story, I am thinking that the current president of Liberia is female – Ellen Johnson Sirleaf – so maybe Iloff was referring to the previous president, Charles Taylor. That Lakewood is beloved of a war criminal convicted of some of the most heinous and brutal crimes in human history would seem a strange way to illustrate the influence wielded by the biggest Church in America.

You can't have a Church as vast as Lakewood without coming in for a lot of criticism from your rivals. Osteen has been attacked for being too tolerant, too intolerant, too Christian, not Christian enough, too dogmatic, not dogmatic enough. But in order to maintain its top spot as America's biggest, the Church can purvey no real message; all it can do is sell itself. The atmosphere is glitzy and the moral compass of the organization not especially strong but its sheer size means it cannot be anything else.

It might be easy to dismiss Lakewood as just a flaky permutation of America's schizophrenic relationship to religion. But England loves Osteen, too. On a midweek afternoon and charging £130 per person, he all but filled the 20,000 seats in London's O2 arena, where he gave the same polished, word-perfect performance to an audience just as eager to stand, hold their arms aloft and sing. Iloff is convinced that England is ready for Osteen because the population is starved of choice.

'It'll happen in England before the rest of Europe. I think England is ready. I have the strongest sense of that.'

I left Lakewood Church numbed by its scale, energy, noise and banality. I had come looking for meaning, in what it did, in what it stood for. But I couldn't find any. As a religious experience, it was as moving as a stay at a large, international chain hotel. For a religious institution, it was morally one of the most vacuous I'd ever encountered. All day I'd been sold to: messages of self-confidence, of happiness and of destiny. I'd been entertained but not enlightened, talked at but not talked to. I was strangely troubled that I was forever exhorted to feel good but never to do good.

I don't believe that the Church's growth was spontaneous, unplanned or God-given. Nobody employs a Chief Strategist without believing in strategy and, while everyone denied the importance of numbers, they all recited them with pride. *Good to Great* was referenced more frequently than the Bible. This influential business book celebrates what it calls Big Hairy Audacious Goals (BHAGs™) but the problem with these is that they tend to overwhelm nuance, subtlety and detail. That's what they're for – to keep eyes on the prize – but that is also the cost that they incur.

The big promise of size is that it imparts invincibility. Organizations hope that being big will eliminate their competitors, allowing them to operate with impunity across a so-called free market. At the very least, they expect scale to command respect. That expectation underlies many, if not most, of the mergers and acquisitions that companies undertake in the face of the data showing that 50 to 80 per cent of such deals fail.

'As a big company, we could drill more wells than a smaller company and hence we could learn far more through greater experience,' John Browne argued when becoming CEO of BP in 1995. 'The bigger we were, the more we could leverage knowledge and experience and do the same things better. So scale and reach seemed like virtues worth having just on this basis.

'But there was more. We believed governments of oil-producing nations would increasingly prefer to work with very big and influential oil companies. They wanted to see a big balance sheet, global political clout and technological prowess and they wanted to be sure that you would be around for a long time.'[11]

With the aim of transforming BP into a 'super major', Browne went shopping, trying and failing to buy Mobil in 1996, successfully buying Amoco in 1998, Atlantic Richfield in 1999 and Castrol in 2000. These deals were big and expensive and garnered big headlines for Browne, large fees for lawyers and left BP with huge amounts of debt. Inevitably, they inaugurated swingeing cost-cutting across the board. Following the Amoco acquisition, the newly combined company ordered a 25 per cent cut in fixed cash costs across all refineries, regardless of the condition of each site. And the cuts continued for the next three years. Everything was cut, it was said, down to the number of pencils.

In 2005, an accident at BP's Texas City refinery resulted in the deaths of fifteen people, with 180 more injured. It was one of the most serious workplace disasters in the United States for twenty years. When the US Chemical Safety and Hazard Investigation Board came to study the accident, cost-cutting was a culprit.[12]

'Cost-cutting and failure to invest in the 1990s by Amoco (who merged with BP in 1998) and then BP, left the Texas City refinery vulnerable to a catastrophe,' the Board wrote. 'BP targeted budget cuts of 25 per cent in 1999 and another 25 per cent in 2005, even though much of the refinery's infrastructure and process equipment were in disrepair. Also, operator training and staffing were downsized.'

One year later, BP had another major industrial accident, this time in Alaska's Prudhoe Bay, where its pipelines leaked 212,252 gallons of oil into the delicate tundra environment – the worst spill ever recorded on Alaska's North Slope. The leak went undetected for as long as five days and, upon analysis, the pipes were found to have been poorly maintained and inspected.[13] And, in 2010, cost-cutting was yet again implicated in the largest accidental marine oil spill in history from BP's Deepwater Horizon rig.

'Whether purposeful or not, many of the decisions that BP, Halliburton, and Transocean made that increased the risk of the Macondo blowout clearly saved those companies significant time (and money).'[14]

The first time that I wrote about BP's cost-cutting and the Texas City refinery, I wondered whether, after the accident, the company had changed any of its views concerning the virtues of scale and reach. I began the delicate negotiations required to secure an interview with the chief executive, Tony Hayward. Yes, I was told, BP had been a mess under Browne, but now, after many years of reflection, discussion, and debate leading to root-and-branch restructuring, the company believed it had finally put its house in order. Perhaps talking to me might be a good way to start to spread that good news. Days later, Deepwater Horizon exploded and I never heard from the company again. BP's immense organizational complexity – which many inside the company had regarded as a competitive advantage and a strategic defence – had rendered the company incapable of fixing itself.

Because it was bigger, Browne imagined it was stronger. Just before Deepwater Horizon exploded, John Browne celebrated his creation of the super-major in his memoir, *Beyond Business:* 'BP Amoco was now a bigger, stronger business. It would become leaner and fitter as it safely pared its activities down to the essential, realizing more than the promised economies of scale.'[15] Even after Texas City and Prudhoe Bay, it seems Browne couldn't see that his infatuation with size was inseparable from the cost-cutting that jeopardized human life and the environment. It seems his appreciation of scale was simplistic and incomplete, overlooking its fundamental corollary: the risk implicit in being very big is that your failures are very big, too.

Yet the quest for size, through mergers and acquisitions, persists. Two thousand and thirteen kicked off with several: American Airlines merging with US Airways, Glencore merged with Xstrata, and Liberty Global bought Virgin Media. The financial press positively crowed – good times were back. Never mind the research that had linked such deals with narcissistic CEOs, never mind the numbers that show the transactions rarely create value. Once M&A came storming back, no CEO wanted to be left behind. 'In the same way that success breeds success,' one Heinz advisor swooned,[16] 'deals breed more deals.' He might more accurately have added 'and failure breeds failure'.

Much merger activity, while dressed up as strategic, represents the pursuit of size for its own sake. 'Once you get to be a $30 billion company,' a former CEO of UPS once said, 'you realize that if you're going to grow 15 per cent next year, you essentially need to create a $4.5 billion business from scratch.'[17] The attraction of size is necessarily tied up with status. Just as the biggest house, the biggest car, the biggest bank balance signify rank in a social pecking order, so companies are led by CEOs who care passionately about their standing in the industrial pecking order. That is what the Fortune 100, 500, 1000 and the FTSE equivalents are all about. The bigger the company, the more status its CEO acquires. To this day, John Browne – now Lord Browne – is regarded in many circles with respect and admiration for having grown his little oil company into a super-major. That so much and so many died along the way is overshadowed by the sheer size of his creation.

Adam Smith saw the quest for size and dominance as inevitable; it is one of the reasons why he feared the growth of joint-stock companies. If there was no limit to a company's size, might it not seek to overwhelm the market? Wouldn't every company aspire to be a monopoly? That, of course, is why anti-trust legislation has tried to curb the egregious abuse of powerful market positions. But what Smith did not foresee was that those instincts might also overwhelm the ability of companies to manage themselves.

Internal sclerosis is one suspect when questions are asked about the failure of big pharmaceuticals to come up with important new drugs. It's been fashionable for these companies to buy competitors and start-ups and then, just like BP, go through several reorganizations and seasons of cost-cutting. But this doesn't improve new drug development. As these companies have grown bigger, the share of experimental drugs that fail has actually risen. The bigger, sadder truth is that every one of these deals leaves behind a workforce traumatized and terrorized by the ever-present threat of layoffs and restructurings.

'Every time you re-org, you lose a couple of years' productivity,' one insider confided in me. 'You can see this in the product pipeline just like you can feel the air bubble in your heating system. A merger, acquisition, re-org is that air bubble; the heat goes out of the system and it's a long time before you get the system up and functional again. In the meanwhile, everyone's running around wondering why – now that we're bigger – we aren't producing more! That is because everyone here is in pain.

'I've survived in this business for nearly fifteen years. But even though I've stayed the course and done well, I know our organization is now so complicated that we get in our own way. Getting anything done is like playing 3D chess. Everyone has become very cynical, they're incredibly defensive because they are so afraid of losing out in the next restructuring.'

The insecurity introduced by mergers and acquisitions generates – or exacerbates – dog-eat-dog behaviours within the new big organizations. Everyone becomes very competitive – even more so when the CEO's personal competitiveness becomes legendary.

'Fred had to win, he always had to win,' Malcolm Woods told me.[18] 'He bullied his direct reports and they bullied others the way they were treated. I learned a new verb: 'to Fred' people because people Fredded each other all the time. He had to win every single encounter – it didn't matter how big or small. He had to dominate. RBS had a very strongly bullying culture. Everything in that bank was competitive.'

Woods came to the Royal Bank of Scotland after nearly two decades in financial services. Neither innocent nor naïve, he had never encountered a culture as ruthlessly competitive as RBS, where he now played a senior role in human resources. That culture, he told me, flowed from the top, from a CEO keenly aware that his bank was a relatively small player in the banking world. Just as Goodwin wanted to bully everyone around him, so he sought to build a bank that could bully the market and, ultimately, national governments.

In 2000, as deputy CEO he launched a hostile takeover bid to buy NatWest Bank – a business three times the size of his own. At £21 billion, the deal was the largest acquisition in UK banking history. The purchase of the big, old British institution by the smaller Scottish bank won Goodwin headlines, prizes (Best Bank CEO and Global Businessman of the Year) and the top job. Harvard Business School duly beatified him with a case study by Nitin Nohria (now dean of the school) that acclaimed RBS 'masters of acquisition'. Goodwin himself revelled in his nickname 'Fred the Shred' as he exercised his much-lauded skills by eliminating 18,000 jobs.

Now RBS was a force to be reckoned with, Goodwin went on a buying spree. Despite the fact that he was relatively new to banking and had no experience in investment banking, insurance, trains or cars, he bought the Irish mortgage provider, First Active, Churchill Insurance, Dixon Motors, Angel Trains and a US investment operation with the world's largest trading floor. By 2004, he had also acquired a knighthood and, of course, he had to have a mammoth 'world headquarters' replete with acres of stone and glass. Like bullying leaders before and since, Goodwin injected a hefty dose of volatility into his big bank.

In 2005, Harvard Business School's Nitin Nohria egged Goodwin on, writing 'Goodwin believed that RBS continued to have multiple options for growth . . . he felt his entire organization was ready to meet this challenge'.[19] Everyone working in RBS read the Harvard case study and some believed it must be true. Eager to live up to that promise, Goodwin paid £8.3 billion to acquire the American bank, Charter One. But shrill notes of criticism were starting to be heard over the chorus of approval.

'Some of our investors,' challenged James Eden of Kleinwort Benson, 'think Fred is a megalomaniac who cares more about size than about shareholder value.'

'Oh yes,' Malcolm Woods laughs, with hindsight. 'Inside the

bank everything was totally about being the biggest bank on the block. You couldn't explain some of the deals any other way. It was all about us, how big we were, how big we were going to be!' That the bank's strategy was driven by a lust for size, and no other reason, was perceived at every level of the organization.

'What did we know about trains? About car companies?' John Berry wondered. Once deals were done, it often fell to him to lead integration projects – to make sure all their systems knitted together. That there was no strategic fit and very little due diligence made his job harder.

'We hadn't finished integrating NatWest – and here we were buying car companies. Angel Trains! Due diligence for Charter One was just about non-existent. We had no idea how to become an international bank – I'd worked in truly global banks before and I can tell you: RBS was not ready to be a global bank. It was just size for its own sake.'

When the RBS board forbade Goodwin from further acquisitions, he visibly chafed – and then found another path to hyper-growth. The investment arm of RBS went 'hell for leather' into structured finance, becoming one of the leading players in the CDO (collateralized debt obligation) market. Here, there were rankings too and, despite being relative novices in the business, RBS raced up them, becoming a top-five player, along with incumbents Lehman Brothers and Bear Stearns. In 2006 alone, CDO volumes increased 134 per cent.[20]

As revenue grew, the board could not deny Goodwin when he came to them with a startling new proposition: he wanted to create an international banking consortium to buy, and then divide, the Dutch bank, ABN AMRO.

For years, ABN AMRO had been struggling with its own internal demons and a wildly over-ambitious CEO, Rijkman Groenink. A big global bank with a complex and cumbersome management structure, it was already in talks with Barclays, which had proposed to buy them outright and merge the two operations fully. Goodwin could not resist the challenge of another hostile takeover. But RBS could not afford to buy all of the Dutch bank, so he created a consortium of Spain's Santander and Belgium's Fortis banks. Together they hoped to buy ABN AMRO and share the spoils: Santander would get Italy and Brazil, Fortis would get the Dutch bank, and RBS would get the rest. The deal would be the most complex as well as, at €71 billion, the biggest banking deal the world had ever seen.

'Lots of people thought it was a bit of a leap,' Bob Weston recalls, 'but there were some good reasons to do the deal.' Weston had only recently joined the bank and brought to it deep global experience. He thought RBS was too dependent on the British economy and that being bigger would enable the bank to spread some of that risk. But he never believed those business reasons lay at the heart of Goodwin's pursuit. That, he knew, was only ever about the status that came with size.

Employees at ABN AMRO were aghast and confused to find themselves at the centre of a big public international fight between RBS and Barclays. Accustomed to a far more sedate style of doing business, they watched with wonder as their fate was determined.

'When the Barclays possibility was announced,' Sunny Uberaii remembers, 'jaws fell about two feet. And then when the RBS consortium came on the scene, jaws fell about four feet! No one had any experience of this kind of thing and people were just in a state of total paralysis.'

The Dutch bank had a worker's council that had to be consulted over any sale. Hans Westerhuis sat on the council, which worked hard not to let their shock overwhelm their thinking. When I met Westerhuis, he brought me a beautifully produced book commemorating the history of the Dutch bank. Today, he remembers the merger as though he's recalling a family tragedy, for which he is still in mourning.

'We talked to all parties involved in the merger. We wanted to understand the strategy in order to know how to implement it. On the RBS side, we had a session with the full board. They obviously expected us to be hardcore trades unionists and to want to discuss redundancies. We just wanted to ask about integration. But the RBS board knew nothing. It was a huge operational risk and they didn't understand a single piece of it.

'We were asked our opinion by the ABN AMRO board and we prepared a long document comparing the two bids. It was a good analysis, which we also sent to investors – pension funds – and it focused on the relative risks of the two scenarios. Some pension funds did read it. But no one could stop Fred.'

Weston, a veteran of takeovers, was less emotional about the unfolding disaster but remained seriously sceptical about what was driving it.

'At the time, regulators and politicians all believed that you would lower risk by being bigger and spread across multiple economies. But somewhere along the line, the arguments faded and the adrenalin of the chase took over. The sheer momentum – the players were so huge that the momentum was too great to be stopped.'

'It was a race,' John Berry recognized. 'The company was – is – stuffed with deeply competitive people and they wanted to win the race. Due diligence? It was a joke – there wasn't any time. Anyone who raised any questions or doubts, they were just treated like wimps.'

Not everyone hated the race. Many found it galvanizing: the thrill of the chase, the size of the prize.

'I am an adrenalin junky,' Sunny Uberaii concedes. 'And this was – it was – exciting. The largest financial services deal in the history of the world! Did that make it exciting? Absolutely. The fact that we would be one of the biggest, one of the top ten banks – which ABN AMRO had once been in the past! We thought, finally we'll be back on the world stage, where we belong.'

'It is very hard to stop these things,' Bob Weston acknowledges. 'There are huge face issues at stake. It's like you go to a dance and meet a girl and she says she never wants to see you again. The risk you take as a man – there is just something in the male psyche that holds that issue. Near completion of a deal, if the market says no, you've failed and you will always be known as a failure. There's just no way that you can walk away and feel a hero. Walking away in financial markets can never be positioned as winning.'

Just as the credit crunch erupted in the autumn of 2007, Goodwin closed in on his prize. Neither the collapse of Northern Rock nor international jitters about the state of the world's economy had dampened his enthusiasm for making RBS the biggest bank in the world. Most wholesale banks did not want to lend him the money to fund his acquisition; the US Federal Reserve and the Bank of England stumped up £100 million.

Goodwin's big deal was the largest cross-border banking takeover in history; with it, Goodwin achieved his dream of creating the world's largest bank. The fallout was predictably enormous too. The Belgian bank, Fortis, collapsed and its part of ABN AMRO had to be nationalized by the Dutch government. Santander fared better; they made a profit by keeping the South American businesses and selling the Italian part of ABN AMRO to Monte dei Paschi di Siena, the world's oldest bank. (That bank too had then to be bailed out in 2013.) And in the UK, in February 2008, RBS announced a loss of £24 billion, the largest annual loss in British corporate history, and had to be rescued by the British government.

In October, Goodwin announced his resignation and, a month later, Stephen Hester was brought in to run RBS. One of his first moves was to chastise, and then eliminate, much of the bank's management. They had not, he told them, been leaders but sheep. The bank wasn't a master of acquisition, after all. Left to knit the pieces together, John Berry was aghast at the mess he still struggles to make functional.

'Five years later, there are huge parts of ABN AMRO that are still not integrated to this day. They will remain unintegrated. Corporate clients who span both banks still have to call two different places for support! We have had to build a complete bank from scratch from IT resources. We've done that – up to a point – but all the legacy work was left. No one wants to touch it.

'They did have a programme going round the world changing offices to blue and white from green and yellow. In some instances, that is all they've done! Had a staff party, changed the signage and the furniture. And when they're done, they have a party and bring over a Scottish piper to play bagpipes through the building to let them know they are now Scottish. It was that crass.'

Stephen Hester worked hard to restore to the bank some sense of connectedness with its customers, with Customer Charters and a policy called 'Helpful Banking'. But trying to inject the organization with some sense of social purpose after years in which it cared only about size proved tough. No one remembered anymore what they were there for; customers had never been on Goodwin's agenda. Re-programming 140,000 traumatized individuals, reminding them what business they were in and why, turned out to be a Sisyphean task for Hester.

There was a severe contradiction at the heart of his mission. On the one hand, he had to stabilize the bank's balance sheet by reducing the size of its bad debt. But one way to stabilize the balance sheet was to make more money – which the investment banking side of the business has continued to do. As a consequence, the bank still isn't small: in 2012, the balance sheet of RBS was the size of the entire British economy.[21] If scale was what Goodwin wanted, he had got it.

In his lust for scale, Goodwin was, of course, not alone: it takes at least two to make competition truly exciting. That Barclays was just as determined to be big and important on the world stage helped to fuel the race. Size alone seems to have been that bank's strategy, too. 'The closest the Barclays Group came to having a single vision was the strategy adopted by Group Chief Executive, John Varley, where he articulated the bank's goal to become a "Top 5" bank,' the Salz inquiry reported. 'While this was a galvanising force, the stated aim was growth and improvement of competitive position ... Winning also extended to a keen interest in Barclays' position on industry league tables. However, we found that, particularly in the investment bank (but also in the retail bank sales force), the interpretation and implementation of "winning" went beyond the simply competitive. It was sometimes underpinned by what appeared to have been an "at all costs" attitude.' The pursuit of size for its own sake devastated the bank's culture. Detail, nuance, ethics went out the window, deemed trivial compared to grandiose schemes and global domination.

One cost of size is insight: knowing what is going on. Organizational silence, inherent in all organizations and exacerbated by steep hierarchies, only gets worse in vast organizations where even those who dare to speak out are often lost in the crowd. Leaders of institutions are surrounded by people who tell them what they want to hear; research shows that 85 per cent of employees have issues or concerns at work that they don't voice, either from fear of recrimination or a belief that they can't make a difference. The larger an institution grows, the more extreme this insight problem becomes until, as many CEOs have told me, you are left relying on the numbers. But those numbers, while they contain a very great deal of information are also dangerous illusions, appearing to capture panoramic detail when in fact all they can convey are thumbnail sketches. In vast institutions, every top-line number summarizes hundreds, thousands of data points, equations and assumptions that themselves contain more. The sheer complexity of the cascade means leaders cannot ever fully know what they are seeing.

The allure of size and dominance, the promise that business will progress more effectively if it can dominate the landscape, turns out to be a fatal chimera. Supersizing buildings or churches, oil companies or financial institutions always comes at a cost: an artistic, moral, social, environmental or financial dysfunction. It must incur that cost because competitive instincts don't stop until they fail. So they must fail in order to stop.

Public commitments to transparency don't get far addressing this systemic issue. In a dazzling forensic analysis of Wells Fargo, one of America's smaller and more conservative banks, Frank Partnoy concluded that 'banks today are bigger and more opaque than ever, and they continue to behave in many of the same ways they did before the crash'.[22] The public accounts that banks file are, in the US, governed by the Financial Accounting Standards Board. Don Young, an FASB board member from 2005 to 2008, now says 'after serving on the board, I no longer trust bank accounting'. Understanding accounts and risks – for this most qualified of assessors – is more fraught than ever. Other board members are adamant that they no longer trust these accounts, either.

Partnoy more than knows his way through a balance sheet. After years of working on Wall Street, he left in disgust and wrote a shockingly honest (and often funny) book, F.I.A.S.C.O, about the madness he had witnessed and sometimes joined. After Enron collapsed, he helped the Senate understand derivatives, and from 2005 onwards he tried to warn anyone who would listen about the ideological blindspots implicit in Alan Greenspan's love affair with deregulation. Now a professor of law and finance, Partnoy is relentless in separating financial rhetoric from reality.

Likening the levels of risk in Wells Fargo to the circles of Dante's Inferno, he argues that each stage is replete with risk and obfuscation. In 2011, Wells had $81 billion in revenue and $16 billion in profit. But it also had $2.8 *trillion* invested in derivatives and $1.5 trillion exposed in entities that did *not* appear on its balance sheet. 'These disclosures make even an ostensibly simple bank like Wells Fargo impossible to understand,' Partnoy concludes. 'Every major bank's financial statements have some or all of these problems; many banks are much worse.'

The CEOs can't trust these statements either. J.P. Morgan's Jamie Dimon, widely regarded as one of the smartest and most trusted of bank CEOs, was blindsided in 2012 by a $6 billion loss. In that context, it is hard to feel comfortable with the knowledge that in RBS (roughly the same size as J.P. Morgan but run by a far less experienced CEO) the UK government finds itself trying to manage a bank as big as its own economy.

In the quest for growth and scale for their own sake, institutions around the world have expanded at a pace and to a size at which their leaders can plausibly deny knowledge of widespread mis-selling, interest rate manipulation and fraud. It may be tempting to imagine that each of these disasters was carefully planned and plotted by avaricious psychopaths but the more prosaic and realistic explanation is that many vital institutions have become both unmanageable and unmanaged. Grandiosity for its own sake breeds complexity and arrogance that allows retail customers to be regarded as 'plankton' and investment bank customers as 'muppets'. When your revenue is larger than many nations' and your power in the marketplace exceeds that of governments, everyone looks small.

Altogether, America's nine biggest bank holding companies have almost 20,000 subsidiaries, with J.P. Morgan Chase having 3,391 subsidiaries, Goldman Sachs 3,115, Morgan Stanley 2,884, and Bank of America 2,019. Does anyone seriously imagine that anyone can run such vast organizations or that any boards can exercise serious and trenchant oversight over them? Bearing in mind that all of these banks operate in at least forty countries, the result – if not the intention – of size is to make regulatory oversight as impossible as governance. As legislators around the world – Sheila Bair in the US, the Vickers Commission in the UK, Erkki Liikanen in the EU – call for the banks to be broken up, the political paralysis that has ensued is a testament to the power these huge institutions have to intimidate reformers and stymie change. Banks bigger than governments wield more power than any legislature can regulate.

It's easy and comforting to imagine that this is a banking problem. It isn't. It's a size problem. The competitive drive to grow bigger and bigger – whether in buildings or pharmaceutical companies – always carries a concentration of risk that makes it ever harder for these organizations to do anything safely or well. Thinking otherwise is hubris. Economies of scale, if they can be achieved, eventually reach a point where they become counterproductive, creating so much complexity, internal and external friction that no one knows any longer how to make them work. The accrual of concentrated power means that no one can interfere – but neither can anyone, any longer, help.

What started as a banking crisis, turned into an economic crisis and may yet develop into a democratic crisis, should have taught us not to expose our most crucial institutions to the risk carried by scale. We should have learned that no organization should be too big to fail and that the corollary of that insight is to keep them small enough to fail with ease. And we should have learned to think more intelligently about growth itself: to see that increasing numbers on a balance sheet or a share price is not necessarily unmitigated good news.

'Being big doesn't protect anyone,' Paul Purcell argues. 'All bigness does is create scale, it doesn't mean you're good. You need to be good at what you do. It is all about whether you are doing a good job for the client and adding value. Look at HSBC right now and Barclays. Did being big help them? You need to break up these institutions.'

Purcell didn't join Occupy Wall Street and he's as far from being a radical as it is possible to get. But, as CEO of Robert W. Baird & Company, he does know what he is talking about. After a lifetime in financial services, he's just reached conclusions somewhat different to those of his peers.

'The whole model is under attack – and so it should be. What's happened is that these big universal banks are too big to manage. The people are the risk. That's why they're losing value and why the government had to step in. They're always saying we have to be global, we have to be vast. But no, you don't. It doesn't work.'

Based in Milwaukee, Wisconsin, Purcell's firm is out of the Wall Street whirlwind and Purcell likes it that way. He keeps up with what other investment houses are doing but feels no compulsion to imitate or compete with them.

'You now have a situation where 10 per cent of the largest institutions own 75 per cent of the assets. By definition, that makes them too large to fail. And the very best of the bankers, Jamie Dimon, even he didn't know what was going on in his institution. You lose six *billion* dollars and you don't know why? That's good evidence that even he can't manage these things.'

Apart from the outspokenness of its CEO, what makes Baird different is that, while it looks like other financial institutions, with investment banking, wealth management, capital markets, private equity and asset management teams in the US, Europe and Asia, the company is owned by its employees. And that, says Purcell, changes its priorities, its pace, its scale and its culture.

'The strength of our model is that every decision we make is long term. Our horizon is at least three to five years. And it is a basic principle here that we are fundamentally client-focused. We don't trade against our clients and we never will.'

In contrast to much larger companies like Goldman Sachs, which earned opprobrium for selling products to its clients while simultaneously betting against them, Baird and its employee shareholders appreciate that their clients are the only source of their revenue and that, therefore, their interests are aligned. The company is run, in effect, like a partnership – as many Wall Street firms used to be before they entered the public markets.

Purcell's passion for the business, and its ownership structure, is hugely influenced by his earlier career at Kidder Peabody. That firm too had been owned by its employees when Purcell joined. After it was sold to GE and became part of a publicly traded company, Kidder Peabody changed dramatically and adventures in derivatives trading quickly destroyed it.

'I saw this terrific firm built and I saw it wrecked – so my passion came from watching that. It galvanized my view that privately held employee ownership is the way to go. Your own money is on the line every day. This year we will achieve a return on equity of eleven to twelve per cent, while most firms will struggle to get to six. We are very metrics-driven because we care passionately about productivity and because we want to be able to pay our people well. But it isn't about bigness. Many banks got big for their own sake. We don't want to be big, we want to be good. Scale alone simply does not work.'

More remarkable than Purcell's statement of principles was the coherence with which it was echoed through the organization. Sue Bellehumeur left her career as a dental hygienist to come to Baird as a receptionist. But she was sufficiently intrigued by what she saw going on around her that (without much encouragement from her immediate, male supervisors) she educated and trained herself to become a financial advisor. For her, organizational silence is not an issue; she has never had any fear of raising problems or challenging the merits of products. Because the bank doesn't sell its own products, there's no conflict of interest. And nobody at Baird would dream of emulating Lehman Brothers' example of posting daily earnings on the wall. What Baird wants, says Bellehumeur, is 'to do what's right for the clients under every circumstance'.

A petite blonde who sparkles with energy, she speaks with passion about her work and has never, she says with a laugh, been afraid to express herself; that's what she has always done.

'If you're an owner, you care about much more than just the money you take home each month. I know that if I have an issue, I can send Paul an email and hear back from him in twenty-four hours. I tell people this and they don't believe me,' she laughs. 'But really: that's how it works here! There is a very strong sense that it is *our* business so we have to keep trying to do the right thing. Intent always matters. You may make a mistake – people do – but what matters is intent. The company is everybody. Big and small producers have skin in the game. You need to be good at what you do – but being big doesn't help you do that.'

The most stunning aspect of Baird's otherwise modest Milwaukee headquarters is the view over Lake Michigan. The frenzy and the hype I'd grown accustomed to in New York was absent; in its place, an unusual eagerness to show how careful the firm was.

'We are very risk-averse,' Dustin Hutter, Baird's assistant con-
troller assured me. 'What has helped me, learning the business here,
is knowing that we are working with our own money. It's our firm
so that influences the strategic thinking. Being privately owned has
allowed more of an entrepreneurial mindset but we approach new
ventures very conservatively. We don't go in head first – we stick
our toes in the water because it is our capital that we are putting
at risk.'

When I asked Hutter whether he ever felt competitive with his
colleagues, he looked stunned and puzzled, unclear what I meant.
I explained how some banks posted daily earnings on the wall, how
hedge fund managers wouldn't talk to each other and he looked at
me as though I was describing a different planet. Perhaps I was.

'If you don't share, you can't learn. What brought me here was
wanting to learn and that's what I've been able to do. What makes
us successful is communication – Paul will share anything.
Everything here is wide open and that's what makes everyone very
successful. Information is there not just to consume but share. The
more I share, the more I learn.'

But if openness and sharing are hallmarks of how Baird does
business, doesn't that mean the company has to be careful about
who it hires? If, as Purcell says, in banking the major risk is the
people, then those people have to be well chosen.

'Gosh yes!' Hutter exclaimed. 'We have been hiring, but I
reckon we only consider about two out of every eighty people who
apply. We have Paul's famous "No asshole" rule. If someone puts
themselves before their client, they stand no chance. If someone
misbehaves after they get here, it doesn't matter if they're a big producer – they're out.

'We did hire some people who came out of GE Healthcare.
They were so full of distrust at first. I think they thought we were
just saying these things but didn't really mean them. It's been hard
for them to break down the walls that they've grown around themselves. But now those same people say there's no way they could
ever go back.'

Choosing people carefully, staying client-focused, not developing proprietary products and giving employees in every function
the chance of skin in the game has made Baird more resilient,

more profitable and more stable. Since 2007, Wall Street has lost 15–18 per cent of its workforce; in the same period, Baird has increased theirs by 12 per cent. Purcell says he does not want to manage his bank 'like an accordion'; he wants to invest – in bonds, equities, companies and in people – for the long term.

Baird did not invest in CDOs nor did it sell sub-prime mortgages. But it's the stories Baird tells about itself that most eloquently articulate the company's values under the stress of large transactions. One of those stories involved the investment banking group's sale of a large consumer services business. As negotiations closed in on a two-horse race, the Baird team grew concerned that one bidder was bound to lose. Should they encourage the losing bidder to keep throwing time and resources at the deal, knowing it would all be wasted? The fetid tradition of auctions says that you should always keep all the players in the game; never mind the cost, you keep the competition going. But the Baird team felt uncomfortable wasting another party's time, effort and good faith. So they let it be known that the deal was all but closed. Their reward was more business both buying for and selling to the company with whom they'd been so straightforward.

People at Baird love telling stories like this – and there are many more – because they're proud of them and recognize that telling them is one way to ensure their lessons are repeated. If that means that Baird must stay a smaller player, that poses no problems for Paul Purcell. It is Baird's smaller scale that makes everything so personal. And because everything is so personal, what you do matters. And that attitude goes from Purcell down to the mail room.

'I just want to do my job well.' A handsome, middle-aged African American in a crisp and spotless white shirt, Stacey Williams is keen to tell me about his sixteen years at Baird.

'I came here as a temp and, when the work was done, I was sad to go but Baird wasn't hiring at the time. Then two years later, I come for an interview. I walk in and the supervisor, Marty, jumps up and says: where you been? We've been looking for you! We remember you, you were a good worker. When can you start?'

Stacey runs much of the back office services; at his supervisor's insistence, he's been promoted often and now runs his own group. He's been an owner for the past nine years.

'Owning makes me feel part of something great. Other companies say everyone matters but they don't really mean it. At other companies where I worked, I worked hard. But you never saw the bosses, they didn't know who you were. Paul knows me and is surprised when I call him Mr Purcell – he looks around and wonders who I'm talking to! It's a blessing working for a company like this. That doesn't mean it's always perfect; there are bad days and people who get upset. But as long as I'm giving 110 per cent, that's okay.'

There are a few banks that work like Baird – William Blair in Chicago, Triodos Bank in Europe – but not enough of them. As I left to go to lunch with some of the Baird team – a quick one, everyone had work to get back to – I reflected that what made the company impressive was not just the people but the fact that the structure of the organization implicitly encouraged them to do the right thing. They didn't need a 'Customer Charter' to remind them of the relationship that they owe to the people they serve. Their obligations to each other, as owners, made their inter-dependency salient and real; the relationship was built into the structure of the organization, not mandated by a management pamphlet. The wild bets and flights of fancy that have characterized many of the giant banks are made more difficult and less abstract when the money is yours and your neighbour's. And it is just harder to make gigantic losses when you aren't gigantic yourself.

Many of the same dynamics can be seen within the peer-to-peer networks that have arisen as alternatives to banks. Zopa, Lending Club and Funding Circle can't do everything that Baird can do but they depend on the same characteristics: sharing, trust and the desire to connect. Similarly, car-sharing, (City Car Club, Greenwheels) house-sharing, (Easyroommate, Airbnb) even pet-sharing (Petstoshare) networks use technology to bring people together who don't want to work with domineering institutions but crave instead personal interaction and the daily experience of being human. Websites like Reddit make it easy for people to ask for – and find – help. This is what Jack (Reddit user Chewy1234) did when he found himself grounded in a snow-bound New York City. A kidney transplant patient, his life depended on medicine that was locked inside a post office. Unable to reach the pills or a hospital, he appealed for help and, through the website, found user

Rockstarames who had pills to spare and, more important, a dry car in a garage, a lifetime's experience of driving in the snow and the desire to help. What all of these technologies do is counter the power of size with the effectiveness of personal, social contact which builds trust and provides a platform for connection.[23]

Size is not what matters. We need organizations that are robust, that can survive the vicissitudes of political, social and economic change. Expecting any vast organization to be infallible is madness or religion. So what we want are organizations that are functional – but can fail safely.

Making them functional could require that they stay small. Robin Dunbar has devoted years to studying the evolution of the human brain as it affects the optimal size of social groupings – known as the 'social brain hypothesis'. Analysing the mathematical relationship between small and large-scale societies, he concluded humans have a cognitive limit of approximately 150 people with whom they can maintain coherent personal relationships. That the number remained roughly the same, regardless of historical period, geography or activity, and its constancy, Dunbar argues, is directly related to the physical size of the neocortex – the part of the brain responsible for higher functions, such as conscious thought, reasoning and language. Brain size limits the number of relationships we can – literally – keep in mind and the size is a function of the groups in which our evolution has occurred. 'Although the evolution of neocortical size is driven by the ecological factors that select for group size, we can use the relationship in reverse to predict group sizes for living species,' he wrote.

This explains, Dunbar argues, the configuration of armies, the world over and throughout history, which are largely constructed thus: platoons of ten to fifteen soldiers, companies of three to four platoons, battalions of three to four companies. 'Could it be,' he asked rhetorically, 'that the army's structures have evolved to mimic the natural hierarchical groups of everyday social structures, thereby optimizing the cognitive processing of within-group interactions?'[24]

Dunbar's work, while widely accepted, isn't without controversy and (like much evolutionary biology) a great deal remains impossible to prove. The breadth, across geography and time, of Dunbar's evidence however is compelling, suggesting that more than culture is at work. However elaborate the systems and technologies we create to manage complex operations, sooner or later they always involve people; therefore the size of organizations and how functional they are may have quite hard cognitive limits that we defy at our peril. This doesn't mean that units can't go beyond 150 – armies quite clearly do. But they depend, for their stability, on a hierarchy of units the smallest of which can't safely go beyond approximately 150.

These numbers have come to be known as 'Dunbar numbers' and many organizations use them as a guide to the maximal efficiency of teams, groups and departments. At the tomato processing company, Morning Star, they are used as a guide to how big the company should get; any bigger and a different entity or structure would be required. At W. L. Gore, no business unit is allowed to go far beyond 150 people. That decision was reached before Dunbar's research but nothing in the company's growth has challenged it. And one reason why the banking crisis in Germany hasn't proved as catastrophic as elsewhere is because 70 per cent of its banking sector comprises small or community banks – in sharp contrast to the UK, where just five banks hold 80 per cent of mortgages and 90 per cent of company accounts.[25]

This doesn't mean that companies can only ever be small but it does mean that, for them to be functional, it might be worth considering how many relationships human beings can manage effectively. I might be able to have hundreds or thousands of friends on Facebook or followers on Twitter but everyone knows that these are not functional relationships and that my life would swiftly reduce to gibberish if I tried to live as if they were. When I look at the wildly complex matrix structures that many corporations design in a desperate attempt to be both efficient and creative, my respect for Dunbar numbers increases. To build organizations that demand greater cognitive capacity than our brains can provide is a perfect definition of hubris.

Geneticists exploring the concept of evolutionarily sustainable systems have come to similar conclusions: namely that for a system to be capable of evolving, it must be robust – and that quality derives, in part, from multiple small parts that are only weakly linked; if one mutates, the whole being doesn't die. That is the premise of the emerging peer-to-peer lending networks like Lending Club, Prosper, Zopa and Funding Circle that enable individuals to lend to individuals. Taken as a whole the networks may be huge but they are really just an aggregate of thousands, maybe one day even millions, of small, more personal transactions. Media rhetoric puffs up the importance of these new lending organizations as deadly rivals of traditional banks however their chief contribution lies in the links they make between individuals but on which the whole system doesn't depend.

Another way to think about this is to look at the design of airplanes, which today are designed with automatic flight-control systems that are typically composed of three modules, each with identical functions but designed differently. The idea here is that there is both redundancy – if one fails, the other takes over – but also that the whole plane doesn't depend on a single technological approach. Whether you are talking about complex biology or engineering, the principle remains the same: multiple small parts, weakly linked, are safer because, when one fails, the system as a whole is not fatally weakened. They are robust because they are small. They are failsafe.

Although technology can't be blamed for the passion for growth, it is a great enabler. We are only just beginning to realize the potential of big data: its capacity to deliver highly customized content and products and to predict human behaviour. The vast accumulation of personal data by Google, Amazon, Apple and national governments promises everything from automated personalized healthcare to preventative law enforcement. But with these tantalizing powers comes, necessarily, big risk. Just as Apple computers used to be safer from viruses because there were relatively few of them – which meant they weren't worth attacking – so the vast accumulation of personal data makes it an irresistible target for hackers and malware. While governments and regulators worry about the personal information stored and exploited by Google, scale is precisely what makes their servers such a tempting target.

While founder, Larry Page may wax lyrical over the thought of all of his customers implanting Google into our brains, you don't have to be a civil-rights campaigner to see that this poses huge risks of extravagant convergence: everyone knowing and thinking the same things, conformity on a scale the world has never seen. Big data today promises to predict behaviours based on the actions and decisions of individuals that share characteristics but just because the data is big doesn't guarantee that it will be right, only that the mistakes will be more damaging.

In 2004, Solafa Batterjee's father, a philanthropist in Saudi Arabia, was placed by the UN Security Council on a terrorist watch list. His habit of travel to dangerous places – Afghanistan, Chechnya – apparently fitted the profile of an Al-Qaeda terrorist. For ten years, her father couldn't function – couldn't work, couldn't access funds – and the family had to sit and watch as their father was rendered impotent and immobile. Under continuous investigation, he could travel nowhere. In January 2013, he was delisted by the United Nations, who had failed to find any substantive information that he was anything other than he said he was: an engineer trying to help people. As the data gets bigger, does it make people smaller?

Companies collecting our data compete with each other; that just increases our risk. As competitors, they've proved loath to share information about mistakes with their customers or about cyber-attacks with regulators or each other. Unlike doctors, who've started to learn the value of mistakes, these data gatherers don't want to reveal their weakness. But since mistakes are learning, their refusal to share leaves everyone more vulnerable.[26] The bigger the data, the more alluring the prize, the greater the secrecy, the bigger the risk.

All of these companies hope that size will protect their commercial interests, while conveniently ignoring the degree to which their size increases their risks and ours. So it isn't just banks that consider themselves too big to fail. In hoping and assuming that governments will take responsibility for data security, most large corporations equally hope to outsource the cost of failure. Or, as one computer security analyst put it, 'No one is expected to provide for their own air defence. We have an army to repel a land invasion, so who is out there protecting the cyber lanes of control?'[27]

Why do we imagine that bigger is better, that size confers some implicit victory? We know that larger organizations struggle to be nimble, to adapt and to innovate. We recognize that power, dangerous in itself, becomes more corrupt and even more destructive as it grows in scale and scope. We have had vivid, living proof from the shores of the Gulf to the boardrooms of the City that vast enterprises acquire the capacity to wreak havoc on a scale previously unimaginable. And we now know that few governments have the resources, insight or political will to rein them in.

I'm not at all convinced that small is beautiful but I am persuaded that big is dangerous. Size does not make organizations invincible – it is what makes them vulnerable. What size does give them, however, is a certain kind of impunity: the confidence that, when things go wrong, only governments can step in. As such, vast enterprises fundamentally outsource their risk to us all. That's the big prize their size confers.

9. HOW LOW CAN WE GO?

> We are unsettled to the roots of our being. We have changed our environment more quickly that we know how to change ourselves.
>
> *Walter Lippmann,* Drift and Mastery: An Attempt to Diagnose the Current Unrest, *1914*

On 25 March 1911, 146 garment workers, mostly women, died as they jumped to their deaths or suffocated in a New York factory fire. The oldest, Providenza Panno was forty-three years old; the youngest were two fourteen-year-old girls, Kate Leone and Rosaria Maltese. Nobody knows whether the fire was started by overheated machines or an illicit cigarette but it spread fast because of the hundreds of pounds of fabric scraps that littered the floor. The doors had been locked to stop the women taking breaks and to enable supervisors to check their purses before they went home. With no access to fire escapes, many workers chose to jump from the building to certain death. In his poem 'Shirt', the American poet Robert Pinsky describes one of their male colleagues helping them out the window as though he were 'helping them up to enter a streetcar and not eternity'.

Just over 100 years later, on 24 April 2013, 1,127 garment workers, mostly women, died when their factory in Bangladesh collapsed on top of them. A day earlier, cracks had appeared in the building and engineer Abdur Razzak Khan had recommended that it be closed. But the company had tough production deadlines to meet; you don't get paid if the goods aren't finished in time, and manufacturers will sue you if you attempt to sell them. Amidst the rubble, photographer Shahidul Alam found a couple embracing each other, their torsos immersed in concrete. Blood ran from the man's eyes, he said, like a tear.[1]

The Triangle Shirtwaist Factory fire in the twentieth century and the Rana Plaza collapse in the twenty-first both derived from the remorseless logic of competition: anything you can make cheap, I can make cheaper. Bangladesh has the lowest labour costs in the world, with the minimum wage for garment workers set at roughly $37 a month. For a consumer to get a bikini from H&M or Walmart for $4.99, costs have to be very low. So wages go right down and safety considerations disappear. This is what economists call the race to the bottom.

Companies like Li & Fung accelerate this race. Acting as a broker between low wage factories and the companies that seek to use them, Li & Fung searches constantly for cheaper labour markets. These days, sub-Saharan Africa is starting to appeal. Sourcing cheap labour is no small-time business – last year, Li & Fung earned $20 billion[2] – and, in theory, brokers like this are supposed also to monitor working conditions. In reality, this poses an impossible conflict of interest. In 2012, Li & Fung was responsible for garments made at Tazreen Fashions, where 112 workers were killed in a fire, having been told to keep working after alarms sounded. But every penny a factory can squeeze from their costs makes them more attractive and eligible to win big contracts.

The problem with the race is that costs do not – cannot – simply vanish; they have to go somewhere. And so mostly they are shifted from those who have power and money to those who have nothing. The cost to the customer of the bikini may be just $4.99 but the cost to its maker is a working day of 14–16 hours, seven days a week in cramped and hazardous conditions. Fires, exacerbated by locked fire escapes, are frequent. Safety is an easy, invisible thing to cut because it might never matter and, when it does, it's too late. As far as possible, the risks of cheap manufacture have been passed down from the corporation to the local contractor, who passes them down to the individual workers. The garment can only be so cheap because its makers and the society they inhabit absorbs the cost of its manufacture. Economists call this externalization: getting costs to move outside the business.

In a less dramatic fashion, you can see this by looking at cheap airlines like Ryanair. When accountant Michael O'Leary took over the running of Ryanair, the first thing he did was run through expenses and eliminate them. The costs of food, luggage, boarding passes and travel agents were all nimbly shifted out of the company – onto the consumer. Costs weren't, in fact, being taken *out*; they were just being moved. The most palatable (and wholly disingenuous) way to present this is as a choice: you have the freedom to choose whether to bring luggage; you have a choice whether to book by phone or online. In reality, you pay for it all. Theoretically the garment workers of Bangladesh have the choice whether to turn up for work or not; in reality, they have no choice to run away when doors are locked.

The competition to drive down costs has become endemic across all industries but perhaps nowhere is it more alarming, and its costs more obvious, than in healthcare. In the belief that competition drives quality and value, many NHS contracts have been put out to tender: essentially a reverse auction in which services win business by charging the lowest price. When the NHS Direct helpline service was put out to tender, successful bidders could keep their prices low by using inexperienced call handlers. But since they lacked medical knowhow, all they could do was follow a script of questions and answers. If they couldn't find a clearcut answer, patients were told to go to A&E or call an ambulance. For the contractor this was a quick, cheap result but, for the NHS, this turned out to be overwhelmingly the most expensive option. And when, in August 2013, providers found that they had bid too low to be able to provide a functional service, they pulled out, leaving the service neither reliable nor trusted.

In a painfully similar scenario, when the security firm G4S found, late in the day, that it could not provide the security guards it had promised for the Olympics, the costs were conveniently externalized to the taxpayer, who funded the military stepping in at the last hour. Competing on price while offering a critical service necessarily produces systems that are too efficient *not* to fail. All the redundancy, the margin for error or change – in other words, all the risk – has been stripped out, to be borne by others.

That competition provokes these rash promises is obvious in

competitive tendering. But the competition to drive down wages and keep them there can be seen across entire countries. In the summer of 2013, low-wage workers across the United States staged one-day strikes to protest against their working conditions. Employees from McDonald's, Subway, Taco Bell, Macy's and Victoria's Secret walked out to protest earnings of $150–350 a week, too little to support themselves. They carried signs proclaiming 'Fight for 15' arguing for a doubling of their salaries. After seven years of working for Taco Bell, Joseph Barrera said he could not yet afford a meal every day, subway fares to work or any new clothes. He did not think that getting married and starting a family was viable. The average fast food worker in New York City gets an annual income of $11,000 – less than one quarter the median household income of $48,631.

The argument in support of low pay is always the same: companies have to stay competitive. To keep food or clothing cheap, wages must stay low. 'We seek to pay competitive wages and benefits,' is how a Macy's vice-president put it. McDonald's insisted 'employees are paid competitive wages and have access to flexible schedules'. The National Restaurant Association claimed that the fast food industry was 'one of the best paths to achieving the American Dream',[3] which might have been true years ago when most fast food workers were teenagers living at home. Now it's just a cruel fantasy as workers are older, more educated and likely to be supporting a family.[4] That these companies can't find any other way (they say) to sustain their business than by keeping pay down merely testifies to the creativity they've lost.

The reference to 'access to flexible schedules' is telling – because, just like Ryanair's luggage policy, it sounds like a choice but in fact is quite the opposite. During the economic crisis, the most popular way to cut costs has been to reduce working hours. Nearly a quarter of Britain's major employers now hire staff on what they euphemistically call a 'zero hours contract' – which means that you might get work or you might not. McDonald's, Wetherspoon, Subway, Boots, Cineworld, Sports Direct, the parliamentary journal *Hansard*, even Buckingham Palace rely on these kinds of agreement whose use increased by 32 per cent in 2012 alone.[5] Under their terms, so-called employees have no choice but to commit to being available; but the employer can choose whether or not to call them a little, a lot or not at all. This makes budgeting impossible and job-seeking risky; no one seeking a permanent job can afford to go to an interview in case they're called in for a few hours of paid employment.

When Amazon built a vast warehouse, the size of nine football pitches, in Rugeley, Staffordshire, hiring was done primarily through temp agencies describing themselves as a 'flexible work solution designed exclusively for each client to optimise the work force and drive cost effectiveness'. What this means in practice is that the labour force is divided into two: the lucky full-time employees wear blue badges, get pensions and the right to shares, while the casual workers wear green badges and get no job security at all. Both carry devices to monitor their productivity at all times. Asked to describe the culture of his company, CEO Jeff Bezos said, 'Our culture is friendly and intense, but if push comes to shove, we'll settle for intense.' [6]

In the US, virtually all the job growth during the recovery has been an increase in the number of temporary jobs, with the result that the US now has more temp workers – 2.7 million – than ever before. In some 'temp towns' where there are, effectively, no permanent jobs, it isn't unusual to find warehouses with no permanent employees. Anyone familiar with the film *On the Waterfront* would recognize the hiring practices that require that everyone turn up for work hoping to be one of the lucky few chosen for work that day. Temporary workers are less likely to have any savings, any pension and (in the US) any healthcare coverage. They're also twice as likely as permanent employees to suffer an injury at work. [7]

In the US, retailers use scheduling software to predict by fifteen-minute increments exactly how many staff members will be needed at what points of the day. Employees may be offered just twelve or fifteen hours a week, sometimes none. This isn't enough to live on but companies like Abercrombie & Fitch, Jamba Juice and Nine West use it to keep their labour costs down. Jamba Juice claims it has saved them millions of dollars a year; the Bureau of Labor Statistics says the practice overall has eliminated over a million jobs. That part-time workers are predominantly parents or students trying to develop a career makes them easy prey: they desperately need the work and dare not baulk at their treatment. But the suggestion that these jobs are the first step on 'the path to achieving the American dream' is belied by the statistics, which show that only about 30 per cent of temp jobs ever lead to permanent positions. If these employees are looking to their frontline workforce for creativity, commitment or innovation – well, they've created the conditions for their own disappointment. In the race to drive down wages, employers burn out and violate all the trust and engagement of people who could make their companies smarter and more dynamic.

What all of these companies are doing is cutting prices by externalizing the costs of their operations onto individual employees, the weakest parts of the system. If they can't earn enough to live on, they have to call on the state for benefits, with the result that, ultimately, the cheap prices are externalized to society at large. At the same time, the companies are aggressive in pursuing tax minimization strategies, so that they absorb as little of their own costs as they can get away with.

Pay cuts have consequences well beyond the companies and industries that impose them – and nowhere has that been more apparent than in the newspaper industry. Until about five years ago, newspapers were profitable businesses. But as the Internet started to siphon off readers, pressure mounted to cut jobs. This race to the bottom started with costs but could not fail to have consequences for editorial standards too.

'Newspapers have been culled for every last bit of money and profit that could be got,' Michelle Stanistreet told me. 'Until five years ago, they made around a twenty per cent profit. But they haven't reinvested that money and, when the economy changed, they just started cutting back. Ownership is a real problem; if they were owned differently they would be moderately profitable and serving a democratic function. But for the most part, that isn't what they are doing right now.'

Stanistreet is the General Secretary of the National Union of Journalists. A former journalist herself, she worked for the *Observer*, *The Times* and *Scotland on Sunday* before working on the *Daily Express* business section. It was there that she became alarmed at the impact of competitive pressures on her colleagues and the newspaper they produced.

'The squeeze on resources – staff numbers and freelance budgets – has been relentless. Inevitably when you chop your budgets and get rid of people the quality of the output is compromised. And that's what we are seeing. It's a real race to the bottom.'

To see just how low this can go, you need only look to the United States, where some newspapers – including the once-respected *Chicago Tribune* and *Houston Chronicle* – were found to have outsourced some of their journalism to the Phillipines. Stories on local events and personalities were written for pennies a time, given fake, American-sounding bylines and printed as though they had originated in their home towns. When the agency responsible, Journatic, was identified, many of its exposed clients hastily withdrew their contracts. But then James Macpherson, a Pasadena publisher, launched a competitor, Journtent, which pays pittances to freelancers in Mexico and the Phillipines to watch and transcribe community meetings that are webcast online. Macpherson said 'This is how I solved the problem of time: I outsource virtually everything. I'm primarily looking for individuals who I can pay a lower rate to do a lot of work.'[8] British editors, Stanistreet tells me, have been eager to go and see how the system works.

The anonymized testimony that Stanistreet presented in evidence to the Leveson inquiry painted a stunning picture of a highly competitive culture in which journalists were all too aware of freelancers and interns competing for their jobs, a contest frequently exploited by their bosses. Insecure in their careers, no one was ever going to argue or debate a questionable editorial decision. Silence and compliance were the inevitable markers of a frightened workforce.

'The atmosphere was poisonous,' one veteran reporter told Stanistreet. 'It was unchecked bullying. When your boss said jump, it was a case of how high and where do you want me to jump from. It wasn't only me, there was talk of the "revolving seat" in the office.'

Another veteran with twenty-five years' experience in print journalism described life within the *News of the World*: 'The way the paper was run was totally dysfunctional. The biggest rival of the news team – was our own features department! If news would bid on a story, features would outbid them. After the features department, the biggest rival to news was the *Sun*. This was the regime that Murdoch created. It's dog-eat-dog. They enjoyed this fighting amongst colleagues. They'd set us off like wild dogs against each other. They thought it was all a great game to keep everyone on their toes. They'd light the touchpaper, sit back and watch them kill each other. It was relentless, you could never rest.'

Working under these conditions, one journalist told me: 'Phone hacking was talked about openly in quite a jovial manner. It wasn't a dirty thing. "Got it off the phone didn't we?" No one thought bad of it. Maybe cheating a bit. The pressure is there and people cave. The temptation to dial a couple of numbers, maybe get a scoop – it was huge. Especially in a hire-and-fire kind of place where you're judged by the number of bylines and column inches you have. Along with a family, a mortgage and bosses breathing down your neck saying you aren't bringing in enough.'

For Stanistreet, this hyper-competitive environment meant no one would refuse to hack a phone or to practise what she called the 'dark arts'. 'It is about delivering the goods. Being first. Not being shown up by a competitor. It is a cumulative pressure that makes people prepared to go to any lengths. The expectation is that you *will* go to any lengths. And if you won't, someone else will.'[9]

Stanistreet's evidence shows editors, under intense pressure to deliver readers, passing their stress along to journalists who compete with each other to do more work with fewer resources and less time, all the while knowing that budgets are shrinking and plenty of aspirants are eager for the opportunity to come and intern for free. Under these circumstances, phones get hacked and editorial standards plummet.

'The ideal of the media holding power to account,' said Richard Peppiatt, 'when you're on the coal face – it just goes out the window. Some buckle up and get on with it, some leave, some embrace it and enjoy the competition. Some like winning at all costs. You get the front page and, if that involves manipulating the facts or lying, some don't mind doing it.'

Peppiatt wasn't speaking theoretically and he very much minded what he was often asked to do as a journalist. When he started, working on the *Mail on Sunday*, he wasn't especially idealistic but had hoped he might be able to move from tabloid journalism to something more serious. In this he was mistaken but, for several years, he decided he'd better stick with it.

'I just gave up the ghost and decided I would fall into line and believe in it because it was easier to live like that. Maybe they are right, I thought, maybe this is the way of the world. I guess you could say that was the point when I lost a sense of who I was.'

Working for Richard Desmond, owner of the *Daily Star* and the *Express* newspapers, he watched as 'chronic under-investment in journalism allowed a corrosive culture to fester. I remember one shift there being just myself and two other reporters to write the whole of a national newspaper. It was so bad we had to use pseudonyms to make it appear there were more of us.'[10]

'"If you won't write it, we'll get someone who will," was the sneer *du jour*, my eyes directed toward a teetering pile of CVs … You may have read some of my other earth-shattering exclusives. "Michael Jackson to attend Jade Goody's funeral". (He didn't.) "Robbie pops pill at heroes concert". (He didn't either.) "Matt Lucas on suicide watch". (He wasn't.) "Jordan turns to Buddha". (She might have, but I doubt it.)'[11]

Peppiatt is a smart, thoughtful guy who willingly admits that he enjoyed the celebrity parties and free champagne. He'd been willing to go along with many of the newspaper's stunts: dressing up in a burka or proposing to Susan Boyle. But it was the newspaper's xenophobia that got to him.

'I nearly walked out the summer when the *Daily Star* got all flushed about taxpayer funded Muslim-only loos. Undeterred by the nuisance of truth, we omitted a few facts, plucked a couple of quotes, and suddenly anyone would think a Rochdale shopping centre had hired Osama bin Laden to stand by the taps, handing out paper towels.'[12]

'Decisions were made by the advertising and accounts departments, not by the editorial floor. Anti-immigrant and anti-Muslim stuff was always good for making money. Inflammatory headlines and then phone lines with questions like: Should we let immigrants take all our jobs? Five thousand readers calling up, each spending two pounds each – that was the real game.'[13]

The race to the bottom that Peppiatt witnessed unnerved him. A newsroom might not look as grim or pose as great a physical danger as a sweatshop, but he came to see that it perpetrated something just as bad. He began to save his money so that he'd be able to leave. But then, one day, he just cracked.

'There was a story saying the English Defence League would become a political party. Front page splash. I sat in the newsroom when it was concocted. It was just not true. But the readers were quite big fans – let's give them something they want. And I thought: there must have been a point in a newsroom in Germany in the 1930s when someone should have asked "why are we running pictures of Jews with hooked noses?" I felt there was a big anti-Muslim sentiment building and we were building it up. And if, one day, it kicks off and there's violence and rioting and people getting killed – well, I can't escape feeling responsible. I played a part whipping that up. There can be no more insidious way to make profit than to whip up hatred and prejudice. That's not how I want to make a living. That's when I decided I didn't care about finances and just did it.'

Peppiatt wrote a long, eloquent and furious letter of resignation to Desmond and left the building.

'As much as I resigned from the *Daily Star* because I'd come to believe it was Islamophobic, my conscience was troubled by another, even more sinister, realization,' he told the Leveson inquiry, 'their hate-mongering wasn't genuine. It was a crude, morally deplorable play on the politics of fear in the pursuit of profit ... It makes victims of the many by exploiting both public and journalist, to line the pockets of the few.'[14]

What Peppiatt recounted was more than just the damage to his hopes and career, more even than the story of a single newspaper that had lost its bearings. He described an industry-wide acceleration: as one newspaper blew through one moral barrier, others raced past to blow through the next one, hitting new lows until few knew any longer where they were or what they stood for. The racist journalism and phone-hacking sensations demonstrated how the race to the bottom had harmed not just the journalists who perpetrated them, or the readers who bought them, but had jeopardized an entire industry and abused the trust of a society that expected to be reliably informed. If few had sympathy for the stress of tabloid journalists, that the institutions of news reporting had been left so frail and discredited left democrats feeling uncertain and afraid.

The corruption of the newspaper industry spread well beyond itself: to the police force, to broadcasters and to parliament. Those not immediately in the race to the bottom found themselves swept up in it, sucked in or trampled as the runners sped past. Because industries don't operate in a vacuum but within a society, the impact of their race may spread far beyond their immediate operations. Nowhere is this more visible than in the meat business.

'I live in America!' Don Webb speaks with disgust and anguish. A big, lumbering man in his seventies, his fierce sentence and lingering stare challenges everything he used to believe in. What kind of America? Whose America? What happened to America, his single sentence seems to ask.

We are sitting inside an old wood-shingled house that once was used to dry tobacco. Outside, it's overcast, humid in the glowering August afternoon. The story that Webb has to tell me is one he's told before, that he will keep telling until he's persuaded that something in America has changed – or until the day he dies. He's a charming, generous man but he is also, palpably, full of rage. For all that he is a lifelong Republican, Webb is strangely reminiscent of Lyndon Johnson, speaking with the same good-ol'-boy drawl and the same raw language.

At six foot four and well over 200 pounds, his powerful physique testifies to an earlier career teaching physical education and coaching the high school football team. But teaching paid poorly and one day, when he was in Kinston, he heard some rich people saying that, if they were younger, they'd go into hog farming. The idea stuck and Webb bought a dozen pigs. He did well from them, so he bought more and more until finally he was raising 4,000 hogs.

'Then one day an elderly black gentleman, Mr Lewis, waved me down. He said, "We can no longer sit on our porch if the wind is blowing in our direction. We can't our use window fans and we don't have air conditioning. There's nights we can't sleep. And we've got a sick little girl at home; she can't sleep either. Can't you do something about the stench?"'

One hog produces three to four times the amount of waste that a human does. Like the farmers around him, Webb threw the faeces and urine into open cesspits, known locally as lagoons. Webb's pigs produced raw sewage roughly equivalent to the waste of a town. Lewis wasn't the only black neighbour to complain and their words, Webb says, bothered him bad.

'I talked to some of the government agents in Winton,' he continued, 'and they said I should put some yeast in my cesspool and stir it up with a ten-horsepower boat. So I did that. I opened up the engine and stirred those two cesspools up good. And then I cleaned my boat off and went home.'

The next time Webb saw his African American neighbours, they were polite but they were still unhappy.

'One more favour,' they asked of him. 'Whatever you did, please don't do it again. It's got worse.'

Webb went home that night and thought hard about his pigs and about his neighbours.

'My home was out of the range of the odour, on nice streets, with curving gutters. Everything was fine in my house. And I remembered how, when I was growing up, we used to live with fans, and I remembered how it was if the fans weren't pulling in enough cool air. Suppose someone did to my mom as I'm doing to those people?

'On that day, well, I didn't feel very highly of myself. My greed – putting too many hogs in one place. Starting with twelve, ending with four thousand. Off the backs of hardworking people who couldn't move and couldn't sell. And I as a decent American could not live with myself. So I shut that operation down.'

But if Don Webb cared about his neighbours, he was pretty isolated. Instead of abandoning the environmental mess that comes with intensive hog farming, big companies piled into it. Between 1992 and 1998, the hog population of North Carolina went from two million to ten million, creating in just one state the waste equivalent of the entire human population of Canada.

Many of the big meat producers moved into North Carolina, where land was inexpensive because it belonged to small farmers, mostly African American, who were in trouble. Tobacco had declined, soybeans weren't very profitable and slaughterhouses, controlled by meat companies, wouldn't give the smallholders access. That meant they sold their farms cheaply to corporations who then stipulated exactly what they could grow and at what price.

Martin is a senior policy advisor at the Johns Hopkins Bloomberg School of Public Health and headed up the Pew Commission inquiry into factory farming. He explained the meat producers' strategy to me.

'The whole idea was to get big, big enough to drive down costs. That meant buying up all the farms to ensure a steady supply to their slaughter facilities which, to be efficient, got bigger and bigger. Individual slaughtering made dismembering the animal too costly so they demanded absolute standardization. They invested in research in order to perfect certain narrow genetic lines of animals. The whole thing was about economies of scale: standardize everything to drive costs down as low as you can go.'

Consolidation was extreme. In 1950, the United States had three million hog farms; by 2007, this was down to 65,640. Big companies producing a standardized product gave rise to CAFOs: concentrated animal feeding operations, also known more colloquially as factory farming. You will find CAFOs all across America, handling hogs, chickens, turkeys and cows. In Europe, intensive farming has been introduced in Poland and Romania and today 50 per cent of the world's pork, 43 per cent of its beef, 74 per cent of its poultry and 68 per cent of its eggs come from CAFOs.[15] Don Webb may be distraught by his country's embrace of factory farming but the American example turned it into a global phenomenon.

The economic premise behind CAFOs is simple: drive down costs. If you put enough animals into a confined space, you need very few people with few skills to look after them. Inject them with antibiotics and also sometimes hormones and the animals will fatten fast so that, after five to six months, you can take them to the slaughterhouse and then start again.[16]

For large meat packers and producers, on the face of it, the race to the bottom has been fantastically successful. Americans are the world's largest consumers of meat and they're eating more than ever, more cheaply than ever. In 1970, the average American spent

4.2 per cent of his or her income on 194 pounds of meat each year. By 2005, consumption had gone up to 221 pounds per person while the cost had halved.

For Smithfield Foods, the world's largest hog producer and pork processor, this has proved tremendously good business. Controlling roughly 75 per cent of the market, the company manufactures more pork than the next five largest producers in the country combined – and it routinely outperforms the stock market.[17] Other large meat producers – Perdue Farms, Tyson Foods, and Cargill – are privately traded so it's hard to gauge just how profitable factory farming has been for them, but they are all large, flourishing enterprises that have made their fortunes by driving down costs to produce cheap meat.

But where did the costs go? Before meeting Don Webb, his friend and colleague Rick Dove took me up in a Cessna 175 Skylark to view one of the most intensive areas of pig farming in the Neuse River basin of North Carolina. Along with pilot Joe Corby, we weren't sightseeing but surveying a landscape that the Environmental Protection Agency has neither the people, the money nor the time to monitor. Dove, a retired Marine, used to be the Waterkeeper of the Neuse River and he knows the area like the palm of his hand.

At first sight, the river and surrounding flood plain look like a Southern idyll: greenery as far as the eye can see, few towns, little traffic. Leaving New Bern, we fly over an elegant marina full of expensive yachts and lavish waterfront homes. A loose skein of canals meander through lush greenery. That this is hog country seems implausible.

But as we move inland, the houses give way to long steel barns sitting on breezeblocks, punctuated with ventilation fans. Inside each barn are up to 10,000 hogs, chickens or turkeys. They are kept permanently indoors, tightly packed together and confined to metal crates. Most animals lack the space to turn around or to lie down. Their feed incorporates antibiotics – penicillin, tetracyclines, macrolides, streptogramins and others – that both accelerate growth and protect against infections, which can travel fast in such intense conditions. Arsenic fulfils a similar purpose for chickens, with the added effect of turning the meat an appealing pink.[18]

Next to the barns, and the length of two or three football fields are what appear, at first glance, to be swimming pools. Except that what fills them isn't blue but a dull maroon brown. These are the lagoons Don Webb described: clay-lined cesspits full of animal urine, faeces, blood and mucus, the waste that runs from the slatted floors of the barns, through pipes and out into the open air. Alongside the lagoons soybeans are being showered by a rotary sprayer that sucks the excrement from the lagoon and atomizes it across the crops, fertilizing them. The United States Department of Agriculture estimates that around 500 million tons of such manure are produced annually by factory farms; that is three times the amount of sanitary waste produced by humans living in America.[19] But this waste isn't treated; 75 times more concentrated than human sewage and 500 times more concentrated than effluent from any municipal wastewater treatment facility, it is sprayed straight onto the crops.[20]

And this is a flood plain, which means that the water table is high, the land laced with small streams and rivulets that feed into the river. Although it is early August and hurricane season hasn't yet begun, the water level is high enough for much of the dispersed spray to be visible, sitting puddled on the soil or running off into the streams. The air we fly through may not be quite as pure as it looks either; up to 80 per cent of the nitrogen in a hog lagoon can be emitted into the air in the form of ammonia, eventually falling back to earth as rain onto crops, waterways and river basins.[21]

The seeping of raw animal waste, together with the antibiotics, arsenic and heavy metal from the lagoons, into the water supply poses serious environmental risks. Not just the 'dead zones' that kill off the fish but what scientists describe as 'objectionable compounds' that can emanate from the livestock facilities: acetic acid, butyric acids, valeric acids, hydrogen sulphide and ammonia. Decomposing manure produces at least 160 gases, of which ammonia, hydrogen sulphide and methane are the most pervasive. One study of chronic exposure to hydrogen sulphide found that it could lead to such abnormalities as impaired balance, hearing, seeing and memory loss. Children living near these farms are more likely to be diagnosed with asthma and other respiratory conditions.

Moreover, meat companies have started to locate large poultry facilities within yards of the hog barns. For Bob Martin, the risk of cross-contamination is the most dangerous development he has seen in years.

'No one is concerned about 250,000 broiler chickens sharing the same ten acres with 25,000 hogs?' he exclaimed. 'These are perfect petri dishes for creating the new strains of avian and human flus!'

The biggest environmental health risk, however, comes from antibiotics being used on such a wide scale to promote growth and prevent disease. According to David Kessler, former Commissioner for the US Food and Drug Administration, 80 per cent of *all* antibiotics sold in 2011 went to the livestock industry.[22] But such profuse applications of antibiotics provoke resistance on a very wide scale. The prolific appearance of MRSA is particularly alarming as it is resistant to all common antibiotics. A form of staphylococcus, it is killed by cooking but can live on the skin, where it causes abscesses that are dangerous and difficult to treat. One study found factory pig farmers 760 times more likely to be colonized with the bacterium than the general population. In Canada, MRSA was found in 24.9 per cent of all pigs tested and one quarter of their farmers.

A 2012 report found an increasing number of pathogens resistant to antibiotics in supermarket meats: 38.2 per cent of chicken breast and 51 per cent of ground turkey hosted forms of salmonella resistant to three or more antimicrobial classes.[23] Health authorities around the world now recognize the rise of antibiotic-resistant organisms as one of the toughest challenges they face today. So the chance of disease increases as our ability to fight the disease decreases.

'It's easy to test for antibiotic-resistant bacteria on grocery store meat,' Bob Martin told me, 'and the results are always shocking. But what happens when it is in the environment, no one can quantify. We know that it is very prolific and gets passed along to other bacteria that have never come into contact with antibiotics. It is amazingly resilient in ground water and carried for miles by flies and in storms. It's really hard to test for that.' What that means is that, even if you don't eat meat at all, the consequences of the way it is produced touches everyone.

Of course, those most immediately at risk from CAFOs are the people who work inside them. The jobs these farms produce are few, unskilled and poorly paid, attracting migrant and often undocumented workers who work long days and long weeks. Although privately they will talk about the smells that make them want to vomit, they have little protection and few have healthcare. Slaughterhouse work is dangerous, with nerve damage, repetitive-stress injuries and accidents common. Surrounded by animals treated without care and often with brutality, they find themselves in the same position: just another means of keeping meat cheap.

This is not the rural America of Aaron Copland or Andrew Wyeth. In North Carolina, 17 per cent of the adult population and a quarter of all children live in poverty.[24] Factory farming didn't create jobs; it undermined the local economy. Centralizing purchasing of feedstuffs and antibiotics keeps costs down but brings no income into the region. Hog farms may produce cheap food but the people who live near them are those most likely to need food stamps.[25]

When we had finished flying over the farms, Rick Dove and I drove around them. Outside the long steel barns would be a pick-up truck, at most two: workers often live onsite and the farms don't require much manpower. We drive through Brown Town, a cluster of houses on the edge of a farm. Refrigerators and rusting farm equipment sit for sale on the grass outside. A few African American men sit on the porch. Kids sit or stand listless on the grass; women don't look up as cars pass. The stillness is eerie. No urgency. No energy. What for? Nothing to do. Nowhere to go. The heat and the smell hang in the air, not moving.

Elsie Herring, an elegant black woman, sat on her porch talking to me about her house. She'd inherited it from her mother, who had it from the plantation owner her father once belonged to. Sometimes the farmers sprayed at night, she said. You couldn't keep the mist or the smell out of the house.

Slavery feels near at hand on these roads, like it was yesterday. The past feels very present but the future is hard to imagine. The region that once grew tobacco and now grows cheap meat finds it hard to attract new high-tech jobs because it isn't clean or skilled enough. The only new industries that want to come here are dirty jobs: recycling batteries and sludge, another form of industrial waste.

'People here are used to suffering in silence and that is what these companies have exploited,' Gary Grant later told me. A former schoolteacher, Grant now runs the North Carolina Environmental Justice Network. Since the big hog farms started in 1991, he has campaigned vigorously against them, arguing that they specifically harm the poor.

'People are very afraid that, if they speak up, they will lose their jobs, they will lose their food stamps, they will just get whipped in the process. It's environmental racism, the last vestiges of Jim Crow.'

For all that he is an outspoken activist, Grant is a soft-spoken, mild-mannered man, with the patience and attention you'd expect of a teacher. He has fought the hog farms and their side effects for years and, in his county, Halifax, he's had a measure of success. That has only meant, however, that the big farms went to counties where the population was more passive or more afraid.

'In one county,' he told me, 'I asked them why they didn't do anything. They just said to me, "It's their land, what can we do?" And I said to them, "But it's your *air*!"'

This was the source of Don Webb's anguish: what the farm had done to his neighbours, to their homes, to his community and to his faith in America. He had tried to help them fight against the farms, breaking into barns to film what he saw, petitioning and protesting in every forum and legislature where he could gain admittance. He was threatened and offered money for his silence. He wouldn't shut up. He still won't.

'I wonder now how much of our world is for sale. When we turn our head away from one American, allow that person to be mistreated, then every man, woman and child in this nation is at risk. I look at it with a sad heart to see that all I worked for all my life can be destroyed.'

Social capital is the term sociologists use to define what Don Webb mourns. It's an academic term for mutual trust, reciprocity and the shared norms that create quality of life and make a society resilient in times of stress. 'Communities with higher levels of social capital,' wrote the Pew Commission into intensive farming, 'tend to have lower poverty rates, fewer incidents of violent crime, and stronger democratic institutions.' Factory farming, the Commission concluded, threatens social capital.

In the race to the bottom, social capital is what is destroyed when people are afraid to speak up and defend themselves. Social capital is what is destroyed when competitive pressures take precedence over community health. And social capital is destroyed when the occupants of Brown Town become invisible and impotent.

'We got to have cheap pork, we have to have cheap chicken – but the people who benefit from it, they don't have to smell it, to eat the flies,' is how Don Webb puts it. You don't need to tell him about power-distance relationships: he lives them, with his neighbours powerless to move and those making decisions a very great distance away. After decades of fighting, he is brokenhearted that his idea of America as a place where everyone mattered and where everyone could be heard has turned out to be a fairytale.

'They don't care about us. They don't care about me and some rural people who don't want to live with faeces factories. My great nation under God with liberty and justice for all does not care for me and my family or for the poor black people who got it the hardest. And I live in America!'

In 2013, the Chinese firm Shuanghui agreed to buy Smithfield Foods for $7.1 billion, the largest ever acquisition of an American company by the Chinese. The deal raised many raised questions – about the safety of the supply of two critical drugs: heparin and clenbuterol, both made from pigs. Contamination of both drugs has been traced to Chinese factories but now, in effect, these issues have been externalized to the new Chinese owners.

It is always easier to push costs down to the poor who can't move away, are afraid to speak up and lack political influence. Threatened with increased regulatory oversight in the US, meat companies have expanded their operations to Europe and South America, where they seek unfettered opportunities to keep up their race to the bottom. In Poland and Romania, they again find populations with a history of silence, afraid to speak up and unaccustomed to the concept of rights. In 1999, Smithfield bought Animex, one of Poland's biggest pork producers, and by 2008, 600,000 Polish hog farmers had lost their livelihoods: consolidation, with its economies of scale keeping meat cheap, then moved on to Romania where 90 per cent of independent farms vanished. Then, in 2010, packets of frozen pork offal, subsidized by the EU, started to appear in African markets. They were so cheap that local farmers found it hard to sell their own products.

It would be comforting to imagine that in Britain we have higher standards of animal welfare and environmental wellbeing. Antibiotic use here is lower than in the US, thanks to European Union legislation, but 30 per cent of antibiotics are used on farm animals, of which 80 per cent is to prevent disease or accelerate growth. In August 2013, Derbyshire County Council will decide whether to approve an indoor pig factory for 25,000 pigs near Foston. So the competitive pressures to intensify meat production and to build intensive 'sty-scrapers' is as powerful here as anywhere.[26] Most of the meat sold in British supermarkets comes from factory farms but, because it tends to be privately-labelled by supermarkets, consumers can't identify its source.

Food activism in the UK tends to be more focused on animal welfare than environmental standards but it still produces problems for large American meat producers who have, by and large, stayed away from production here. When I interviewed the Chief Sustainability Officer of Smithfield Foods, Dennis Leary, he was clear about the degree to which it is hard for his company to do business in the UK, and openly contemptuous of British fastidiousness when it comes to food supply.

'I hear a lot from UK activists, saying, "our meat is the best in the world, everyone should do what we do. Importing US meat with lower standards is a bad thing; everyone should come to us." But that's not how it works − it works the other way! What the United States enjoys − and the United Kingdom is suffering in this regard − is high-quality, low-cost food. We produce the highest quality at the lowest cost because of the nature of the systems and inventiveness of folks in this business. Our challenge here is to keep the price low so that we are competitive worldwide.'[27]

Leary is frequently the spokesman provided by Smithfield Foods. A former environmental regulator, he is now an executive vice-president who also acts as treasurer for the company's political action committee.[28] We met, not in North Carolina, but in Washington DC in the heart of the political lobbying district. Giving the world the 'choice' of cheap meat is the company's strategic agenda.

'To feed the world,' Leary argues, 'modern intensive agriculture is the only way to go. Our task is to (I'm trying to avoid sounding noble here) make products that are sustainable so everyone enjoys the same thing. How are we going to feed people? Low prices are fundamental, so you have to start thinking about sustainable intensification. That is the current thought. That is where we all need to go.'

Leary may be the Chief Sustainability Officer and happy to talk about 'sustainable intensification' but he can't and won't define sustainability and he discourages his staff from even trying.[29] Although the company's annual report proudly describes itself as combining 'leading brands and a commitment to sustainability to produce good food responsibly',[30] the company is at pains to stress that sustainability must be pursued as part of 'value creation' – in other words, it must never interfere with making money. 2011 and 2012 were the company's most profitable years ever, but the sustainability initiatives they boasted of in their annual report seem trivial: reduced packaging at some plants, the replacement of cardboard bins with collapsible plastic ones and donations to breast cancer research and the Red Cross.[31] New waste management technologies have been installed in some Missouri farms (where the company faces multiple lawsuits) and the company sponsored a livestock-judging contest. It also boasts of having conformed to recent legislation that calls for phasing out gestation crates – the metal frames that hold pregnant sows before and during pregnancy – and replacing them with 'group housing', which doubles the tiny space available for each sow. New lagoons can no longer be built in North Carolina but the old ones remain. Antibiotic use is up but food donations are down. At no point does Leary articulate any connection between business and the society that supports it.

'It's hard enough,' Leary writes, 'to run a business even without considering the social concerns that have been injected in recent years.'[32]

'Sustainable intensification' is the kind of oxymoron Orwell would have relished, since many – including the Pew Commission – argue that intensification is inherently unsustainable because of the pollution, health problems and cruelty it creates. But for Leary, a genial blowsy man who has clearly rehearsed these same arguments for years, any other approach is just romantic.

'I understand the romantic concept of the idealized farm; I live on a farm myself and buy from farmers' markets occasionally. That's our choice. But my wife can barely feed us from this small operation. And the people who believe in that stuff, they're always monied. Our job at Smithfield is to meet the expectations of a demanding population. That's where our planning comes from. And people want cheap meat.'

Smithfield Foods is just one contestant among many in the race to the bottom; along with other private companies – Tyson, Cargill, JBS – they all compete fiercely on price. Leary insists that, while the company isn't obsessed with its competition, there's no point resisting consumer demand: someone is going to fill it and it might as well be them.

The true cost of cheap meat is poverty (which we all pay for), environmental degradation (which we all pay for), healthcare risks (to which we are all exposed) and the destruction of the social fabric on which we all depend. Even if you aren't a meat eater, you inhabit a society riven, stressed and divided by the costs of producing it. In externalizing their costs to society while retaining profits for themselves and their shareholders, these businesses hope to win the race. To do so, they fundamentally sever their connection to the world in which they operate. And if a corporation is big enough, there may be nothing that anyone can, or is willing to, do about it. This leaves such companies and their leaders feeling they can do what they want with the environment.

'To me ecology's just a source for raw materials and the place to (legally) flush our wastes.'

That was Ray Anderson's view at one time and, having become one of the largest carpet manufacturers in the world, he thought he had every reason to feel self-satisfied.

'So what if each day just one of my plants sent six tons of carpet trimmings to the local landfill? It was someone else's problem, not mine. That's what landfills were for.'[33]

Ray Anderson's soft Georgia accent and good-ol'-boy style could be deceptive; he described himself as a driven, cold-eyed businessman. After his college football career was cut short by injury, he studied industrial engineering and, in 1973, started his carpet-tile business, Interface. Carpet tiles turned out to be a perfect solution for the new economy, in which companies come, go and change every week, and Interface built alliances with architects and interior designers who loved the product. But then some of those architects and interior designers started asking: what is the company doing about the environment? Anderson's answer then was much the same as Smithfield's today: we comply with the law.

'We took it all for granted at that time,' he recalled.[34] 'That's just the way it was. The energy was all coming from fossil fuels. The process is very energy-intensive and in some cases very abusive to the environment. That meant effluent going into the water system, maybe not treated. And with lots of chemicals in the process: dyes and surfactants.'

Customers and employees kept nagging Anderson for his environmental vision; he didn't have one. Recognizing that he had to come up with something more motivating than compliance, he happened to pick up *The Ecology of Commerce*. Because it was written by another successful businessman, Paul Hawken, he reckoned it would at least be pragmatic. Instead it galvanized him.

'I stood indicted as a plunderer, a destroyer of the earth, a thief, stealing my own grandchildren's future,' Anderson later wrote. 'And I thought, *My God, someday what I do here will be illegal. Someday they'll send people like me to jail.*'

Many of Anderson's employees thought he'd gone mad but his epiphany set a new agenda for his company. Heretofore a huge consumer of fossil fuels and a generator of vast amounts of waste with tons of carpet going to landfill each year, Anderson decided that his company would no longer take anything from the earth that could not easily be renewed. Unlike Smithfield's Dennis Leary, Anderson could define sustainability.

'Sustainability,' Anderson wrote, 'is all about coming up with ways to meet our needs (not wants – needs) today without undermining the ability of other folks to meet their needs tomorrow.' For his own business, he made it even simpler: 'Take nothing. Do no harm.'[35]

Most companies, he realized, were externalizing machines. In traditional businesses, when costs came down, they were imposed on people and places powerless to respond. That, Anderson determined, had to change. Businesses needed to identify all of their costs and then they had to find or invent ways to eliminate them completely and permanently – not just pass them along.

In contrast to the race to the bottom, Anderson talked about 'climbing Mount Sustainability' and challenged everyone to create 'the first company that, by its deeds, shows the entire industrial world what sustainability is in all its dimensions: People, process, product, place and profits'. Mission Zero meant that the company aimed to eliminate *all* negative environmental impact by 2020.

At the time, Anderson really had no idea how hard it would be to accomplish his vision, but he never wavered. His mission required completely different thinking about the full impact of the company on the environment and everyone who lived within it. In other words, Anderson vowed that he would no longer externalize anything. And he put his money where his mouth was.

'Make no mistake. Mission Zero is hard, hard, work. It is not a "program of the month". And nobody is making us do it. We're under no pressure from our competitors to achieve sustainability.'

Anderson wasn't driven by a passion to lower prices but by a determination that his company would accept all the responsibilities that its business incurred. Instead of seeing Interface as separate from society, he viewed it is integrally connected to the entire world. For a free market truly to exist, everyone would do this.

Interface is a billion dollar, publicly traded business, operating in 110 countries. Changing a company this size would, Anderson knew, involve a lot more than creating a sustainability officer or a specialized team; every single person in the business had to get involved and contribute. His mission unleashed a whirlwind of innovation, leading the company to invent new processes and new technologies. Setting the bar high, not low, galvanized that creativity. It also forced everyone in the company to become collaborators. In place of dog-eat-dog politics and departmental silos, the entire business could not be transformed without, as Anderson describes it, 'a corporate "ecosystem" to borrow a term from nature, with cooperation replacing confrontation'. In everything the company learned along the way, Anderson found new lessons, ideas and processes to share. Instead of keeping his discoveries to himself, he shared them broadly with anyone who would listen – Anheuser-Busch, PepsiCo, Google, Epson, Toyota, Bayer, Cisco – inciting them all to set new standards. After all, a free market would only ever be truly free if everyone stopped externalizing and instead absorbed the full cost of their activity.

Key to Interface's success was the determination not to out-source responsibility but to embrace it. Instead of trusting their suppliers to eliminate toxic substances, company chemists and engineers analysed every material Interface used. Instead of trust-ing government lists detailing safety and side effects of substances, they developed their own chemical screening protocol. At every step of the way, instead of passing responsibility along to depend-ent suppliers, the company grabbed responsibility and set their own standards. 'Trust but verify' is how Anderson summed it up.

Didn't this cost a fortune? It didn't. It made the business both more efficient and more creative. The idea that harm to people and the planet was the inevitable price paid for a successful business was one that Anderson repeatedly – and successfully – disproved.

'Any evaluation that concludes that it is cheaper and more cost-efficient to cause serious harm to the only world we have is not particularly logical,' Anderson wrote. 'You can be sure that exter-nalities of some kind are disguising the true economics.'

And he kept proving he wasn't a dreamer. Greenhouse gas emis-sions were reduced by 99 per cent; water usage was down by 74 per cent. In Europe, the use of all heavy metals was entirely eliminated. Since 2003, the company has sold eighty-three million square yards of one particular product – Cool Carpet – that has zero net global warming effect to the earth. It has been a runaway best-seller.

Not only did Anderson's radical approach to the environment make his business more successful and more influential, it also made the company itself more resilient because of the quality of com-mitment everyone working for Interface brought to their work.

'It has had a profound effect on organizational cohesiveness,' he said. 'A shared higher purpose will do that.'[36]

Interface's Mission Zero was full of creativity like this: breaking rules about what could and could not be economic, finding or inventing new technologies to solve problems everyone assumed just had to be accepted. And the more that the company innovated, the more lessons they had to teach – and wanted to teach – anyone who would listen.

Tragically, Anderson died on 8 August 2011, before he could see his company ascend the summit of Mount Sustainability. But Interface continues to challenge itself to meet Anderson's 2020 goal and to prove to the world at large that externalizing can and must be a thing of the past. Anderson didn't try to win the race to the bottom; he just called it off.

'Will the new business model – investing in a truly sustainable future, a future characterized by new thinking, new products and new profits – see us through the economic downturn?' Anderson wrote. 'I say, yes, and my money – my personal investment – is where my mouth is. And if we can do it, anybody can. And if anybody can, everybody can.'

Although his leadership was uniquely inspiring, Anderson isn't the only business leader who has vigorously refuted the notion that the only way is down. At American Apparel, founder Dov Charney vigorously rejects the idea that making clothing requires sweatshops.

'Fast fashion is crass and cheap and sits on the backs of other people,' Charney insisted. 'It looks sexy but it is basically stolen goods, hot goods. Twenty cents an hour is slavery.'[37]

American Apparel proudly labels itself 'Sweatshop Free'. The company eschews outsourcing and operates the single largest garment factory in America, where it pays nearly twice the minimum wage.[38] Employees are also offered subsidized public transport and meals, low-cost health insurance and can participate in a bike-lending scheme. All of this is aimed at keeping better, more committed workers and better quality control.

'I believe in bringing the worker *into* the company, knowing the face of the worker. Not relentlessly pursuing low wages. A $4.99 bikini doesn't exist unless you're screwing somebody. Focus on a better product!'

Charney is clearly capable of whipping up controversy about almost anything – he calls himself 'a complicated freak' – and he clearly enjoys pushing boundaries. But he also means it when he urges consumers to reject sweatshop labour, comparing cheap clothes to the Outspan oranges his mother would never let him eat because they symbolized the injustice of apartheid. By refusing to outsource, Charney can bring everyone involved in the business under one roof where they can share ideas and "sculpt a sustainable business model that doesn't rely on exploitation."

But his argument against sweatshops goes beyond hating them because they represent a form of slavery. He also thinks that the race to the bottom is doomed. It isn't just that low wages are offensive – he doesn't think they're financially sustainable either. Today's low-wage countries, like Bangladesh, will become tomorrow's middle-class societies. Transport costs will rise. Sooner or later prices will go up. It's to the long-term advantage of any business not to get cheaper but to get smarter about what consumers really want and how to make it well. Instead of cutting the wages of the least skilled, put pressure on the most skilled to be more creative.

Marketing American Apparel as 'sweatshop free' doesn't, Charney believes, make more than 1 per cent difference to his customers. But it proves that fashion doesn't have to be cheap and sweatshops aren't a competitive necessity. And he uses his company to show that businesses don't have to race to the bottom, they don't have to outsource and they don't have to destroy the environment. The wall of colourful bow ties displayed in the stores illustrate the company's 'Creative Reuse' strategy that, instead of wasting offcuts or leaving them on the floor to cause fire hazards, turns scraps into smaller items like tank tops, ties and hairbands. His factory is solar-powered and a whole range of clothing is made from organic cotton. He believes in what he calls 'win-win business' and is determined to prove that it works.

Emma Bridgewater's is a far quieter style than Charney's but their passion is shared. She had started making mugs in 1985 when she couldn't find a gift for her mother's birthday. What began as a hobby soon became a business but, instead of doing what most entrepreneurs do – work from home until growth forces expansion into nearby industrial units – she sat down and thought about what kind of a business to build.

She knew her history. Aware that Stoke-on-Trent had once led the world in the production of both fine china and more homely pottery, that seemed the natural home for her new company. But contemporary Stoke was full of warnings about the desperate business that making pottery had become. Where once the British had led the world in manufacturing and designing fine china and tableware, now the town was covered in abandoned warehouses, empty streets and vacant houses: the Detroit of the pottery world.

Brands that had once been world-famous were now only just hanging on. Most had begun outsourcing the cheap labour to China, although they found that doing so lowered the value of once-famous names: Minton, Royal Doulton, Wedgwood. But her first visit to Stoke was daunting.

'I was astonished by what I found: a post-industrial wasteland, really a desolate scene. There were only two manufacturers here who could supply the kind of clay we needed – it wasn't clear that they were going to be around all that long. We could only get the glazes we needed from one company so that felt pretty risky, too. And I knew we could get things done more cheaply abroad. But at the same time, I realized that this was where it had all started! And right from the start, I felt this business could grow from the grass-roots. If it meant we were going to have high costs, so be it. That's what the brand would have to stand for. We would have to make things that had high value to people: because they were beautiful, well made, with great design and worth the money.'

Bridgewater wasn't blind; all around her, she could see the car-casses of dead businesses. But the lesson she took from them was that the race to the bottom was doomed. Those companies had cut costs and outsourced jobs – and it hadn't worked. Customers didn't want to buy British pottery made in Malaysia.

'Exporting a labour problem is just such crap; why aren't we ashamed to do that? Ashamed that we can't run our own busi-nesses – the businesses we *invented* – well enough to make them work? As a new company, we couldn't cut costs – we didn't have any yet! So we had to be in tune with our customers. And what they wanted was really great design but something much more modern, less formal than the old manufacturers had produced. We just had to think hard, and think creatively, about how to be rele-vant.'

Walking through the Emma Bridgewater factory in Stoke today is an eye-opening experience. Crisply decorated bright mugs are still being hand-printed; plates are being handled by people, not machines. There's an air of cheerful concentration about the place. When you stop and talk to women painting polka dots, applying transfers, or men removing bowls from firing ovens, they're happy to chat about anything – but they don't ever stop working.

The factory is spotless and visitors can take tours, stay for lunch or just fill their baskets at the shop. Even mid-week in a bleak winter, the atmosphere buzzes with visitors and the background hum of furnaces. Many visitors are shocked to see that their favourite mugs and plates are produced this way: by hand, by a person. But once she decided not to race to the bottom, to set up in Stoke and make it work, Bridgewater simply refused to compromise.

'Cutting your prices isn't a strategy. It isn't even thinking. Whenever you buy or sell something cheap – well, someone else must be paying, being exploited somehow. The environmental impact of buying crap is huge. When you buy a plate for two pounds, you have to think that someone somewhere is paying so you can do that. The race to the bottom – it's just total suicide.'

Bridgewater runs the business with her husband, Matthew Rice, a talented furniture and print designer. They've doubled the firm's revenue in the last five years – straight through the recession – but the numbers didn't seem to excite them as much as the impact the company can make on its community. As we sat in the factory kitchen, he talked about the thrill he got watching the company thrive.

'Companies are starting to come back to Stoke now – it's fantastic! It's as though we've given them courage. And of course, just being here, you keep suppliers in business. That means you don't lose the crafts, the talents, the skills you need for an industry like this. So if you can keep going – everyone can keep going.'

Rice and Bridgewater have moved in some pretty swanky circles; Rice's partner in his furniture business was Viscount Linley. But up in Stoke, it didn't seem that glamour and the social whirl were uppermost in his mind.

'You know what makes me happy?' Rice asked rhetorically. 'What makes me happy is knowing that, the better we do, the more jobs we can create. We *like* employing people. That's what it is all about.'

After I left Stoke-on-Trent, I reflected that I hadn't heard anyone in business say that they actually *liked* employing people. Had I ever heard it? After decades of working in the US and the UK, almost all I'd ever heard were around cutting costs, cutting people. The race to the bottom had become so ubiquitous, its central tenets so pervasive and unquestioned, that most business leaders had entirely forgotten what companies were for.

Although wildly different in their businesses and personae, Ray Anderson, Dov Charney and Emma Bridgewater all follow firmly in the footsteps of Henry Ford. Ford maintained that all business exists to serve others and that, to do so, it had to observe these principles: fearlessness, a disregard for competition and the putting of service before profit. He also insisted that manufacturing was not about buying low, selling high, speculation, gambling or 'sharp dealing', and had a pronounced disdain for financiers.

But Ford caused greatest consternation when he doubled the wages of his factory workers. He did so in order to reduce staff turnover; to him, labour flexibility was not an efficiency but a waste. He considered every employee a partner – 'the boss is the partner of his worker, the worker is the partner of his boss' – and insisted that any good business would aspire to keep good employees, train them and pay them more.

'It ought to be the employer's ambition, as leader, to pay better wages than any similar line of business, and it ought to be the workman's ambition to make this possible ... What good is industry if it be so unskillfully managed as not to return a living to everyone concerned?'

Ford maintained these passionate principles because he believed absolutely in the value of human labour. But he also understood that, when he paid his workers more, he enabled them to earn enough money to buy his cars. You could say that Ford was the first evangelist for 'trickle-up' economics: the argument that if you pay well at the bottom of the market, the whole economy will expand.

'If we can distribute high wages, then that money is going to be spent and it will serve to make storekeepers and distributors and manufacturers and workers in other lines more prosperous and their prosperity will be reflected in our sales. Country-wide high wages spell country-wide prosperity.'[39]

Now that we know trickle-down doesn't work, it's an interesting thought that a 'trickle-up' world might prove strikingly more successful. Instead of the entire economy sinking to the bottom, we could do better raising everyone's boat. As much as the poor may be shut off from view – across the world or working strange hours in places we don't see – and as much as the rich may shut themselves away in limousines and private jets, the stability of society and the health of the planet are ultimately requirements for all safe and healthy lives. What Anderson, Charney, Bridgewater and Henry Ford share is a vision of business in which nobody is left out. Everyone counts and the secret of success lies not in being an expert at exploiting people and the planet but in being smarter about getting them to work creatively together. Shortly before he died, Ray Anderson recorded a video message for his workforce, celebrating the thirty-eighth birthday of his carpet company. He did not know whether he would live to see it achieve the audacious goal that had made it both successful and famous. But he knew what he wanted for the world he left behind.

'I can't say whether I'll see the view from the top of Mount Sustainability but I want you to see it. And I want you to see the day when the Interface model has become the accepted business model of the most successful companies on earth. I want you to feel the joy of having led the transformation of the worldwide industrial system. I want you to appreciate the wisdom of doing well by doing good and the huge shift in thinking that has led to this journey.'

10. TOP OF THE WORLD

The more we sweat in peace, the less we bleed in war.

Vijaya Lakshmi Pandit

China, India, Germany, and South Korea are not playing
for second place. And neither should we. The United
States of America, we play for first place.

Barack Obama

In 2009, Brett Pierce disconcerted his family by making regular
trips to Iraq. He was neither a spy nor serving with the military.
Having spent most of his professional life as a producer on *Sesame
Street*, Pierce was on a mission to use television to educate Iraqi
teenagers in communication, collaboration and peace-building. His
format of choice was a game show.

In *Salam Shabab* (which means Peace, Youth) six regions fielded
four teams of three kids each and they competed to go through to
a national final. A series of sports challenges, mental puzzles, film-
making and performance exercises were designed to teach
collaboration through competition. Pierce ruled out anything too
preachy. Years of making TV shows for kids, he told me, had taught
him that, if they sensed an iota of didacticism, they would tune out.
The fact that girls and boys would be working together was radical enough.

'Keep in mind: the idea of putting a girl next to a boy where
their knees might touch – it was mind-blowing! We didn't know

how the kids would respond. They had never experienced this freedom before! It was a big thing for them to experience so much freedom, to think freely and to find a voice.'

Building tricycles from spare bike parts, throwing water balloons, painting from memory: all of these challenges were designed to be met through collaborative interaction. Soloists would make teams fail. And, in the first regional rounds, the kids thrived. These were not the media-savvy, polished products of *The X Factor* but eager, shy, excited teenagers who felt lucky to be involved. Watching the shows, every participant came across with a highly distinct personality, energy and sense of humour. Everyone was eager to do well; there's palpable pleasure in the experience as a whole. The prize was kept deliberately low-key – a laptop and a video camera for the team – because the reward wasn't the focus of the experience.

'It mattered that it didn't matter,' Pierce told me. 'There wasn't a lot at stake. That was deliberate. Being part of the show was enough. So the kids were very spirited but not mean. There was no nastiness, no rivalry – because they were all on such a unique trip.'

Every challenge was part play, part work. The experience was supposed to be fun – and it's certainly fun to watch. The film-making and performance sequences attract the largest number of points and in these the results were voted on by the audience. It is a strange and moving sight to see the teenagers place their votes in a ballot box and then swipe their fingers with ink: for many this is their first experience of democracy.

But, in the final round, Pierce had introduced into the game what he called 'the switch'. At this point, the regional teams that had gone forward were broken up into new teams: black, white, red and green, the colours of the Iraqi flag. Each team was now comprised of members from different parts of the country. In the very first series of the show, this had had dramatic consequences. Many of the kids had become sullen, resistant. What had been fun became seriously difficult and they were visibly angry at being made to collaborate with people from other parts of Iraq, some Shia, some Sunni, some Kurdish.

The first series aired on Iraqi television in 2011. By the third season, shot in 2012, everyone knew that the switch was coming, so it wasn't such a shock. Most of the kids took it in their stride, looking nervous of their new teammates but intrigued, prepared to give them a chance. Some even looked quite excited, smiling shyly at their new friends.

'I'm convinced my team is strong – and the rest is for God and us to decide.'

But not in the white team. There, one young woman from Tigris named Baraa decided that she simply could not get along with her teammate Fatma from Najaf. What was especially peculiar about this reaction was that, as part of her regional team, Baraa had been a great contributor. Alone among the teams, hers had scored in a water-balloon challenge because she gave her teammate excellent support and advice. When they had struggled to make a boat from straws and hollowed-out eggs – and mostly failed – she conceded that 'it was my mistake and next time I'll listen to them'. Fatma too had done well in her regional team, particularly in the performance exercise, which attracted a large number of points.

But Baraa was adamant that she could not work with Fatma. The girl from Tigris was too quiet, she was bound to let the team down. Baraa started to cry as she explained – in front of Fatma – that she was sure 'this girl from Najaf' would make her lose.

Given odds and ends from bicycles, they were challenged to build a vehicle that could carry all three of the team. The white team couldn't decide on their design and Baraa pinned all her hopes on the weakness of the other teams. All the Heath Robinson creations that emerged were quirky and clumsy – but most still worked. The white team's vehicle, however, only loosely connected with string, could not hold together. A perfect image for the disjointed vulnerability of their teamwork, the machine lacked all coordination and the three limped last across the finishing line. All through the semi-final, whenever there was a break between challenges, Fatma and Baraa both retreated quickly to their regional friends.

In a subsequent challenge, the teams had to look at a grid of nine images, try to remember them all and paint them. Once again, the dissentious white team struggled.

'I told her to draw a mountain – and she just drew a triangle,' Baraa complains. The more she berated Fatma, the more withdrawn and sullen Fatma became. As Baraa took charge, the other girl relinquished responsibility to contribute. And as the contest progressed, the inability of the team to function, the failure of the teenagers to relish their once-in-a-lifetime experience, became increasingly pronounced.

In the musical challenge, the three had to compose and play a piece of music using a rough assortment of pan lids, bottles and sticks. The other teams quickly figured out that, in addition to the props they'd been given, they also had their own voices. What emerged was hilarious but charming cacophony. But the white team never saw their own voices as instruments. Lacking any melody, they hammered out a joyless series of rhythms that lacked structure, vigour, finesse.

The best teams quickly resolved their individual difficulties. Some relished the chance to meet kids from other parts of the country, to learn a few words of Kurdish or hear about different foods and styles of dress. But the white team never figured this out. The more dominant Baraa became, the more Fatma withdrew, leaving her other teammate, Buraq, puzzled, isolated and ineffective.

Salam Shabab won the Unesco Special Prize at Prix Jeunesse in 2012 for its contribution in teaching the skills of collaboration and conflict resolution. It's easy to see why. On this small scale, with no high stakes and the lightest of oversight, the difficulty and potential of collaboration played out in miniature just as it plays out in life. It can feel quite easy and natural to work alongside people with whom you have much in common. The same work becomes far more difficult, contentious and irrational when regional or national differences come into play. People are territorial animals and that sense of defensiveness – irrational and counter-productive – can make the complex work of collaboration harder still. And the teams where one member tries to dominate lose.

Competitions always need a way to keep score. In *Salam Shabab*, it's done with points and votes. Schools, colleges, hospitals have rankings and league tables, athletes use time, and companies compare stock-price rises and market share. When it comes to international competition, nations use Gross Domestic Product (GDP) to show

how big their economies are and how energetic their growth rate. Just like all competitive measures, GDP defines the game by what it measures – and what it doesn't. Like any single instrument trying to capture the value of a complex activity, it leaves a lot out. No one has summed this up better than Robert Kennedy in 1968, seven weeks before he died.

'Gross National Product, if we judge the United States of America by that ... counts air pollution and cigarette advertising, and ambulances to clear our highways of carnage. It counts special locks for our doors and the jails for the people who break them. It counts the destruction of the redwoods and the loss of our natural wonder, and chaotic sprawl. It counts napalm and it counts nuclear warheads and armoured cars for the police to fight the riots in our cities. It counts Whitman's rifle and Speck's knife*, and the television programs that glorify violence in order to sell toys to our children.

'Yet the gross national product does not allow for the health of our children or the quality of their education, or the joy of their play. It does not include the beauty of our poetry or the strength of our marriages, the intelligence of our public debate or the integrity of our public officials. It measures neither our wit nor our courage, neither our wisdom nor our learning, neither our compassion nor our devotion to our country. It measures everything, in short, except that which makes life worthwhile and it can tell us everything about America except why we are proud that we are American.'

Had Kennedy been in Britain today, he might have added that current gross domestic product will include the war in Afghanistan, the cost of flooding, the medical care of injured athletes, the cost of steroids and anti-depressants, of legal services in mergers and acquisitions, divorces and litigation, and the food banks proliferating across the countryside. Because it represents total spending, GDP goes up in the wake of disasters but does not go down when fracking pollutes the water table, when gases evaporate from pig slurry pits or athletes bow out with their injuries. In GDP terms, it might

---

* In 1966, Charles Whitman killed sixteen and wounded thirty-two people in Austin, Texas, while in the same year Richard Speck raped and killed eight student nurses.

be better for Tewkesbury and the Somerset levels to be flooded regularly than to install effective drains and defences. GDP doesn't reflect the lost capacity of kids who gave up on education (or who were abandoned by it) or the creative energy siphoned off by forced ranking and office infighting. Nor can it reflect the efforts parents invest in their children or looking after their own parents and neighbours; or the time they devote to volunteering or community participation. Like all scores, it draws attention to one thing – spending – and erases the rest.

The inventor of GDP recognized this. Before the 1930s, governments had only a ragbag of data – stock-price indices, freight-train loadings – which made economic planning both impossible and highly susceptible to political manipulation or wishful thinking. With the onset of the Great Depression, what had been a chronic problem became acute, so the US Department of Commerce commissioned a Russian econometrician, Simon Kuznets, to design a method for measuring economic output. During World War Two, the metric came into its own, in the planning and financing of wartime production. When, in 1944, the Bretton Woods Conference attempted to create a new monetary order throughout the world, GDP was adopted as the standard measure of a country's economy.

Kuznets himself, however, wasn't entirely gratified by this wholesale adoption of his work. A meticulous econometrician, he believed that a true measure of national output ought to include unpaid work – like housework. It made no sense that a parent cooking dinner for the family contributed only the ingredient costs to the economy, while a business executive dining alone apparently contributed more. The Commerce Department didn't take the distinction seriously and refused to incorporate the value of unpaid labour, so Kuznets moved on to study inequality – but not before warning Congress that 'the welfare of a nation can scarcely be inferred from a measure of national income'.

GDP is tweaked every five years; in 2013, the US Commerce Department decided to give greater weight to intellectual property like movies, TV shows and books. But discontent with GDP has persisted: GDP doesn't capture externalities, physical or mental health and it doesn't reflect educational attainment, economic inequality, social stability or environmental degradation. Nevertheless, in 1999, the Department of Commerce threw a party to celebrate the invention of GDP as 'its achievement of the century'. Alan Greenspan, then the Chairman of the Federal Reserve, crowed, 'I personally would be inclined to say that the accuracy and conceptual rigour of our underlying data systems are more powerful and important than is commonly understood.'

Other countries occasionally toyed with alternative measures – as early as 1972, Bhutan proposed measuring gross national happiness; thirty years later, France and Great Britain did likewise. It turns out that happiness is a little complicated, in part because different cultures interpret questions about happiness in radically different ways and because surveys show up quite troubling anomalies. There is, for example, no relationship between increased gender equality and happiness while there is a positive relationship between happiness and violent crime in the USA but it seems unlikely any policymaker would use that data to campaign for more gender inequality accompanied by more murder.[1] The happiness indices, as a consequence, turned out not to provide much insight into the drivers of social welfare. In 2006, the Chinese introduced a 'green GDP' that, applied to its own economy in 2004, would have knocked 3 per cent off its growth rate. But still GDP has been the measure that has stuck. And because everyone uses it, countries can do what individuals and companies do: compare and compete.

What an insidious effect this has had. Every year, every quarter, even every week, just like companies on the stock market, countries compare their GDP numbers and growth figures to see who is winning. In recent years these numbers have incited something approaching panic, as Chinese GDP creeps closer and closer to that of the United States. As journalists wrote about the 'last few years of America's historic GDP reign', the 2012 presidential election echoed with candidates whipping up hysteria and promising bold action in the global competition.

'I want to beat China,' Republican Senator Rick Santorum said. 'I want to go to war with China and make America the most attractive place in the world to do business.'

'We can't just sit back and let China run all over us,' Mitt Romney argued. 'People say "you'll start a trade war!" There's one going on right now, folks! They're stealing our jobs and we're going to stand up to China.'

Even the President has weighed in, using (as he often does) a sports analogy to insist that 'the United States of America plays for first place'.

While pundits placed bets about the exact year in which Chinese GDP would overtake America's, the public was already way ahead of them. Since 2011, Gallup polls have shown that China is widely regarded by most Americans as the world's top economic power.[2]

'Few would argue that China's rocketing economic growth looms as a formidable challenge to the United States' global economic leadership,' Gallup commented. 'However, the majority of Americans believe the US has already lost the challenge, and relatively few are confident that the situation will be reversed in 20 years.'[3]

But what challenge is this? When the United States is not at war, lower defence spending brings down GDP but that does not necessarily make American lives poorer or Chinese lives any richer. If there are no further oil spills in the Gulf of Mexico, it's hard to see this as a national calamity. Moreover, if American employment increases and those in work now can afford iPhones and iPads, the fact that the Foxconn factory that makes them has more work does not make the US economy weaker. National economies are not zero-sum games in which one gain is another's loss. In fact, as we've seen throughout the economic crisis, quite the reverse: one failure provokes multiple failures.

Yet, world leaders endlessly talk about nations competing with one another. In the presidential debates, Obama argued about competing with China in education – as though well-educated Chinese children hurt American students. Conservative rhetoric for at least one season was dominated by the phrase 'global race', appearing in David Cameron's 2013 New Year message, in party political broadcasts, set speeches and informal remarks.[4] This rhetoric of competition plays to bias and prejudice, enflaming fear and distrust while illuminating nothing about why or how education needs to be improved for the children who receive it. The reason to upgrade schools or healthcare or road safety isn't to make the Chinese stupid or sick or dangerous; it is for their own sake, because these are the right things to do and because they make a society socially and environmentally sustainable. The America Creating Opportunities to Meaningfully Promote Excellence in Technology, Education, and Science Act makes perfect (if inelegant) sense; what seems spurious is its alternative title: America Competes.

It's hard to imagine what 'winning' an economic war would look like. If, as Romney opined, the war has already started, what will 'winning' look like? Will Americans truly thrill to see China languish in poverty, debt and civil unrest? Would they feel safer if poverty in India grew and the youth of Algeria and Egypt were less well educated? Just what kind of victory do these evangelists for global competition have in mind? The drama of competitiveness attracts attention and engagement because it appears to simplify relationships that are, in fact, complex and delicate. It's far easier to demonize others than to improve ourselves. Crude political rhetoric studiously discourages awkward questions or rigorous insight. And the tropes of winning and losing are so pervasive and ancient that we assume they must mean something.

GDP is a poor indicator of national wellbeing but it isn't the only culprit. All the global indices are sophisticated pecking orders that both represent and confer status. But they all contain agendas. Ever since 1979, the *Global Competitiveness Report* has been assembled and published by the World Economic Forum, the organization best known for its annual conference of government leaders and chief executives at Davos. The *Competitiveness Report* is a rich mix of hard data (numbers like government debt and deficits) together with a broad array of opinion that comes from 'top management leaders'. Nobody at the World Economic Forum would tell me who these leaders were or what companies they came from, only that they all worked in the private sector. But whoever they are, it is their opinions that drive the data concerning the 'twelve pillars of competitiveness'. These include, among other things, infrastructure, financial-market development, education, healthcare and labour efficiency. It is when you start to drill down into these pillars that what looks like hard data starts to feel a little squishy.

Top management leaders addressing labour market efficiency, for example, are asked how easy or hard it is to hire and fire employees, what the costs of redundancy are and to what extent pay is linked to productivity. The countries where hiring and firing is 'flexibly determined by employers' top the list; countries where the cost of redundancy is nothing and countries that do relate pay to productivity top the list. In other words, a labour market is deemed efficient where employers can hire and fire people at will and reward them according to performance. Yet there is no evidence that performance-related pay works, that it generates higher levels of productivity, creativity, engagement or innovation – in fact, there is much evidence that it has quite the opposite effect.

Moreover, we also know that being able to hire and fire people at will is negatively correlated to company performance. Swapping people in and out of jobs is expensive – you have to find, hire and train them; it harms corporate reputations and loses companies a great deal of knowledge, commitment and efficiency.[5] While bringing new people into a business can be inspiring and galvanizing, turnover rates can get too high not just because, as Henry Ford found, training is expensive but because layoffs may damage corporate standing and erode the relationships that make work meaningful, creative, efficient and engaging.[6] It's a rare company that spends a fortune recruiting talented employees because they want to be able to fire them quickly. And while zero-hours contracts create an illusion of efficiency, the fact that the workers on those contracts can't even afford to buy lunch restricts economic growth.

To get to the top of the competitiveness index, therefore, requires that a country and its larger corporations conform to a very particular business model of a kind that is, at the very least, highly debatable. Having investigated many aspects of the index, Australian academic Harald Bergsteiner concluded that the *Report* is ideology masquerading as data.

'I remember reading the *Report* some years ago,' Bergsteiner told me, 'and thinking, this didn't make sense. There is more than one way to run an effective business but the research really only looks for one model and puts that forward as though it's the only thing that works. So I sat down and looked at their metrics and discovered that many of them were ideologically biased. Then when you remove those questions from the questionnaire and add questions they should have had in there, distortions become huge.

This stinks. Its poor science and someone has to say that it's wrong.'

Bergsteiner diagnoses a biased feedback loop, that over-emphasizes policies valued by dominant nations while not questioning alternatives practised by less influential countries. This, he says, produces the global equivalent of a Matthew effect: the dominant 'efficient labour markets' are rewarded by a high ranking while those who might dare to diverge from such thinking are condemned to languish further down the pecking order. The index, therefore, really measures how far a country conforms to a very specific agenda rather than to any objective definition of economic success. And because the World Economic Forum makes a big noise in the world, and leaders command respect at Davos according to the size and success of their economies, the *Global Competitiveness Report* has come to represent an authoritative report card on how well politicians and their economies are doing.

Much in the composition of the *Report* provokes debate – or should. Not all citizens, not even all economists would argue that foreign ownership of companies is infinitely beneficial; there must come a point at which the dominance of an economy by outsiders presents significant democratic and social challenges. But openness to foreign investment pulls countries up the league tables. Questions around such issues aren't posed, or explored, by the *Global Competitiveness Index*. Instead, for all the sophistication of the statistical analysis, what emerges is a doctrinaire picture of a thriving state in which anonymous management thinkers determine what constitutes a successful economy. Yet these scores form the basis of political rhetoric and policy.

That an economy is distinct from a society has only just begun to emerge within the rhetoric of the *Report*. Growing discomfort with the implications of the World Economic Forum's formula for success led in 2013 to the first of its sustainability rankings. But even these affect little change in the overall rankings, although the degree to which countries are making little or no significant progress in social or environmental sustainability makes for demoralizing reading. Mostly what these supplementary league tables demonstrate is how poorly such rigid thinking maps onto the rich complexity of social communities.

Boston Consulting Group, a privately held advisory firm, has attempted to do better, creating a *Sustainable Economic Development Assessment* (*SEDA*), which distinguishes between different kinds of growth: the growth that improves wellbeing for everyone versus the growth that benefits just a few. 'What is important,' its authors maintain, 'is for rising national income to translate into greater well-being ... countries with higher GDPs are not necessarily the best at converting their wealth into well-being for their citizens. A number of eastern European nations, such as Albania and Romania, and such Southeast Asian countries as Indonesia, the Philippines, and Vietnam, score particularly high in converting wealth into well-being.' What *SEDA* demonstrates, that other metrics cannot, is that a pro-poor approach to growth can make a positive impact without proportionate GDP growth.

'Brazil's record has been particularly impressive in this regard. While it averaged GDP growth of 5.1 per cent over the past five years, Brazil generated gains in living standards that would be expected of an economy expanding by an average of more than 13 per cent per year. New Zealand and Poland are among the other countries whose recent progress in improving well-being is greater than their GDP growth rates would suggest.'

One thing Boston Consulting Group did *not* do was to generate a league table with their data. In part, this is because the way they've constructed their findings doesn't lend itself to so simplistic a display; more acid commentators have surmised that the company simply wished not to annoy prospective government clients (after all, these reports all have to be paid for somehow). But the main lesson of *SEDA* is that not all growth is equal and therefore growth alone isn't a useful measure.

Everyone knows – has known for over half a century – that GDP doesn't work and that the *Global Competitiveness Report* has its own agenda. So why does GDP persist, in the mouths of politicians, economists and policymakers? In part, it's a game of chicken: no one wants to turn away first. As long as the prevailing systems can somehow be gamed, and dominant countries can stay on top, who wants to risk a different measure?

But the rhetoric of competition and the alluring fantasies of victory impede our thinking about what meaningful progress might look like or require. It's simply impossible to frame effective policy when using a competitive metaphor even when it is incomprehensible. We know that the well-being of any nation depends on the stability and well-being of others but competitive language omits dependencies, implying that winners live in a world untouched by the losers. Even those who might wish this to be true know that it is not.

Moreover the competitive mindset focused exclusively on GDP blinds us to other issues crying out for critical attention. We should be thinking about sustainable energy and food sources, but GDP doesn't draw attention to those issues. When, as recently, the cost of solar energy starts to plunge, this shouldn't register as a negative effect if it simultaneously reduces dependence on fossil fuels. The complex trade-offs between the longer-term benefit of sustainable technologies and the shorter-term benefits of extraction industries require a more sophisticated mindset than win/lose can ever provide.

As new technologies continue to disrupt and eliminate entire industries, we need to think about how comfortable we are with the rising inequality that follows in its wake. As Jaron Lanier has described so eloquently in *Who Owns the Future?*, advances in technology will make it easier and cheaper to automate a whole range of industries from healthcare to transportation, leaving more and more people without work. But at the same time, because the population continues to grow by one billion people every twelve years, GDP will rise. But a growing population with fewer and fewer job prospects should give anyone pause. As long as you consider GDP through a competitive mindset, however, these challenges don't even surface and cannot be addressed.

Once we recognize that even winning states have to co-exist with everyone else, it becomes clear that the true challenge isn't competition at all: some nation will always be the winner, as Britain was until it was overtaken by America around 1880. But one dominant nation doesn't make the others vanish – or even leave them powerless or poor. It does mean that those societies that can't define their place in the world by being the biggest or the richest, the most aggressive or threatening, seek alternative forms of identification. Like siblings, they must find their niche and, if they want to be productive, learn to play well with others. The challenge of cooperation and collaboration, it turns out, may be more demanding and subtle than dominance.

David Skilling argues that small countries tend to be better at addressing these questions because they have to be. Without the sheer economic dominance of the US or China, they can't derive a sense of comfort or security through sheer size. Even if bigger were better, they have no choice. Finland, Switzerland, Singapore and the Nordic countries are, he argues, more exposed – and that exposure makes them more alert.

'Small countries,' Skilling told me, 'have less margin for error if you don't get things right. One small misstep and the ground falls away. If you're big, like the US, the size of your economy means that you can keep blundering along for quite a long time. Your size protects you. But small countries don't have that luxury, if you will. That makes policy-making much sharper. They're closer to the edge.'

Skilling, a lanky New Zealander, knows what he's talking about. His own country is doubly disadvantaged: both small and remote. These days, he spends much of his time in Singapore, where he advises policymakers keen to ensure that the tiny country makes as much as it can of its landmass and population. He's been struck by the similarities between small nations around the world, countries that thrive because of their smaller size.

'They know,' Skilling says, 'that they can't be the biggest voice at the table. Therefore they have to be allies, great partners and collaborators. They're under no illusion as to their own importance so they have had to develop relationships – with other countries and with regional and global organizations like ASEAN or WTO – that give them insight and influence. They invest a lot of time and effort in making these institutions work for them.'

The greatest creativity, therefore, in large countries like the United States, may be more likely to be found at state level. It is here, after all, that the toughest gun laws have been quickly passed and here that the greatest steps have been taken to reduce carbon emissions and energy consumption.

'In the United States, you don't see this on a global scale but you are starting to see it within the individual states and in some cities,' says Skilling. It is at that level – not the federal level – where you're starting to see the really creative initiatives and the ability to collaborate with one another. It's really at the level of smaller states and local economies that you're seeing innovation and reform.'

Skilling sees the dynamic between small and large economies as analogous to Clayton Christensen's innovator's dilemma. In his classic business book, *The Innovator's Dilemma*, Christensen argued that large corporations – like Kodak – did not respond to disruptive technologies like digital photography because, when they first appeared in the market, they represented a trivial challenge; they just didn't seem to warrant a strategic response and might, indeed, have gone away. By the time the challenge loomed large, change was too late and too expensive. Small companies, like Method, can challenge big incumbents like Procter & Gamble, because being adroit and creative is how they make their mark in the world. Pursuing this analogy, small countries have to be clever and think ahead because they don't have the comfort or economic cushion afforded by scale. An example of such foresight is Norway which, despite sitting on vast oil reserves, produces 99 per cent of its energy from hydropower not, obviously, because it has to – but because small countries learn to look ahead, knowing that sheer size or market heft will not protect them.[7]

'Small countries have developed a keen understanding of best practice and rapid learning. They're always looking, searching for new ideas and bringing them in whenever they can. Singapore – it's a small country on steroids, constantly on the lookout for innovation in education, in healthcare, in technology. It's easier to introduce on a small scale, of course. But the benefit of being small is that you *have* to be more engaged with the world outside your own.'

You can see this, Skilling says, when you look at the number of people carrying passports or speaking other languages. And engagement with the world as a whole shows up nowhere more starkly than in exports.

'The US exports just over 15 per cent,' says Skilling. 'But the average for a small country is 55 per cent. The UK does reasonably well but it's still in the 20 per cent range, which is well short of Norway or Denmark. So these countries are, and know they are, highly dependent on how they relate to all the economies around them. The world cannot be binary for them. So it works two ways:

they are more exposed to the pressures around them – and they know they have to develop the capacity internally to be excellent collaborators. That dominance isn't an option is what makes them nimble.'

The cultural and psychological difficulty that Britain has experienced in adapting to and defining its post-imperial identity testifies to the challenge. The United Kingdom has chosen to adopt what foreign policy analysts call a 'lieutenant strategy': deriving reflected power from its so-called special relationship with the United States. Increasingly this seems something of a proxy identity: neither inspiring in its own right nor meaningfully reciprocated. One of the most striking features of Danny Boyle's London Olympics opening ceremony was the degree to which he seemed able to articulate the shared values of British society in a way which no government or party leader since the Second World War had ever quite mastered. That it appeared largely incomprehensible to the rest of the world proved its point: Britain was its own place, neither the servant nor the master of another.

Politically however, a century of dominance followed by a half century of good lieutenantship has left Britain strangely isolated: neither commanding in its economic presence nor adroit in its capacity to collaborate with others. Skilling says that you can see this within British politics: the Chancellor, George Osborne, manages the economy as though the UK were a small country while David Cameron's rhetoric suggests it is still a world power. Such a misalignment makes coherent policy and patient partnering impossible and goes a long way towards explaining Britain's dysfunctional relationship with the EU. Like Baraa in *Salam Shabab*, Britain's schizophrenic attitude to the EU prevents it from becoming an influential or valued member of a successful team. Smaller nations, however, have had to adapt perforce. Lacking imperial power or sheer financial muscle, they've had no choice but to become super-collaborators: partners to the world at large. And, in very many instances, this has served them well. But make no mistake. If personal collaboration is hard – and everything about office politics and laboratory pecking orders suggest that it is – global cooperation is even harder.

'The Human Genome Project had to be international for all

kinds of reasons,' John Sulston told me. 'Everyone wanted to contribute; that was a good reason. Everyone knew that a big public project was the best way to overcome intellectual property rights issues. That was a good reason. And some people wanted to make sure America didn't sweep the board with the whole thing. That was a less good reason.'

Sulston is invariably described as self-effacing, gentlemanly, someone keen not to step on toes. He's respected for his part in sequencing the genome of the worm, *C. elegans*, for which he was awarded the Nobel Prize. But what he's most famous for is the role he played in the Human Genome Project.

'He is the archetypal ethical, selfless scientist', according to Linda Partridge. 'What he did with the project was quite altruistic insofar as it was extremely hard, terribly labour-intensive and, for a scientist, somewhat unrewarding in the sense that the *science* wasn't the problem! The problem was getting everyone to work together.'

A genial, shaggy man, accessible in his language and broad in his interests and friendships, Sulston comes across as someone rather amazed and delighted to have been able to make a living doing what he loves. He had no great life plan, no conscious ambition, just endless curiosity about what could be discovered. In his autobiography, he makes it clear that he'd never really imagined a life as an institutional manager or politician; the job fell on his shoulders as the publicly funded project to sequence the human genome needed a home, a leader and a fundraiser. Sulston, it turned out, was gifted in all of these areas. He had a talent for making people want to produce excellent work; he was also quite (although not infinitely) patient, thoughtful and difficult to provoke.

The Project had begun in 1990 as a collaboration between American scientists funded by the National Institutes of Health and an international consortium led by Sulston and funded by the Medical Research Council and Wellcome Trust, the world's largest medical charity. The overarching goal was to map the whole of the human genome, but most scientists preferred to do this as a loose collaboration, with groups around the world contributing their data, rather than as a big science project, masterminded by a single individual. Although personalities often clashed and conflicts over methodology were rife, the international group was united in its conviction that all of the data had to be published and shared as fast as it was produced. Their commitment to open data generated the trust required to collaborate. This sometimes made the Project look chaotic or slow but it also provided scale and diversity.

In 1994, Sulston received from his collaborator Bob Waterston an email entitled 'An Indecent Proposal' which, in effect, proposed a concerted push to complete the entire genome by 2001. The plan was stunningly ambitious, not least because it included sequencing everything – including so-called 'junk DNA' because Sulston believed (correctly) that it would turn out to be important. As audacious as the intellectual goal was so too was the Project's price tag: some $3 billion. Since no one organization or even nation would foot the bill, the Project could only survive if funded internationally. And Sulston excelled at bringing massive UK funding to the table on a scale that compelled the United States to join in.

All of that was thrown into jeopardy in 1998 when a fellow scientist, Craig Venter, announced that his commercially funded venture (eventually named Celera) could and would sequence the human genome better, faster and with no cost to the public. Venter's methodology wasn't as thorough as that proposed by the Human Genome Project but, he argued, it would be good enough. The stage was set for a competition the likes of which the media adored. The public project was portrayed as old, stodgy, academic and impractical; Celera was positioned as the youthful upstart: brash, ruthless and practical. National stereotypes sharpened the contrast: the public project featured British scientists (code for old-fashioned) while the American initiative was all about crass moneymaking. That all of this took place in the white heat of the Internet boom only fuelled the drama. An historic moment in which breakthrough technologies produced millionaires overnight focused all eyes on a wildly rising stock market that made heroes of the young men breaking conventions and the corpses of the institutional figures who stood in their way. In that context, Sulston played a fuddy-duddy Goliath to Venter's pugnacious David.

Although everyone followed the money with avid interest, what was at stake was more important and long-lasting. Venter attracted investors who hoped to be able to patent thousands of genes and create a business of renting out the data about them to researchers and drug developers. The idea was that Celera would become somewhat akin to Microsoft: an operating system for gene research, without which no research group could function. Sulston feared and fought this. He believed that genes were inherently not patentable, being a discovery and not an invention, and that charging for access to the information would both slow down subsequent research and make it all the more costly. Moreover, if different companies 'owned' different genes, research would become balkanized, making it more difficult to combine knowledge, insight and research. The law offered little clarity because the field was simply too new. So the heated contest, between the public and the private projects, represented far more than the personality or culture clash the media relished. At stake was not just whether a vast knowledge base would be privately owned or publicly shared – that was important enough – but whether a large, diffuse international collaboration could prove more effective than a single dominant (even domineering) player.

'There's only one human genome, one basic human reference genome,' Sulston reflected. 'Why compete over it? It's crazy! You want to pool resources, and it's not just a matter of getting the job done. It is very difficult to organize a consortium – we all know that. The point is, scientifically and psychologically and in terms of ownership, it's much much better to bring everybody into the same tent and to share the data. It was positioned as a race but there's only one thing that matters: and that is the issue of data release.'

Passions around sharing data ran explosively high. At one point, James Watson, the man most closely associated with DNA and the emerging field of genomics, compared the struggle to the Second World War. Venter's attempt to take over genome sequencing was analogous to Hitler's seizure of Poland, and the scientific community badly wanted a Churchill, not a Chamberlain.

'As I saw it,' Watson said, 'Craig [Venter] wanted to own the human genome the way Hitler wanted to own the world. And that was unacceptable for any person.'[8]

In the contest between the global project and the American project, agreement was finally reached whereby Celera would agree to share its data but only after a one-month delay; the public project, meanwhile, would continue to release its data daily and to everyone – including Celera. By combining the public data with their own, Celera would have everything – but the company refused to reciprocate. Anyone wanting access to their full data set would have to pay for it and would be forbidden from redistributing it. Either way, eventually all of the information would enter the public domain but Celera could charge for access to its data because of its proprietary analysis and formatting. Moreover, that one-month delay gave the company crucial time to secure its intellectual property. Celera – whose tagline was 'Speed matters. Discovery can't wait' – quickly perfected its ability to read a gene sequence in the morning and have the patent application in a lawyer's office by the afternoon.

Because his method was quicker and less granular than the consortium's, in effect Venter was externalizing much of the detail; that's how he was going to win. But rather than emulating his land grab, Sulston recognized that his best hope of reinforcing and protecting the public ownership of the information was to involve as many groups in generating and funding it as possible. The international consortium offered the advantage both of increased funding and broader ownership, and labs across the United States, United Kingdom, France, Germany and Japan did not want to be left out. But, of course, that also made the Project a bear to manage, with scientists, governments, lawyers and politicians around the world piling into what was rapidly becoming a gold rush. If the public research weren't well managed, duplication and waste would be extreme – and Venter's claim that public projects were bloated, wasteful and duplicative would be validated.

'Of course it was harder that the Project was an international collaboration. Of course it was. But it had to be. It was too big to be owned by anyone, by a company or a country. And the spirit of the Project had to be about sharing: the genome that we all share. It isn't yours or mine; it's ours.'

Rhetoric around the two initiatives presented them as a race: who would be first to complete their map of the human genome? Privately, Sulston felt that the contest was ridiculous – after all, the human genome wasn't going anywhere and new technologies kept accelerating and simplifying the task. But he devoted the next six years of his life to shepherding the public project through to completion and – most important of all – publication. Through this period, what's remarkable is the amount of time this eminent scientist – and many of his peers around the world – devoted not to the science but to media management. Press releases were more carefully drafted and reviewed than scientific papers. Public appearances had to be carefully stage-managed and rehearsed. That Venter turned out to have a great knack for publicity exacerbated the rivalry. Journalists loved the fact that Celera's headquarters were full of foosball tables, Nerf guns and plastic Viking helmets. Wagner's 'Ride of the Valkyries' blasting out of loudspeakers reinforced his image as the heroic soloist, singlehandedly taking on both the scientific establishment and the human genome and wrestling both to the ground. When a *New Yorker* profile opened with the words 'Craig Venter is an asshole', his fame was assured.[9]

Academic attempts at such colour could not hope to capture the same kind of breathless attention. The Human Genome Project wasn't one superman but thousands of scientists, technicians, software engineers and administrators performing precise, often dull repetitive tasks, day after day. It didn't have a heroic leader but multiple advisors, evangelists and silent partners. As Sulston shuttled between England and America clearing up misunderstandings, keeping everyone aligned, committed and focused, he found, much to his astonishment, that he had entered the world of politics.

'I was interviewed on the *Today* programme on BBC Radio and pointed out that our problem was that Celera not only collected their own data but would hoover up all of ours – which of course was publicly available – call it their own and charge others for using it. "It's a sort of con-job, if that's not too rude a word," I added. From its place deep inside the interview *BBC Online* pulled out the word "con-job" and flashed it around the world, to be seized on by journalists. And what did people say? Some approved. But many accused me of mud-slinging, jealousy, protecting my turf. I had been heard, but the world by and large divided along party lines.'[10]

The party lines, roughly, were those who believed absolutely in private, competitive commerce – as represented by Venter – versus the public, international cooperation represented by Sulston,

Watson and the National Institutes of Health. Every prejudice against government involvement sprang to the surface; every fear of corporate dominance flowered there, too.

Although Venter proved the superior showman, his life at Celera was not plain sailing. The company's aims competed with themselves. Investors and executives pursued a higher stock price and an expensive bioinformatics product while the scientists concentrated on doing the same difficult work as their academic peers, but with less time, more pressure and more showbiz. Caught in the crossfire between the scientific and the commercial missions, Venter's antagonistic relationship with the company's management left him abrasive, pugnacious and often paranoid. His research team showed immense personal loyalty but some days work ground to a halt when researchers watched in stunned silence as their net worth reached millions of dollars. And Venter felt his outsider status keenly; while he used this to whip up popular support, the personal animus he and the media drummed up made any meaningful collaboration impossible.

That it also put more pressure on the Project was part of Venter's intent, but Sulston persevered. Together with his counterpart Francis Collins at America's National Institutes of Health, he kept the Project funded and shielded while scientists around the world just kept their nerve on academic salaries. (Sulston once said he saw no reason why scientists should be paid more than dustmen.) But the politics of the contest were becoming disruptive.

'The negative side,' Sulston told me, 'was that we started going for the wrong goal. We had to do a very stagey announcement with Blair and Clinton, saying what a great thing it was – like going to the moon, terribly OTT blah de blah – when it wasn't even finished at that point! But the reason for doing it was to make sure there was some kind of peaceful accord in the US. It was an election year for Clinton – and we wanted to ensure that we got some kind of publicity out to secure the intellectual property. But it was a slightly fake goal and quite a phenomenal waste of time.'

Despite the ambient noise, Sulston and Collins fought the political fires together while work progressed at ever-increasing speed as the technology for gene-sequencing kept improving. But had anyone ever asked who was running the public project, it might have been hard to provide an answer. Venter openly sniped at it, calling it 'the Liar's Club' and claiming that 'it's just a bunch of disorganized academics and we [Celera] are the organized company'. But the collaborators themselves thought differently. 'Had any one party been able to dictate how the Project was done,' one commented, 'I think it would have failed.'[11]

In the end, Celera never made a business model out of charging subscriptions to its data and Venter was eventually fired by the management, who'd found him unworkably antagonistic. One year after the famous press conference, the public project published all of its data in *Nature* and Celera was compelled to publish theirs in *Science*. The mapping of the human genome was complete, Venter had made millions and went on to run well funded biotech businesses, and Celera (which is now part of Quest Diagnostics) still owns the patents on 6,500 genes. Sulston hadn't made any money but was, at last, able to retire from his role as super-collaborator. In 2004, along with Sydney Brenner and Bob Horvitz, he was awarded the Nobel Prize in recognition of his work on the genetic map of the worm, *C. elegans*. Many of his colleagues muttered that he might equally have been a strong candidate for the Peace prize. Ten years on, I asked him whether competition had made the science any better?

'I don't think so. Competition didn't make it any faster or any cheaper. And you can't make it better because, well, it is what it is. What is worrying is that we do now have a situation where several thousand genes have already been patented. Myriad, for example, is a company that has patented BRCA1 and 2, which are small genes for breast cancer. They're very important in testing for family risks. If you want to be tested for this, you have to go to Myriad, which charges three thousand dollars. That puts up the cost of healthcare. Many countries outside the US simply refuse to have anything to do with it. This is exactly why we wanted the Project to be international and the data to be free. It does not seem in any way right that a country – any country – can own a patent on something which anyone, anywhere might carry in their body.'

In 2009, the American Civil Liberties Union took Myriad to court over the extreme level of patent protection it claimed. Four years and as many court cases later, the Supreme Court ruled that the patents were invalid. But about 20 per cent of human genes are now patented and all that we know is that, as long as those patents are upheld, research will be more expensive, more cumbersome and the promise of genetic medicine will be slowed. Had the Human Genome Project continued unchallenged, the problem would never have arisen.

'What we had originally wanted was to hold all of the human genome inside a public database that could be added to and annotated all the time, enriched by knowledge that researchers everywhere were uncovering – just like Wikipedia. But once genes were patented, then – well, the whole area of whether you even can, or should, patent a gene still remains unclear. This makes multigenic testing very difficult, a real roadblock. And it will make future collaborations a great deal more difficult. If you can't share the data, you can't build trust; the work suffers and the research suffers.'

The Human Genome Project showed what could be achieved through international collaboration – but it also vividly demonstrated how hard it is, and how much talent it takes, to make them work. Sulston believes, and the ongoing legal wrangles continue to reflect, what happens when coordination gives way to competition. Where there might have been an open, steadily improving and refined knowledge base, there is now an infinite progression of contracts, negotiation and lawsuits.

Everyone who has worked with Sulston – and thousands of scientists have, one way or another – talk about his fairness, patience and ability to keep in mind a broad cross-section of interests: personal, political, national, scientific. More eager to tell me about the achievements of his grandchildren than about his Nobel Prize, he seems to epitomize many of the values John Abele observed in great collaborators: humility, patience, curiosity. Perhaps that explains why he was asked, and agreed to lead, a more recent project commissioned by the Royal Society: People and the Planet.

'The idea was to look at how we are all going to live on this planet that gains a billion more people every twelve years. How do we work together, share resources? My perception is that in my lifetime, and especially over the last ten years, people have become more and more competitive. The recession has made that worse –

but that was a result of competition, too. All our governments do is tell us that we have to compete for growth, but this is becoming ridiculous; we can't all grow faster and faster. There are resource limits. So the idea of the Royal Society report was to think about this destructive competition and how we might find a way to adjust.'

By now, you might have thought that Sulston had had his fill of destructive competition. But his experience of the Project had heightened his sense of how profoundly the world needed to find better ways together to tackle the problems and threats that grow by the day. Characteristically, he drew together a wide array of disciplines – scientists, economists, sociologists, demographers, theologians and thinkers from all over the world: China, India, Egypt, Brazil, Ethiopia, Cameroon, Malawi, the United Kingdom and the United States. The report that they produced is detailed and thoughtful. But although it is the product of many minds, Sulston's experience, living through fifteen years of full-throttle naked competition, hovers over the work.

Consumption in the developed world, the report argues, has to be reduced. The extravagance and exhibitionism of pecking order anxiety incurs too great a cost to be trivialized or ignored. Obesity, the by-product of over-consumption, now represents a significant mortality risk. Gross inequalities – in education and in healthcare – represent a waste of human potential and talent. Trickledown doesn't deliver. Most of the healthcare issues discussed by the report are susceptible to low-tech solutions and medications – but these are the kinds of challenges that competitive businesses currently dodge. Environmental degradation of the kind perpetrated by externalizing pollution will only become increasingly expensive and difficult to repair. Whatever the carrying capacity of the planet turns out to be, we know that it is limited and this challenges all of us, and our institutions, to devise constructive ways to share its wealth. Competition isn't solving these problems; if anything, it is making them worse faster.

One way or another, the critical issues in *People and the Planet* concern resource allocation: how to share what we have and how to handle the externalities that we generate. The report is fairly gloomy about our chances of resolving them, seeing each one as exemplifying the tragedy of the commons. That parable, first described by ecologist Garrett Hardin, described common land where, given the freedom to graze, shepherds eventually graze the green to destruction. Confronted with a global tragedy of the commons, Sulston's report argues passionately for statesmen, legislators and populations to think beyond competitive interests. 'So long as an excess of competition between nations continues,' the report concludes, 'the future of humanity is in doubt.'

When Hardin published his paper *The Tragedy of the Commons* in 1968, it was immediately controversial for his conclusion that there was no technical solution to the problem of resource allocation.[12] The only way forward was what Hardin called 'a fundamental extension of morality' and this enraged people, in part because it seemed implausible and also because so philosophical a position seemed out of place in the pristinely objective pages of *Science*. For the most part, however, the tragedy of the commons came to be accepted as inevitable.

When taken together with game theory, these two landmark concepts illustrated, in abstract, the destructiveness of competitive self-interest. Whenever individuals compete by placing their individual interests above the common good, they prove collectively destructive. Believing that to be the case encourages people to imagine that their only choice – and chance – is to get there first, or with more force – or both. In a dog-eat-dog world, you could be bigger, better, faster, cheaper – or you could cheat. That, fundamentally, has been the sermon read out to all of us from free-market pulpits around the world for the last fifty years.

But then an economist came along who insisted on arguing not from theory but from observation. Elinor Ostrom wondered whether Hardin's tragedies, where they existed in real life, really were inevitable or whether they could be averted. Could she find examples where the tragedy had been circumvented – and, if so, how? Even today, it remains surprisingly uncommon for economists to adopt an empirical approach, but that is what she did.

At an early age, nobody would have picked out Elinor Ostrom as a winner. Coming from a poor family in Los Angeles, neither of her parents had attended university and she'd been steered away from studying mathematics because she was a girl. Further dissuaded from studying political science because she stood no chance of getting a good university position, she found that, as a graduate, the only jobs she was offered were secretarial. And when she was offered a university post, it required teaching a class at 7.30 a.m. (the kind of assignment no one wanted). But she took on the challenge and never looked back.

Ostrom was the least owl-like of researchers. She and her husband Vincent worked, not in the grand palaces of Harvard or Oxford, but at Indiana University. An exceptional collaborator, she saw the polarization between public and private; state and market; politics and economics as an impoverished debate, unhelpfully contradictory and contentious.[13] Ideologues liked to dismiss arguments about the commons as archaic; surely now all property was private. But Ostrom drew attention to intricate areas of cooperation in all our lives – whether in the management of condominiums, the Internet, school boards or businesses.

One of her earliest studies boldly questioned the belief that big organizations, with hierarchies and economies of scale, delivered services that, because they were cheaper, were therefore better. She compared two different forms of policing in and around Indianapolis: one ran a big, centralized organization, and the other was run with small, autonomous units. What she found both surprised her and laid the groundwork for her future work. The police forces of twenty-five to fifty officers proved more effective in every way than metropolitan teams of one hundred or more. Citizens were more likely to interact with the smaller teams, to report a crime, and to meet citizen demands for protection. Big wasn't better; hierarchies didn't help.

A cheerful but rigorous iconoclast, Ostrom delighted in smashing silos, creating workshops and organizations where different disciplines could collaborate – to study collaboration. One of the many examples she analysed concerned the provision of sanitation to poor communities in Brazil. A decade of large-scale public projects had failed, with the result that the absolute number of city dwellers without adequate sanitation had risen by 70 million. Putting large projects out to private contractors had created opportunities for bribery and corruption but left just 37 per cent of Brazilian urban populations with access to sewerage services.

Rejecting the brutal simplification of market economics, Ostrom analysed a Brazilian reform plan for sanitation that started with block meetings; if half of the households on the block didn't attend, the meeting was called off: inhabitants had to be involved. Residents decided on the layout they wanted, affecting the cost of the system and the charges they would end up paying. Before construction started, residents had to sign a formal petition requesting the system they themselves had chosen and committing themselves to the payment of fees. The process wasn't quick – it could take four to six months to get the necessary agreement – but once a block was complete, other blocks learned from it and the process picked up momentum. Critically, the planners learned that they couldn't restrict the process to only the issues they thought belonged on the agenda. The residents knew their needs better than anyone and the give-and-take in negotiations improved the design of the schemes.

Once designed, the water systems weren't built by large multinational contractors with political connections to national leaders but no long-term commitment to the community. Instead, construction came from medium-sized local contractors who built better-performing systems because they cared about their reputation for high-quality work and were bound to encounter the users of their work in the future.

At every stage, Ostrom observed, the process encountered difficulties: some neighbourhood groups were more cooperative than others; monitoring the performance of contractors wasn't always easy. But the process dramatically increased the availability of lower-cost services to the poorest neighbourhoods in Brazilian cities – and was subsequently emulated in Kenya, Paraguay and Indonesia. Critical to this success was the contribution of citizens who honoured their promises, and good communication and collaboration between citizens and local-government agencies. Knowledge-sharing, reciprocity, shared standards and autonomy both required but also developed large amounts of social capital.

Similarly, Ostrom's study of irrigation systems in Nepal found that those built and governed by the farmers were in better repair, delivered more water and had higher agricultural productivity than the modern, commercial permanent systems funded by donors and constructed by professional engineering firms. On many such projects, farmers face perverse incentives: to over-consume and under-contribute. But where they have been instrumental in designing both the systems, the sanctions and the rewards, incentives, motivations and understanding were all aligned.

Ostrom's work proved to her that what worked best was collaborative pluralism: lots of different solutions, applied and devised locally by those with immediate, personal investment. Left to their own devices, human beings could create solutions together that were superior to those imposed by external authorities or managing agents. Studying community projects as far apart as policing in Indianapolis, irrigation systems in Spain, mountain villages in Switzerland and Japan, fisheries in Maine and Indonesia, and condominiums in the United States, she found that human beings could and already did collaborate effectively in the management of shared, limited resources – and did so without tragic consequences. The commons, she argued, need not be a tragedy: the commons posed an opportunity.

She called this 'polycentrism' and what she meant was that the hard problem of managing limited resources creatively was best organized from the ground up in ways that fitted with, and articulated, social norms. Communities were, it turned out, very good at organizing themselves, but design principles applied. Discussion had to be face to face because it depended on and deepened trust. Smaller units worked better than large ones. The solution to the vast ecological and environmental problems we face could be solved, not by a single over-arching agreement but by thousands of individual efforts at city, regional, national and international initiatives. Operating across multiple levels was both more sustainable and more robust. 'Such an evolutionary approach to policy provides essential safety nets should one or more policies fail.' At all levels, collaboration was key but even the finest collaborations would fall apart if individual participants came to dominate the group or if they started to form elites. The community had to be self-monitoring and had to design its own sanctions. Conflict was bound to occur – she was, after all, describing real life, not theory – but low-cost conflict-resolution mechanisms could resolve them.[14]

As she came to outline the principles discerned in effective collaborations around the world, she might have been describing many of the organizations described in this book. The emphasis on personal relationships, self-management, the absolute requirement of trust, the sharing of resources and denial of dominance lie at the heart of all successful collaborations. They succeed not because they pursue a competitive agenda but because they define and develop fundamentally social goals. They refuse to choose between business serving society or society serving business; instead they insist on keeping the two aligned. There can be no successful business that is anti-social; there is no successful society where work can't get done.

Most of all, Ostrom insisted that there weren't any simple answers. Following the example of the successful social projects she studied, she created workshops and institutes in which researchers from a whole range of different disciplines could share their knowledge in the search for common solutions. 'No panaceas' was her mantra. Perhaps that's one reason why, after celebrating the fact that she was the first woman ever to win the Nobel Prize for economics, so little public attention was paid to her work. She kept insisting that collaboration was hard – but that it solved problems better than any other way. She kept insisting that trust lay at the heart of all effective work – but that meant that everyone needed not to compete with one another. She kept insisting that, working together, groups achieved optimal outcomes – but that meant there couldn't be winners or losers. She saw that we thrive when we acknowledge our mutual dependency – but that means we all have to pull our weight and not try to buy our way out of social relationships.

In 2011, Elinor Ostrom was asked whether, given the vast problems the world faced, she was still optimistic.

'If we keep to our current theories, no,' she replied. 'If we can slowly but surely change the way we think about these problems, there are ways of doing much better multilevel thinking and understanding the diversity and the complexity and not rejecting it. So I think there's a good chance. But if we stay with our current narrow ways of thinking about the world, no, I'm very discouraged.'[15]

On the day that she died in 2012, Elinor Ostrom published her last article. In 'Green from the Grassroots' she reiterated her faith in collaborative projects, but insisted that 'everyone must have a stake in establishing them: countries, states, cities, organizations, companies, and people everywhere. Success will hinge on developing many overlapping policies to achieve the goals.' And as a lifelong student of resource allocation, she left with one final observation.

'Time is the natural resource in shortest supply.'

11. A BIGGER PRIZE

An era can be said to end when its basic
illusions are exhausted.

Arthur Miller

Following the events of 11 September 2001, Kenneth Feinberg was
appointed special master of the Victim Compensation Fund. The
statute establishing the Fund was unlike anything enacted before,
providing tax-free compensation to families of those who had been
killed and to those who had been injured on 9/11. Implicit in the
fund were two aims. The nation as a whole, and the government
as its voice, wished to help, console and support victims of the
attack. More pragmatic however was the recognition that, without
federal compensation, the airlines would be bankrupted by ensu-
ing lawsuits. The prospect of courtrooms filled for years with
bereaved families and maimed victims reliving their trauma was
financially, politically and culturally unacceptable. In these circumstances, the head-to-head contest of the courts was too
grotesque for anyone to contemplate and mediation was the only
remedy that would both respect the individuals' lives and preserve
a nation's transportation system. So urgent was the demand to
address these issues with sensitivity and decorum that no cap was
put on the amount of money Feinberg could give.[1]

It's telling that, under extreme pressure, no one believed
competition would work. The sorrow and pity of events remained
so vivid that public contests over the value of life felt obscene.
Knowing that the rich, with ample resources, were bound to fare
better than those with none threatened to exacerbate the tragedy.

That mediation was embraced as a better process was the culmination of several decades during which the gladiatorial showdowns of the legal system had come increasingly to look like slow, expensive and inhumane mockeries of justice. For years, Feinberg had championed mediation as an effective, fast and human alternative to epic courtroom pugilism. In his resolution of cases involving Vietnam veterans and Agent Orange, asbestos, fraud and a wide range of industrial accidents, he demonstrated how much faster and more humane it could be. His appointment to lead the Victim Compensation Fund paid tribute to his achievement in positioning mediation as a true alternative to legal contests.

In 1990, impressed by the growth of mediation, London lawyer Eileen Carroll had travelled to the US to become a qualified mediator. Returning as an energetic convert to the values of mediation, she set up the Centre for Effective Dispute Resolution right in the heart of the British legal establishment, where it's grown ever since.

'People spend a lot of time in life positioning themselves – where they stand in the pecking order, making sure they're seen, they're important enough. It means we stop seeing one another as people! And when conflict blows up, we don't know who we're dealing with – and we're so keen to win, we don't stop to think what that means. You see it in families all the time. Everyone's so concerned to win, they don't stop to think about the consequences.'

Carroll described one case involving siblings who had inherited their father's business on his death. They'd been unable to resolve issues of control and day-to-day management, with feelings running so high that everyone stopped talking to each other. Their eighty-year-old mother desperately wanted the issue resolved before she died because she wanted to be able, once again, to spend time with her grandchildren. But she knew that a conventional courtroom battle could take too long for her. She also wanted a viable business left in good hands fit for the future, something else a lawsuit could not guarantee. So she turned to mediation. Emotions ran very high; there was, Carroll told me, an incredible amount of tension in the room.

'These were the ground rules: don't interrupt; and be prepared to tell your story. They had to listen to each other and think about what they'd heard. It was an amazingly powerful session. You want to interrupt! You don't want to listen! So, having a mediator was vital. We then had sessions in the afternoon and the thing was settled by midnight. For the first time in four years, the business was on a firm footing. And the matriarch was going to see some of her grandchildren for the first time; that's how bad it had been and how much distance everyone travelled.'

Listening to each other's stories and taking time, Carroll told me, changed everyone's perspectives, knowledge and understanding. They started to see how much their standoff cost them – and to appreciate all they had in common. Finding a resolution pulled the family back together where competition had torn it apart. What Carroll had been able to do was to retrieve their humanity and the value they had for each other.

'In mediation, you have to be patient and leave your ego behind. You have to be able to develop a relationship and to develop effective empathy with a broad range of people, to build trust. Trust is big so that other people feel confidence in you, will open up and say what is important to them.

'There is another quality: you have to be able to be comfortable with conflict and not avoid it. Because mediation isn't an absence of conflict; it's a creative approach to resolving it. So you must be willing to come up with ideas that other people can take and own. You are aiming at a solution that is for them, not just for you. You don't want winners; you strive for success.'

In our long, tortured love affair with competition, we have forgotten the qualities Carroll practises and that she tries to resuscitate in her clients. Abjuring competition is not about avoiding conflict but learning to do it well: thinking vigorously together in search of new ideas. Social connections and interdependence both enable and require this. But once the dialogue is framed as a tournament in which there must be a winner and a loser, the quality of the exchange gets hollowed out. Communication becomes positioning. Dialogue turns into point-scoring. No one listens.

Nowhere is that impoverishment of communication more costly than in what is so appropriately labelled the political 'arena'. The absurd schoolboy slugfest that is Prime Minister's Questions requires days of preparation for a ritual that is followed avidly within political circles but seen as narcissistic and embarrassing outside them. It's hard to imagine a less meaningful way of judging solutions to complex problems than people screaming at each other across a table, egged on by rowdy followers.

That the contest is fatuous ritual is bad enough; that it stymies creative thinking about critical problems is one of its biggest costs. Competitive positions inevitably produce constrained thinking – just the opposite of the divergent mindset required for creativity. Our politics are stalled because our problems are complex and our means of addressing them are crude and rigid. That the coalition and cabinets of all parties have been characterized by whispering campaigns against their own members, briefings for and against so-called colleagues, only demonstrates how profoundly ill-equipped government is for the listening and creativity our problems demand. In the looming face-off between business, government and society a competitive mindset can frame the contest, but doing so destroys all the mental maps showing how we might find a solution. The problem is not a failure of imagination but of courage: the willingness to relinquish fantasies of winning in exchange for the bigger prize of joint achievement and progress.

But the global rise of mediation marks a sea-change, a moment when the competitive strains that have so exhausted our institutions give way to the cooperative, collaborative talents that have lain in wait all these years.

Competition has proved so disappointing because it is effective, under only some, but by no means all, conditions. Speaking in 1912, President Roosevelt argued that 'competition has been shown to be useful up to a certain point and no further'. It is a great way to focus on short-term problems and to enliven monotonous repetitive work. In small doses, competition adds spice to what might otherwise be mundane and dreary. And when the stakes are low, it can be an inspiring way to get things started, to galvanize participation and spark the imagination.

But when the stakes are high, and competition becomes the dominant driver, it backfires spectacularly, undermining exactly what it hopes to build. Competitive thinking, constrained by benchmarks, scorecards and comparisons, cannot wander and explore new territory but stays fettered to old ideas and models. Cheating, corruption, subversion, silence, disenchantment and the unwinding of the social fabric are not perverse but inevitable outcomes of societies captive to the competitive mindset and the ephemeral pleasures of winning.

But competition isn't the only source of our inspiration. Children given support and encouragement learn from, respect and enjoy their siblings' differences. Schools can inspire and develop a love of learning that doesn't die on graduation but adapts and grows as the world changes. Friends and couples find in each other an understanding of one another and of themselves that enriches, connects and renews social bonds. Games and sport can teach fairness, integrity, stamina, self-discipline and community when they're played for fun. These are bigger prizes, available to everyone for a lifetime.

Innovative institutions and organizations thrive not because they pick and breed superstars but because they cherish, nurture and support the vast range of talents, personalities and skills that true creativity requires. Collaboration is a habit of mind, solidified by routine and predicated on openness, generosity, rigour and patience. It requires precise and fearless communication, without status, awe or intimidation. It's hard because it allows no passengers: everyone must bring their best. And failure is part of the deal: mistakes, failed prototypes, dead ends and clouds are a necessary and inevitable part of the process, to be greeted with support, encouragement and faith. The safest hospitals are those where it's easiest to acknowledge error. These are bigger prizes that grow as they're shared.

Conflict is inevitable because that's how new ideas emerge. So great collaborators do conflict well. 'Scrapping' as the Wright brothers called it, is how we stretch, test and develop new ideas and possibilities. The conflict-averse can't do this well and those who love a fight can't either. But the mediators, listeners and scrappers enjoy unfettered exploration, sure in the knowledge that intellectual risks and experiments are how new ideas emerge.

The impresarios of creativity make great breakthroughs because they support and unleash the genius and energy of the people around them. Like the pianist Fou Ts'ong, they recognize that the greatest originality comes from serving the needs and brilliance of others. These are prizes that unite the past with the future.

It's hard to create a climate of safety in times that feel so dangerous. But the failure to inculcate the habit of collaboration may be the biggest organizational, social and political risk we face today. It's why companies hire armies of brilliant people, only to feel disappointed by what they produce; it's why citizens feel so disillusioned by politicians eager to attack but paralysed when asked to work together. We don't lack for talent but organizational silence and stalemates persist when the cost of honesty and sharing remains too high.

It would be wonderful to conclude this book with the perfect blueprint for collaboration. But the engineering concept of robust systems offers a cautionary tale here: single dominant models are dangerous. Safety lies in plurality. For a collaborative mindset to take hold, we need multiple systems – different sizes, shapes, ambitions and goals. They have different forms of hierarchy but they share salient characteristics. Extremes of power and distance are carefully, and structurally, avoided. Trust is valued more highly than secrets because giving ideas away is what makes them proliferate. Success is measured across two, three, four generations, by the impact and legacy left for children, grandchildren and great-grandchildren. Success isn't pursued, like the Purdue chickens, by selecting superstars and seeing which is the last left standing; instead true champions are fiercely protective of the principle that no one gets left out and that no one else pays the price of success. Just like the Finnish schools, they start and finish on the principle that success is only meaningful when everyone owns it. Instead of trophies for a few, collaborators seek the bigger prize.

The reason employee ownership matters, and why it is so powerful, is because it motivates and rewards mutual assistance and support, openness and honesty. While every business leader says people are a company's most precious asset, employee ownership makes this a structural reality, creating the conditions in which trust derives from mutual interest and success is shared. Cooperatives do this too and their resilience through the economic downturn illustrates the degree to which embracing our interdependence isn't weakness but strength. Brilliant innovations in technology demonstrate that we can radically reduce the costs of cooperation, making it easier to solve any problem, harming no one, if that's how we choose to define our goals.

We have science on our side. A team of scientists recently revisited game theory, challenging mathematician John Nash's original conclusion that selfishness must always prevail. If Nash were right, why was it that cooperation prevailed – in the animal kingdom, the microbial world and in human society? That answer turned out to be what Nash had left out of his equations: communication. Being able to talk to one another, bring in a wide range of opinion and expertise to debate, argue and negotiate, changes the game.[2]

That's what super-collaborators excel at: they listen, make connections and share. They're the people who keep family members in touch with each other, who make neighborhoods safe and functional, who make organizations smart and responsive. They've more tools with which to reach out than ever before. Some act on instinct, others because they enjoy social contact but, unsung and often invisible, they make things work and drive change.

People giving each other time and respect is what makes organizations like Morning Star, Gore, Eileen Fisher, Ocean Spray, Interface and Boston Scientific so creative. It's why Uri Alon's learning from improv, Mike North's lessons from comedy, Travis Tygart's crusade for real sport and the classrooms of Martti Helström are so important. When the world has more teachers like Koh Thiam Seng or Beau Lotto, and more organizations like Gripple, Arup, TechShop, Lending Club, Mozilla and Punchdrunk, our children will see for themselves that they can succeed without cheating, without gaming the system and without making their friends lose.

As I was finishing this book, I was in Boston, Massachusetts, where I'd once lived and run technology companies. Just a few months before my visit, a bomb killed three people and injured 264. Walking through familiar streets that had witnessed panic and mayhem, I thought about my friends and colleagues who had been at the scene that day. All of their accounts had been saturated with a strange emotion. Yes, the day had been tragic and frightening and, yes, everyone had been angry and upset. But when they talked to me, that wasn't what I heard. What I heard was pride. Their stories told about what they'd done to help, who they'd put up for the night or the week, how generous everyone had been, the kindness of strangers. It was as though, in the moment of disaster, they'd all been given permission to stop competing and to do instead what human beings are so great at: help one another. What I heard was freedom.

Those feelings didn't last for ever. But we don't need such tragedies to liberate the generosity latent in us all. The hopeful sign that I took from these stories – and they were everywhere – was the pent-up yearning people feel to connect, communicate, collaborate. They're just waiting for permission to live and work in ways that feel so much better than winning. That would be the biggest prize of all.

NOTES

1. Oh, Brother!

1 http://www.childhoodpoverty.org/

2 Hart, S. and H. Carrington (2002) 'Jealousy in 6-month-old infants', *Infancy* Vol. 3, Issue 3

3 Finkelhor, D., H. Turner, R. Ormrod (2006) 'Kid's Stuff: the nature and impact of peer and sibling violence on younger and older children', *Journal of Child Abuse and Neglect* 30, 1401–21 http://www.unh.edu/ccrc/pdf/CV133.pdf

4 Kluger, Jeffrey, *The Sibling Effect: What the Bonds Among Brothers and Sisters Reveal About Us*, Riverhead Books, 2011

5 Wiehe, V. R. (2000) 'Sibling abuse' in H. Henderson (ed.) *Domestic violence and child abuse sourcebook*, pp. 409–92. Detroit, MI: Omnigraphics.

6 National Crime Prevention Council (1995) *Helping Kids Handle Conflict*. A guide for students ages 5–12 on how to handle conflict

7 Ryckman, Richard M., Cary R. Libby, Bart van den Borne, Joel A. Gold and Marc A. Lindner (1997) 'Values of Hypercompetitive and Personal Development Competitive Individuals', *Journal of Personality Assessment* 69(2), 271–83

8 Bing, Mark N. (1999) 'Hypercompetitiveness in Academia: Achieving Criterion-Related Validity from Item Context Specificity', *Journal of Personality Assessment* Vol. 73 (1), p. 80

9 Mazur, Allan and Alan Booth (1998) 'Testosterone and dominance in men', *Behavioral and Brain Sciences* 21, 353–63

10 Van Honk, Jack, Dennis J. Schutter, Peter A. Bos, Anne-Wil Kruijt, Eef G. Lentjes and Simon Baron-Cohen (2011) 'Testosterone administration impairs cognitive empathy in women depending on second-to-fourth digit ratio' *PNAS*, Vol. 8, No. 8, 3448–52

11 Wright, Nicholas D., Bahador Bahrami, Emily Johnson, Gina Di Malta, Geraint Rees, Christopher D. Frith and Raymond J. Dolan (2011) 'Testosterone disrupts human collaboration by increasing egocentric choices' *Proceedings of the Royal Society of Biological Sciences,* Vol. 279, No. 1736, 2275–80

12 Yildirim, Baris O., and Jan J. L.Derksen (2012) 'A review on the relationship between testosterone and life-course persistent antisocial behavior', *Psychiatry Research*

13 Perner, Josef and Ted Ruffman (1994) 'Theory of Mind is Contagious: You Catch It From Your Sibs', *Child Development* Vol. 65 (4)

14 Sulloway, Frank J., *Born to Rebel,* Little, Brown & Co., New York, 1996, p. 594. See also *On the Origin of Species,* in which Darwin explored one of the keystones of his theory: the principle of divergence which causes 'differences, at first barely appreciable, steadily to increase, and the breeds to diverge in character both from each other and from their common parent ... The truth of the principle, that the greatest amount of life can be supported by great diversification of structure, is seen under many natural circumstances.'

15 http://www.nytimes.com/2007/06/22/science/22sibling.html? pagewanted=all Kristensen, Petter and Tor Bjerkedal, 'Explaining the Relation Between Birth Order and Intelligence', *Science* 22 June 2007: Vol. 316, no. 5832, p. 1717

16 It's important to acknowledge that, as in most scientific studies, general conclusions on vast topics like birth order may be meaningful about groups while meaningless when applied to individuals. And all studies of siblings suffer from small group size and (except in a few rare cases) periods of study that are short compared to the span of a human life

17 Hertwig, Ralph, Jennifer Nerissa Davis and Frank J. Sulloway (2002) Parental Investment: How an Equity Motive Can Produce Inequality, *Psychological Bulletin* 128, No. 5, pp. 728–45

18 Ibid.

19 Sulloway, Frank and R. L. Zweigenhaft (2010) 'Birth Order and Risk Taking in Athletics: A Meta-Analysis and Study of Major League Baseball', *Personality and Social Psychology Review*, 14(4) 402–16

20 Sulloway, Frank, *Born to Rebel*. It's important to point out that many don't accept these birth-order hypotheses. It isn't at all clear whether the source of the difference lies primarily with parents or with

siblings themselves and, of course, large patterns won't necessarily map to individual cases. But what all of historical and psychological data does point to is the persistence and heat of this competition: a conflict not just between siblings but also between love and hate

2. Making the Grade

1 'Young adults falling behind rest of the world on the 3Rs', *Guardian*, 9 October, 2013, p. 1

2 Alon, Uri, 'How to Build a Motivated Research Group', *Molecular Cell*, 29 January 2010, DOI: 10.1016/j.molcel.2010.01.011

3 Fasko, Daniel Jr. (2000–1) 'Education and Creativity', *Creativity Research Journal*, Vol. 13, Nos. 3 & 4, pp. 317–27

4 Ibid. See also their other papers

5 http://www.standard.co.uk/news/education/michael-gove-passing-exams-make-children-happy-and-satisfied-8315529.html accessed 26 February 2013

6 Xu, K., M. Ernst, D. Goldman (2006) 'Imaging genomics applied to anxiety, stress response, and resiliency', *Neuroinformatics* 4, pp. 51–64. See also: http://mbldownloads.com/1006CNS_Stein.pdf: Warriors Versus Worriers: The Role of COMT Gene Variants by Dan J. Stein, Timothy K. Newman, Jonathan Savitz, and Rajkumar Ramesar © MBL Communications Inc. October 2006

7 Cohen, Roger, 'The competition drug', *New York Times*, 4 March 2013

8 http://www.nytimes.com/2012/09/26/education/stuyvesant-high-school-students-describe-rationale-for-cheating.html?pagewanted=all

9 Paton, Graeme, 'Schools bribing pupils to cheat Ofsted inspections', *Daily Telegraph*, 6 January 2012

10 http://www.telegraph.co.uk/education/educationnews/7840969/Half-of-university-students-willing-to-cheat-study-finds.html

11 OECD Pisa 2010 Singapore report

12 For the full details of this project, together with the published scientific paper, see http://www.lottolab.org/articles/blackawtonbees.asp. Further details of Beau Lotto's work are also on this website

13 Sample PISA questions can be found here: http://pisa-sq.acer.edu.au/

14 Quoted from Charles Moore's biography of Margaret Thatcher in '1979 and All That' by John Lanchester, *New Yorker*, 5 August 2013

15 http://www.theatlanticcities.com/technology/2011/10/worlds-leading-nations-innovation-and-technology/224/

3. The Morning After

1 In January 2005, when the president of Harvard University, Larry Summers asked 'whether innate differences between men and women might be one reason fewer women succeed in science and math careers'. He subsequently left the university in the wake of a no-confidence vote

2 Pearson, M., and B. C. Schipper, 'Menstrual Cycle and Competitive Bidding', (2009), Working Papers, University of California, Department of Economics, No. 11, 10 http://www.econstor.eu/bitstream/10419/58389/1/717283119.pdf

3 Zethraeus, N., L. Kocoska-Maras, T. Ellingsen, B. von Schoultz, A. L. Hirschberg and M. Johannesson, 'A randomized trial of the effect of estrogen and testosterone on economic behavior, *PNAS*, 21 April 2009, 106(16): 6535–8

4 Cotton, Christopher, Frank McIntyre, Joseph Price, 'Gender differerences in repeated competition: Evidence from school math contests', *Journal of Economic Behaviour and Organization*, available online 3 January 2013

5 Croson, R., and Gneezy, U. (2009) 'Gender Differences in Preferences', *Journal of Economic Literature* 47: 2 1–27. Niederle, M. and L. Vesterlund, 'Do women shy away from competition? Do men compete too much?' *Quarterly Journal of Economics*, August 2007, 1067–101. Dreber, A., E. von Essen and E. Ranehill, 'Outrunning the Gender Gap – Boys and Girls Compete Equally', *Institute for Financial Research*, March 2010

6 Gneezy, U., K. L. Leonard and J. A. List (2009) 'Gender Differences in Competition: Evidence from a Matrilineal and a Patriarchal Society', *Econometrica* 77(5): 1637–64

7 http://stanley-siegel.com/2012/02/13/penis-envy/

8 Ibid.

9 Ryan, Christopher and Cacilda Jetha, *Sex at Dawn: How We Mate, Why We Stray and What It Means for Modern Relationships*, Harper Perennial, 2010

10 *Economist*, 'Married to the Mortgage', 13 July 2013, p. 49

11 *Why Women Have Sex*

12 Buss, David M. and David P. Schmitt (2001) 'Human Mate Poaching: Tactics and Temptations for Infiltrating Existing Mateships', *Journal of Personality and Social Psychology*, Vol. 80, No. 6, 894–917

13   Author interview. But see also *My Years with Ayn Rand* by Nathaniel Branden and *The Passion of Ayn Rand* by Barbara Branden

14   http://www.ft.com/cms/s/0/7a185746-c869-11e2-acc6-00144feab7de.html

15   Klinenberg, Eric, *Going Solo*, Kindle edition, Duckworth Overlook, 2013

4. Angry Birds

1   Price, John (1995) 'A Remembrance of Thorleif Schjeldereup-Ebbe', *Human Ethology Bulletin*, 10(1)

2   'Contributions to the Social Psychology of the Domestic Chicken' translated by Monika Schleidt and Wolfgang M. Schleidt

3   This also derives from 'Further biological observations of *Gallus domesticus*' by Thorvald Schjelderup-Ebbe, own translation

4   Zink, C. F., Yunxia Tong, Qiang Chen, D. S. Bassett, J. L. Stein and A. Meyer-Lindenberg (2008) 'Know your place: neural processing of social hierarchy in humans' *Neuron*, 58(2) 273–83

5   Bales, Robert Freed (1955) 'How People Interact in Conferences', *Scientific American* Vol. 192, No. 3, refs 841 and 842

6   Kalma, Akko (1991) 'Hierarchisation and dominance assessment at first glance', *European Journal of Social Psychology* Vol. 21, pp. 165–81

7   http://www.ted.com/talks/amy_cuddy_your_body_language_shapes_who_you_are.html

8   Ibid.

9   Gregory, Stanford W. and Stephen Webster (1996) 'A Nonverbal Signal in Voices of Interview Partners Effectively Predicts Communication Accommodation and Social Status Perceptions', *Journal of Personality and Social Psychology* Vol. 70, No. 6, 1231–40

10   Gregory, Stanford W. and Timothy J. Gallagher (2002) 'Spectral Analysis of Candidates' Nonverbal Vocal Communication: Predicting US Presidential Election Outcomes', *Social Psychology Quarterly* Vol. 65, No. 3, 298–308

11   Michell, Lynn and Amanda Amos (1997) 'Girls, Pecking Order and Smoking', *Social Science and Medicine* 44(12) 1861–9

12   Ibid.

13   Author interview

14   http://www.cityweekend.com.cn/beijing/articles/blogs-beijing/expat-life/eating-disorders-on-the-rise-in-china/

15 http://www.guardian.co.uk/technology/2011/aug/29/world-of-warcraft-video-game-addict

16 Curtis, Polly, 'Why has executive pay increased so drastically?', *Guardian* 22 November 2011

17 http://www.culturegps.com/

18 Zink, op. cit.

19 Sapolsky, R. M. (2004) 'Social status and health in humans and other animals' *Annual Review of Anthropology* 33, 393–418

20 Mudrack, Peter E., James M. Bloodgood and W. H. Turnley (2011) 'Some Ethical Implications of Individual Competitiveness', *Journal of Business Ethics*, DOI: 10.1007/s10551-011-1094-4

21 Keltner, Dacher D. H. Gruenfeld, C. Anderson (2003) 'Power, Approach and Inhibition' *Psychological Review*, 110(2) 265–84

22 Hofstede, Geert, *Culture's Consequences: Comparing Values, Behaviors, Institutions and Organizations Across Nations*, Sage Publications, 2001, p. 135

23 Hofstede, Geert, Gert Jan Hofstede and Michael Minkov, *Cultures and Organizations*, McGraw Hill, 2010, p. 87

24 Smith, Adam, *The Theory of Moral Sentiments*, Oxford University Press, 1979, pp. 308–13

25 Piketty, Thomas, Emmanuel Saez, and Stefanie Stantcheva, 'Optimal Taxation of Top Labor Incomes: A Tale of Three Elasticities', NBER Working Paper No. 17616, November 2011, revised March 2013, JEL No. H21

26 The Valve staff handbook can be found at http://newcdn.flame-haus.com/Valve_Handbook_LowRes.pdf

5. Keeping Score

1 Hopkins, Keith and Mary Beard, *The Colosseum*, Profile Books (London) 2011

2 This quote only: http://gulfnews.com/gntv/sport/interview-with-daigreene-olympic-captain-of-great-britain-s-athletics-team-1.1047740

3 http://trackandfieldathletesassociation.org/blog/how-much-money-do-track-and-field-athletes-make/

4 http://fs.ncaa.org/Docs/eligibility_center/Athletics_Information/Probability_of_Competing_Past_High_School.pdf

5 http://chronicle.com/article/Need-3-Quick-Credits-to-Play/135690/

6 *Desert Island Discs*, BBC Radio 4, first broadcast 10 February 2012

7   Agassi, Andre, *Open*, (2010) Vintage Books, p. 214

8   http://www.unc.edu/depts/nccsi/2011Allsport.pdf

9   Mueller, Frederick O. and Bob Colgate (2012) 'Annual Survey of Football Injury Research, American Football Coaches Association

10 *Science Daily*, 5 September 2012

11 http://thinkprogress.org/alyssa/2013/01/04/1395771/how-jadeveon-clowneys-smashing-hit-demonstrates-footballs-existential-crisis/ accessed 23 February 2013

12 http://www.concussiontreatment.com/concussionfacts.html

13 http://www.escardio.org/about/press/press-releases/pr-11/Pages/endurance-exercise-right-ventricle.aspx European Society of Cardiology 7 December 2011

14 Tinley, Scott, *Racing the Sunset*, Lyons Press, 2003

15 http://espn.go.com/nfl/story/_/id/8316638/anonymous-nfl-players-share-secrets-player-safety-concussions-scandals-espn-magazine accessed 23 February 2013

16 Goldman, Bob, *Death in the Locker Room*, Icarus Press, 1984

17 Gibson, Owen, 'Doping: Now worse than it's ever been', *Guardian*, 16 February 2013

18 Connor, J. M. and J. Mazanov (2009) 'Would You Dope? A general population test of the Goldman dilemma', *British Journal of Sports Medicine* 43: 871–2

19 http://www.huffingtonpost.co.uk/will-carling/cheating-in-sport_b_2439325.html accessed 25 March 2013

20 World Economic Forum http://www.euractiv.com/sports/davos-underlines-economic-value-news-221098

21 Interviewed by Martin Bashir on *20/20*. Available on YouTube

22 'The use of performance-enhancing drugs like steroids in baseball, football, and other sports is dangerous, and it sends the wrong message – that there are shortcuts to accomplishment, and that performance is more important than character. So tonight I call on team owners, union representatives, coaches and players to take the lead, to send the right signal, to get tough, and to get rid of steroids now.' http://edition.cnn.com/2004/SPORT/01/21/bush.doping/

23 http://www.bbc.co.uk/news/education-22126301 published 14 April 2013; accessed 24 July 2013

24 Haynes, Jill 'Socio-economic impact of the Sydney 2000 Olympic Games', paper given to the 2001 seminar of the International Chair in Olympism. http://olympicstudies.uab.es/pdf/OD013_eng.pdf

25 Chatterjee, A. and Donald Hambrick (2006) 'It's All About Me' http://www.bus.umich.edu/Academics/Departments/Strategy/pdf/F06Hambrick.pdf

26 Rattner, Steve, *Overhaul: An Insider's Account of the Obama Administration's Emergency Rescue of the Auto Industry*, Mariner Books, 2011

27 http://www.forbes.com/sites/boblutz/2013/02/28/how-ed-whitacre-saved-gm-in-just-10-months-and-other-fables/

28 If you are interested in the science of fatigue, please see chapter 3 of my *Wilful Blindness* for more detail and references

29 Virtanen, M., S. A. Stansfeld, R. Fuhrer, J. E. Ferrie, M. Kivimäki (2012) 'Overtime Work as a Predictor of Major Depressive Episode: A 5-Year Follow-Up of the Whitehall II Study'. PLoS ONE 7(1): e30719, DOI: 10.1371/journal.pone.0030719 and 'Long Working Hours and Cognitive Function The Whitehall II Study', DOI: 10.1093/aje/kwn382
Marianna Virtanen, Archana Singh-Manoux, Jane E. Ferrie, David Gimeno, Michael G. Marmot, Marko Elovainio, Markus Jokela, Jussi Vahtera and Mika Kivimäki, initially submitted 5 June 2008; accepted for publication 3 November 2008

30 Stout, Lynn (2013) 'The Toxic Side Effects of Shareholder Primacy', *University of Pennsylvania Law Review*, 161: 2003

31 Foster, Richard, Sarah Kaplan, *Creative Destruction: Why companies that are built to last under-perform the market – and how to successfully transform them*, Crown Business, 2001

32 Stout, Lynn, *The Shareholder Value Myth*, Berrett-Koehler, San Francisco, 2012

33 Martin, Roger, *Fixing the Game: Bubbles, Crashes, and What Capitalism Can Learn from the NFL*, Harvard Business Review Press, 2011

34 Guerrera, Francesco, 'Welch Condemns Share Price Focus', *Financial Times*, 12 March 2009

35 Erdal, David, *Beyond the Corporation: Humanity Working*, Bodley Head, London, 2011

6. Only the Impresarios Succeed

1 Djerassi, Carl, *The Pill, Pygmy Chimps and Degas' Horse*, pp. 33–4

2 Ibid.

3 Ibid., p. 43

4 Ibid., p. 44

5   Sloan Wilson, David *Evolution for Everyone,* Random House, New York, 2007, p. 33

6   Goodstein, D. (2002) 'Scientific misconduct', *Academe* 88, 28–31

7   Rajan, T. V. 'Biomedical Scientists are engaged in a pyramid scheme', *The Chronicle of Higher Education,* 3 June 2005

8   Anderson, Melissa S., E. A. Ronning, R. de Vries and B. C. Martinson (2007) 'The Perverse Effects of Competition on Scientists' Work and Relationships', *Science and Engineering Ethics,* 13: 437–61

9   Walsh, John P. Wei Hong, 'Secrecy is increasing in step with competition', *Nature* Vol. 422, 24 April 2003

10 de Vries, Raymond, Melissa S. Anderson and Brian C. Martinson, published in final edited form as 'Normal Misbehavior: Scientists Talk About the Ethics of Research', *J Empir Res Hum Res Ethics,* March 2006; 1(1): 43–50

11 Anderson et al., op. cit.

12 Matthew 25: 29

13 Mullis, Kary, 'The Unusual Origin of the Polymerase Chain Reaction', *Scientific American,* April 1990

14 Fang, F. C. (2011) 'Reforming Science: Structural reforms', *Infection and Immunity* 80(3): 897–901

15 Reich, Eugenie Samuel, *Plastic Fantastic,* Palgrave Macmillan, 2009, p. 109

16 http://www.salon.com/2002/09/16/physics/

17 http://www2.technologyreview.com/tr35/profile.aspx?TRID=395

18 *Plastic Fantastic,* p. 150

19 Ibid., p. 117

20 Ibid., p. 131

21 Ibid., p.176

22 http://www.ukrio.org/ukR10htre/misconduct-in-research-who-is-responsible.pdf

23 http://www.dfg.de/download/pdf/dfg_im_profil/reden_stellungnahmen/2004/ha_jhschoen_1004_en.pdf

24 Bhattacharjee, Yudhijit, 'The Mind of a Con Man', New York Times, 26 April 2013

25 http://www.nature.com/news/2011/111005/full/478026a.html

26 Steen, R. Grant, A. Casadevall and F. C. Fang, (2013) 'Why has the Number of Scientific Retractions Increased?' http://www.plosone.org/article/info%3Adoi%2F10.1371%2Fjournal.pone.0068397

27 Ibid.

28 Korpela, K. M. (2010) 'How long does it take for the scientific literature to purge itself of fraudulent material? The Breuning case revisited', *Current Medical Research and Opinion*, 26(4): 843–7

29 Kalichman, M. W. and P. J. Friedman (1992) 'A pilot study of biomedical trainees' perceptions concerning research ethics'. *Academic Medicine* 67: 769–75, DOI: 10.1097/00001888-199211000-00015

30 Fang, op. cit.

31 I wrote at greater length about Ruderman's ethical journey in *Wilful Blindness*

32 For more on cognitive limits and some of the experiments which explain them, see chapter 4 of *Wilful Blindness*

33 Terpstra, David E., M. G. C. Reyes and D. W. Bokor, 'Predictors of Ethical Decisions regarding Insider Trading', *Journal of Business Ethics*, 10(9): 699–710

34 You can see Alon singing the Scoop song at http://www.youtube.com/watch?v=RVoz_pEeV8I

35 Abele, John, Bringing Minds Together, *Harvard Business Review*, July–August 2011

36 See Bronson, Po and Ashley Merryman, *Top Dog*, p. 207

37 To be absolutely precise, there are a few other places in which cranberries have grown, notably Northern Ireland and some parts of China. But these bogs have been small and have not been farmed

38 Avorn, Jerry, Mark Monane, Jerry H. Gurwitz, Robert J. Glynn, Igor Choodnovskiy, Lewis A. Lipsitz (1994) 'Reduction of Bacteriuria and Pyuria After Ingestion of Cranberry Juice' *JAMA* 271(10): 751–4, DOI: 10.1001/jama.1994.03510340041031

39 I am indebted to John Restakis and Ed Mayo for introducing me to the cooperatives of Emilia Romagna

40 http://www.uk.coop/performance-co-operative-economy

7. Clone Wars

 1 http://thatgrapejuice.net/2011/02/neyo-slams-autotune-singers-training-wheels/

 2 http://thepoweroffilm.com/pages/contradictions-in-the-system/

 3 For more on this, read the first chapter of *Wilful Blindness*

 4 Munos, Bernard, 'Lessons from 60 years of pharmaceutical innovation', *Nature Reviews Drug Discovery*, Vol. 8, December 2009, p. 959

 5 Goldacre, Ben, *Bad Pharma*, Fourth Estate, 2012, pp. 146–8

6 Cockburn, I., A. H. Anis (1998) 'Hedonic Analysis of Arthritis Drugs', NBER Working Paper 6574

7 Azoulay, P. (2002) 'Do Pharmaceutical Sales Respond to Scientific Evidence?' *Journal of Economics & Management Strategy* 11(4): 551–94

8 Love, James (2003) 'Evidence Regarding Research and Development Investments in Innovative and Non-Innovative Medicines', http://www.cptech.org/ip/health/rnd/evidenceregardingrnd.pdf accessed 5 February 2013

9 Clarke, Tom, 'Drug companies snub antibiotics as pipeline threatens to run dry', *Nature* Vol. 425, 18 September 2003, p. 225

10 Kaufman, Fred, 'How Goldman Sachs Created the Food Crisis', *Foreign Policy*, 27 April 2011. See also his book *Bet the Farm*, published in 2012

11 http://necsi.edu/research/social/foodcrises.html

12 http://www.hsgac.senate.gov//imo/media/doc/052008Masters.pdf?attempt=2

13 http://www.ted.com/talks/lee_cronin_print_your_own_medicine.html

14 The idea that the way to influence a market is by giving your ideas away isn't new. Andrea Palladio became the most influential architect in the world by publishing all of his ideas and designs in his *Quattro Libri dell architettura*. Had he not done so, his thinking might have remained obscure, as few of his buildings were in big public spaces; most of his villas are in obscure parts of the Veneto where, to this day, they're rarely visited. It was the books, however, that changed Western architecture for ever

15 His brilliant video series can be seen at www.allremix.ru

8. Supersize Everything

1 Dupre, Judith, *Skyscrapers,* with an introductory interview with Philip Johnson, Black Dog and Leventhall Publishers, New York, 1996, p. 36

2 Ibid., p. 7

3 Glendinning, Miles, *Architecture's Evil Empire*, 2012

4 http://www.christianpost.com/news/joel-osteen-finally-gets-to-the-truth-of-sin-with-piers-morgan-48685/#EetpxqSIaiiP91rj.99

5 http://www.christianpost.com/news/pastor-joel-osteen-addresses-gun-control-after-conn-school-shooting-86807/

6 http://www.youtube.com/watch?v=rXktvy4Uv5Y

7 Baumeister, R. F., J. D. Campbell, J. I. Krueger and K. D. Vohs, 'Does High Self-Esteem Cause Better Performance, Interpersonal Success, Happiness or Healthier Lifestyles?' *Psychological Science in the Public Interest*. http://www.irc.csom.umn.edu/Assets/53495.pdf See also Carol Dweck's *Mindset: The New Psychology of Success*, Ballantine Books, 2007

8 Twenge, Jean and W. Keith Campbell, *The Narcissism Epidemic*, Free Press, New York, 2009, loc 229 in e-book

9 Ibid., loc 114

10 Forsyth, Donelson R., Natalie K. Lawrence, Jeni L. Burnette, Roy F. Baumeister (2007) 'Attempting to Improve the Academic Performance of Struggling College Students by Bolstering Their Self-Esteem: An Intervention That Backfired', *Journal of Social and Clinical Psychology*, Vol. 26, No. 4, pp. 447–59

11 Browne, John, *Beyond Business*, Weidenfeld & Nicolson, London, 2010, pp. 68–9

12 http://www.csb.gov/assets/document/CSBFinalReportBP.pdf

13 White House Oil Commission report on Deepwater Horizon

14 Ibid.

15 Browne, op. cit., p. 74

16 Lattman, Peter, 'Confidence on Upswing, Mergers Make Comeback', *New York Times*, 14 February 2013

17 Meyer, Christopher with Julia Kirby, *Standing on the Sun*, Harvard Business School Press, 2012, p. 136

18 Some of the interviewees in this account of RBS have been given pseudonyms to protect their identity

19 Nohria, Nitin and James Weber, *The Royal Bank of Scotland: Masters of Integration*, Harvard Business School Press, 2005

20 Fraser, Ian, 'Loss of Trust', *Signet Magazine*, July 2012

21 http://www.guardian.co.uk/business/blog/2012/jan/12/rbs-balance-sheet-uk-economy accessed 12 October 2012

22 Partnoy, Frank and Jesse Eisinger, 'What's Inside America's Banks', *Atlantic*, February 2013

23 For more details on this story, and on digital altruism, see Aleks Krotowski's Radio 4 series, *Digital Human*: http://www.bbc.co.uk/programmes/b01n7094

24 Zhou, W.-X., D. Sornette, R. A. Hill and R. I. M. Dunbar (2005) 'Discrete hierarchical organization of social groups sizes', *Proceedings of the Royal Society*, 272, 439–44 and Dunbar, R. I. M. (1993)

'Coevolution of neocortical size, group size and language in humans', *Behavioral and Brain Sciences* 16, 681–694

25 Simms, Andrew, 'Let's play fantasy economics', *Observer*, 17 February 2013, Business p. 53

26 Adams, Tim, 'I Still Haven't Found What I'm Looking For', *Observer*, 20 January 2013, p. 8

27 'War on Terabytes', *Economist*, 2 February 2013, p. 64

9. How Low Can We Go?

1 http://lightbox.time.com/2013/05/08/a-final-embrace-the-most-haunting-photograph-from-bangladesh/#1 accessed 31 July 2013

2 Urbina, Ian and Keith Bradsher, 'Linking Factories to the Malls, Middleman Pushes Low Costs', *New York Times*, 8 August 2013, p. A1

3 https://www.commondreams.org/view/2013/04/11-1

4 http://www.cepr.net/documents/publications/min-wage3-2012-04.pdf

5 http://www.ft.com/intl/cms/s/0/46b6c682-fa94-11e2-a7aa-00144feabdc0.html#axzz2apTfkDFw

6 O'Connor, Sarah, 'Amazon Unpacked', *Financial Times*, 8 February 2013 http://www.ft.com/intl/cms/s/2/ed6a985c-70bd-11e2-85d0-00144feab49a.html#slide0 accessed 15 March 2013

7 http://www.propublica.org/article/the-expendables-how-the-temps-who-power-corporate-giants-are-getting-crushed

8 Sheffield, Hazel, 'Pasadena publisher launches a system for outsourcing local news', *Columbia Journalism Review*, 27 August 2012 http://www.cjr.org/behind_the_news/pasadena_publisher_launches_a.php. accessed 30 March 2013

9 The accumulated evidence can be found at http://www.levesoninquiry.org.uk/wp-content/uploads/2012/02/MS-Exhibit-11.pdf last accessed 3 April 2013

10 Testimony by Richard Peppiatt to the Leveson inquiry, Seminar 1: 'The Competitive Pressures on the Press and the Impact on Journalism', 6 October 2011

11 Richard Peppiatt's letter of resignation, reprinted in the *Guardian*, 4 March 2011, can be accessed here: http://www.guardian.co.uk/media/2011/mar/04/daily-star-reporter-letter-full

12 Ibid.

13 Author interview

14 Testimony by Richard Peppiatt to the Leveson Inquiry, op. cit.

15 http://www.worldwatch.org/towards-happier-meals-globalized-world

16 Since the EU banned the administration of drugs for growth-promoting purposes in 2006, levels of antibiotic resistance (in humans and animals) have decreased

17 http://www.forbes.com/lists/2006/12/UQDU.html

18 http://www.nytimes.com/2012/04/05/opinion/kristof-arsenic-in-our-chicken.html?_r=0. See also 'Putting Meat on the Table', a report of the Pew Commission on Industrial Farm Animal Production, a project of the Pew Charitable Trust and Johns Hopkins Bloomberg School of Public Health, 2008. http://www.ncifap.org/about/
In October 2013, the FDA rescinded approval for three of the four arsenic-based drugs used in animal feeds after high levels of arsenic from poultry faeces were found in rice

19 Environmental Protection Agency (2007b). US EPA 2008 Compliance and Enforcement: Clean Water Act, pp. 1–3, quoted in Pew, p. 23

20 Pew, p. 25

21 *Animal Factory*, p. 84

22 Kessler, David A., 'Antibiotics and the Meat We Eat', *New York Times*, 28 March 2013, p. A25.

23 http://www.fda.gov/downloads/AnimalVeterinary/SafetyHealth/AntimicrobialResistance/NationalAntimicrobialResistanceMonitoringSystem/UCM237120.pdf

24 http://www.ers.usda.gov/data-products/county-level-data-sets/poverty.aspx

25 Pew, p. 41

26 Pretty, J. N., C. Brett, D. Gee, R. E. Hine, C. F. Mason, J. I. L. Morison, H. Raven, M. D. Rayment, G. van der Bijl (2000) 'An assessment of the total external costs of UK agriculture', *Agricultural Systems* 65, 113–36

27 In 2004, Smithfield Foods entered the British market by purchasing Ridpath Pek and the Norwich Food Company. Ridpath Pek supplies chopped pork and Polish deli meats to major supermarkets; the Norwich Food Company imports turkey, chicken and game. Now merged into Smithfield Foods UK, I've been unable to gain any information from supermarkets or the company itself about where

exactly, and which products, they sell here. While emphasizing supply relationships with Smithfield's operations in Poland, the company press release at the time merely stated 'Smithfield Foods Ltd will provide retail and food service customers in the UK with a full line of fresh meats and further processed chilled and canned meat products developed for the UK market'. David Cameron is on record insisting that Britain would not import food produced with lower animal-welfare standards than are applied nationally – 'any more than cars with lower emission standards' – but the truth is that we have little insight into much of the meat that we purchase

28 http://www.opensecrets.org/pacs/lookup2.php?strID=C00359075
29 Smithfield Foods annual report, 2012, p. 4
30 Ibid., cover
31 Ibid., p. 47
32 Ibid.
33 Anderson, Ray C., *Confessions of a Radical Industrialist*, p. 8
34 http://www.youtube.com/watch?v=HRkHJxQKM8A
35 *Confessions of a Radical Industrialist*
36 http://www.youtube.com/watch?v=oedz4E9vlDU
37 http://www.youtube.com/watch?v=CG_T1fY3KTk
38 http://www.nytimes.com/2006/04/23/magazine/23apparel.html accessed 1 August 2013
39 All Ford quotes come from his book *Henry Ford – My Life and Work* published online: http://www.gutenberg.org/cache/epub/7213/pg7213.html

10. Top of the World

1 Johns, Helen and Paul Ormerod, *Happiness, Economics and Public Policy*, Institute of Economic Affairs, 1 August 2007
2 http://www.gallup.com/poll/160724/majority-names-china-top-economic-power.aspx accessed 18 March 2013
3 http://politicalticker.blogs.cnn.com/2011/02/14/china-the-top-world-economy-americans-say/ accessed 15 March 2013
4 Beckett, Andy, 'What is the "global race"?' *Guardian*, 22 September 2013
5 Michie, Jonathan and M. Sheehan-Quinn (2001), 'Labour market flexibility, human resource management and corporate performance', *British Journal of Management* 12(4), 287–306
6 Glebbeek, A. C. and E. H. Bax (2004) 'Is high employee turnover

really harmful? An empirical test using company records',
Academy of Management Journal, 47(2), 277–86. Hillmer, S., B.
Hillmer and G. McRoberts (2004) 'The real costs of turnover:
Lessons from a call center', *Human Resource Planning* 27(3), 34–41

7   Norwegian Ministry of Petroleum and Energy http://www.
regjeringen.no/en/dep/oed/Subject/energy-in-norway.
html?id=86981

8   Sulston, John, *The Common Thread*, Transworld, 2002, p. 154

9   Preston, Richard, 'The Genome Warrior', *New Yorker*, 12 June 2000

10 Sulston, *The Common Thread*, pp. 218–19

11 McElheny, Victor K., *Drawing the Map of Life: Inside the Human
Genome Project*, Basic Books, 2010, p. 153

12 The full text of the original article can be found here:
http://www.sciencemag.org/content/162/3859/1243.full

13 Interview with Elinor Ostrom, http://www.mercatus.org/
uploadedFiles/Mercatus/Publications/Rethinking%20Institutional%
20Analysis%20-%20Interviews%20with%20Vincent%20and%
20Elinor%20Ostrom.pdf accessed 20 March 2013.

14 Ostrom, Elinor, *Governing The Commons: The Evolution of Institutions
for Collective Action*, Cambridge University Press, 1990

15 http://oecdinsights.org/2011/07/01/a-lesson-in-resources-
management-from-elinor-ostrom/ accessed 30 March 2013

11. A Bigger Prize

1   Feinberg wrote a tremendous account of running the Fund in *What
is Life Worth?*

2   Adami, Christoph and Arend Hintze, 'Evolutionary instability of
zero-determinant strategies demonstrates that winning is not everything', *Nature Communications*, 1 August 2013, 4, Article number:
2193, DOI: 10.1038/ncomms3193

BIBLIOGRAPHY

Adams, Tim. 'When Politics Is in the Blood', *Observer*, 2010

Adewunmi, Bim, and Patrick Kingsley. 'A Whole New Ball Game', *Guardian*, 2011

Adler, Nancy. 'The Arts and Leadership: Now That We Can Do Anything, What Will We Do?', *Academy of Management Learning and Education* Vol. 5, No. 4, 486–99, 2006

Adner, Ron. *The Wide Lens: A New Strategy for Innovation*, Portfolio, 2012

Agassi, Andre. *Open: An Autobiography*, Harper Collins, 2009

Ahmadi, Sanaz Saeed, Mohammad Ali Besharat, Korosh Azizi, and Roja Larijani. 'The Relationship between Dimensions of Anger and Aggression in Contact and Noncontact Sports', *Procedia – Social and Behavioral Sciences* Vol. 30, 247–51, 2011

Ailing, Abigail, and Mark Nelson. *Life under Glass: The inside Story of Biosphere 2*, Biosphere Press, 1993

Akerlof, George, and Rachel Kranton. 'It Is Time to Treat Wall Street Like Main Street', *Financial Times*, 24 February 2010

Almas, Ingvild, A. W. Cappelen, K. G. Salvanes, E. O. Sorensen, B. Tungodden. 'Explaining Gender Differences in Competitiveness', (2011) www.aeaweb.org/aea/2012conference/program/retrieve.php?pdfid=51

Alon, Uri. 'How to Build a Motivated Research Group', *Molecular Cell* Vol. 37, 2010

Anderson, Melissa S., Emily A. Ronning, Raymond De Vries, and Brian C. Martinson. 'The Perverse Effects of Competition on Scientists' Work and Relationships', *Science and Engineering Ethics* Vol. 13, 437–61, 2006

Anderson, Ray. *Confessions of a Radical Industrialist*, Cornerstone Digital, 2010

Anderson, Stephen, Erwin Bulte, Uri Gneezy, and John A. List. 'Do Women Supply More Public Goods Than Men? Preliminary Experimental Evidence from Matrilineal and Patriarchal Societies', *American Economic Review: Papers & Proceedings* Vol. 98, No. 2, 376–81, 2008

Andeweg, Rudy B., and Steef B. Van Den Berg. 'Linking Birth Order to Political Leadership: The Impact of Parents or Sibling Interaction?', *Political Psychology* Vol. 24, No. 3, 605–23, 2003

Anon. 'The Secret Teacher Writes an Honest Letter Home', *Guardian*, 2012

Armstrong, Lance. *It's Not About the Bike*, Yellow Jersey Press, 2001

Asthana, Anushka. 'The Secret of a Happy Child: No Irritating Siblings to Get in the Way', *Observer*, 2010

Auger, Pat, and Timothy M. Devinney. 'Do What Consumers Say Matter? The Misalignment of Preferences with Unconstrained Ethical Intentions', *Journal of Business Ethics* Vol. 76, No. 4, 361–83, 2007

Austin, Elizabeth J., Daniel Farrelly, Carolyn Black, and Helen Moore. 'Emotional Intelligence, Machiavellianism and Emotional Manipulation: Does EI Have a Dark Side?', *Personality and Individual Differences* Vol. 43, No. 1, 179–89, 2007

Baden-Fuller, Charles, and Mary S. Morgan. 'Business Models as Models', *Long Range Planning* Vol. 43, No. 2–3, 156–71, 2010

Baird, Benjamin, Jonathan Smallwood, Michael D. Mrazek, Julia W. Y. Kam, Michael S. Franklin, and Jonathan W. Schooler. 'Inspired by Distraction: Mind Wandering Facilitates Creative Incubation', *Psychological Science* Vol. 23, No. 10, 1117–22, 2012

Baker, Mike. 'Should We Rank Pupils Instead of Grading Them?', *Guardian*, 2012

Bales, Robert F. 'A Set of Categories for the Analysis of Small Group Interaction', *American Sociological Review* Vol. 15, No. 2, 257–63, 1950

———. 'How People Interact in Conferences', *Scientific American* Vol. 192, No. 3, 31–5, 1955

Ball, Philip. 'The H-Index, Also Known as the Stag's Antlers', *Guardian*, 2012

Barrett, David. 'The Cheating Epidemic at Britain's Universities', *Daily Telegraph*, http://www.telegraph.co.uk/education/educationnews/8363345/The-cheating-epidemic-at-Britains-universities.html

Basu, Paroma. 'Where Are They Now?', *Nature Medicine* Vol. 12, 492–3

Bedford, Victoria Hilkevitch. 'Sibling Relationship Troubles and Well-Being in Middle and Old Age', *Family Relations* Vol. 47, No. 4, 369–76, 1998

Beenstock, Michael. 'Deconstructing the Sibling Correlation: How Families Increase Inequality', *Journal of Family and Economic Issues* Vol. 29, No. 3, 325–45, 2008

Beggan, James K., David M. Messick, and Scott T. Allison. 'Social Values and Egocentric Bias: Two Tests of the Might over Morality Hypothesis', *Journal of Personality and Social Psychology* Vol. 55, No. 4, 606–11, 1988

Bell, Jarrett. 'Vilma, Others Silent as NFL Makes Its Case', *USA Today*, 2012, http://usatoday30.usatoday.com/sports/usaedition/2012-06-19-saintshearing_st_u.htm

Bellafante, Ginia. 'Forget the Downturn; Punish the Lazybones', *New York Times*, 2010, http://www.nytimes.com/2010/10/17/arts/television/17bellafante.html?pagewanted=all&_r=0

Benenson, Joyce F., Timothy J. Antonellis, Benjamin J. Cotton, Kathleen E. Noddin, and Kristin A. Campbell. 'Sex Differences in Children's Formation of Exclusionary Alliances under Scarce Resource Conditions', *Animal Behaviour* Vol. 76, No. 2, 497–505, 2008

Benjamin, Alison. 'A Wider View of the Welfare State', *Guardian*, 2012

Bennet, Catherine. 'Games Mothers Make Tiger Moms Look Like Pussycats', *Observer*, 2012

Bensinger, Greg. 'Sprint Abandons Blackberry Tablet', *Wall Street Journal*, 2011

Berns, Gregory. 'The Biology of Cultural Conflict', *Philosophical Transactions of the Royal Society B: Biological Sciences*, No. 367, 633–9

Bernstein, Richard. 'The Chinese Are Coming!', *New York Review of Books*, 2012

Bidgood, Jess. 'Chicken Chain Says Stop, but T-Shirt Maker Balks', *New York Times*, 2011

Bing, Mark N. 'Hypercompetiveness in Academia: Achieving Criterion-Related Validity from Item Context Specificicity', *Journal of Personality Assessment*, 1999

Birkinshaw, Julian. 'Strategies for Managing Internal Competition', *California Management Review* Vol. 44, No. 1, 21–38, 2001

Blitz, Roger. 'Clubs with Contrasting Resources Fight to Stay Up', *Financial Times*, 2012

Blow, Charles M. 'For Jobs, It's War', *New York Times*, 2011, http://www.nytimes.com/2011/09/17/opinion/blow-for-jobs-its-war.html

Blythe, Anne. 'Hog Farm Fine to Clean River', *News & Observer* (Raleigh), 2012, http://www.newsobserver.com/2012/07/25/2221356/1-million-from-hog-farm-case-to.html

Boksem, Maarten A. S., Evelien Kostermans, and David De Cremer. 'Failing Where Others Have Succeeded: Medial Frontal Negativity Tracks Failure in a Social Context', *Psychophysiology* Vol. 48, No. 7, 973–9, 2011

———, Evelien Kostermans, Branka Milivojevic, and David De Cremer. 'Social Status Determines How We Monitor and Evaluate Our Performance', *Social Cognitive and Affective Neuroscience* Vol. 7, No. 3, 304–13, 2012

Booth, Alan, Douglas A. Granger, Allan Mazur, and Katie T. Kivlighan. 'Testosterone and Social Behavior', *Social Forces* Vol. 85, No. 1, 167–91, 2006

Boothman, Richard C. *Journal of Health and Life Sciences Law* Vol. 2, No. 2, 2009

Borgatta, Edgar F., and Robert F. Bales. 'Sociometric Status Patterns and Characteristics of Interaction', *Journal of Social Psychology* Vol. 43, No. 2, 289–97, 1956

Borger, Julian. 'Who Creates Harmony the World Over? Women. Who Signs Peace Deals? Men', *Guardian*, 2012

Bos, Peter A., David Terburg, Jack van Honk, and Bruce S. McEwen. 'Testosterone Decreases Trust in Socially Naïve Humans', *Proceedings of the National Academy of Sciences of the United States of America* Vol. 107, No. 22, 9991–5, 2010

Boseley, Sarah. 'NHS Director to Review Cosmetic Surgery Safety', *Guardian*, 2012

———. 'Eye Doctor Resigns from US University after Research Fraud', *Guardian*, 2012

Boshoff, Alison. 'The Other Winslet Girls', *Daily Mail*, 2009

Bowers, Simon. 'Glencore X-Strata Deal Threatened by Unimpressed Shareholders', *Guardian*, 2012

Bowles, Hannah Riley, Linda Babcock, and Lei Lai. 'Social Incentives for Gender Differences in the Propensity to Initiate Negotiations: Sometimes It Does Hurt to Ask', *Organizational Behavior and Human Decision Processes* Vol. 103, No. 1, 84–103, 2007

Bowles, Samuel. 'Group Competition, Reproductive Leveling and the Evolution of Human Altruism', *Science* Vol. 314, 1569–72, 2006

———. 'Genetically Capitalist?', *Science* Vol. 318, 394–5, 2007

———. 'Policies Designed for Self-Interested Citizens May Undermine "The Moral Sentiments": Evidence from Economic Experiments', *Science* Vol. 320, No. 5883, 1605–9, 2008

———. 'Did Warfare among Ancestral Hunter-Gatherers Affect the Evolution of Human Social Behaviors?', *Science* Vol. 324, 1293–8, 2009

———, and Herbert Gintis. 'Cooperation', *The New Palgrave Dictionary of Economics*, 2007

———, and Yongjin Park. 'Emulation, Inequality and Work Hours: Was Thorsten Veblen Right?', *Economic Journal* Vol. 115, No. 507, November, 397–412, 2005

Bradbury, Jane. 'Social Opportunity Produces Brain Changes in Fish', *PLOS*, 2005

Branden, Barbara. *The Passion of Ayn Rand*, Anchor Books, 1986

Branden, Nathaniel. *My Years with Ayn Rand*, Jossey-Bass, 1999

Bray, Elizabeth. 'Behind Every Female Superstar ...', *Independent*, 2012

Brickman, Barbara Jane. 'Brothers, Sisters, and Chainsaws: The Slasher Film as Locus for Sibling Rivalry', *Quarterly Review of Film and Video* Vol. 28, No. 2, 135–54, 2011

Broad, William J. 'North Korea's Performance Anxiety', *New York Times*, 2012

Brody, Gene H. 'Sibling Relationship Quality: Its Causes and Consequences', *Annual Review of Psychology* Vol. 49, 1–24, 1998

Bronson, Po, and Ashley Merryman. *Top Dog: The Science of Winning and Losing*, Twelve, 2013

Brooks, David. 'Testing the Teachers', *New York Times*, 2012

Brown, D. J., D. L. Ferris, D. Heller, and L. M. Keeping. 'Antecedents and Consequences of the Frequency of Upward and Downward Social Comparisons at Work', *Organizational Behavior and Human Decision Processes* Vol. 102, No. 1, 59–75, 2007

Brown, Helen Gurley. *Sex and the Single Girl*, Open Road Media Iconic Ebooks, 2012

Browne, John. *Beyond Business: An Inspirational Memoir from a Visionary Leader*, Weidenfeld & Nicolson, 2010

Bruck, Connie. 'The Art of the Billionaire', *New Yorker*, 2010

Buettner, Russ. 'State Panel to Review Pay of Leaders of Nonprofits', *New York Times*, 2011

Buhrmester, Duane and Wyndol Furman. 'Perceptions of Sibling Relationships During Middle Childhood and Adolescence', *Child Development* Vol. 61, No. 5, 1387–98, 1990

Bull, Andy. 'Greene's Gold Silences the Critics', *Guardian*, 2011

———. 'Bolt Knows He Can Be Beaten – but Only by Himself', *Guardian*, 2011

———. 'Fast Learner', *Observer*, 2011

Burckle, Michelle A., Richard M. Ryckman, Joel A. Gold, Bill Thornton, and Roberta J. Audesse. 'Forms of Competitive Attitude and Achievement Orientation in Relation to Disordered Eating', *Sex Roles* Vol. 40, No. 11–12, 853–70, 1999

Buser, Thomas, Muriel Niederle. 'Gender, Competitiveness and Career Choices', 2012, http://www.nber.org/papers/w18576

Bussey, John. 'Subsidy Nation: Can Firms in U.S. Compete with China', *Wall Street Journal*, 2011

Butler, Patrick. 'Making an Impact', *Guardian*, 2011

Buunk, Abraham P., and Frederick X. Gibbons. 'Social Comparison: The End of a Theory and the Emergence of a Field', *Organizational Behavior and Human Decision Processes* Vol. 102, No. 1, 3–21, 2007

Byrne, John A. 'B-Schools with the Most Competitive Students', http://poetsandquants.com/2012/03/01/b-schools-with-the-most-competitive-students/

Cadwalladr, Carole. 'Have an Idea as Good as Jamie Oliver's and Win 1m to Make It Happen', *Guardian*, 2012

Calapinto, John. 'Looking Good', *New Yorker*, 2012

Callahan, David. *The Cheating Culture: Why More Americans Are Doing Wrong to Get Ahead*, Harcourt Inc., 2004

Cambers, Simon. 'Why Does the Women's Game Seem a Shadow of Its Former Self?', *Guardian*, 2011

———. 'Pushy Parents Have Not Gone Away', *Guardian*, 2011

Cardenas, Juan-Camilo, Anna Dreber, Emma von Essen, and Eva Ranehill. 'Gender Differences in Competitiveness and Risk Taking: Comparing Children in Colombia and Sweden', *Research Papers in Economics*, No. 18, 2010

Cashdan, Elizabeth. 'Hormones and Competitive Aggression in Women', *Aggressive Behavior* Vol. 29, No. 2, 107–15, 2003

Cassidy, John. 'After the Blow-Up', *New Yorker*, 22 January 2010

————. 'Mastering the Machine', *New Yorker*, 25 July 2011

Centre for Effective Dispute Resolution. 'Tough Times, Tough Talk', 2011

Chang, Yang-Ming. 'Transfers and Bequests: A Portfolio Analysis in a Nash Game', *Annals of Finance* Vol. 3, No. 2, 277–295, 2007

————. 'Strategic Altruistic Transfers and Rent Seeking within the Family', *Journal of Population Economics* Vol. 22, No. 4, 1081–98, 2009

Cheshire Fair. 'Brochure', 2011

Cho, Adrian. 'Particle Physicists' New Extreme Teams', *Science* Vol. 333, 2011

Choi, Jung-Kyoo, and Samuel Bowles. 'The Coevolution of Parochial Altruism and War', *Science* Vol. 318, 636–9, 2007

Cicirelli, Victor G. 'Feelings of Attachment to Siblings and Well-Being in Later Life', *Psychology and Aging* Vol. 4, No. 2, 211, 1989

Citigroup. 'Revisiting Plutonomy: The Rich Get Richer', 25 March 2006

Clark, Alex, and Peter Stanford. 'Should Charities Use Shock Tactics', *Observer*, 2012

Colapinto, John. 'Meet Trevor Neilson', *Observer*, 29 July 2012

Cole, Daniel. 'Elinor Ostrom', *Guardian*, 15 June 2012

Coll, Steve. 'Gusher', *New Yorker*, 9 April 2012

Collier, Paul. 'Don't Look to China for Economic Salvation', *Observer*, 11 March 2012

Collins, Laura. 'England, Their England', *New Yorker*, 4 July 2011, 28–34

Colt, George Howe. *Brothers*, Scribner, 2012

Coman, Julian. 'The King and I', *Observer*, 25 March 2012

Conerly, Rachel. 'The Collaborative Organization', 2011

Conley, Dalton. *The Pecking Order: Which Siblings Survive and Why*, Pantheon Books, 2004

Conn, David. 'Inspire a Generation?', *Guardian*, 2012

Connor, J. M. 'Would You Dope? A General Population Test of the Goldman Dilemma', *British Journal of Sports Medicine* Vol. 43, No. 11, 871–2, 2009

Cook, Chris. 'Oaksey House: The Service Station That Helps Bruised and Battered Jockeys Back in the Saddle', *Guardian*, 2011

Cookson, Clive. 'Synthetic Life: The Revolution Begins', *Financial Times magazine*, 28/29 July 2012

Cooper, Chris. 'What If We Tested Athletes for Genes Instead of Drugs?', *Observer*, 6 May 2012

Corbett, J., Barwood, Ouzounoglou, Thelwell, Dicks. 'Influence of Competition on Performance and Pacing During Cycling Excercise', *University of Portsmouth*, 2012

Coy, Peter. 'You're So Bain', *Bloomberg Business Week*, 16 January 2012

Crawford, Leslie. 'Does Homework Really Work?', *Great Schools*

Crocker, Jennifer, and Lora E. Park. 'The Costly Pursuit of Self-Esteem', *Psychological Bulletin* Vol. 130, No. 3, 392–414, 2004

Croson, Rachel, and Uri Gneezy. 'Gender Differences in Preferences', *Journal of Economic Literature* Vol. 47, No. 2, 1–27, 2009

Curtis, Guy J. 'An Examination of Factors Related to Plagiarism and a Five-Year Follow-up of Plagiarism at an Australian University', *International Journal for Educational Integrity* Vol. 7, No. 1, 30–42

Cyranoski, David. 'Your Cheatin' Heart', *Nature Medicine* Vol. 12, No. 5, 490, 2006

Dalisay, Francis, Jay D. Hmielowski, Matthew James Kushin, Masahiro Yamamoto. 'Social Capital and the Spiral of Silence', *International Journal of Public Opinion*, 2012

Daly, M., Margo Wilson, Catherine A. Salmon, M. Hiraiwa-Hasegawa, and T. Hasegawa. 'Siblicide and Seniority', *Homicide Studies* Vol. 5, 30–45, 2001

Darwin, Charles. *The Origin of Species*, John Murray, 1859

———. *The Descent of Man and Selection in Relation to Sex*, John Murray, 1922

Das, Andrew. 'Less Is More: Less Practice Equals More Medals', *New York Times*, 5 August 2012

Davies, William. 'All of Our Business: Why Britain Needs More Private Sector Employee Ownership', Employee Ownership Association, 2012

Davis, Anna, and Pippa Crerar. 'Gold Club of Elite Schools to Put London Pupils on Top', *Evening Standard*, 18 October 2012

Davis, Jennifer. 'Birth Order, Sibship Size, and Status in Modern Canada', *Human Nature* Vol. 8, No. 3, 205–30, 1997

Dawkins, Richard. *The Selfish Gene: 30th Anniversary Edition – with a New Introduction by the Author*, Oxford University Press, 2006

de Botton, Alain. *Status Anxiety*, Hamish Hamilton, 2004

de Dreu, Carsten K. W., Lindred L. Greer, Michel J. J. Handgraaf, Shaul Shalvi, Gerben Van Kleef, Matthijs Baas, Femke S. Ten Velden, Eric Van Dijk, and Sander W. W. Feith. 'The Neuropeptide Oxytocin

Regulates Parochial Altruism in Intergroup Conflict among Humans', *Science* Vol. 328, 1408–11, 2010

de Waal, Frans. *Chimpanzee Politics: Power and Sex among Apes*, Jonathan Cape, 1982

———. *Our Inner Ape: The Best and Worst of Human Nature*, Granta Books, 2005

Decety, Jean, Philip L. Jackson, Jessica A. Sommerville, Thierry Chaminade, and Andrew N. Meltzoff. 'The Neural Bases of Cooperation and Competition: An fMRI Investigation', *Neuro-Image* Vol. 23, No. 2, 744–51, 2004

Dehart, Tracy, Brett Pelham, Luke Fiedorowicz, Mauricio Carvallo, and Shira Gabriel. 'Including Others in the Implicit Self: Implicit Evaluation of Significant Others', *Self and Identity* Vol. 10, No. 1, 127–35, 2011

Delaney, Kevin. 'In the Outgoing and the Introverted, Yin and Yang', *New York Times,* 11 March 2012

———. 'Change the World? Game On', *New York Times*, 8 July 2012

Delios, Andrew. 'How Can Organizations Be Competitive but Dare to Care?', *Academy of Management Perspectives*, 24–35, 2010

Denrell, Jerker, and Chengwei Liu. 'Top Performers Are Not the Most Impressive When Extreme Performance Indicates Unreliability', *PNAS* Vol. 109, No. 24, 9331–6

Depner, Charlene E., and Berit Ingersoll-Dayton. 'Supportive Relationships in Later Life', *Psychology and Aging* Vol. 3, No. 4, 348–57, 1988

Devine, Cathy. 'We Should Not Fetishise Competitive School Sport', *Guardian*, 10 December 2010

Djerassi, Carl. *Cantor's Dilemma*, Penguin Books, 1989

———. *The Pill, Pygmy Chimps and Degas' Horse*, Basic Books, 1992

———. *This Man's Pill*, Oxford University Press, 2001

Do Young Choi, Kun Chang Lee, and Seong Wook Chae. 'The Effect of Individual Psychological Characteristics on Creativity Revelation: Emphasis with Psychological Empowerment and Intrinsic Motivation', *Brain Informatics*, Springer Berlin Heidelberg, 2012

Doorn, G. Sander Van, Geerten M. Hengeveld, and Franz J. Weissing. 'The Evolution of Social Dominance I: Two-Player Models', *Behaviour* Vol. 140, No. 10, 1305–32, 2003

Dreber, Anna, Emma von Essen, and Eva Ranehill. 'Outrunning the Gender Gap – Boys and Girls Compete Equally', *Institute for Financial Research*, 2010

Dunn, Judy. *Siblings: Love, Envy and Understanding*, McIntyre, 1982

———. *Sisters and Brothers*, Fontana, 1984

———. *The Beginnings of Social Understanding*, Athenaeum Press, 1997

———. 'Sibling Relationships: Theory and Issues for Practice, *Children & Society* Vol. 19, No. 4, 339–40, 2005

Dwyer, Jim. 'A Billionaire Philanthropist Struggles to Go Broke', *New York Times*, 8 August 2012

Dysvik, Anders, and Bård Kuvaas. 'Intrinsic and Extrinsic Motivation as Predictors of Work Effort: The Moderating Role of Achievement Goals', *British Journal of Social Psychology* Vol. 52, 2012

Economist. 'Move over, Dalton', 1 September 2012

———.'Class Acts', 15 September 2012

———.'Working the System', 29 September 2012

———.'Body Politic', 6 October 2012

———. 'Who's Shrugging Now?', 20 October 2012

Edmondson, Amy C. 'Learning from Mistakes Is Easier Said Than Done: Group and Organizational Influences on the Detection and Correction of Human Error', *Journal of Applied Behavioral Science* Vol. 32, No. 1, 5–28, 1996

Edsall, Thomas B. 'The Reinvention of Political Morality', *New York Times*, 5 December 2011

———.'Is This the End of Market Democracy?', *New York Times*, 19 February 2012, http://campaignstops.blogs.nytimes.com/2012/02/19/is-this-the-end-of-market-democracy/

Edward, Joyce. 'Sibling Discord: A Force for Growth and Conflict', *Clinical Social Work Journal* Vol. 41, March 2013, 77

Eichenwald, Kurt. 'Microsoft's Lost Decade', *Vanity Fair*, August 2012

eLearners. 'Student Dropout Rates Linked to High Stress over Finances', *eLearners.com*

Employee Ownership Association. 'Case Study: Gripple', *www.gripple.com*, 2011

Enrich, David and David Gauthier-Villars. 'Struggling French Banks Fought to Avoid Oversight', *Wall Street Journal*, 2011

Erat, Sanjiv, and Uri Gneezy. 'White Lies', *University of California*, 2011

Erdal, David. *Beyond the Corporation: Humanity Working*, Bodley Head, 2011

Evans, Rhonda. 'Is the Canadian Model Right for UK Schools?', *Guardian*, 4 January 2011

Falbo, Toni, and Dudley L. Poston, Jr. 'The Academic, Personality, and Physical Outcomes of Only Children in China', *Child Development* Vol. 64, No. 1, 18–35, 1993

Farrer, Martin. 'Olympics Effect on Economy May Be Short Lived, Says King', *Guardian*, 13 August 2012

Feinberg, Kenneth. *What Is Life Worth? The Unprecedented Effort to Compensate the Victims of 9/11*, Public Affairs, 2005

Feinberg, Mark E., Susan M. McHale, Ann C. Crouter, and Patricio Cumsille. 'Sibling Differentiation: Sibling and Parent Relationship Trajectories in Adolescence', *Child Development* Vol. 74, No. 5, 1261–74, 2003

———, Anna Solmeyer, and Susan M. McHale. 'The Third Rail of Family Systems: Sibling Relationships, Mental and Behavioral Health, and Preventive Intervention in Childhood and Adolescence', *Clinical Child and Family Psychology Review* Vol. 15, March 2012

Felson, Richard, B. 'Aggression and Violence between Siblings', *Social Psychology Quarterly* Vol. 46, No. 4, 271–85, 1983

Fernandez-Araoz. 'The Coming Fight for Executive Talent', *Bloomberg Business Week*, 7 December 2009

Festinger, Leon. 'A Theory of Social Comparison Processes', *Human Relations* Vol. 7, No. 2, 117–40, 1954

Finkelhor, David, Heather Turner, and Richard Ormrod. 'Kid's Stuff: The Nature and Impact of Peer and Sibling Violence on Younger and Older Children', *Child Abuse & Neglect* Vol. 30, No. 12, 1401–21, 2006

Finnegan, William. 'The Storm', *New Yorker*, 5 March 2012

Fowden, A. L., and T. Moore. 'Maternal-Fetal Resource Allocation: Co-Operation and Conflict', *Placenta*, 2012. 10.1016/j.placenta.2012.05.002

Frank, Robert H., *The Darwin Economy: Liberty, Competition and the Common Good*, Princeton University Press, 2011

———. 'Will the Skillful Win?', *New York Times*, 5 August 2012

———, and Philip J. Cook. *The Winner-Takes-All Society: How More and More Americans Compete for Ever Fewer and Bigger Prizes, Encouraging Economic Waste, Income Inequality and an Improverished Cultural Life*, Free Press, 1995

———, Thomas Gilovich, and Dennis T. Regan. 'Does Studying Economics Inhibit Cooperation?', *The Journal of Economic Perspectives* Vol. 7, No. 2, 159-171, 1993

Franken, R. E., Ross Hill, and James Kierstead. 'Sport Interest as Predicted by the Personality Measures of Competitiveness, Mastery, Instrumentality, Expressivity, and Sensation Seeking', *Personality and Individual Differences* Vol. 17, No. 4, 467–476, 1994

Fraser, Giles. 'Loose Canon', *Guardian*, 21 July 2012

Frazier, Ian. 'Out of the Bronx', *New Yorker,* 6 February 2012

Freedland, Jonathan. 'The Markets Distrust Democracy', *Guardian*, 16 November 2011.

Freeman, Richard, Eric Weinstein, Elizabeth Marincola, Janet Rosenbaum, and Frank Solomon. 'Competition and Careers in Biosciences', *Science* Vol. 294, No. 5550, 2293–4, 2001

Frere-Jones, Sasha. 'The Gerbil's Revenge', *New Yorker*, 9 June 2008

Frick, Bernd. 'Gender Differences in Competitiveness: Empirical Evidence from Professional Distance Running', *Labour Economics* Vol. 18, No. 3, 389–98, 2011

———. 'Gender Differences in Competitive Orientations: Empirical Evidence from Ultramarathon Running', *Journal of Sports Economics* Vol. 12, No. 3, 317–40, 2011

Friedman, George. 'The Rise of Britain', *Geopolitical Weekly*, 2012

Friedman Stewart, D. 'Sibling Relationships and Intergenerational Succession in Family Firms', *Family Business Review* Vol. 4, No. 1, 3–20, 1991

Friedman, Thomas L., and Michael Mandelbaum. *That Used to Be Us: What Went Wrong with America – and How It Can Come Back*, Little, Brown & Co., 2011

Furnham, Adrian, D. Kirkcaldy Bruce, and Richard Lynn. 'National Attitudes to Competitiveness, Money, and Work among Young People: First, Second, and Third World Differences', *Human Relations* Vol. 47, No. 1, 119–32, 1994

Gagne J. J., Choudhry N. K. 'How Many "Me-Too" Drugs Is Too Many?', *JAMA* Vol. 305, No. 7, 711–12, 2011

Garcia, S. M., and A. Tor. 'Rankings, Standards, and Competition: Task Vs. Scale Comparisons', *Organizational Behavior and Human Decision Processes* Vol. 102, No. 1, 95–108, 2007

Garcia-Martinez, Jose Antonio. 'Competitiveness, Cooperation and Strategic Interaction: A Classroom Experiment on Oligopoly', *Revista Internacional de Sociologia* Vol. 70, 168–87, 2012

Gay, Jason. 'A Long, Amazing Ride to the Olympics', *Wall Street Journal*, 2012

Gefter, Amanda. 'The Blessing of Great Enemies', *New Scientist*, 2009, http://www.newscientist.com/article/dn17771-wilson-vs-watson-the-blessing-of-great-enemies.html

Gibbons, Frederick X. 'Social Comparison and Depression: Company's Effect on Misery', *Journal of Personality and Social Psychology* Vol. 51, No. 1, 140–8, 1986

Gibson, Owen. 'Fewer Young People Playing Sport, Research Reveals', *Guardian*, 23 June 2012

———. 'The Host Country Has Claimed Gold in Even More Sports Than the US Has', 9 August 2012

———, and Patrick Wintour. 'This Generation of Parents May Be Fitter Than Their Children, Says Coe', *Guardian*, 11 August 2012

Gilbert, Paul, John Price, and Steven Allan. 'Social Comparison, Social Attractiveness and Evolution: How Might They Be Related?', *New Ideas in Psychology* Vol. 13, No. 2, 149–65, 1995

Glendinning, Miles. *Architecture's Evil Empire: The Triumph and Tragedy of Global Modernism*, Reaktion Books, 2012

Glucksberg, S. A. M. 'Problem Solving: Response Competition and the Influence of Drive', *Psychological Reports* Vol. 15, No. 3, 939–42, 1964

Gneezy, Ayelet, and Daniel M. T. Fessler. 'Combat and Cooperation', *Royal Society* 2012

———, Alex Imas, Amber Brown, Leif D. Nelson, and Michael Norton. 'Paying to Be Nice: Consistency and Costly Prosocial Behaviour', *Harvard Business School*, 2011

Gneezy, Uri, Kenneth L. Leonard, and John A. List. 'Gender Differences in Competition: Evidence from a Matrilineal and a Patriarchal Society', *Econometrica* Vol. 77, No. 5, 1637–64, 2009

———, Muriel Niederle, and Aldo Rustichini. 'Performance in Competitive Environments: Gender Differences', *Quarterly Journal of Economics*, 2003

———, and Aldo Rustichini. 'Gender and Competition at a Young Age', *American Economic Review* Vol. 94, No. 2, 2004

Gogarty, Paul and Ian Williamson. *Winning at All Costs: Sporting Gods and Their Demons*, J.R. Books, 2009

Goldacre, Ben. *Bad Pharma: How Drug Companies Mislead Doctors and Harm Patients*, Fourth Estate, 2012

Gonzalez-Bono, E., A. Salvador, J. Ricarte, M. A. Serrano, and M. Arnedo. 'Testosterone and Attribution of Successful Competition', *Aggressive Behavior* Vol. 26, No. 3, 235–40, 2000

Goodley, Simon. 'Meltdown in the City', *Guardian*, 10 September 2011

Goodman, P. S., and E. Haisley. 'Social Comparison Processes in an Organizational Context: New Directions', *Organizational Behavior and Human Decision Processes* Vol. 102, No. 1, 109–25, 2007

Gopnik, Alison, and Adam Gopnik. 'Mom Always Liked You Best', *New York Times Book Review*, 23 September 2011

Graf, Lorenz, Andreas König, Albrecht Enders, and Harald Hungenberg. 'Debiasing Competitive Irrationality: How Managers Can Be Prevented from Trading Off Absolute for Relative Profit', *European Management Journal* Vol. 30, No. 4, 386–403, 2012

Grafton, Anthony. 'Our Universities: Why Are They Failing?', *New York Review of Books* 24 November 2011

Grandjean, Guy, Matthew Taylor and Paul Lewis. 'Deportation Contractor Faces Litany of Abuse Claims against Staff', *Guardian*, 14 April 2012

Grant, Adam M. *Give and Take: A Revolutionary Approach to Success*, Viking, 2013

———, and Sabine Sonnentag. 'Doing Good Buffers against Feeling Bad: Prosocial Impact Compensates for Negative Task and Self-Evaluations', *Organizational Behavior and Human Decision Processes* Vol. 111, 13–22, 2010

Gray, Peter. 'As Children's Freedom Has Declined, So Has Their Creativity', *Psychology Today*, 2012

Graziano, William G., Elizabeth C. Hair, and John F. Finch. 'Competitiveness Mediates the Link between Personality and Group Performance', *Journal of Personality and Social Psychology* Vol. 73, No. 6, 1394–408, 1997

Greenbaum, L. 'Sibling Rivalry', *Lancet* (British edition) Vol. 354, No. 9186, 1312, 1999

Gregory, S. W. Jr., and Timothy J. Gallagher. 'Spectral Analysis of Candidates' Nonverbal Vocal Communication: Predicting U.S. Presidential Election Outcomes', *Social Psychology Quarterly* Vol. 65, No. 3, 298–308, 2002

Guala, Francesco. 'Reciprocity: Weak or Strong? What Punishment Experiments Do (and Do Not) Demonstrate', *Behavioral and Brain Sciences*, 2012

Hacker, Andrew 'We're More Unequal Than You Think', *New York Review of Books*, 23 April 2012

Hacker, Jacob S., and Paul Pierson. *Winner-Take-All Politics*, Harper Paperbacks, 2010

Hahn, Avital Louria. 'Baird Revels in Its Independence', *Investment Dealers Digest*, 2005

Hamedani, MarYam G., Hazel Rose Markus, and Alyssa S. Fu. 'My Nation, My Self: Divergent Framings of America Influence American Selves', *Personality and Social Psychology Bulletin* Vol. 37, No. 3, 350–64, 2011

Hamel, Gary. 'First, Let's Fire All the Managers', *Harvard Business Review*, 2011

Hamilton, W. D. 'The Genetical Evolution of Social Behaviour', *Journal of Theoretical Biology* Vol. 7, 1964

Hamlin, J. Kiley, Karen Wynn, and Paul Bloom. 'Social Evaluation by Preverbal Infants', *Science* Vol. 450, No. 22, 557–8, 2007

Harris, Judith Rich. *The Nurture Assumption: Why Children Turn out the Way They Do*, Bloomsbury, 1998

Hasan, Mehdi. 'The Schools Exam System Is No Longer Fit for Purpose', *Guardian*, 17 December 2011

Hatemi, Peter K., and Rose McDermott. 'The Genetics of Politics: Discovery, Challenges, and Progress', *Trends in Genetics* Vol. 28, No. 10, 525–33, 2012

Hayes, Christopher. *The Twilight of the Elites: America after Meritocracy*, Crown, 2012

Heffernan, Margaret. *Wilful Blindess: Why we ignore the obvious at our peril*, Simon & Schuster, 2011

Heller, Nathan. 'The Disconnect', *New Yorker*, 16 April 2012

Hemming, Henry. *Together: How Small Groups Achieve Big Things*, John Murray, 2011

Hertwig, Ralph, Jennifer Nerissa Davis, and Frank J. Sulloway. 'Parental Investment: How an Equity Motive Can Produce Inequality', *Psychological Bulletin* Vol. 128, No. 5, 728–45, 2002

Hibbard, David R., and Duane Buhrmester. 'Competitiveness, Gender, and Adjustment among Adolescents', *Sex Roles* Vol. 63, No. 5, 412–24, 2010

Ho, Violet. 'Interpersonal Counterproductive Work Behaviors: Distinguishing between Person-Focused Versus Task-Focused Behaviors and Their Antecedents', *Journal of Business and Psychology*, 1–16, 1 December 2012

Hoare, Stephen. 'In the Market for MAS', *Guardian*, 27 March 2012

Hochschild, Arlie Russell. 'The Outsourced Life', *New York Times*, 6 May 2012

Hofstede, Geert. *Culture's Consequences* (Second Edition), Sage Publications, 2001

————, Gert Jan Hofstede, and Michael Minkov. *Cultures and Organizations: Software of the Mind: Intercultural Cooperation and Its Importance for Survival*, McGraw Hill, 2010

Hopkins, Keith, and Mary Beard. *The Colosseum*, Profile Books, 2011

Hopkins, Nick. 'G4S Using Untrained Staff to Screen Visitors', 7 August 2012

Hornbacher, Marya. *Wasted: Coming Back From an Addiction to Starvation*, Fourth Estate, 2010

Houston, John M., Sandra A. Mcintire, Judy Kinnie, and Christeine Terry. 'A Factorial Analysis of Scales Measuring Competitiveness', *Educational and Psychological Measurement* Vol. 62, No. 2, 284–98, 2002

Hughes, Claire, Alexandra L. Cutting, and Judy Dunn. 'Acting Nasty in the Face of Failure? Longitudinal Observations of "Hard-to-Manage" Children Playing a Rigged Competitive Game with a Friend', *Journal of Abnormal Child Psychology* Vol. 29, No. 5, 403–16, 2001

Inman, Philip. 'Brazil Passes UK to Become World's 6th Largest Economy', *Guardian*, 26 December 2011

————. 'Skyscraper Craze Shows Chinese May Be Heading for a Fall', *Guardian*, 12 January 2012

Insley, Jill. 'Farmers Fear Supermarket Offers Threaten British Food', *Guardian*, 12 August 2012

Iryin, Nancy, Carol Leonard, Ronald Clyman, Roberta A. Ballard. '60 Follow up of Siblings Present at Birth in an Alternative Birth Center', *Pediatric Research*, 1981

Jackson, Nate. 'The NFLs Concussion Culture', *Nation*, 2011

Jacobs, Andrew. 'Heavy Burden on Athletes Takes Joy Away from China's Olympic Success', *New York Times*, 7 August 2012

Jacques, Martin 'Why Do We Continue to Ignore China's Rise', *Observer*, 24 March 2012

Jamshidi, Akbar, Talebi Hossien, Seed Saeed Sajadi, Khalil Safari, and Ghasem Zare. 'The Relationship between Sport Orientation and Competitive Anxiety in Elite Athletes', *Procedia – Social and Behavioral Sciences* Vol. 30, 1161–5, 2011

Janssen, Marco A. 'Elinor Ostrom', *Nature* Vol. 487, 2012

Jayson, Sharon. 'From Brain to Mouth: The Psychology of Obesity', *USA Today*, 2012

Jena, Anupam B., John E. Calfee, Edward C. Mansley, and Tomas J. Philipson. '"Me-Too" Innovation in Pharmaceutical Markets', *Forum for Health Economics & Policy* Vol. 12, No. 1, 1–19, 2009

Jha, Alok. 'Being Social "Gave Humans Larger Brains"', *Guardian*, 22 June 2011

———. 'Research Fraud Forces Psychology to Take a Hard Look at Itself', *Guardian*, 13 September 2012

Johnson, Diane. 'Finish That Homework!', *New York Review of Books*, 18 August 2011

Judson, Horace Freeland. *The Great Betrayal: Fraud in Science*, Harcourt Inc., 2004

Kahn, Jennifer. 'The Perfect Stride', *New Yorker*, 8 November 2010

Kalma, Akko. 'Hierarchisation and Dominance Assessment at First Glance', *European Journal of Social Psychology* Vol. 21, No. 2, 165–81, 1991

Kapner, Suzanne. 'After Grueling Woes, CompUSA's Revival Efforts Fail to Spark Faith', *The Street*, 30 December 1999

Karavasilis Karos, Leigh, Nina Howe, and Jasmin Aquan-Assee. 'Reciprocal and Complementary Sibling Interactions, Relationship Quality and Socio-Emotional Problem Solving', *Infant and Child Development* Vol. 16, No. 6, 577–96, 2007

Kaufman, Frederick. *Bet the Farm: How Food Stopped Being Food*, John Wiley & Sons, 2012

Kaufman, Scott Barry. *Ungifted: Intelligence Redefined*, Basic Books, 2013

Keltner, Dacher, Deborah H. Gruenfeld, and Cameron Anderson. 'Power, Approach, and Inhibition', *Psychological Review* Vol. 110, No. 2, 265–84, 2003

Kennedy, Maev. 'Why Cross the South Pole in Winter? It's Just What I Do', *Guardian*, 18 September 2012

Kessel, Anna. 'Athletics Is All I Ever Think About – It's Like Being Young and Falling in Love', *Guardian*, 1 May 2012

Kessler, David A., Janet L. Rose, Robert J. Temple, Renie Schapiro, and Joseph P. Griffin. 'Therapeutic-Class Wars – Drug Promotion in a Competitive Marketplace', *New England Journal of Medicine* Vol. 331, No. 20, 1350–3, 1994

Khoja, Faiza. 'Is Sibling Rivalry Good or Bad for High Technology Organizations?', *Journal of High Technology Management Research* Vol. 19, No. 1, 11–20, 2008

Kidder, Rushworth. 'Ask Not for Whom the Students Cheat: They Cheat for Thee', 2011 Institute for Global Ethics

King, Ronnel B., Dennis M. McInerney, and David A. Watkins. 'Competitiveness Is Not That Bad ... at Least in the East: Testing the Hierarchical Model of Achievement Motivation in the Asian Setting', *International Journal of Intercultural Relations* Vol. 36, No. 3, 446–57, 2012

Kirby, David. *Animal Factory: The Looming Threat of Industrial Pig, Dairy, and Poultry Farms to Humans and the Environment*, St Martin's Press, 2010

Kirkpatrick, Doug. 'Does Power Corrupt? Science Says Yes', Morning Star Self-Management Institute, 2012

Korelitz, Jean Hanff. *Admission: A Novel*, Grand Central Publishing, 2009

Koretz, Gene. 'Are Women Less Competitive?', *Business Week*, 9 December 2002

Korpela, K. M. 'How Long Does It Take for the Scientific Literature to Purge Itself of Fraudulent Material? The Breuning Case Revisited', *Current Medical Research & Opinion* Vol. 26, No. 4, 843–7, 2010

Koster, Raph. *A Theory of Fun for Game Design*, Paraglyph Press, 2005

KPMG. 'Profile of a Fraudster', 2011

Kraus, Michael W., Paul K. Piff, and Dacher Keltner. 'Social Class as Culture: The Convergence of Resources and Rank in the Social Realm', *Current Directions in Psychological Science* Vol. 20, No. 4, 246–50, 2011

Kushner, David. 'Machine Politics', *New Yorker*, 7 May 2012

Lafsky, Melissa. 'Are Men Really More Competitive Than Women?', *New York Times*, 6 February 2008

Lanier, Jaron. *Who Owns the Future?*, Simon & Schuster, 2013

Larrick, Richard P., Katherine A. Burson, and Jack B. Soll. 'Social Comparison and Confidence: When Thinking You're Better Than Average Predicts Overconfidence (and When It Does Not)', *Organizational Behavior and Human Decision Processes* Vol. 102, No. 1, 76–94, 2007

Lashewicz, Bonnie, and Norah Keating. 'Tensions among Siblings in Parent Care', *European Journal of Ageing* Vol. 6, No. 2, 127–35, 2009

Lawrence, Peter, A. 'The Politics of Publication', *Nature* Vol. 422, No. 6929, 259–61, 2003

Lehmann, Laurent, and François Rousset. 'How Life History and Demography Promote or Inhibit the Evolution of Helping Behaviours', *Philosophical Transactions of the Royal Society B: Biological Sciences* Vol. 365, No. 1553, 2599–617, 2010

Lepper, Mark R., David Greene, and Richard E. Nisbett. 'Undermining Children's Intrinsic Interest with Extrinsic Reward: A Test of the "Overjustification" Hypothesis', *Journal of Personality and Social Psychology* Vol. 28, No. 1, 129–37, 1973

Levine, George. *Darwin Loves You*, Princeton University Press, 2008

Levy, David M. 'The Hostile Act', *Psychological Review* Vol. 48, No. 4, 356–61, 1941

———, and A. Ruckmick Christian. 'Studies in Sibling Rivalry', *American Journal of Psychology* Vol. 49, No. 4, 691, 1937

Lewis, Anthony. 'The Shame of America', *New York Review of Books*, 12 January 2012

Lewontin, Richard. 'It's Even Less in Your Genes', *New York Review of Books*, 26 May 2011

Lindquist, Gabriella Sjorgen, Jenny Save-Soderbergh. '"Girls Will Be Girls" – Especially among Boys: Competitive Behavior in the "Daily Double" On *Jeopardy*' *Economics Letters*, August 2011

Littlemore, Sue. 'Universities "Need to Explain What Plagiarism Is"', *Guardian*, 12 June 2012

Longman, Jere. 'For Female Athletes, A.C.L. Injuries Take a Toll', *New York Times*, 27 March 2011

Lott, Tim. 'As a Child, I Always Sought My Older Brother's Approval', *Observer*, 24 March 2012

———. 'Did We Damage Each Other?', *Guardian*, 30 March 2012

———. 'Get over It Guys', *Observer*, 18 August 2012

———. *Under the Same Stars*, Simon and Schuster, 2012

Ludwig, Sandra and Thoma, Carmen. 'Do Women Have More Shame Than Men? An Experiment on Self-Assessment and the Shame of Overestimating Oneself', *Discussion Paper No. 2012–15, Department of Economics, University of Munich*, 2012

Lunn, Peter. *Basic Instincts: Human Nature and the New Economics*, Marshall Cavendish, 2008

Machi, Ethel. 'Improving U.S. Competitiveness with K-12 Education and Training', *Heritage Foundation*, 2008

Macilwain, Colin. 'What Science Is Really Worth', *Nature*, 9 June 2010

Magagna, Jeanne. 'Transformation: From Twin to Individual', *Journal of Child Psychotherapy* Vol. 33, No. 1, 51–69, 2007

Majendie, Matt. 'The Brains Behind Our Mind Games', *Evening Standard*, 17 November 2011

Martens, Rainer, Robin S. Vealey, and Damon Burton. *Competitive Anxiety in Sport*, Human Kinetics, 1990

Martin, Roger L. *Fixing the Game: Bubbles, Crashes and What Capitalism Can Learn from the NFL*, Harvard Business Review Press, 2011

Mathiason, Nick. 'Square Mile in Spotlight as Tax Avoidance Trade "Cheats" Europe', *Observer*, 18 December 2011

Matthews, Karen A., and Julio Angula. 'Measurement of the Type A Behavior Pattern in Children: Assessment of Children's Competitiveness, Impatience-Anger, and Aggression', *Child Development* Vol. 51, No. 2, 1980

Mayr, Ulrich, Dave Wozniak, Casey Davidson, David Kuhns, and William T. Harbaugh. 'Competitiveness across the Life Span: The Feisty Fifties', *Psychology and Aging* Vol. 27, No. 2, 278–85, 2012

Mazur, Allan. 'Sex Difference in Testosterone Response to a Video Game Contest', *Evolution and Human Behavior* Vol. 18, No. 5, 317–26, 1997

———, and Alan Booth. 'Testosterone and Dominance in Men', *Behavioral and Brain Sciences* Vol. 21, No. 3, 353–63, 1998

McCormick, Neil. 'I Love My Brother ... I Just Can't Stand to Be with Him', *Evening Standard*, 13 October 2011

McElheny, Victor K. *Drawing the Map of Life: Inside the Human Genome Project*, Basic Books, 2010

McGrath, Ben. 'Queen of the D-League', *New Yorker*, 25 April 2011

McIntyre, Matthew H. 'The Use of Digit Ratios as Markers for Perinatal Androgen Action', *Reproductive Biology and Endocrinology* Vol. 4, No. 10, 2006

McKie. 'Why We Are All in This Together', *Observer*, 11 March 2012

McWilliams, James E. 'The Myth of Sustainable Meat', *New York Times*, 12 April 2012

Meggyesy, David and Dave Zirin. 'How Players Won the NFL Lockout', *Nation*, 20–1, 2011

Mehta, Pranjal H., Amanda C. Jones, and Robert A. Josephs. 'The Social Endocrinology of Dominance: Basal Testosterone Predicts Cortisol Changes and Behavior Following Victory and Defeat', *Journal of Personality and Social Psychology* Vol. 94, No. 6, 1078–93, 2008

Meikle, James. 'Cricketer Admits Being Bribed to Give Away Runs', *Guardian* 13 January 2012

Melis, Alicia P., and Dirk Semmann. 'How Is Human Cooperation Different?', *Philosophical Transactions of the Royal Society B: Biological Sciences* Vol. 365, No. 1553, 2663–74, 2010

Meston, Cindy, and David M. Buss. *Why Women Have Sex: Understanding Sexual Motivation from Adventure to Revenge*, Vintage Digital, 2010

Meyer, Christopher, and Julia Kirby. 'Runaway Capitalism', *Harvard Business Review*, January 2012

Michell, Lynn, and Amanda Amos. 'Girls, Pecking Order and Smoking', *Social Science & Medicine* Vol. 44, No. 12, 1861–9, 1997

Midgley, Mary. *The Solitary Self: Darwin and the Selfish Gene*, Acumen, 2010

———. 'No Gain without Pain', *London Business School Alumni News*, No. 127, 34–5, 2012

Millar, David. *Racing through the Dark: The Fall and Rise of David Millar*, Orion Books, 2011

Miller, Geoffrey. *The Mating Game: How Sexual Choice Shaped the Evolution of Human Nature*, Vintage, 2001

Miller, Greg. 'The Prickly Side of Oxytocin', *Science* Vol. 328, 1343, 2010

———. 'Social Savvy Boosts the Collective Intelligence of Groups', *Science* Vol. 330, 22, 2010

Mitchell, Heidi. 'Competing for Scholarships on the Field and Online', *Wall Street Journal*, 7 August 2012

Mock, D. W., and G. A. Parker. 'Siblicide, Family Conflict and the Evolutionary Limits of Selfishness', *Animal Behaviour* Vol. 56, No. 1, 1–10, 1998

Moore, D. A. 'Not So above Average after All: When People Believe They Are Worse Than Average and Its Implications for Theories of Bias in Social Comparison', *Organizational Behavior and Human Decision Processes* Vol. 102, No. 1, 42–58, 2007

Morgan, Mary, S. 'Economic Man as Model Man: Ideal Types, Idealization and Caricatures', *Journal of the History of Economic Thought* Vol. 28, No. 1, 1–27, 2006

Morning Star Self-Management Institute. 'Newsletter', 2011

Mowen, John C. 'Exploring the Trait of Competitiveness and Its Consumer Behavior Consequences', *Journal of Consumer Psychology* Vol. 14, No. 1/2, 52–63, 2004

Mudrack, Peter E., James M. Bloodgood, and William H. Turnley. 'Some Ethical Implications of Individual Competitiveness', *Journal of Business Ethics* Vol. 108, No. 3, 2011

Mueller, Frederick O. 'Annual Survey of Football Injury Research', *American Football Coaches Association*, 2011

Muir, William M. 'Incorporation of Competitive Effects in Forest Tree or Animal Breeding Programs', *Genetics* Vol. 170, No. 3, 1247–59, 2005

Murayama, Kou, and Andrew J. Elliot. 'The Competition–Performance Relation: A Meta-Analytic Review and Test of the Opposing Processes Model of Competition and Performance', *Psychological Bulletin* Vol. 138, No. 6, 1035, 2012

Narain, Jaya. 'Three Teachers at Award-Winning School Suspended "for Helping Students Cheat in GCSEs"', *Mail Online*, http://www.dailymail.co.uk/news/article-1205521/Three-teachers-award-winning-school-suspended-helping-students-cheat-GCSEs.html

Neville, Lukas. 'Do Economic Equality and Generalized Trust Inhibit Academic Dishonesty? Evidence from State-Level Search-Engine Queries', *Psychological Science* Vol. 23, No. 4, 339–45, 2012

Niederle, Muriel, and Lise Vesterland. 'Do Women Shy Away from Competition: Do Men Compete Too Much?', *Quarterly Journal of Economics*, 2007

Niman, Nicolette Hahn. *Righteous Porkchop: Finding a Life and Good Food Beyond Factory Farms*, Harper, 2009

Nowak, Martin. *Super-Cooperators*, Canongate, 2011

Okasha, Samir. 'Altruism Rsearchers Must Cooperate', *Nature* Vol. 467, 2010

Orr, H. Allen. 'Is Goodness in Your Genes?', *New York Review of Books*, 14 October 2010

———. 'The Science of Right and Wrong', *New York Review of Books*, 12 May 2011

Osnos, Evan. 'The Han Dynasty', *New Yorker*, 4 July 2011

———. 'Meet Dr. Freud', *New Yorker*, 10 January 2011

———. 'Boss Rail', *New Yorker*, 22 October 2012

Paserman, M. Daniele. 'Gender-Linked Performance Differences in Competitive Environments: Evidence from Pro Tennis', *VOX*, 2007

Patil, Anita. 'Don't Fight It, Crowd-Source It', *New York Times*, 4 March 2012

————. 'Status Anxiety Vs Status Updates', *New York Times*, 4 December 2011

Paton, Graeme. 'Schools "Bribing Pupils" to Cheat Ofsted Inspections', *Daily Telegraph*, 17 January 2012

Pearson, Matthew, and Burkhard C. Schipper. 'Menstrual Cycle and Competitive Bidding', *SSRN eLibrary*, 2009. http://ssrn.com/paper=1441665

Peng, Wei, and Gary Hsieh. 'The Influence of Competition, Cooperation, and Player Relationship in a Motor Performance Centered Computer Game', *Computers in Human Behavior*, http://www.sciencedirect.com/science/article/pii/S0747563212001641

Pepitone, Emmy A. *Children in Cooperation and Competition*, Lexington Books, 1980

Perlman, Michal, and Hildy, S. Ross. 'The Benefits of Parent Intervention in Children's Disputes: An Examination of Concurrent Changes in Children's Fighting Styles', *Child Development* Vol. 68, No. 4, 690–700, 1997

Perner, Josef, Ted Ruffman, and Susan R. Leekam. 'Theory of Mind Is Contagious: You Catch It from Your Sibs', *Child Development* Vol. 65, No. 4, 1228–38, 1994

Petrecca, Laura. 'Bullying by the Boss is Common but Hard to Fix', *USA Today*, 2010

Pettit, Nathan C. 'The Eyes and Ears of Status: How Status Colors Perceptual Judgment', *Personality and Social Psychology Bulletin*, 2012

Pfeiffer, Thomas, Lily Tran, Coco Krumme, and David Rand. 'The Value of Reputation', *Royal Society Interface*, 2012

Piff, Paul K., Daniel M. Stancato, Stephane Cote, Rodolfo Mendoza-Denton, and Dacher Keltner. 'Higher Social Class Predicts Increased Unethical Behavior', *PNAS* Vol. 109, No. 11, 2012

Pinto-Gouveia, José, Cláudia Ferreira, and Cristiana Duarte. 'Thinness in the Pursuit for Social Safeness: An Integrative Model of Social Rank Mentality to Explain Eating Psychopathology', *Clinical Psychology & Psychotherapy*, 2012

Porter, Michael E. *Competitive Strategy*, Free Press, 1998

————. 'Clusters and the New Economics of Competition', *Harvard Business Review*, 1998

————, and Mark R. Kramer. 'Shared Value: How to Reinvent Capitalism – and Unleash a Wave of Innovation and Growth', *Harvard Business Review*, 2011

Price, J., L. Sloman, R. Gardner, P. Gilbert, and P. Rohde. 'The Social Competition Hypothesis of Depression', *British Journal of Psychiatry* Vol. 164, No. 3, 309–15, 1994

Price, John S. 'A Remembrance of Thorleif Schjelderup-Ebbe', *Human Ethology Bulletin* Vol. 10, No. 1

———, and Leon Sloman. 'Depression as Yielding Behavior: An Animal Model Based on Schjelderup-Ebbe's Pecking Order', *Ethology and Sociobiology* Vol. 8, Supplement 1, 85–98, 1987

Puffer, Sheila M. 'CompUSA's CEO James Halpin on Technology, Rewards and Commitment', *Academy of Management Executive* Vol. 13, No. 2, 29, 1999

Quasem, Himaya. 'Small Nations Can Also Be Tech Giants', *Straits Times*, 2011

Rajan, T. V. 'Biomedical Scientists Are Engaged in a Pyramid Scheme', *Chronicle of Higher Education*, 2005

Ramesh, Randeep. 'Britain Risks Catching the "US Disease"', *Guardian*, 7 December 2011

Rand, David. 'The Value of Reputation', *Interface: Journal of the Royal Society*, 2012

———. 'Slow to Anger and Fast to Forgive', *American Economic Review* Vol. 102, No. 2, 720–49, 2012

Recchia, Holly E., Hildy S. Ross, and Marcia Vickar. 'Power and Conflict Resolution in Sibling, Parent–Child, and Spousal Negotiations', *Journal of Family Psychology* Vol. 24, No. 5, 605–15, 2010

Reginato, James. 'The World's Most Expensive House', *Vanity Fair* Vol. 622, 2012

Reich, Eugenie Samuel. *Plastic Fantastic: How the Biggest Fraud in Physics Shook the Scientific World*, Palgrave Macmillan, 2009

Reidy, Tess, and Conal Urquhart. 'Sixth-Formers Pay up to £350 in Bid to Cheat University Admissions System', *Observer*, 13 October 2012

Repak, Nick. 'Emotional Fatigue: Coping with Economic Pressure' Grad Resources

Reynolds, Gretchen. 'Phys Ed: Will Olympic Athletes Dope If They Know It Might Kill Them?', *New York Times*, 2010

Ricarte, J., A. Salvador, R. Costa, M. J. Torres, and M. Subirats. 'Heart Rate and Blood Pressure Responses to a Competitive Role-Playing Game', *Aggressive Behavior* Vol. 27, No. 5, 351–9, 2001

Richmond, Riva. 'Web Site Ranks Hacks and Bestows Bragging Rights', *New York Times*, 21 August 2011

Ridley, Matt. *The Red Queen: Sex and the Evolution of Human Nature*, Harper Perennial, 2003

Rifkin, Jeremy. *The Empathic Civilization*, Polity Press, 2009

Robbins, Alexandra. *The Over-Achievers: The Secret Lives of Driven Kids*, Hyperion, 2006

Robertson, Ian. *The Winner Effect: How Power Affects Your Brain*, Bloomsbury, 2012

Ronay, Barney. 'Wheldon's Death in Las Vegas Leaves an English Village Grieving over a Favourite Son', *Guardian*, 17 October 2011

Ronay, Richard, and Dana R. Carney. 'Testosterone's Negative Relationship with Empathic Accuracy and Perceived Leadership Ability', *Social Psychological and Personality Science* Vol. 4, No. 1, 92–9, 2013

Rosenthal, Elizabeth. 'Troubled Marriage? Sibling Relations May Be at Fault', *New York Times*, 19 August 1992

Rothstein, Jesse. 'Does Competition among Public Schools Benefit Students and Taxpayers? A Comment on Hoxley', *American Economic Review* Vol. 97, No. 5, 2026–37, 2007

Rowe, Dorothy. *My Dearest Enemy, My Dangerous Friend: Making and Breaking Sibling Bonds*, Routledge, 2007

Rustin, Margaret. 'Taking Account of Siblings – a View from Child Psychotherapy', *Journal of Child Psychotherapy* Vol. 33, No. 1, 21–35, 2007

Royal Society. *Theme Issue: Cooperation and Deception*, 2010

Ryan, Richard M., and Edward L. Deci. 'Intrinsic and Extrinsic Motivations: Classic Definitions and New Directions', *Contemporary Educational Psychology* Vol. 25, 56–67, 2000

Ryckman, Richard M., Cary R. Libby, Bart van den Borne, Joel A. Gold, and Marc A. Lindner. 'Values of Hypercompetitive and Personal Development Competitive Individuals', *Journal of Personality Assessment* Vol. 69, No. 2, 271, 1997

———, Bill Thornton, and J. Corey Butler. 'Personality Correlates of the Hypercompetitive Attitude Scale: Validity Tests of Horney's Theory of Neurosis', *Journal of Personality Assessment* Vol. 62, No. 1, 84, 1994

Saavedra, Serguei, Kathleen Hagerty, and Brian Uzzi. 'Synchronicity, Instant Messaging, and Performance among Financial Traders', *Proceedings of the National Academy of Sciences* Vol. 108, No. 13, 5296–301, 2011

Sahlberg, Pasi. 'Education Reform for Raising Economic Competitiveness', *Journal of Educational Change*, 2006

————. *Finnish Lessons: What Can the World Learn from Educational Change in Finland?*, Teachers College Press, 2010

Salmon, Catherine A. 'Birth Order and Relationships', *Human Nature* Vol. 14, No. 1, 73–88, 2003

————, and M. Daly. 'Birth Order and Familial Sentiment – Birth Order, Family Dynamics, and Creative Lives', *Evolution and Human Behavior* Vol. 19, No. 5, 299–312, 1998

Santora, Marc. 'Amid Inquiry into Cheating, Stuyvesant Principal Will Retire', *New York Times*, 4 August 2012

Savikhin, Anya C. 'Is There a Gender Gap in Preschoolers' Competitiveness? An Experiment in the U.S.', 2011, http://www.sciencedirect.com/science/article/pii/S0167268113001091

Schachter, Frances F., Ellen Shore, Susan Feldman-Rotman, Ruth E. Marquis, and Susan Campbell. 'Sibling Deidentification', *Developmental Psychology* Vol. 12, No. 5, 418–27, 1976

Schjelderup-Ebbe, Thorleif. 'Fortgesetzte Biologische Beobachtungen Des Gallus Domesticus', *Psychological Research* Vol. 5, No. 1, 343–55, 1924

Schleien, Sara, Hildy Ross, and Michael Ross. 'Young Children's Apologies to Their Siblings', *Social Development* Vol. 19, No. 1, 170–86, 2010

Schneier, Bruce. *Liars & Outliers*, John Wiley & Sons, 2012

Schroth, Raymond A. 'The Plagiarism Plague', *America: National Catholic Weekly*, 2012

Schwartzapfel, Beth. 'The Brothers Moynihan', *Brown Alumni Magazine*, 2010

Schwarz, Alan. 'From Big Leagues, Hints at Sibling Behaviour', *New York Times*, 24 May 2010

————. 'Risky Rise of the Good-Grade Pill', *New York Times*, 24 June 2012

Segal, David. 'They Win Gold, but a Pot of It Rarely Follows', *New York Times*, 4 August 2012

Segal, Nancy L., and Scott L. Hershberger. 'Cooperation and Competition between Twins: Findings from a Prisoner's Dilemma Game' *Evolution and Human Behaviour* Vol. 20, 29–51, 1999

————, Shirley A. McGuire, Steven A. Miller, and June Havlena. 'Tacit Coordination in Monozygotic Twins, Dizygotic Twins and

Virtual Twins: Effects and Implications of Genetic Relatedness', *Personality and Individual Differences* Vol. 45, No. 7, 607–12, 2008

Sennett, Richard. *Together: The Rituals, Pleasures and Politics of Cooperation*, Allen Lane, 2012

Sequino, Stephanie and Thomas Stevens, Mark A. Lutz. 'Gender and Cooperative Behavior: Economic *Man* Rides Alone', *Feminist Economics* Vol. 2, No. 1, 1–21, 1996

Shreeve, James. *The Genome War*, Alfred A. Knopf, 2004

Sides-Moore, Lauren, Karin Tochkov. 'The Thinner the Better? Competiveness, Depression and Body Image Among College Student Women', *College Student Journal Publisher* Vol. 45

Silverman, Rachel Emma and Leslie Kwoh. 'Performance Review Facebook Style', *Wall Street Journal*, 2012

Skilling, David. *Observer newsletter*, http://landfallstrategy.com/about/david-skilling/

Smit, Jeroen. *The Perfect Prey: The Fall of ABN Amro, or What Went Wrong in the Banking Industry*, Quercus, 2009

Smith, Julie, and Hildy Ross. 'Training Parents to Mediate Sibling Disputes Affects Children's Negotiation and Conflict Understanding', *Child Development* Vol. 78, No. 3, 790–805, 2007

Smither, Robert D., and John M. Houston. 'The Nature of Competitiveness: The Development and Validation of the Competitiveness Index', *Educational and Psychological Measurement* Vol. 52, No. 2, 407–18, 1992

Solomon, Yvette, Jo Warin, and Charlie Lewis. 'Helping with Homework? Homework as a Site of Tension for Parents and Teenagers', *British Educational Research Journal* Vol. 28, No. 4, 603–22, 2002

Son Hing, Leanne S., D. Ramona Bobocel, Mark P. Zanna, and Maxine V. McBride. 'Authoritarian Dynamics and Unethical Decision Making: High Social Dominance Orientation Leaders and High Right-Wing Authoritarianism Followers', *Journal of Personality and Social Psychology* Vol. 92, No. 1, 67–81, 2007

Stadler, Christian. 'The Four Principles of Enduring Success', *Harvard Business Review*, 2007

Stapel, Diederik A., and Willem Koomen. 'Competition, Cooperation, and the Effects of Others on Me', *Journal of Personality and Social Psychology*, vol. 88, 2005

Steen, R. Grant. 'Retractions in the Scientific Literature: Do Authors Deliberately Commit Research Fraud?', 2010

———. 'Retractions in the Scientific Literature: Is the Incidence of Research Fraud Increasing?', *Journal of Medical Ethics* Vol. 37, No. 4, 249–53, 2011

Steinberg, Jacques. 'Feeling Anxious, and Applying Now', *New York Times*, 2010

Steinberg, Julie, Aaron Lucchetti, and Mike Spector. 'At MF Global: Rush to Move Cash', *Wall Street Journal*, 23 February 2012

Stevenson, Joan C. 'The Evolution of Sibling Rivalry', *American Journal of Human Biology* Vol. 12, No. 5, 720, 2000

Stewart, James B. *Tangled Webs: How False Statements Are Undermining America: From Martha Stewart to Bernie Madoff*, Penguin Books, 2011

Stillwell, Robin, and Judy Dunn. 'Continuities in Sibling Relationships: Patterns of Aggression and Friendliness', *Journal of Child Psychology and Psychiatry* Vol. 26, No. 4, 627–37, 1985

Stocker, Clare M., and Lise Youngblade. 'Marital Conflict and Parental Hostility: Links with Children's Sibling and Peer Relationships', *Journal of Family Psychology* Vol. 13, No. 4, 598, 1999

Stout, Lynn. *The Shareholder Value Myth: How Putting Shareholders First Harms Investors, Corporations and the Public*, Berrett-Koehler Publishers, 2012

Stross, Randall. 'The Algorithm Didn't Like My Essay', *New York Times*, 9 June 2012

Stuart, Keith. 'Game Changers', *Guardian*, 9 December 2011

Sulloway, Frank J. *Born to Rebel: Birth Order, Family Dynamics, and Creative Lives*, Little, Brown & Company, 1996

———. 'Birth Order and Intelligence', 2007, http://www.sulloway. org/BirthOrder&Intelligence-Science2007.pdf

———. 'Why Siblings Are Like Darwin's Finches: Birth Order, Sibling Competition and Adaptive Divergence within Family', in David M. Buss and Patricia H. Hawley (eds), *The Evolution of Personality and Individual Differences*, OUP, 2010

Sulston, John, and Georgina Ferry. *The Common Threat: A Story of Science, Politics, Ethics and the Human Genome*, Bantam Press, 2002

Sutton, Bob. 'Self Awareness, Competitiveness and Cooperation', *Psychology Today* website, 2010

Tauer, John M., and Judith M. Harackiewicz. 'Winning Isn't Everything: Competition, Achievement Orientation, and Intrinsic Motivation', *Journal of Experimental Social Psychology* Vol. 35, No. 3, 209–38, 1999

Terpstra, David E., Mario G. C. Reyes, and Donald W. Bokor. 'Predictors of Ethical Decisions Regarding Insider Trading', *Journal of Business Ethics* Vol. 10, No. 9, 699–710, 1991

Tharp, Twyla. *The Collaborative Habit: Life Lessons for Working Together*, Simon & Schuster, 2009

Thamotheram, Raj, and Maxime Le Floc'h. 'The BP Crisis as a "Preventable Surprise": Lessons for Institutional Investors', *Rotman International Journal of Pension Management*, Vol. 5, 2012

Thornton, Bill, Richard M. Ryckman, Joel A. Gold. 'Competitive Orientations and the Type A Behavior Type', *Psychology* Vol. 2, No. 5, 411–15, 2011

Tietz, Jeff. 'Boss Hog', *Rolling Stone*, 2006

Tignor, Stephen. *High Strung: Bjorn Borg, John McEnroe and the Untold Story of Tennis's Fiercest Rivalry*, Harper Collins, 2011

Tilton, Sarah and Juliet Chung. 'Mogulopoly', *Wall Street Journal*, 2011

Tinley, Scott. *Racing the Sun: An Athlete's Quest for Life after Sport*, Lyon's Press, 2003

Trilling, Bernie, and Charles Fadel. *21st Century Skills: Learning for Life in Our Times*, Jossey-Bass, 2009

Tsai, Terence, Michael Young, and Bor-shiuan Cheng. 'Confucian Business Practices and Firm Competitiveness: The Case of Sinyi Real Estate', *Frontiers of Business Research in China* Vol. 5, No. 3, 317–43, 2011

Tucker, Corinna, Genevieve Cox, Erin Sharp, Karen Van Gundy, Cesar Rebellon, and Nena Stracuzzi. 'Sibling Proactive and Reactive Aggression in Adolescence', *Journal of Family Violence*, 1–12

Tugend, Alina. 'Experts' Advice to the Goal-Oriented: Don't Overdo It', *New York Times*, 5 October 2012

Ungrady, Dave. 'From 10,000 Meters to 26.2 Miles in New York', *New York Times*, 14 October 2010

Vaillancourt, Tracy, Denys deCatanzaro, Eric Duku, and Cameron Muir. 'Androgen Dynamics in the Context of Children's Peer Relations: An Examination of the Links between Testosterone and Peer Victimization', *Aggressive Behavior* Vol. 35, No. 1, 103–13, 2009

van Beest, Ilja, and Kipling D. Williams. 'When Inclusion Costs and Ostracism Pays, Ostracism Still Hurts', *Journal of Personality and Social Psychology* Vol. 91, No. 5, 918–28, 2006

Venter, J. Craig. *A Life Decoded: My Genome: My Life*, Allen Lane, 2007

Vidal, Catherine. 'Brain, Sex and Ideology', *Diogenes* Vol. 52, No. 4, 127–33, 2005

———. 'The Sexed Brain: Between Science and Ideology', *Neuroethics*, 1 December 2012

Virtanen, Marianna, Archana Singh-Manoux, Jane E. Ferrie, David Gimeno, Michael G. Marmot, Marko Elovainio, Markus Jokela, Jussi Vahtera, and Mika Kivimäki. 'Long Working Hours and Cognitive Function: The Whitehall II Study', *American Journal of Epidemiology*, 2009

Vivian, Dent. 'Reply to Commentary by Juliet Mitchell: Siblings in Clinical Work', *Psychoanalytic Dialogues: The International Journal of Relational Perspectives* Vol. 19, No. 2, 171–4, 2009

Vivona, Jeanine M. 'Sibling Differentiation, Identity Development, and the Lateral Dimension of Psychic Life', *Journal of the American Psychoanalytic Association* Vol. 55, No. 4, 1191–215, 2007

Walker, Stuart H. *Winning: The Psychology of Competition*, W.W. Norton & Co., 1980

Warneken, Felix, Frances Chen, and Michael Tomasello. 'Cooperative Activities in Young Children and Chimpanzees', *Child Development* Vol. 77, No. 3, 640–63, 2006

———, and Michael Tomasello. 'Varieties of Altruism in Children and Chimpanzees', *Trends in Cognitive Sciences* Vol. 13, No. 9, 397–402, 2009

———. 'The Roots of Human Altruism', *British Journal of Psychology* Vol. 100, No. 3, 455–71, 2009

Watson, Michael. 'The Secret World of Male Anorexia', *Guardian*, 9 September 2012

Wei, David. 'The Long Game', *Insights* (Alumni magazine of London Business School), No. 123, 2010

Weiner, Jonathan. *The Beak of the Finch: A Story of Evolution in Our Time*, Jonathan Cape, 1994

Whittemore, Irving C. 'The Influence of Competition on Performance: An Experimental Study', *Journal of Abnormal and Social Psychology* Vol. 19, No. 3, 236–53, 1924

———. 'The Influence of Competition on Performance', *Journal of Abnormal and Social Psychology* Vol. 20, 17–33, 1925

Wiehe, V. R. *Sibling Abuse*, Sage Publications, 1991

Wilkinson, Richard, and Kate Pickett. *The Spirit Level: Why Equality Is Better for Everyone*, Penguin Books, 2010

Williams, Martin and John Plunkett. 'X Factor Takes 15 Places in Top 100 Ofcom Complaints', *Guardian*, 2011

Wills, Garry. 'Verdi & Boito: The Great Collaboration', *New York Review of Books*, 24 March 2011

Wilson, David Sloan. *Evolution for Everyone: How Darwin's Theory Can Change the Way We Think About Our Lives*, Delacorte Press, Random House, 2007

Windschitl, Paul D., Justin Kruger, and Ericka Nus Simms. 'The Influence of Egocentrism and Focalism on People's Optimism in Competitions: When What Affects Us Equally Affects Me More', http://www.ncbi.nlm.nih.gov/pubmed/14498778

Winerip, Michael. 'When a Hazing Goes Very Wrong', *New York Times*, 12 April 2012

Wingfield, Nick. 'Why Microsoft Chose to Make a Tablet PC', *New York Times*, 8 July 2012

Winnicott, D.W. *The Child, the Family and the Outside World*, Penguin Books, 1964

Wood, Greg. 'Gillespie Determined That Whip Rules Row Will Not Overshadow Cheltenham Festival', *Guardian*, 2012

Wozniak, David. 'Gender Differences in a Market with Relative Performance Feedback: Professional Tennis Players', *Journal of Economic Behavior & Organization*, Vol. 83, 158–71, 2012

Wright, Nicholas D., Bahador Bahrami, Emily Johnson, Gina Di Malta, Geraint Rees, Christopher D. Frith, and Raymond J. Dolan. 'Testosterone Disrupts Human Collaboration by Increasing Egocentric Choices', *Proceedings of the Royal Society B: Biological Sciences* Vol. 279, No. 1736, 2275–80, 2012

Wright, Robert. *The Moral Animal: Evolutionary Psychology and Everyday Life*, Little, Brown & Co., 1995

Wylie, Ian. 'Schools Have the Final Word on Plagiarism', *Financial Times*, 2012, http://www.ft.com/intl/cms/s/2/97a2c816-57ca-11e1-ae89-00144feabdc0.html

Yildirim, Baris O., and Jan J. L. Derksen. 'A Review on the Relationship between Testosterone and the Interpersonal/Affective Facet of Psychopathy', *Psychiatry Research* Vol. 197, No. 3, 181–198, 2012

Young, Ed. 'Girls Are as Competitive as Boys – Just More Subtle', *New Scientist*, 2008

Yücel, Murat, Alex Fornito, George Youssef, Dominic Dwyer, Sarah Whittle, Stephen J. Wood, Dan I. Lubman, Julian Simmons, Christos Pantelis, and Nicholas B. Allen. 'Inhibitory Control in Young Adolescents: The Role of Sex, Intelligence, and Temperament', *Neuropsychology* Vol. 26, No. 3, 347–56, 2012

Zaimov, Stoyan. 'Joel Osteen Asked by Interviewer: Was Jesus Poor?', *Christian Today*, 2012

Zethraeus, Niklas, Ljiljana Kocoska-Maras, Tore Ellingsen, Bo von Schoultz, Angelica Lindén Hirschberg, and Magnus Johannesson. 'A Randomized Trial of the Effect of Estrogen and Testosterone on Economic Behavior', *Proceedings of the National Academy of Sciences* Vol. 106, No. 16, 6535–8, 2009

Zimmer, Carl. 'A Sharp Rise in Retractions Prompts Calls for Reform', *New York Times*, 16 April 2012

Zimmerman, Jenn, Tara Malone, and Jennifer Delgado. 'More Top High Schools Eliminate Class Rank', *Chicago Tribune*, 2011

Zink, Caroline F., Yunxia Tong, Qiang Chen, Danielle S. Bassett, Jason L. Stein, and Andreas Meyer-Lindenberg. 'Know Your Place: Neural Processing of Social Hierarchy in Humans', *Neuron* Vol. 58, No. 2, 273–83, 2008

Zitek, Emily M., and Benoît Monin. '"That's the One I Wanted": When Do Competitors Copy Their Opponents' Choices?', *Journal of Applied Social Psychology*, 2013

Zoltners, Andris A., P. K. Sinha, and Sally E. Lorimer. 'How to Manage Forced Sales Rankings', *Harvard Business Review*, July 2011

INDEX

ACKNOWLEDGEMENTS

Writing may appear to be the ultimate solo activity but every author knows it is really a collaboration. And I've been fortunate in the many men, women and children who have helped me to understand how we manage our feelings of competitiveness and develop our ability to work together. Chief among these are my agent, Natasha Fairweather, and my editor, Mike Jones. They both had faith in this book early and throughout, offering excellent questions, challenges and ideas that have made it richer.

I've also been very fortunate to work again with Isobel Eaton, a gifted and imaginative researcher who seems to have a strong stomach for tough assignments and I'm indebted to her for finding many of the remarkable people who have talked to me so honestly about their experiences of the competitive and collaborative life.

Everyone in these pages – many of them recognizable only to themselves – gave their time generously, offering insight, reflection, and openness of a kind that it was a privilege to share. But many others form a deep, unseen foundation to my thinking: Philip Auger, Kate Bernhardt, Guy and Lidia Bradley, Charlotte Calkin, John Carlisle, Judith Derbyshire, Jane Drabble, Paul Duggan, Tony Falbo, Clarissa Farr, Eileen Fisher, Mia Gray, Ava Griffith, Ginger Hardage, Erin Hoffman, Saj-Nicole Joni, the late Rush Kidder, Stef Kranendijk, Bernard Litaer, Donald Low, Ed Mayo, Christopher Meyer, Paul Moore, Patrick Moynihan, Bill Nemtin, Hilary Old, Daniel Oran, Frank Partnoy, Jessica Ronane, Rachel Rosenblum, Michael Smith all contributed to much that is in this book.

As I discovered, competitiveness or collaboration can be found everywhere, and I'm grateful to many guides who showed me the impact these two forces make on their lives: Father Aidan Bellinger, Edmund Newell and Dr. Anthony White on the church; Neil Tully on the world of wine; Mary King and Ferdi Alberg on competitive horse-riding; Gisela Stewart on party politics; Leonor Stjepic on competition among charities; Graham White on the law; Jo Hawes and Jessica Ronane on child actors. Matthew Rock stopped me from speaking foolishly about cricket.

Kathy August, Clarissa Farr, Chuck Finkle, Beth Weiner, Elaine Goldberg and Charles Fadel helped me find my way through the thickets of current education while students from many schools, including Manchester Academy, Norton Hill and Millfield were frank in sharing their thoughts and experiences with me. I'm also grateful to the Royal Academy of Dramatic Art and their audition candidates for letting me sit in on their very careful selection process. Nicolette Hahn Niman and Rick Dove were unstinting in showing me how the meat industry works. Simon Middlemass, Steve Phillips, Stephane Diagana, Ian Williamson and Annie Skinner showed understanding and insight into sport that opened my eyes.

Alexandra and Caroline Paul, together with Prophecy Coles, Rosalind Edwards, Kate Gilbert, Albert Roux, Jan Seriff and Tim and Jeff Lott shed a great deal of light on sibling rivalry for me. My sister, Pamela Stewart, continues to show me how precious and wise a sibling can be.

As always, Albert Bandura was a great source of wisdom, support and encouragement and Robert Burton helped me distinguish the signal from the noise of neuroscience. Nick Bicat, Iona Bird, Dorothy Nancekievill, Lizzie Tocknell, Adam Tudhope and John Williams were all terrific guides through the world of music. I am also indebted to Ben and Peter Stocks, who, together with David Erdal taught me a great deal about the history and future of employee ownership. In Finland, Raila Pirinen together with Glenn and Carita Orlando were wonderful hosts as well as sources.

Many business organizations allowed me to explore and test some of my ideas at an early stage, in particular Footdown, the Caux Institute for Change and Merryck & Co. The insights of those on the coalface of business provided essential reality tests. At the University of Bath, I am fortunate in outstanding colleagues, especially Glynis Breakwell, Veronica Hope-Haley, Michael Mayer,

Stephen Rangecroft and Bruce Rayton. Their support of my work has proved a wonderful collaboration.

Like any researcher, I'm indebted to libraries and librarians, especially those at the University of Bath, Bristol University and the wonderful London Library.

Criss-crossing the world was made very much more enjoyable, thanks to the warm welcome, curiosity and hospitality from Beth Edwards, Cindy Solomon, Cinta Burgos, Pam Esty, Witney Beals and Rob and Fiona Wilson. Thank you for offering a warm and welcome respite from hotel rooms. I'm also indebted to Rebecca Lynn-Nicholson, David and Denise Nicholson for their endless patience and support.

For the study of competition and collaboration, there is no laboratory as intense (or uncontrolled) as my family. I would like to say that my children, Felix and Leonora Nicholson, were patient with my enquiries but they were better than that: fierce, argumentative, at turns furious, hilarious and chastening. I continue to learn a lot from them and I hope that they feel they've learned something from me too.

If at times, during the darker moments of this book, I began to lose faith in human generosity, I needed to look no further than my husband Lindsay for inspiration. His willingness to engage in exploration, debate, doubt and challenge was inexhaustible, punctilious and illuminating, proof, if it were needed, that altruism is not always self-interested.

Boston and Farrington Gurney
2013